MONOGRAPH 49

Perspectives on Ancient Maya Rural Complexity

Edited by Gyles Iannone and Samuel V. Connell

The Cotsen Institute of Archaeology
University of California, Los Angeles
2003

The Cotsen Institute of Archaeology at UCLA
Charles Stanish, Director
Brenda Johnson-Grau, Managing Editor

Edited by ZoAnna Carrol, Rita Demsetz, Marilyn Gatto, Beverly Godwin, and Kathy Talley-Jones
Designed by Brenda Johnson-Grau
Production by Erin Carter, Petya Hristova, Merlin Ramsey, Karla Saenz, Keomanee Vilaythong, and Alice Wang

Library of Congress Cataloging-in-Publication Data

Perspectives on ancient Maya rural complexity / edited by Gyles Iannone
and Samuel V. Connell.
   p. cm. -- (Monograph series ; v. 49)
Includes bibliographical references.
ISBN 1-931745-06-4
 1. Mayas--Land tenure. 2. Mayas--Dwellings. 3. Mayas--Antiquities.
4. Human settlements--Central America. 5. Land settlement patterns,
Prehistoric--Central America. 6. Social archaeology--Central America.
7. Demographic archaeology--Central America. 8. Rural
population--Central America. 9. Central America--Antiquities. I.
Iannone, Gyles. II. Connell, Samuel V. III. Monograph (Cotsen Institute
of Archaeology at UCLA) ; 49.
F1 435.3.L35 P47 2003
97 2.8'01--dc21
                                              2002012657

To the people of Belize

Contents

Preface

TOURING THROUGH THE MAYA HEARTLAND, one cannot help but be struck by the incredible density and variability of ancient mounds visible throughout the countryside. Although one of the earliest settlement surveys in the Maya area did recognize a complex mosaic of site types, highlighted by middle-level settlements called "minor centers" (Bullard 1960), archaeological research has instead been focused on either complex major urban centers or, more recently, small-scale rural households. Influenced by "core/periphery" models, the urban/rural dichotomy that has long held sway in the social sciences has profoundly affected Maya archaeology. A direct result of the emphasis on these antipodes is that a whole range of settlement lying along the continuum between and visible to the naked eye throughout the Maya heartland still receives little academic attention. A number of scholars, however, have recently begun to consider the importance of exploring settlements of medium size and complexity. This attitude has led to greater concentration on the ubiquitous, but little understood, collection of sites that since Bullard's survey more than forty years ago have traditionally fallen under the category of minor center. In particular, there has been a growing awareness that these settlements play a key role in articulating the truly urban and the genuinely rural. As exemplified by the various chapters in this volume, scholars have recently begun to focus their attention on "rural complexity" as a means to generate a more holistic understanding of ancient Maya sociopolitical and socioeconomic integration.

The majority of essays in this volume derive from a symposium, entitled "The Social Implications of Ancient Maya Rural Complexity," which was convened at the 63rd Annual Meeting of the Society for American Archaeology (Seattle, 1998). The contributions to this volume underscore the existence of ancient Maya rural complexity, discuss the methodological and theoretical issues relevant to the analysis of rural complexity, provide case studies to highlight the variability exhibited by complex rural settlements, and explore the implications of this variability for the study of ancient Maya social, economic, and political organization. With the exception of Wendy Ashmore's general discussion of settlement issues, and Edward Schortman and Patricia Urban's concluding analysis, the majority of research presented here has been pursued in Belize (see figure 1). We believe, however, that the insights generated through these case studies have much broader relevance and that they will, therefore, be appealing to all students of the archaic state, regardless of where one's research interests lie.

The chapters in this volume indicate that although there is some convergence of opinion with respect to spatial patterning and site function, there is less agreement concerning the sociopolitical and socioeconomic significance of middle-level settlement variability. Some researchers suggest that the evidence implies the ancient Maya lived in poorly integrated, decentralized polities. Others provide data more indicative of tightly integrated, centralized Maya states. Still others suggest that the information derived from the middle level of settlement is more evocative of political fluctuations between centralization and decentralization. In part, these contrasting conclusions reflect the different scales, regions, time periods, and theoretical perspectives of individual contributors. The differences of opinion also point to the fact that we must expand our database before we can hope to discern a greater range of patterning. In addition, it is also clear that we must make a more concerted effort to contextualize these sites by situating them within their broader regional contexts.

It is acknowledged that, for the most part, the data presented within this volume derive from only a small portion of a single culture area. The conclusions, we feel, are far

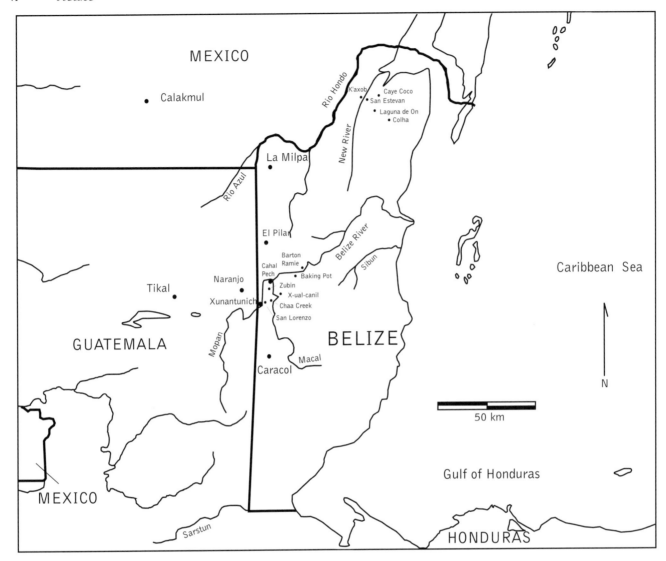

Figure 1 Map of Belize

reaching. Clearly, the investigation of rural complexity has the potential to provide new and intriguing insights into all societies, not just that of the ancient Maya. In particular, studies of this sort have the capacity to not only review and expand upon the urban/rural dichotomy prevailing within Maya archaeology but also to synthesize new interpretations of rural complexity for the social sciences. If one overwhelming conclusion may be drawn from these chapters, it is that past social relations were much more fluid than our models have traditionally assumed.

All the contributors have conducted research in Belize. We would thus like to begin by thanking the Department of Archaeology in Belmopan for promoting middle-level settlement research over the years. We thank the funding agencies that have seen fit to support this type of research.

The editors are grateful for the hard work that all the participants put into both the original Society of American Archaeology symposium and the final book chapters. We are also appreciative of the various comments made by a number of anonymous reviewers, as well as those provided by Edward Schortman and Patricia Urban. Finally, we thank Marilyn Beaudry-Corbett, Brenda Johnson-Grau, Tara Carter, Beverly Godwin, Marilyn Gatto, Petya Hristova, ZoAnna Carrol, and Alice Wang, from the Publications Unit of the Cotsen Institute of Archaeology at UCLA, for allowing us to take this topic to a wider audience.

- Gyles Iannone
- Samuel V. Connell

1 Perspectives on Ancient Maya Rural Complexity

An Introduction

Gyles Iannone and Samuel V. Connell

IN THEIR APPROACHES TO SOCIETAL ANALYSIS, most social scientists have tended to emphasize the urban/rural dichotomy. Within sociocultural anthropology, the emphasis on these antipodes has been most explicitly articulated in the works of political economists. For example, in his seminal work, Robert Redfield (1971) contrasted the literate and religious character of the urban realm, or "great tradition," with the oral and magical qualities of the rural realm, or "little tradition" (see also chapter 8). Recently, a number of studies have begun to question the viability of this urban/rural distinction (see various papers in Ching and Creed 1997; see also chapter 8). It has been pointed out that the urban/rural dichotomy is false because " 'purely rural' and 'purely urban' spaces make up only a portion of the various places in which people live and form their identities" (Creed and Ching 1997:15; see also Schwartz and Falconer 1994a). Advocates of this opinion have underscored the fact that a middle ground has been ignored in social science research. Anthropologist Rhoda Halperin has attempted to deal with this problem by differentiating between the traditional "deep rural" and the "shallow rural," the latter referring to more complex rural settlements, or "the middle ground between country and city" (1990:4). The term *rurban* has been resurrected in some studies to refer to the mixing of rural and urban characteristics that these pluralistic communities exhibit. Regardless of the term employed, there is general acceptance that, in most contemporary social landscapes, communities exist which exhibit a mixing of urban and rural characteristics and that these communities have been under explored when compared to the truly urban and genuinely rural poles of the settlement continuum.

Like their social science colleagues, Maya archaeologists have tended to work within an analytical framework that gives precedence to the urban/rural dichotomy. Much of the early research in the Maya area focused on the urban component. Traditional long-term research projects have been carried out at such major centers as Tikal, Copan, Uaxactun, Caracol, Chichen Itza, and Seibal. In response to this urban bias, "settlement archaeology" shifted some focus to rural settlements. These rural-based settlement studies concentrated primarily on Halperin's deep rural, as noted above. This emphasis is clearly stated in an early call to arms by Willey et al. in which it was suggested that settlement archaeology was aimed at exploring the "'ordinary dwellings', 'houses of the people', or 'housemounds'" (1965:7). For the most part, this methodological dichotomy between exploration of urban centers and rural settlement has continued to the present. In theoretical terms, some Mayanists have even adopted the analytical framework of political economists such as Redfield and have thus underscored the distinction between the great tradition and the little tradition of Maya society (Gossen and Leventhal 1989; see also Webster 1998:10, 29). It is only recently that scholars have begun to call for more detailed investigation of the complex rural settlements that lay between the urban and rural extremes of the ancient Maya settlement continuum (Gonlin 1994; King and Potter 1994).

This volume marks the beginnings of this research endeavor. As volume editors, we have identified particular themes drawn out by the various contributors:

- a recognition within their research that not only do these complex settlements exhibit a high degree of variability but they also have a syncretic quality in that they display a mixing of urban and rural characteristics, allowing us to explore more satisfactorily the concept of rural complexity for the Maya;
- the idea that minor centers do not constitute a homogenous site type but rather are best viewed as elements within a highly variable middle level of settlement;
- the point that minor centers, and other middle-level

settlements, have received little attention in past considerations of ancient Maya sociopolitical and socioeconomic interaction; and

- the position that although most middle-level settlements were the loci for a variety of residential, administrative, and ritual activities, there is considerable divergence with respect to which function was primary at any given site.

In chapter 12, Edward Schortman and Patricia Urban provide a more extensive summary of the important issues the individual contributors raised.

Rural Complexity in Maya Studies

As the majority of the authors in this volume underscore, notions of shallow rural or rurban settlements have played a limited role in the interpretation of ancient Maya social, economic, and political organization (in particular, see chapters 2, 3, 5, and 10). That is not to say that Mayanists have not recognized the existence of more complex rural communities. As far back as the mid-twentieth century, investigators such as Willey, Bullard, and Glass, were referring to the presence of "minor ceremonial centers" (1955:24). Shortly thereafter, Bullard was in his Petén study (1960) the first to state clearly that a level of rural complexity (minor centers) lay between the fully urban (major centers) and the genuinely rural (house mounds). According to Bullard, these sites were appreciably larger and more complex than the more frequent house-mound groups, but comparatively smaller and not so grandiose in design as the less frequent, but more intensively studied, major centers. The diversity of minor center plans (Bullard 1960: 360, Fig. 3) was a significant aspect of the study. Subsequent researchers (for example, Hammond 1975; Puleston 1983:25) highlighted the variable quality of these settlements. Recent studies have also underscored this variability in noting that contrary to Bullard's more general assertions, sites of this size and complexity sometimes have stelae, altars, ballcourts, and causeways (for example, Garber et al. 1994:13–14; Iannone 1996; in this volume, see chapters 3, 4, 7, 9, and 11).

Such features were traditionally thought to have been restricted to the confines of major centers. Their presence in minor centers is important for two reasons. First, it attests to the syncretic quality of these sites in that they exhibit a mixing of urban and rural characteristics (see also chapter 9). Second, the uneven distribution of these features contributes to the overall variability of this settlement level. As a result of this syncretism and variability, our study of minor centers becomes doubly difficult. There is simply no consistent pattern in the form and context of these sites that can be used as a model from which hypotheses about Maya social organization can be built and projected to other sites and regions.

The term *rural complexity* is used here to delineate this

syncretism and variability and to review the outdated notion of an urban/rural dichotomy. In the extreme case, the suggestion has been to drop the term because of its associations with the social evolutionary paradigm (chapter 8). Nevertheless, this rural complexity is significant, and a concerted effort must be made to both explore and explain the potential implications of this combined syncretism and variability. The importance of this endeavor has been stressed in a number of recent discussions. To quote King and Potter (1994:84), "By not expecting social, economic, or political complexity from small sites, we disregard possible important sources of information on the Lowland Maya world." Also, as Gonlin has concluded, "if we do not fully understand rural complexity, we cannot convincingly speak of complexity in general for the ancient Maya" (1994:195).

Settlement Type versus Settlement Level: Introducing the Middle Level

Although most Mayanists would undoubtedly accept the presence of minor centers, there has been little agreement concerning how these sites should be classified or interpreted. Bullard's (1960) settlement typology for the Petén region—as well as those of Hammond (1975) for northern Belize and Puleston (1983:25) for the vicinity of Tikal—have tended to focus on the qualitative aspects of minor centers. These settlement typologies refer to the presence or absence of certain features (stela, temples of a certain size) and specifically highlight the quality of the site as opposed to its overall size. The generalizing, or polythetic, quality of some of these classifications is advantageous (for example, Bullard 1960) in that it highlights the overall variability of this settlement level. The more specific, or monothetic, of these typologies (for example, Hammond 1975) are, however, often of limited use outside their regional contexts (de Montmollin 1988a:151).

In contrast to the aforementioned qualitative endeavors, others have attempted to classify minor centers and other settlements using quantitative schemes (R.E.W. Adams 1981, 1982; R.E.W. Adams and Jones 1981; Guderjan 1991; Turner, Turner, and Adams 1981). The quantitative typologies focus mainly on site size and the quantity of certain elements, such as the number of courtyards and stelae. These approaches do, however, tend to homogenize settlement variability by converting minor centers (and other sites) into a numerical format for comparative purposes. Ultimately, these inquiries hinder the exploration of settlement differences beyond gross measures of settlement size and complexity (see also Iannone 1996:51).

In our view, the most successful characterizations of ancient Maya settlement are based on bundled continua of variation (chapter 2; de Montmollin 1988a, 1989; see Easton 1959 for a more general discussion). They suggest ancient

Maya settlement does not consist of a series of discrete site types; rather, settlement is best viewed as a continuum of variation (D.Z. Chase, A.F. Chase, Haviland 1990:500; Culbert 1991:328; Haviland 1970:190). For this reason, Iannone (1996:53–55) has found it profitable to amalgamate minor centers within a highly variable "middle level of settlement." Although the middle level is not a discretely defined settlement unit, there are survey data and specific structure forms and layouts that can help identify a range of sites as part of a middle level.

We therefore propose that on the basis of settlement data, middle-level settlements are those arrangements of Maya mounds (sites) that lie at the top of hinterland settlement hierarchies (Connell 2000). This proposal necessitates full regional coverage of rural communities to define the top rungs of settlement. Middle-level settlement begins with what Hammond has called "minimal ceremonial center[s]" (1975:41) (see also Ford 1981:57; P.M. Thomas 1981:108). In his definition, Hammond stresses that although such sites replicate many of the features present in lower-level settlements (housemounds, patio groups, and smaller plazuela groups), they differ in that they also include at least one large nonresidential structure. A large "civic" structure suggests that these sites had a degree of religious, political, and economic control. Following this progression, one reaches the first genuine minor centers, as originally discussed by Bullard (1960; see also Ford 1981:57; Hammond 1975:42; P.M. Thomas 1981:108). Their greater size (that is, spatial extent and structure volume) and complexity of overall site plan readily separate such sites from lower-level settlements. An increase in the number of apparently nonresidential structures also attests to significant differences between these and the lower-level sites. Hammond (1975:42) has noted that at this point on the continuum, sites begin to show clear differentiation between plaza or courtyard function. Whereas one courtyard may serve primarily a residential function, others may be the focus of religious and/or administrative activities. With this functional distinction, these smaller sites begin to exhibit a characteristic of upper-level sites, or major centers (see Ashmore 1992). The presence of other distinctive architectural configurations within these middle-level settlement units, such as ballcourts, causeways, eastern ancestor shrines, and restricted access plazas, also attests to the replication of upper-level traits (as does the sporadic occurrence of stelae and altars).

In the end, the middle level of settlement forms a *fuzzy set* (chapter 3), a term Laughlin (1993:18) has used to define "categories with graded membership." By adopting the notion of a fuzzy set of middle-level settlement, we allow ourselves to deal with a polythetic level within a settlement continuum (in this volume see chapters 2, 3, 4, 5, 9, and 11), rather than an idealized, monothetic site type within a settlement hierarchy (see also de Montmollin 1988a:151). As de Montmollin has pointed out, "...it is analytically most useful to avoid squeezing actual settlement distributions into the small number of rigidly-defined, synthetic ideal types usually associated with idealized settlement-scale hierarchies" (1988a:165). Just as the original Bullard (1960) classification continues to have general utility, the notion of a middle level of settlement is advantageous because it highlights both the highly variable and syncretic quality of complex rural settlements without being regionally specific or overly homogenizing. Deriving as they do from the full range of middle-level settlement possibilities, the various case studies presented here appear to confirm the utility of this settlement level concept. It is also important to stress at this juncture that the criteria for recognizing such sites may change over time (chapter 11), and this situation must be considered when assigning sites to a particular level within a settlement continuum.

Social Implications of Complex Rural Settlements

Clearly, it is not enough to recognize that middle-level settlements are highly variable and syncretic in character. As the majority of the authors in this volume point out, the social implications of this syncretism and variability must be explored. In fact, some of the authors have gone so far as to state that the middle level of settlement may hold the key to understanding ancient Maya socioeconomic and sociopolitical organization (chapters 3, 4, and 10). Unfortunately, sites of this size and complexity remain the least investigated of all ancient Maya settlements. For this reason, there has been a tendency to interpret these settlements solely on surface configurations and models of ideal settlement types (in this volume see chapters 3, 5, 6, and 10). Specifically, many Mayanists have adopted an essentialist perspective within which minor centers have been conceptualized as an idealized site type, with little effort made to account for extant variability (for a discussion of essentialism see O'Brien and Holland 1990:61). As a result, although it is generally recognized that middle-level settlements are highly variable, this variability is given less consideration in most models than is overall site size (chapter 6; Gonlin 1994; Iannone 1996, chapter 3; King and Potter 1994; see also Schwartz and Falconer 1994a:2; chapter 5) and/or the settlement's proximity to, or spatial arrangement around, larger centers (for example, Garber, Driver, and Sullivan 1993:6–7; see also chapters 3 and 5).

A corollary of this approach to middle-level settlement analysis is that owing to the lack of excavations (Gonlin 1994:195) and the rather blatant reliance on surface features, our current understanding of rural complexity is heavily biased toward the synchronic scale (Iannone 1996). As a result, there has been little regard for developmental sequences (see Bawden 1982:181; Gonlin 1994; Hendon 1992:37; Iannone 1996; King and Potter 1994:66–67; and chapters 3,

5, 6, 7, and 10). As Yaeger (chapter 5) has underscored, just as surface reconnaissance has highlighted the range of variability that exists among sites within the middle level of settlement, excavations have revealed a wide range of divergent developmental trajectories (see also Iannone 1996). This developmental variability is clearly significant, and future research must strive not only to document these developmental sequences but also to explore the broader implications of "diachronic complexity" (chapter 5). The importance of reconstructing developmental sequences is crucial for a number of reasons, not the least of which relates to the fact that, within specific developmental trajectories, middle-level settlements may have grown into important and powerful upper-level settlements (chapter 10). For the purposes of sociopolitical and socioeconomic analyses, it is therefore imperative to understand when and why such transformations took place. In sum, research cannot focus only on those middle-level settlements that are readily discernible on the contemporary landscape. We must also take on the difficult task of investigating middle-level settlements that lie buried beneath the overburden of larger and more complex upper-level settlements.

Given the aforementioned issues, it is not surprising that our interpretations of rural complexity have been guided primarily by the tenets of overarching models. For the most part, strong emphasis has been placed on the functional roles that minor centers played within the overall settlement hierarchy (for example, Ball and Taschek 1991:158; Borhegyi 1956:105; Bullard 1960:368; W.R. Coe and M.D. Coe 1956:381; Culbert 1974:67; Hammond 1975:41–42, 1982:168; Marcus 1983b:469; Puleston 1983:25; P.M. Thomas 1981:108; Tourtellot 1970:410; Willey 1956a:778; Willey, Bullard, and Glass 1955:25; Willey et al. 1965:579). Specifically, a review of the literature indicates that our interpretations of minor centers have tended to proceed through two stages. First, we have confounded a diverse array of complex rural settlements into an idealized site type (see also Schwartz and Falconer 1994a:3). Then, we have assigned the same functional roles to these centers based on the postulated position of this homogenized site type within a rather static settlement hierarchy. As underscored by King and Potter, "By expecting centers to be functionally similar, we fail to explore variability and fail to discern the intricate relations that must have existed among them, particularly the kinds of interactions that are not spoken of in the glyphs" (1994:84) (see also Iannone 1996, and chapters 10, 6, 4, and 5).

In the end, we have often assumed that the inhabitants of middle-level settlements carried out a consistent range of functional roles and that these roles were defined by the needs of those living within both the urban and rural components of a settlement hierarchy (see comments in Schwartz and Falconer 1994a:3). Few have stressed that the overall variability within this settlement level might indicate that the inhabitants of middle-level settlements played numerous, diverse roles within ancient Maya society. It is this very point that the majority of the contributors to this volume underscore. Those who espouse the traditional interpretation suggest that all middle-level settlements had multiple functions tied to the production and redistribution of agrarian and craft goods within an economic hierarchy. Others argue that although middle-level settlements were often the loci for a whole range of activities, they also tended to have primary functions, such as feasting, and may have evolved to complement one and another (chapter 4). Within the different case studies here, the primary functions of particular middle-level settlements included residences for nonelite (chapters 3, 5, and 8), "subelite" (chapters 3, 4, 5, 6, 7, and 9), and elite lineages (chapters 4, 6, and 10); markets (chapter 10); administrative nodes, some of which focused on water management (chapter 3), agricultural production and storage (chapters 3, 4, 6, 7, 9, and 10), and border, or "control point" management (chapters 9 and 10); feasting sites (chapters 4 and 9) ; and ritual loci (chapters 3, 4, and 9). Potential secondary functions include activities tied to trade (chapters 7 and 11), and craft specialization (chapter 11). Given the variability within this settlement level, such a broad range of functional roles seems fitting.

In some ways, the recognition of this functional variability moves us away from the old and rather tired "shared function" argument described above. In other ways, however, the contributors to this volume have tried to be careful not to view middle-level settlements almost as if the sites themselves were human actors. Although for the most part we have continued to view these sites with respect to their roles or functions within a socioeconomic and/or sociopolitical hierarchy, we have also begun to populate the sites with people (chapters 4 and 10).

The potential autonomous, or semiautonomous, quality of some middle-level settlements is something that many of the volume contributors hint at. Social groups inhabiting middle-level settlements may have had their own motivations, ambitions, agendas, and goals (chapters 2, 3, and 5). External relations with individuals who commanded greater and lesser political and economic powers would have required constant negotiation by people populating middle-level settlements (chapters 3 and 6). Perhaps by striving to "populate" these sites we can fully capture the fluidity of the social interaction that was likely played out within this settlement level.

The Notion of Heterarchy

A sense of the fluidity in social relations, especially at the middle level of settlement, carries our research closer to operationalizing the concept of heterarchy. Chase and Chase (chapter 10) have aptly noted that the term *minor center*, in and of itself, implies the presence of a hierarchy. In reaction to the traditional stance of functional/hierarchical models that has often been invoked to interpret middle-level settlements, a number of scholars (both in the Maya area and elsewhere) have, however, recently advocated the notion of heterarchy (see various papers in Ehrenreich, Crumley, and Levy 1995; in this volume, see chapters 2, 3, and 8). As Crumley points out, "Most geometric models of settlement are informed by theories of both biological and social complexity that rely almost exclusively on a single type of structure: hierarchy," but "many structures, both biological and social, are not organized hierarchically" (1995:2). She defines heterarchy "as the relation of elements to one another when they are "or when they possess the potential for being ranked in a number of different ways" (Crumley 1995:3).

Studies in Maya heterarchy would be "concerned with functional complexity along both vertical and horizontal dimensions" (Potter and King 1995:17). In other words, the strength of heterarchical models lies in the fact that they can accommodate variability over both time and space (Levy 1995:47; chapter 8). Importantly, the adoption of a heterarchical approach does not in any way negate the existence of hierarchical relationships. Rather, it is accepted that most social or settlement systems have both heterarchical and hierarchical qualities (Levy 1995:47; see also Feinman and Marcus 1998:11). In some cases for the Maya (Marcus 1993) and elsewhere (McGuire and Saitta 1996), it has also been suggested that either can be subsumed within the other. For the purposes of studying ancient Maya rural complexity, sites that are hierarchically equivalent may have very different functions (see Wailes 1995:68; chapter 4). As Crumley points out, "three cities might be the same size but draw their importance from three different realms: one hosts a military base, one a manufacturing center, and the third is home to a great university" (1995:3). Given the variable nature of the middle level of settlement, we must be more open to the possibility that a similarly diverse range of heterarchical relationships is manifest within this segment of the ancient Maya settlement continuum. In the sense that our proposed middle level of settlement is a fuzzy set, we have left the door open to incorporating the notion of heterarchical relations in our understandings of not only ancient Maya regional organization, but also as an example for scholars working in other culture areas both past and present.

Summary

The term *rural complexity* has been employed here to challenge the urban/rural dichotomy that has been prevalent in Maya research to date (but compare chapter 8). On one level, the notion of rural complexity has been used to underscore the syncretism, or plurality, that is the hallmark of these sites (that is, the mixing of characteristics from upper- and lower-level settlements). On another level, the idea of rural complexity has been used to highlight the variability that existed within the middle level of settlement as a whole, the heterogeneity present within specific middle-level settlements, and the divergences in individual developmental sequences. With regard to the types of activities that may have been carried out within the confines of middle-level settlements, the contributors to this volume have suggested a variety of primary and secondary functions. Specifically, evidence has been marshaled to argue for a wide range of administrative, residential, and ritual roles. It is apparent that these various functions manifest themselves in a variety of ways within the middle level of the ancient Maya settlement continuum. This diversity in potential site roles fits well with the multiplicity of site plans, site inventories, and developmental sequences exhibited by sites of this size and complexity. Clearly, a diverse array of socioeconomic and sociopolitical transactions were played out within these complex rural settlements.

Conclusion

As Schwartz and Falconer conclude, "Rural studies are compelling not only because they may be unorthodox but also because they allow us to reject, revise, and refine previous interpretations of ancient societies in a way we cannot always anticipate" (1994a:7). The analyses of ancient Maya rural complexity contained within this volume attest to the validity of this statement. Although the various contributors underscore the degree of variability inherent within the middle level of the ancient Maya settlement continuum, there is little agreement as to the socioeconomic or sociopolitical significance of this variability. Some contributors imply that the evidence from the middle level of settlement is indicative of a segmentary, or decentralized state (chapters 4, 6, and 11). Others suggest the opposite—that the middle level of settlement is more indicative of a centralized, or unitary state (chapters 9 and 10). Some have adopted a middle-of-the-road position in which the data derived from the investigation of middle-level settlements are considered to be reflective of both decentralizing and centralizing processes (chapters 3 and 5), a stance considered to be consistent with the tenets of Marcus' (1992, 1993, 1998) "dynamic model" (chapter 3).

These divergences in opinion quite likely arise for a number of reasons having to do with the methodological and theoretical strategies individual researchers employed. For example, they could be reflective of a particular segment of the middle-level continuum that contributors have chosen to research. Some plazuela and patio groups may be middle-level sites that reflect decentralized control versus other minor sites that reflect centralized models. This same difference in interpretation may also arise from choices concerning different scales of analysis (microregional vs. regional) and the specific time period emphasized (Classic versus Postclassic). What we do know, however, is that at this moment the study of rural complexity does not lend itself to simple generalizations. Given the variation within the middle level of settlement, it seems reasonable that differences of opinion will abound for the time being and into the distant future. Still, within the chaos, some patterning is presented, as seen in the overlapping functional interpretations for middle-level settlements and in the possible regularized spacing of such sites (chapters 8, 9, and 10). As more research is conducted within the middle level of settlement, this sort of patterning will provide new and important insights into ancient Maya sociopolitical and socioeconomic interaction. As some of the chapters (4, 8, 9, and 10) demonstrate, regional analyses may be a particularly fruitful means through which such patterning may be recognized.

In closing, it is our contention that middle-level settlement units, and specifically minor centers, provide one of the best laboratories for exploring ancient Maya social, economic, and political organization. The variability encompassed by this settlement level attests to important divergences in site development, which, in turn, implies that the inhabitants of such sites carried out a complex network of socioeconomic and sociopolitical transactions. The contributors to this volume explore this complexity in various ways. As Maya archaeologists, we must begin to approach the question of socioeconomic and sociopolitical organization in a far more sophisticated manner if we are going to paint an accurate picture of Maya society. As anthropologists, the intricacies of dealing with this middle level of settlement are very likely to be the same as they are in other culture areas. In methodological terms, we must strive to produce a more representative database, one that includes data from the highly variable middle level of settlement. In culture-historical and theoretical terms, the formulation of greater understanding of the various factors behind this rural complexity will produce a more comprehensive knowledge of societies such as the ancient Maya.

2 Aspects of Maya Settlement Archaeology, 1999

Wendy Ashmore

*I*N 1977, approximately a *katun* after Gordon Willey's pathbreaking Belize Valley fieldwork (Willey et al. 1965), a small group of archaeologists took stock of emerging data, method, and theory in the study of lowland Maya settlement patterns (Ashmore 1981a). Although it seemed clear then that such study was steadily increasing in quantity, quality, and interpretive recognition, the energetic optimism of the time was tempered with a sense that theory and method had a long way to go to realize fully the interpretive potentials of Maya settlement data (for example, Ashmore 1981a; Marcus 1983b; Sabloff 1983; Willey 1981). Even Willey felt that the state of the art at that point remained rather confused (Willey 1980, as cited by Sabloff 1983: 413).

Another katun has passed since that general stocktaking, and the editors of this volume invited me to consider some of the intervening changes in Maya settlement archaeology. This essay is not intended as being comprehensive in any sense, neither for interpretive trends nor substantive findings. Fortunately, several recent articles provide critical reviews of the state of the art in relevant cross-cutting domains, and I refer especially to critiques and prognoses for Maya archaeology by William Fash (1994) and Joyce Marcus (1995) and to Deborah Nichols' (1996) assessment of thirty-five years of Mesoamerican settlement surveys.

My goal here is simply to highlight aspects of Maya settlement archaeology in which I see important change. All are works in progress and find differential expression in the work of any individual or project, including some in this volume. Although one might choose to highlight many aspects (for example, Sabloff and Ashmore 2001), I have selected the following interrelated set of three: (1), our conceptualization of the analytic domain has become much broader and more diversified; (2), our interpretive models are becoming more socially informed; and (3), we invoke a more complex array of potential determinants for observed settlement patterns. I briefly discuss each

aspect, in turn, alluding to both accomplishment and the need for further development. Attention to rural complexity is relevant to and affected by all.

Conceptualizing the Analytic Domain

In parallel with archaeologists elsewhere, Mayanists have come to examine a far larger and more continuous range of settlement traces, those more diverse in their form, function, and articulation. This examination has involved moving beyond sites and mounds as foci of study and looking more closely at how varied our recorded sites actually are. Underlying such methodological changes are significant shifts in thinking about how people inhabit, use, and modify the land. That is, to deal with a greater diversity of activities and people potentially represented by physical traces, the nature of settlement evidence has become both a broader domain, and one more textured in what it encompasses.

Maya settlement surveys customarily emphasize recording discrete, often clustered features that are the most obtrusive elements on the landscape, and such sites most often have comprised collapsed ruins of ancient buildings. Such focus on hot spots of occupation has tended, perhaps, to stifle comprehensive examination of the settlement record for at least two reasons. First, such a focus steered us away from dealing effectively with areas in between and connections among those places we traditionally designated—or isolated—as sites. Surely Mayanists' increasing encounters in the 1970s with extensive tracts of agricultural features, such as terraces or ridged fields, were strong, albeit only partial, stimulus to expand the effective scope of settlement study beyond traditional sites (for example, Harrison and Turner 1978). The frequent complexity and sheer extent of agricultural, water-management and other kinds of landscape modification now require a more inclusive perspective regarding what constitutes evidence of settlement and how we detect, record, and analyze such data (for example, Dunning and Beach 1994; Dunning et al. 1999; Fedick 1996;

Scarborough 1993). Roads or causeways, too, have gained increasing attention as features worthy of concerted study, whether articulating areas within continuous settlement zones or connecting distinct places, often many kilometers apart (for example, Folan, Marcus, and Miller 1995; Keller 1995a; Kurjack and Andrews 1976; Trombold 1991; see also chapter 10). To borrow a phrase from Amos Rapoport (1990), we have begun to appreciate wider, more diverse, and complicated systems of settings to map more comprehensively the multiple sets of activities through which people lived their lives.

At the same time, Mayanists look more closely at seemingly empty areas within and between sites. Vacant terrain and hidden house-mound studies are far from new in Maya studies (for example, Haviland 1966), but they have been substantially amplified in recent years, as at Nohmul, Sayil, and Xunantunich (for example, Braswell 1998; Killion et al. 1989; Pyburn 1989; Robin 1998). The goal is potential discovery of settlement traces where none are obvious at ground level. Actual detection involves adding methods, such as post-hole or phosphate testing; more critical is the underlying conceptual change, again broadening the range of what we look for and where. In some cases, this broadening involves recognition that formal and social continua may have been truncated by differential physical survival: Even the least imposing remains visible now at surface level may not mark the least imposing constructions created in ancient times. For example, Webster and Gonlin's (1988) important study of the humblest Maya at Copan dealt with traces of simple household compounds on the far rural outskirts of that city. The sites studied were smaller than the smallest units recognized anywhere within the urban core (Willey and Leventhal 1979), yet because the use of platforms was so pervasive to Copan-area house building (Webster and Gonlin 1988: 185) even these unimposing structures involved basal stone construction. Pyburn's (1989) work at Nohmul, Wilk and Wilhite's (1991) at Cuello, and others' studies elsewhere have revealed that the truly humblest of Maya domestic remains might at times neither be visible above the modern ground surface nor involve imperishable construction of any sort. To the extent that architectural elaboration is a measure of social or economic standing (for example, Arnold and Ford 1980; Webster 1999; Willey and Leventhal 1979; but see Haviland 1982; Tourtellot, Sabloff, and Carmean 1992), earlier analysts may have missed a significant chunk of society altogether because it was not sought in the first place.

As fundamental a truncation is the omission of outdoor areas as repositories of settlement traces. Whether or not architecture left readily tangible traces, many activities— indeed, probably the majority—took place beyond the confines of formal buildings (for example, Braswell 1998; Killion et al. 1989; Robin 1999). Even without the extraordinary site of Ceren, where volcanic eruption entombed traces of both indoor and outdoor activities now preserved in exquisite detail (Sheets 1992, 1998; Sweely 1998; Webster, Gonlin, and Sheets 1997), ethnographic and ethnoarchaeological studies testify amply to the importance of house lots and other outdoor settings in tropical or other hot climates. Robin's (1999) studies of domestic compounds near Xunantunich, Belize, drew jointly on Killion's (1992; Killion et al. 1989) house-lot model and her own ethnoarchaeological research at Sisbecchen, Yucatan, to interpret distinctive combinations of artifacts, ecofacts, and features as material signatures of recurring sets of household activities.

Although fully siteless or off-site survey of the sort advocated by Dunnell, Foley, and others (for example, Dunnell and Dancey 1983; Foley 1981) might be misplaced in Maya studies, we now do give markedly more attention to landscape modification in less discrete site-like forms that may be quite extensive, subtle, or both. Mounds, sites, and even construction simply do not encompass the range of traces appropriate for study, because people do not confine their lives to such spatially restricted frames.

Sites and mounds do remain useful analytic entities. To compare and contrast them, we draw on various sorts of typologies. These important tools remain problematic in application for at least two reasons. One is the perpetual risk of conflating archaeological types with anciently recognized units. Marcus (1983b) rightly called colleagues to task for drawing too infrequently on the Maya settlement descriptions contained in richly informative ethnohistoric documents. The danger always remains, however, that the interpretive pendulum can swing too far to uncritical reliance on these sources: Analogs of any sort always require demonstration, not assumption (for example, Ashmore and Wilk 1988; Sharer 1993).

A second enduring problem with typologies is that reducing an assemblage of settlement units to types can obscure variability at least as much as it can spur comparison. One of the principal arguments of Haviland's (1981) Tikal Group 7F-1 discussion was that much of the compound's interpretive importance stems from its historical uniqueness, and that this uniqueness becomes completely lost in the compound's settlement-type designation as a minor center. Although labels such as *minor* or *midrange* draw attention to a potentially informative class of sites, an increasing number of analysts actively recognize the need to scrutinize the diversities, as well as the uniformities, of these sites in their form, function, and social significance (for example, Ehret 1997, 1998; Iannone 1996, 1997, chapter 3).

Indeed, this volume on rural complexity reflects interest in breaking apart a pair of related and long-standing typological dichotomies. One is the contrast between urban and nonurban, and the other, more subtle and incidental, between site and settlement. The question of whether the ancient Maya had an urban tradition and lived in cities has had a long and hotly argued history (for example, Becker 1979). Most now agree that Maya centers could be truly urban in size, density, and organizational intricacy, although the nature of Maya cities and urbanism certainly remains contested (for example, D.Z. Chase, A.F. Chase, and Haviland 1990; Sanders and Webster 1988). Moreover, whatever the definitions used for those terms, not all of what had been thought of as vacant ceremonial centers should now automatically be considered urban places. The situation appears far more complex and variable (for example, Ball and Taschek 1991; Tourtellot 1993). One creative and flexible approach is de Montmollin's (1989, 1995) replacement of categorical types with dimensional variation, highlighting what he calls "bundled continua" of characteristics. It is also important to note, particularly in the context of this volume, that nonurban or rural settlement components have remained underdefined, in formal, as well as organizational, terms. Closer examination by contributors here, as well as elsewhere, is welcome.

Perhaps a more fundamental, if unintended, typological dichotomy is embodied, in my view, in the terms *site* and *settlement*, as they have come to be used informally by Mayanists and others. In the wake of Willey and his colleagues' (1965) Belize Valley research, settlement-pattern studies were appropriately hailed as balancing the attention traditionally paid to centers, providing views of ancient domestic remains as counterparts to the temples and palaces of civic precincts (compare Haviland 1966); this has certainly proven true. But whereas the ultimate goal is treating a larger physical and social whole more comprehensively (for example, Sabloff and Ashmore 2001; Sabloff and Tourtellot 1991), I would argue that we have sometimes created an unnecessary terminological divide, contrasting sites (by which we have mostly meant the centers and elite-occupied buildings) with settlement (by which we have mostly meant places outside the civic core, and especially farmers' homesteads) as if they were distinct and perhaps somewhat unrelated phenomena. In practice, field crews are often usefully organized logistically along such a divide, although even that distinction is far from absolute, and settlement research may take place within the urban core of a site (for example, Haviland 1963; Sanders 1986–90). Nevertheless, William Coe's (1966) review of the Belize Valley monograph raised concern over what he saw as disjunctive study of Barton Ramie without equivalent examination of its presumed governing center, Baking Pot. The contributions of the Barton Ramie study far outweigh this criticism, but the risk of unintentionally reifying distinctions is still with us.

In rethinking the scope and analytic subdivision of settlement archaeology, we begin to gain a fuller appreciation of continuities of spatial scale in settlement traces. Even scalar typologies in discussions by Clarke (1977), Parsons (1972),

Rouse (1972), or Trigger (1968) simultaneously emphasize the wide scalar span of settlement studies, ranging variously from individual features and their components to such aggregates of features as sites, settled landscapes, and regions. Just as landscapes are emerging as worthy of study, so features smaller than buildings are important as settlement traces (for example, Chase and Chase 1985), especially when found away from structures. Larger units are more than simple enlargements or mechanical sums of their constituent parts, and there are surely distinctions in the kinds of social, symbolic, economic, or other information conveyed most readily or commonly by features of different size and form. That does not, however, reduce the need to encompass a fuller range of forms nor the need to study them less disjunctively (compare J. Thomas 1991). Although we still tend to privilege the most obvious forms, and especially those in urban cores, exploring variability in rural Maya contexts is a significant step in domain expansion, as is addressing the variable formal and social complexity embodied within the range of settings.

Socially Informed Interpretive Models

The latter comment leads to the second point: Our interpretive models have grown more socially informed. Models twenty years ago dealt principally with settlement as cultural systems and adaptation; now one reads increasingly of social relations and people. Maya settlement studies have begun to follow what Hendon (1996: 55) exhorted in a related context "to think in terms of social actors rather than abstract entities such as adaptive mechanisms." Concepts of agency- and actor-based models, practice approaches, and structuration theory are prominent in archaeology more generally, of course, as are moves to balance or—for some archaeologists—even replace long-term systemic and evolutionary models with greater emphasis on understanding closer to the scale of individual lives.

This emphasis is evident most clearly, perhaps, in the context of household archaeology. In the work quoted above, Hendon urges archaeologists generally to consider more closely the social consequences of how cooking, weaving, or other domestic tasks were organized (for example, Brumfiel 1991), and she describes such efforts in the Maya area as still very few (for example, Hendon 1997; Joyce 1993). Other aspects of household archaeology are beginning, as well, to yield social inferences. Family and household developmental cycle models, for example, have offered fruitful avenues for exploring observed diversity of settlement forms in social terms, of what the size or composition of the resident group may have been, and of what this seemingly passive construct may imply about active household strategies (for example, Haviland 1988; Robin 1997; Tourtellot 1988a; Yaeger 1995). Other analyses have looked productively at the social implications of variably elaborate house construction, diversity of compound arrangement, or differential hosting of communal feasts (for example, D.S. Rice 1988; Robin 1999; Yaeger 2000a; chapter 5; Yaeger and LeCount 1995). As reflections of household-based decisions (for example, Blanton 1994; Wilk 1990, 1991), these actions mark deliberate strategies for articulating household members and their neighbors, with the goals and consequences of these strategies either enhancing or impeding integration of the larger social groups (for example, Ashmore, Yaeger, and Robin 2001; Tourtellot, Sabloff, and Carmean 1992).

A related development of crucial interpretive importance is the documentation of variability and flux within ancient Maya social classes. From what was once a two-class model of ancient Maya society, we have moved to understanding the social pyramid as having been built of more complicated and diverse tiers. Although inferences of variability among nobility and royalty stem from glyphic decipherment of titles and analysis of portrait imagery (for example, Joyce 1992; Stuart 1993; Webster et al. 1998), such inferences across the entire social range derive perhaps most strongly from settlement studies (for example, Becker 1971; Bullard 1964; A.F. Chase and D.Z. Chase 1992; Gonlin 1994; Hendon 1991; King and Potter 1994; Webster 1999; Willey and Leventhal 1979). The kinds of studies cited in the preceding paragraph are symptomatic of variation in household composition, domestic organizational strategies, and social standing. Other inquiries begin to outline mobility and competition within class ranks and not solely among royalty and nobility (for example, Ashmore, Yaeger, and Robin 2001; Webster 1999). From the foregoing and such summary assessments as are already available—including McAnany's (1993) review of eighth-century Maya household economics; Pyburn's (1998) consideration of diverse commoner statuses and organization at Nohmul, at Chau Hiix, and on Albion Island; and collected essays in D.Z. Chase and A.F. Chase's (1992) volume on Mesoamerican elites, it is clear that models of ancient Maya society must, and increasingly do, accommodate more variability within social classes.

Also noteworthy is the enhanced attention being given to entities larger than households. Yaeger and Canuto (2000) urge, especially, a new emphasis on communities as a crucial but understudied level of social integration between household and polity. At the level of polities, Marcus (1983a: 206–208) called attention long ago to indigenous definitions for Mesoamerican polities and their capitals in which governance and community identity were embodied in the person of the ruler. More recently, Quezada's (1993) reconsideration of Yucatec political organization at the time of the Spanish conquest supports complementing, if not replacing, Roys's (1957) territorial formulations with models in which polity constituents are tethered to their capitals and rulers, as radii to a center, but probably lack firm territorial boundaries encompassing them on the ground. More-

over, such radial models are intriguingly compatible with emerging evidence for radial causeway systems known at such major sites as Caracol and Calakmul (for example, A.F Chase and D.Z. Chase 1987; chapter 10; Folan et al. 1995).

In Maya contexts, wider trends toward socially informed models are abetted most dramatically by the development of a conjunctive methodology, especially as that methodology conjoins deciphered political history with material evidence (for example, W.L. Fash 1988; Fash and Sharer 1991; C. Jones 1977, 1991; Marcus 1983b; Schele and Freidel 1990). To take just one example, architectural, iconographic, and textual data from Copan's Str. 10L-22A allows its identification as a *popol nah* (council house), and as a reflection of royal strategy to share authority and thereby shore up dynastic strength following beheading of the thirteenth ruler (B. Fash et al. 1992). The same building also seems to name subdivisions of the Copan polity, which then constitute an emic resource for modeling settlement organization—when and as the units named are identified on the ground. In the context of settlement archaeology, however, it is important to remember that texts and iconography are associated mostly with works of royalty or elites, the people with the wherewithal to commission text-bearing buildings and belongings. The most crucial aspect of a conjunctive approach, then, is not inclusion of texts or images, per se, but consideration of the broadest possible range of relevant evidence of whatever (critically examined) source.

A nascent area of inquiry is the analysis of time. We begin—but as yet only begin—to recognize the differential interpretive implications of temporality and tradition on settlement archaeology (compare R. Bradley 1987; Ingold 1993; Knapp 1992). Certainly, we recognize that the material remains we encounter are a palimpsest, representing myriad cumulative traces of discrete individual decisions, acts, and days with which we can disaggregate with variable success. The whole includes traces of both cyclical and unique occurrences, all conflated through what we recognize as linear time. The temporal interval of cycles may be daily, as in mundane domestic activities (for example, Robin 1999), or it may be seasonal, as in farming regimens or ritual observances. Some cycles are annual, such as the community seating rituals discussed by Michael Coe (1965) and Diane Chase (1986). Yet other intervals may be longer or more irregular, as in some pilgrimages (for example, Brady and Ashmore 1999; Freidel 1981; Keller 1995a).

Sorting among periodicities is often difficult at best, particularly with shorter intervals. Writing of Aztec domestic contexts, Michael Smith (1992:51) offers the term *household series* to acknowledge the inevitable condensing of lifetimes and generations in even finely analyzed domestic settlement traces. One correlate of recognizing the differing periodicities noted above is positing alternating uses and meanings for settlement units. For example, identifying the remains of a household-based feast does not mean that the locale involved was used constantly or solely as a feasting site. Single-function spaces are surely the exception, not the rule (for example, Kent 1990). This is the temporal aspect of Rapoport's system of settings: we need to seek and recognize the people using and moving through the spaces (for example, Rapoport 1990; Robin 1998).

Reciprocally, we need to recognize—but are only just beginning to do so—the impact of tradition and historical continuity and discontinuity. A homestead is founded or a shrine is created and, as each continues in use it becomes a repository for memory (for example, Basso 1996). Settlement aspects of tradition and memory have been examined most widely at house and landscape scales (for example, Ashmore and Knapp 1999; Blanton 1994; Bourdieu 1973; Hirsch and O'Hanlon 1995; Schama 1995). As memories accrue to a place, further use or abandonment is conditioned in part by what went before (for example, J. Barrett 1999; Bradley 1987). I believe, for example, that the location of the hilltop site of Xunantunich reflects, in part, a social strategy drawing on the accumulated traditional sacredness of the location; the somewhat upstart founders of Xunantunich invoked the sacred authority of the place to enhance their tenuous claims to legitimacy (for example, Ashmore 1998). Others have described the special importance attached to founders' homes and ancestors' burial sites as foci for social continuity and the potential creation of *axes mundii* (for example, Haviland 1988; McAnany 1995; Sharer 1978; Sharer et al. 1999; Tourtellot 1988a; Webster 1999). Alternatively, destruction of places may be an index of change, of attempts to disrupt memory (for example, Chapman 1994; Low 1995). We still tend too often, however, to lose sight of the importance of such links across time. We strip history from settlement studies by reifying otherwise quite useful sequential occupation phases as nearly discrete segments of a series rather than as a continuous—or discontinuous—flow in human social occupation and memory (compare J. Barrett 1999; Bender 1998; Gamble 1998).

Determinants of Settlement Patterns

This continuous flow leads to the third of the points I want to highlight: the greater complexity in what we entertain as determinants of settlement location, form, and distribution. Twenty years ago the dominant settlement models in Maya archaeology were economic, ecological, and/or social in nature (Ashmore 1981a; D.S. Rice and P.M. Rice 1980). To explain the distribution and evolution of observed settlement patterns, we looked to the roles of cultural ecological opportunities and risks; of local and long-distance networks for production, exchange, and consumption; of carrying capacity and subsistence systems; and of social organiza-

tional models. Not only have current models continued to explore these factors, often incorporating the kinds of dynamism described earlier, but the range of influences on choice, form, and change of settlement has grown. Most dramatically, and in keeping with approaches pervading archaeology more widely, we look to ancient political considerations and constraints and to the roles of both ritual and symbolic expression in shaping settlement form and distribution.

Marcus (1992, 1993), for example, considers what had been portrayed as static alternative forms of political organization and their settlement correlates, and recasts them as variants among which polities shifted through time and with particular kinds of historical circumstance. In the Petexbatun and at Caracol, respectively, Demarest (1997) and the Chases (A.F. Chase and D.Z. Chase 1989, 1998a) looked at the specific impact of warfare, combining textual reference to military events with research aimed conjunctively at recognizing war's short- and long-term local effects on settlement form, economic prosperity, and social integration. De Montmollin (1989, 1995) has offered new ways of looking for and at the political aspects of ancient settlement. Importantly, he portrays alternative solutions as dimensions of fairly continuous variation—such as degrees in centralization of administrative authority—rather than as discrete either/or categories of form, structure, and organization. He also urges attention to political strategies, including efforts at both control and resistance, as shaping settlement configurations on local and regional scales (for example, de Montmollin 1987).

Among the varied impacts of political strategizing that de Montmollin examines, the expressive potentials of settlement elements, such as architectural emulation in planning buildings and open spaces, and in establishing new civic centers are highlighted. In this way, those who commission the architecture can express affiliation with distant and revered others, potentially enhancing their local prestige and legitimacy, or perhaps manifesting colonial subordination (for example, Agrinier 1983; de Montmollin 1995). I have drawn on similar arguments in discussions of the establishment of Xunantunich, inferring that its founders alluded architecturally and in other ways to political ties with the older and larger center of Naranjo, as well as perhaps Calakmul (Ashmore 1998; R. Bradley 1987). Alternatively, distinct spatial orders can convey competitive political interaction and strategies, as Schortman and Nakamura (1991) have proposed for the peoples in the sierras and valleys northeast of Copan and Quirigua. I have applied related models to understanding strategies behind spatial orders at Quirigua and Copan (Ashmore 1989, 1991); Houk (1996; Dunning et al. 1999) has extended the application to Dos Hombres in northern Belize. More recently, Sabloff and I have sought to isolate the conditions under which different such strategies are invoked more generally (Ashmore and Sabloff 1997).

Another interpretive area overdue for consideration by settlement archaeologists is the seemingly unmodified landscape. Extensive, if sometimes subtle, modifications were discussed earlier as new foci of study. For much longer, we have known the landscape to be meaningfully constituted for Maya residents today. We have been slow, however, to examine the role of such features as caves in conditioning settlement in space and time (for example, Brady 1997; Vogt 1976, 1981, 1983). Caves and bodies of water are frequent correlates of Maya settlement location, and where they are absent naturally, they are often created artificially (for example, Brady 1997). This is the case at the household-level and commoner settings, as well as in elite and civic contexts, and reflects more than simply economic concerns (for example, Brady and Ashmore 1999; Robin 1999; Scarborough 1998). As cave specialists would agree, I am sure, it is not enough to simply add caves to the mix. Bringing together several foregoing themes, we need to embed such features within what we understand to be an actively occupied, actively traversed, continuously reconsidered, cognized landscape (for example, Brady and Ashmore 1999; Dunning et al. 1999; Knapp and Ashmore 1999; Scarborough 1998; Schele and Mathews 1998).

Conclusion

We have come a long way, indeed, even if we still have a good long way to go. Comparing Maya settlement research and writing today with antecedents of two decades ago, I see much that is different along the three related lines highlighted here:

- our conceptualization of the analytic domain has become much broader and more diversified;
- our interpretive models are becoming more socially informed; and
- we invoke a more complex array of potential determinants for observed settlement patterns.

Despite truly exciting developments along all these lines, we can and should do more. We need to integrate more fully the maximum range of archaeological features, not to make all Maya archaeology a subset of settlement archaeology but to break down the artificial analytic boundaries among individual features, connective areas, larger aggregates at various scales, and the range of contexts in which occupation and settlement occur. There are undeniable differences among a cache, a house, an acropolis, a managed watershed, and the city of Tikal, but we must keep the whole array in mind more effectively, as context, when examining each individually.

We should encourage trends toward greater recognition of temporality, tradition, and social strategy in settlement studies. I believe we also need to recognize more effectively the intricacies and mutability of social roles among those whose lives are attested in the archaeological record. Gender, class, and factionalism are only three of the dimensions of social differentiation receiving nascent attention among Mayanists and with respect to settlement remains (for example, D.Z. Chase and A.F. Chase 1992; Claassen and Joyce 1997; J.W. Fox 1994; E. Graham 1991). Recognizing the interplay among roles and strategies of individual actors yields a view of ancient society—in this case, lowland Maya society—that potentially comes closer than before to modeling the intricacy of life as anciently lived. Attending to these dimensions and to the actors who occupied them need not require that we cast older models wholly aside (for example, Brumfiel 1992), but I agree that the resultant interpretations are significantly transformed by, to paraphrase Flannery (1967), looking again and in new ways at the people behind the system behind the artifacts. Close consideration of the complexities in rural settlement can contribute significantly to these and other goals. I look forward to what Mayanists will think of theory in settlement archaeology another katun from now.

Acknowledgments. An earlier version of this essay was presented at the 1998 Annual Meeting of the Society for American Archaeology, in the symposium out of which this volume grew. Thanks to Gyles Iannone and Sam Connell for inviting my participation in the session and in its publication, and to Tom Patterson, Jerry Sabloff, Ed Schortman, Pat Urban, and two anonymous reviewers for helpful comments on previous drafts. I am also indebted to colleagues in the field, especially members of the Xunantunich Archaeological Project, from whom I continue to learn much about ancient Maya settlement.

3 Rural Complexity in the Cahal Pech Microregion
Analysis and Implications

Gyles Iannone

APPROACHES TO ANCIENT MAYA RURAL COMPLEXITY turn on four key issues (Iannone 1996). First, a review of the literature indicates that the vast majority of Maya research has focused on the urban and rural poles of the settlement continuum, even though it has long been recognized that numerous complex rural settlements existed between these antipodes (for example, Bullard 1960; Willey 1956a:778; Willey, Bullard, and Glass 1955:24–25; Willey et al. 1965:249). Second, Mayanists have often adopted an essentialist perspective and, in doing so, have treated "minor centers" and other complex rural settlements as if they were representative of an "ideal" site type (Gonlin 1994:177). In reality, the variability exhibited by sites of this size and complexity suggests that, more strictly speaking, they comprise a "fuzzy set" of "graded membership" (see Laughlin 1993:18). Thus, it is more accurate to view these sites as variable elements within the "middle level" of an ancient Maya settlement continuum (Iannone 1996). Third, we have often erroneously assumed that all middle-level settlements shared similar or identical functional roles based on the perceived needs of the inhabitants of upper- (urban) and lower-level (rural) settlements (see also Schwartz and Falconer 1994:3; chapter 5). As a result, not only have we homogenized these sites by assuming consistent, shared functions (Gonlin 1994:177, 195; King and Potter 1994:67; chapter 5; see also Schwartz and Falconer 1994:2), but we have in a sense "depopulated" them by not taking into account that the inhabitants of such sites may have had their own motivations, ambitions, agendas, and goals (King and Potter 1994:84; see also chapters 2 and 5). Finally, as a direct result of this approach, we have been inclined to interpret middle-level settlements with reference to their position within a settlement hierarchy (chapter 5; see also Schwartz and Falconer 1994:3). As such, we have downplayed the fact that the overall variability within this settlement level is probably reflective of the diverse roles that the inhabitants

of these sites played within ancient Maya society, something more successfully captured by a heterarchical model (Potter and King 1995; see also chapter 5).

An acceptance of these ideas has led a number of Mayanists to take up the study of rural complexity (for example, Gonlin 1994; King and Potter 1994). Gonlin has even gone so far as to state that "if we do not fully understand rural complexity, we cannot convincingly speak of complexity in general for the ancient Maya"(1994:195). This chapter aims to contribute to this effort by outlining the results of a long-term study (1992 to 1998) conducted within two middle-level settlements located in the upper Belize River region. My goals are to highlight the variability exhibited by these complex rural settlements and explore the implications of this variability with regard to the study of ancient Maya sociopolitical and socioeconomic integration.

Rural Complexity within the Cahal Pech Microregion

The following case study focuses on two middle-level settlements located in the upper Belize River region (figure 3.1). The two sites, Zubin (Iannone 1996) and X-ual-canil (also known as Cayo Y), are situated in the undulating foothills zone, on opposite sides of the Macal River, between 2 and 3 km from the upper-level settlement of Cahal Pech (figures 3.1–3.5). The research design for the investigation of these two sites was very much inductive in orientation. The principal goals were to generate a multifaceted, diachronically sensitive, comparative database that could be used to isolate similarities and differences between the two middle-level settlements; and explore the social, economic, and political implications of these affinities and divergences. A comparable excavation strategy was employed in both instances. An effort was made to test as many site core features as possible. At Zubin, excavations were carried out within seven of the nine site core structures

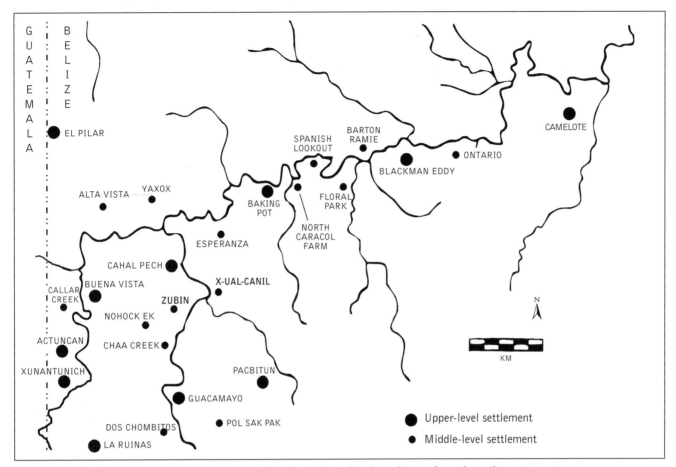

3.1 Map of the upper Belize River region showing the location of Cahal Pech, Zubin, and X-ual-canil. Map by Gyles Iannone

(78%); the X-ual-canil excavations were conducted within twelve of fifteen site core structures (80%). At both sites, a similar excavation strategy was employed, with larger, horizontal excavations (generally 4 x 4 or 2 x 4 m units) providing a detailed understanding of terminal architecture, and smaller, vertical probes (usually 2 x 2 m units) revealing architectural sequences, sealed ceramic lots, and ritual deposits. Investigations within the peripheries of the two sites were limited to mapping and small-scale test excavations to develop a basic understanding of the growth of the respective support populations.

In broad terms, Zubin and X-ual-canil share similar ecological and social contexts. They also exhibit significant differences, however. For one, the Zubin site core (50 x 100 m) was roughly half the size of its X-ual-canil (80 x 200 m) counterpart. The two sites also differ with respect to length of occupation. Zubin was occupied from roughly 850 BC to AD 875. It is important to note, however, that the earliest use of the site was as a hilltop shrine, and it did not take on its residential aspect until the Late Classic (AD 600 to 900). In contrast, although there is evidence for Terminal Preclassic (AD 100 to 400) and Early Classic (AD 400 to 600) settlement within the X-ual-canil periphery, the site core itself exhibits a relatively short Late Classic occupation. The following

comparative analysis therefore focuses on the Late Classic period, as this is the time when both sites received their most intensive and sustained use. To highlight the similarities and differences between these two sites, I discuss the following data categories: architecture (ritual/ceremonial, residential, administrative), artifacts, mortuary remains, and settlement.

ARCHITECTURAL COMPARISON
Comparison of ritual/ceremonial architecture. Pyramidal, or shrine structures, were long part of the Zubin site plan (figure 3.2). The earliest shrine, structure C9, dates to the Middle Preclassic (approximately 850 BC). This structure would be joined by a second pyramidal structure, A1, during the Late Preclassic (300 BC to AD 400). Structure A1's placement on the eastern side of the Ac courtyard suggests it may have been a precursor to the eastern ancestor shrines of the Classic period (Becker 1971; A.F. Chase and D.Z. Chase 1994a:53–54; Iannone 1996:394; McAnany 1995:53; Welsh 1988:190). Both of these early structures contained mortuary and cache offerings suggestive of shrine-related rituals. It is important, however, to reiterate that there is no evidence of residential occupation of Zubin before the Late Classic. It would appear, therefore, that prior to the Late

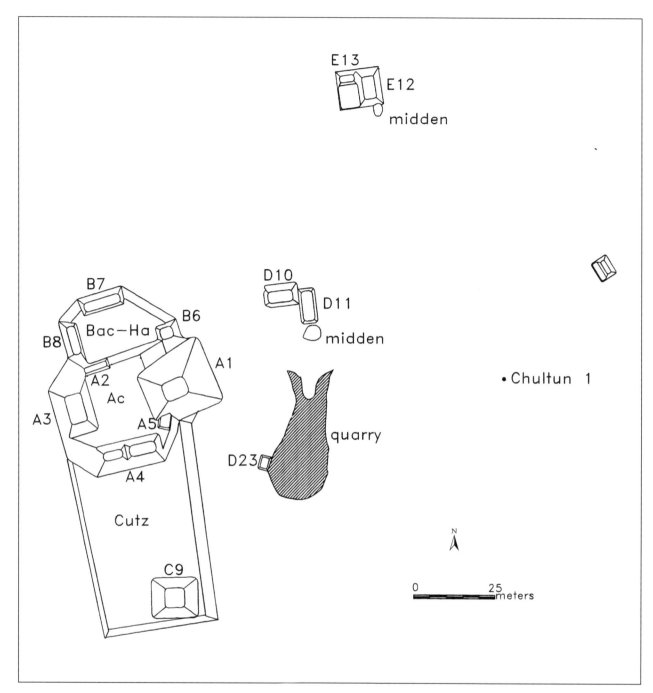

3.2 Map of the Zubin site core. *Survey and map by Shawn Brisbin and Gyles Iannone*

Classic, structures C9 and A1 were not typical localized lineage shrines. Rather, it seems as if these early shrines may have had broader microregional importance, not unlike the "pilgrimage" shrines described by Vogt (1970:98–99) for the contemporary Zinacantan Maya.

The character of the ritual architecture at Zubin would change dramatically during the Late Classic period. Sometime around AD 675 we see the first evidence of residential occupation. The newly founded residential corporate group appears to have gone to great lengths to transform the structure A1 shrine from one that may have previously emphasized broader microregional affiliations to a more localized, eastern ancestor shrine used to legitimize the new occupant's claim to social space. Specifically, during the Late Classic a significant degree of construction was undertaken in association with the shrine. This construction created a larger (roughly 5-m high), more impressive edifice from which claims to social space could be conducted and visually displayed to outsiders. In conjunction with these modifications, ritual activity was undertaken to augment the claims sym-

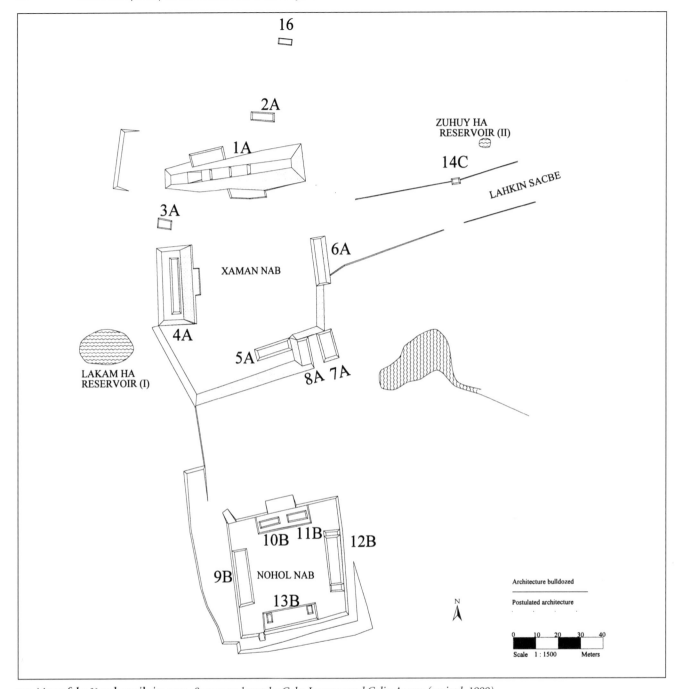

3.3 Map of the X-ual-canil site core. *Survey and map by Gyles Iannone and Colin Agnew (revised, 1999)*

bolized by the structure itself. These rituals included the interment of at least ten different graves (Iannone 1996:417). These interments range widely in terms of both the degree of elaboration of the grave chamber and the quantity and quality of the grave goods included. Clearly, the Late Classic residential group adopted a multifaceted approach to claim the ancestor shrine as theirs and, subsequently, to employ it as a means to define and control their newly acquired social space.

In contrast to Zubin, X-ual-canil has no pyramidal shrine structures. The site does, however, contain significant ritual

architecture. In particular, the site has both a ballcourt and a causeway complex, two features more commonly associated with upper-level settlements. The ballcourt was first recognized in 1995 in a recessed corner in direct association with the Xaman Nab raised platform (figure 3.3). Structures 7A and 8A comprising the court had been built in one construction phase during the Late Classic period. Our investigations exposed sloping aprons and veneer stones, features that confirmed that these structures did indeed comprise a ballcourt. Excavations within the alley failed, however, to produce a ballcourt marker, or any cache

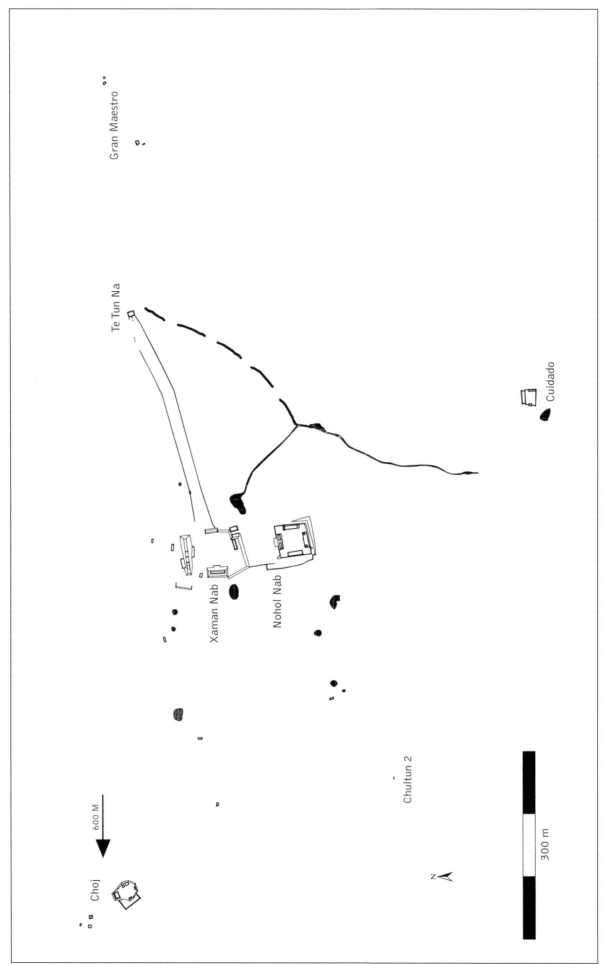

3.4 Map of the X-ual-canil site core and periphery. Survey and map by Gyles Iannone and Colin Agnew

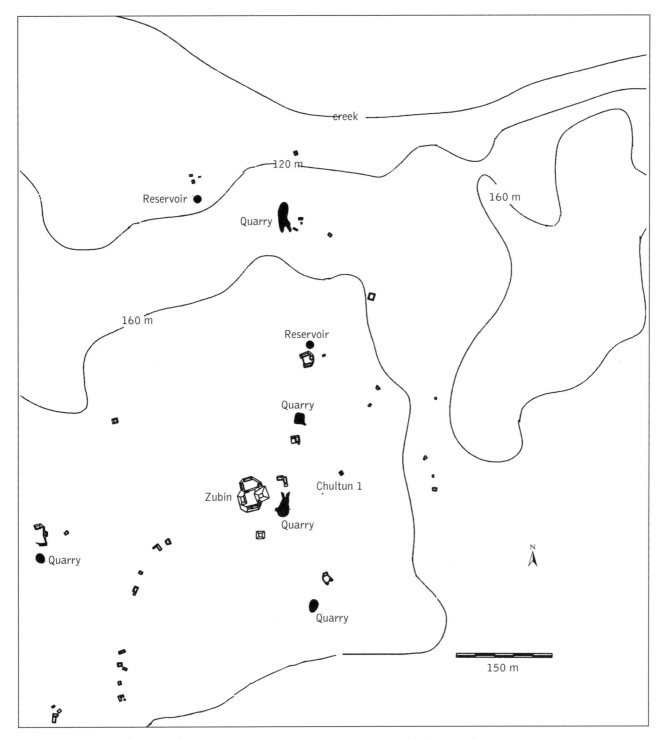

3.5 Map of the Zubin site core and periphery. *Survey (1991–92,94) and map (1994) by Shawn Brisbin*

offerings. Regardless, X-ual-canil is one of the few sites in the upper Belize River region, besides Ontario Village (Garber et al. 1994), that has a ballcourt but which cannot be readily classified as an upper-level settlement or major center. As such, it provides a good example of the syncretism exhibited by some middle-level settlements. The existence of a ballcourt also implies that a certain amount of

specialized ritual activity was carried out at X-ual-canil. Specifically, it suggests that the cyclical rituals of fertility, normally ascribed to the ball game (for example, Freidel, Schele, and Parker 1993), were being conducted.

A second example of syncretism at X-ual-canil is the occurrence of a large *sacbe* (causeway) with an associated termini complex (figures 3.3, 3.4). The Lahkin Sacbe, at approximately 19 m across, represents one of the widest features of this type in the upper Belize River region. The sacbe begins between structures 1A and 6A on the eastern side of the Xaman Nab plaza. From this point, it runs roughly 363 m east by northeast, following a long, narrow, natural ridge to its termination. The termini complex, designated Te Tun Na, consists of a relatively small performative platform (15C) fronted by both a stela (stela 1) and an altar (altar 1). Excavations within the 15C platform, and beneath the stela and altar, failed to produce any dedicatory offerings. These excavations did, however, confirm a Late Classic construction date.

Investigations just east of the entrance to the X-ual-canil's Xaman Nab plaza also exposed large portions of structure 14C, which straddles the northern wall of the Lahkin Sacbe (figure 3.3). These explorations suggested that structure 14C had a small inset stair that led to a C-shaped platform. Considered together, this building's location and morphology imply that the structure may have served as a "reviewing stand" for the processions conducted along the causeway (Schwake 1999).

In summary, a comparison of the ritual architecture at Zubin and X-ual-canil indicates that these two centers had little in common. Zubin, with its eastern shrine, appears to conform to the ritual practices shared by a wide cross section of ancient lowland Maya society—from small housemound groups to large, upper-level settlements. Zubin's emphasis on rituals associated with an eastern ancestor shrine therefore allies it with many other social groups that were striving to initiate and maintain ties to lineage land holdings (McAnany 1995).

In contrast, the failure to exhibit an eastern shrine structure, as well as the burials and caches normally associated with such buildings, implies that ancestor-related ritual activity was not imperative to X-ual-canil's claim to land. Rather, the absence of these features and activities suggests that the inhabitants of X-ual-canil were sanctioned by another, more firmly established political unit that did not require localized ancestor veneration rituals to validate its claim to X-ual-canil and its environs. Still, rituals were conducted at X-ual-canil. These activities, which probably manifest themselves in fertility rituals in the ballcourt and processions along the causeway, are reflective of some of the more specialized ceremonies undertaken by the elite who inhabited upper-level settlements. It is plausible that these activities were not so much concerned with claims to land; rather they were aimed at controlling the production of land through cyclical, fertility-based rituals of the ball game and ceremonial processions.

Comparison of residential components. At X-ual-canil, the Nohol Nab courtyard represents the primary residential unit (Seibert 2000; figure 3.3). Formal entry was gained via an approximately 9-m–wide stair centrally located on the north side of the courtyard. Upon ascending to the summit of the raised platform, the visitor would first pass between two flanking structures (structures 10B and 11B) and then down a small step formed by the platform that sustained these two architectural features. We were unable to determine whether the two flanking structures were employed as open platforms or whether they were surmounted by pole-and-thatch or wattle-and-daub superstructures. Given the formal nature of the entrance, the latter appears more likely. The western side of the courtyard was bounded by a large building (roughly 24 m long) with a masonry substructure (structure 9B). Low, double-faced masonry walls were partially exposed on the surface of this building. Indications are that the upper walls and roof were originally constructed of perishable materials such as pole-and-thatch or wattle-and-daub. No residential features, such as benches or room walls, were encountered during excavations of this building. The lack of such features, and the large interior space, suggest that this building may have served as a storage facility. Unfortunately, because of the paucity of artifacts recovered during excavations, this interpretation cannot be confirmed.

A slightly different structure is located opposite structure 9B on the eastern side of the courtyard. This structure, 12B, likely contained two or three rooms. Excavations uncovered parts of the frontal terrace; portions of a low, double-faced masonry wall; and a section of a room interior and associated bench. These attributes, combined with its setting at the site (within the site's only moderately restricted access courtyard), suggest that structure 12B was probably a residential building. The building itself would have been comprised of a masonry substructure, double-faced masonry lower walls, either pole-and-thatch or wattle-and-daub upper walls, and a perishable roof.

The southern boundary of the courtyard is defined by another problematic architectural feature. This structure, 13B, had a masonry substructure, as well as front and side walls of double-faced masonry construction. The upper walls were apparently constructed of either poles or wattle-and-daub. In contrast, there was no evidence of masonry walls in the rear of the structure. Rather, the rear wall appears to have been constructed entirely of poles or wattle-and-daub. This material suggests that a "cheaper" form of construction was employed in areas that would have been visually hidden from visitors. Two entrances were located along the front face of the building near its western and eastern ends. No interior walls or benches were found in this 24-m–long structure. As with structure 9B, there is nothing to suggest that this building was a residence. Once again, the lack of residential features and the large interior space are both suggestive of a storage function.

Like X-ual-canil, Zubin's residential component dates to the Late Classic period (Iannone 1996:426–429). Within the site core, residential structures were established in both Ac, the central courtyard (structure A4), and in the adjacent Bac-Ha courtyard (structure B8; figure 3.2). The primary Zubin residence was structure A4, located on the southern side of the Ac courtyard. Excavations indicated that, in its final form, structure A4 comprised a three-room building fronted by a terrace. The substructure employed masonry walls. In contrast, the superstructure was constructed entirely of pole-and-thatch or wattle-and daub, except for the far western room, which had low, double-faced masonry walls. Each of the rooms had masonry benches, although, once again, the western room stands out as having had a bench of greater overall height.

A second, smaller residence (structure B8) was situated on the western side of Zubin's lower Bac-Ha courtyard. Excavations indicated that structure B8 comprised at least one large room, with one low bench. The room was fronted by a terrace, and the substructure employed masonry walls. The superstructure was entirely of perishable construction (wattle-and-daub or pole-and-thatch). Given its slightly smaller size and slightly less complex construction (lack of clear room definition and double-faced masonry walls), structure B8 appears to have been a secondary residence representative of slightly less status and prestige than structure 4A.

In summary, if we compare the most elaborate residential features at X-ual-canil (structure 12B) and Zubin (structure 4A, western room), we see a great deal of overlap. Both sites have "improved" architectural forms (Abrams 1994) in that there is evidence of masonry substructures; low, double-faced masonry walls; and interior benches. These houses, however, are clearly not representative of the highest status, as they fail to employ vaulted roofs (Abrams 1994; Kurjack 1976). Rather, because the most elaborate residences from both sites are very simple examples of Abrams (1994) "Improved C" form, they likely represent intermediate, rather than high, status households (see Abrams 1994:85). Access into these residential groups is also comparable: Both exhibit relatively restricted formal access but are only moderately restricted with regard to visual access. This level of access again suggests an intermediate position between comparatively open, low-status house-mound groups and highly restricted elite residences.

Finally, although there appears to be a significant degree of similarity between the residential components of Zubin and X-ual-canil, there is one fundamental difference. In terms of the configuration of residential spaces, it is important to note that Zubin's residences share ambient space with ritual features (the structure A1 shrine). Specifically, there is a blending of residential and ancestor-based ritual features. This blending implies that lineage, or kinship-based, activities were an important determinant of the settlement plan at Zubin. In contrast, the residential and administra-tive/ritual components at X-ual-canil are clearly separated from each other, suggesting a distinction between the institutions of kinship (residential) and kingship (administration, processions, and the ball game).

Comparison of administrative architecture. At X-ual-canil, the Xaman Nab plaza is dominated by two long, multiroomed, "range-type" structures, designated 1A and 4A (figure 3.3). Structure 1A is situated on the northern side of the plaza. Excavations on the summit of this building indicated that it was never vaulted; it does, however, exhibit many of the characteristics of administrative buildings, given the criteria presented by Kowalski (1987:85). Structure 1A has a broad, central staircase; contains multiple rooms; and fronts a large public plaza. As a result, although it fails to display all the criteria for an administrative building (it is missing an axially aligned throne feature), structure 1A generally fits the administrative category.

Structure 4A overlooks the western portion of X-ual-canil's Xaman Nab plaza (figure 3.3). Investigations at the base of this building exposed the basal portion of the terminal staircase and portions of an associated frontal sustaining platform. Excavations on the summit of structure 4A, along the primary access, exposed two vaulted rooms separated by a thick spine wall. The smaller, more restricted inner room was dominated by a C-shaped bench. The larger, and more open, frontal room contained two bench features. Taken together, the placement of the large 4A building within the main public plaza, its wide staircase, spacious frontal room, and smaller interior room with its "throne-like" bench, all suggest that this structure was X-ual-canil's principal administrative building.

In contrast to X-ual-canil, Zubin has only one questionable administrative construction, structure A3. This structure, located on the west side of the Ac courtyard (figure 3.2), exhibits a large substructure with the typical broad staircase. Its superstructure was comprised of a long, narrow room with low, double-faced masonry walls and a perishable roof. The room itself was too narrow to accommodate people (it was only 0.75 cm wide); thus, it apparently could not have served as a residence. Similarly, excavations along the building's primary axis failed to uncover any burials or cache offerings, ruling out a ritual role. As a result, this structure appears to have had a special function; however, the only feature suggestive of administration is the broad staircase. In the end, structure A3 may have had some administrative purpose, but this interpretation is based more on the absence of certain characteristics (no residential rooms or ritual deposits) rather than on the presence of well-defined administrative features.

In summary, the administrative qualities of X-ual-canil and Zubin are very different. Zubin has only one very questionable administrative building (structure A3), suggesting that Zubin's integrative tools were kinship based rather than bureaucratic (kingship). X-ual-canil, on the other hand, has two likely administrative buildings (structures 1A and 4A). In particular, structure 4A is consistent in many ways with administrative buildings found within upper-level settlements. As such, it appears that X-ual-canil's officials administered subordinate populations through the same bureaucratic mechanisms and edifices that the elite from upper-level settlements used. Clearly, Zubin was much farther down the administrative ladder.

ARTIFACTUAL COMPARISON

In looking at the material culture assemblages of the middle-level settlements of X-ual-canil and Zubin, the first significant difference that presents itself is that X-ual-canil has a relative paucity of artifacts and a limited number of artifact types, whereas Zubin has both a plethora of artifacts and a wide range of artifact types. These differences partially reflect contrasting occupational durations. The divergences in artifact inventories are, however, suggestive of the fact that different activities were carried out at these sites.

The Late Classic components of both sites exhibit a wide range of utilitarian artifacts, such as ceramics, obsidian blades, chipped-stone tools (bifaces, choppers, scrapers), manos, and metates. The main differences in utilitarian assemblages lay in the significantly smaller number of artifacts at X-ual-canil. As indicated above, this small number is likely a reflection of divergences in the intensity and duration of occupation.

The most important artifactual differences between the two sites concerns the presence of ritual deposits. Both cache and grave offerings were discovered at Zubin. The majority of caches consisted of partial vessel termination offerings. Partial vessel caches were encountered in ritual contexts (in front of the structure A1 shrine), residential contexts (within structure A4), and beneath the staircase between the Ac and Bac-Ha courtyards. None of the ceramics recovered from these partial vessel caches can be considered "elite" varieties. In one instance, portions of a well-made Orange-Walk Incised: Orange-Walk Variety cylinder vase were discovered. Although this is not an elite type, the relatively high quality, form, and elaborate designs on such vessels suggest that they may have been "subelite" wares.

Common Late Classic grave goods at Zubin included obsidian blades, small jadeite beads, small conch shell beads, disks, adornos (small *Spondylus* shell beads, inlays, rosettes), and ceramic vessels. Although these items do signify some elevated status, their small number, size, and inferior quality are indicative of either nonelite, or subelite, status. This status is particularly evident when the objects are compared to examples of similar materials recovered from more elaborate graves within both the Cahal Pech site core (see Reents-Budet 1994:349) and its immediate periphery (Cheetham 1994; Conlon 1992; Conlon and Awe 1991). The ceramic as-

semblage recovered from mortuary contexts at Zubin included plates, dishes, bowls, and cylinder vases. Once again, many of these vessels are of varieties not considered elite wares; these include various Dolphin Head Red, Belize Red, and Mount Maloney-type varieties. Other examples, however, may potentially be indicative of subelite types, such as Orange-Walk Incised, Saxche Orange Polychrome, and Montego Polychrome. The subelite classification for these vessels is once again postulated because although the vessels are very well made and exhibit fairly elaborate decoration, they are not of the same quality as vessels found in more elaborate graves within Cahal Pech's immediate periphery (Cheetham 1994; Conlon 1992; Conlon and Awe 1991). It is particularly telling that the Zubin polychromes have pseudoglyphs, a possible indicator of nonelite or subelite mimicry of elite characteristics (Reents-Budet 1994:139–140, 184, 227).

In contrast to Zubin, investigations within the X-ual-canil site core failed to produce any ritual assemblages. Excavations in prime locations for such deposits, such as along the primary axis of various buildings, below stela 1 and altar 1 at the Te Tun Na termini group, and within the ballcourt alley, produced nothing in the way of artifactual offerings. The absence of such deposits is intriguing. Specifically, although there was great effort to create the stage for large processions and ceremonies at X-ual-canil, the normal practice of conducting dedicatory and termination rituals to sanctify this sacred space does not appear to have been required.

In summary, the utilitarian artifact assemblages from X-ual-canil and Zubin are comparable. The main difference revolves around the relative paucity of utilitarian artifacts at X-ual-canil. This incongruity mainly reflects the site's comparatively limited intensity and duration of occupation. In contrast, more substantial differences exist in the ritual assemblages at the two sites. In particular, whereas Zubin shows a wide range of material offerings, X-ual-canil fails to exhibit similar deposits. This situation suggests that the ritual activities carried out at these sites diverged significantly. At Zubin, grave offerings and caches were likely employed as part of dedicatory and termination offerings aimed at maintaining and solidifying control over lineage landholdings. At X-ual-canil, materially constituted offerings were clearly not required to lay claim to social space. This condition implies that the occupants of X-ual-canil sanctified and legitimized their claims to social space through nonmaterial means (that is, through administration and ceremonies) and/or that the use of the site was sanctified by a more powerful external force. Whether or not this more powerful center was the nearby Cahal Pech remains hard to determine. Regardless, the X-ual-canil data suggest that the use of the center was materially sanctioned at some place other than the site itself.

MORTUARY COMPARISON

During the Late Classic period, at least ten different interments were placed within the structure A1 eastern shrine at Zubin (figure 3.2; Iannone 1996:417). These burials range widely in terms of both the degree of elaboration exhibited by the grave chamber itself, and the number and quality of goods interred. Differences in body orientation (that is, supine versus prone) and the timing of the interment, suggest further lines of distinction. Overall, a pattern exists showing that burials associated with major construction phases (often found within the structure itself) tended to have more elaborate grave goods (jadeite beads, ceramic vessels, marine shell items, obsidian blades), a moderate level of grave chamber elaboration (they exhibit simple crypts, that is, graves comprised of a stone-lined chamber slightly larger than the body itself; Welsh [1988]), and supine body position. Some of the other burials, given their timing (they were interred at the same time as the more elaborate graves) and placement (often in front of the structure itself), appear to have been dedicatory "caches" or offerings, following the arguments of Becker (1992). These offerings were associated with simple crypt graves, as well as less elaborate forms such as capped pits, haphazard cists, and head cists (see Welsh 1988). They also contained few, if any, grave goods, and exhibited prone body positions. Finally, at least one burial discovered in the plaza fronting the structure A1 shrine appears to have been a large-scale sacrificial offering consisting of five superimposed individuals interred in prone positions, with a relative paucity of grave goods (one partial vessel). Thus, the structure A1 burial assemblage represents various status differences. Social proximity to the head of the residential corporate group may have been the definitive factor in determining one's status, and this proximity may have been reflected in the way in which one was interred in association with the ancestor shrine.

In contrast to Zubin, X-ual-canil fails to exhibit an eastern ancestor shrine. That burials were still interred at the site, in association with nonshrine contexts, is indicated by the simple crypt burial in the structure 4A range-type building. Unfortunately, this interment was affected by recent bulldozing, and its contents remain a mystery. Based on the degree of elaboration (simple crypt), the grave suggests that this individual held moderate status within the microregional community. The lack of burials and an eastern shrine structure suggest that mortuary rituals were not a significant activity at X-ual-canil.

In summary, Zubin appears to have employed the tried-and-true method through which ancestral ties to the landscape were initiated and reaffirmed. The abundant evidence of mortuary activity associated with the site's eastern ancestor shrine (structure A1) confirms this. In contrast, the limited evidence for mortuary activity at X-ual-canil, coupled with the lack of an eastern ancestor shrine, suggests that the inhabitants of this center must have had a very different connection to their social space. It also indicates that X-ual-canil had few, if any, ancestors that warranted veneration. These differences suggest that Zubin and X-ual-canil had very different "place-making" strategies.

In terms of similarities, the single disturbed burial in structure A4 at X-ual-canil exhibits a grave form that is consistent with the more elaborate graves at Zubin, particularly with regard to labor investment (simple crypt). This form indicates that inhabitants of the two sites may have had comparable status. In general, the degree of labor investment represented by the simple crypt grave form appears to be indicative of moderate status. It clearly lies between a number of simpler burial types and more elaborate crypt and tomb varieties, as presented in the Welsh (1988) typology. The fact that some of these less elaborate grave forms (capped pits, head cists, haphazard cists) also exist at Zubin implies that this corporate group was internally differentiated. These social differences are reaffirmed by the location of individual burials vis-à-vis the ancestor shrine itself (that is, within the structure or in the plaza fronting it). That the lineage heads at Zubin held moderate status (nonelite or subelite) is also confirmed by the grave goods recovered during excavations. This moderate status is particularly evident when the Zubin grave-goods assemblages are compared with the more elaborate offerings discovered in graves both within the Cahal Pech site core (Reents-Budet 1994:349) and its immediate periphery (Cheetham 1994; Conlon 1992; Conlon and Awe 1991).

SETTLEMENT COMPARISON

During the Late Classic period, a relatively dense peripheral population formed around the Zubin site core (figure 3.5). This settlement consisted of numerous smaller mounds and mound clusters, forming a continuum beginning with small solitary structures and concluding with a number of larger patio or plazuela-type configurations (see Ashmore, ed. 1981a). Test excavations within a number of these peripheral groups indicated that these residences were not as elaborate as those in the Zubin site core. Specifically, they were smaller and did not contain bench features or double-faced masonry walls. They are all classifiable as Abram's (1994:63) Category D buildings (masonry substructure, perishable superstructure). The less elaborate peripheral residences suggest that there were status differences between the inhabitants of the Zubin site core and the peripheral population, as confirmed by other lines of evidence. Specifically, although the peripheral population was clearly focused on the center of Zubin, the architecture of the main group restricted access to the site core and its inhabitants. Once again, this restriction implies that there were significant status differences between the inhabitants of the site core and those who occupied its periphery. In terms of the broader settlement context of Zubin, the site is located on a high hill within the undulating foothills zone. The surrounding terrain comprises moderate slopes and small valleys, both of which would have been ideal for swidden agriculture. That agriculture was an important activity at Zubin is confirmed by the numerous chipped-stone farming implements (bifacial) we discovered during our excavations (n = 83). There is no evidence, however, of such intensive agricultural pursuits as terracing.

In contrast to Zubin, the hilltop area immediately surrounding the X-ual-canil site core was apparently sparsely populated (see figure 3.4). With the exception of a few small, two-mound groups, the settlement inventory is characterized by solitary mounds. All the hilltop peripheral structures are once again classifiable as Abram's (1994) Category D residences. As a result, it is implied that the inhabitants of the site's periphery were of a lower status than X-ual-canil's principal site core occupants. Test excavations within the Gran Maestro group, and the collection of sherds from the surface and within looters' trenches in the other peripheral structures, indicated that most of these hilltop groups were probably established during the Late Classic period. Within the valley at the base of the X-ual-canil hill a different type of settlement was encountered. Reconnaissance in this area led to the discovery of two substantial plazuela groups, Choj and Cuidado. These groups were larger and more complex than any of the peripheral settlements on the X-ual-canil hilltop. For the most part, however, the Choj and Cuidado residences also fall neatly into Abram's (1994) Category D buildings.

Another difference between the hilltop and valley settlements is that the valley plazuelas were occupied much earlier. Excavations within Chultun 1 at Choj (Gray 2000) indicated that this group was occupied as early as the Terminal Preclassic. Similarly, test excavations within structure 21D at Cuidado suggested that this group was established during the Early Classic. In sum, not only are the hilltop and valley sites different with regard to group size and complexity (mostly solitary mounds on the hill, larger plazuela groups restricted to the valley), but they also display differences in the timing of initial occupation (Late Classic on the hill, Terminal Preclassic and Early Classic in the valley).

The two groups of peripheral settlements are linked by one of X-ual-canil's most intriguing features: a modified drainage system. The major components of the drainage system are a number of dry reservoirs located on the X-ual-canil hilltop. Given the small size of the hilltop population (as suggested by the limited quantity of mounded architecture), it would appear that these features had another purpose besides the collection of potable water. Specifically, although the reservoirs may have begun as quarries for construction stone, they may have subsequently been used to regulate water flow. In some cases, funnel channels and rock walls appear to have been used to divert water into the reservoirs. The reservoirs tend to be located at the heads of natural gullies that would have distributed water among a series of natural drainage channels located at the saddles between hills. Exploration of these drainage channels indicated that they encircled the X-ual-canil hill.

The extent of this drainage network allowed us to carry out only a detailed study of the southern drainage. Indications are that one arm of this channel began in the open area between the Nohol Nab courtyard and the Xaman Nab plaza, near the ballcourt (figure 3.4). The western boundary of this intervening surface is demarcated by a retaining wall that is 0.50 m high. From this point, the surface slopes toward the east, where the architecture and surrounding landscape seem to have been utilized to drain water into an ancient drainage ditch located 10 to 15 m southeast of the ballcourt. Thus, at least some of the X-ual-canil architecture and natural topography appears to have been employed in controlling drainage, as Scarborough has proposed for other lowland Maya sites (1994, 1998). Additional water would have been carried to the channel via the various gullies along its course. A second channel begins near the Te Tun Na termini group (figure 3.4). Thus, the two primary ritual features at the site (the ballcourt and the Te Tun Na stela/altar complex) are associated with the principal channels of the southern drainage system; this is likely more than coincidence. As Houston (1998:359) has pointed out, a growing body of evidence suggests that ballcourts were often considered the origin point for water used in irrigation. If the processions along the causeway were also fertility based, the location of the second drainage channel may also be explained in this manner.

Reconnaissance along the drainage channel suggests partial modification through the use of check-dams. In combination, the check-dams and reservoirs appear to have been constructed at key points along the drainage to control flow and amass larger volumes of water in the areas adjacent to a large agricultural field system situated at the base of the X-ual-canil hill. The small peripheral population on the ridge itself, which appears to consist primarily of solitary structures situated in close proximity to reservoirs, was potentially involved in the maintenance and daily operation of the drainage.

During the 1997 field season, the effects of a tropical storm permitted us to see the drainage system in action. Indications are that the system would have transported a great volume of water to the agricultural sectors at the base of the X-ual-canil hill. Research in the vicinity of the field system has led to independent confirmation of the agricultural potential. Specifically, a series of phosphate tests on the soil from beneath the fields produced highly positive results, indicating extensive prehistoric use. In addition, in 1998 we discovered and excavated a series of agricultural terraces to the northwest of the site, near the Choj group (figure 3.4). Associated ceramics allowed us to date these terraces to the Late Classic period. The presence of these agricultural features, considered along side the other field systems already explored, confirmed the notion that the base of the X-ual-canil ridge was the locus for intensive agricultural production during the Late Classic period. Given that earlier settlements, such as Choj and Cuidado, existed in the vicinity of these features, it is clear that the area itself had a long history of agricultural use.

In summary, the settlement micropatterns of Zubin and X-ual-canil are very different. Zubin appears to have comprised a large, internally differentiated residential corporate group, as defined by Hayden and Cannon (1982). Its associated settlement consisted of a fairly dense and diverse range of settlement units, from solitary mounds to larger plazuela groups. This settlement, including that of the site core itself, was established during the Late Classic period. There is no indication that any specialized economic activities, beyond swidden agriculture, were carried out.

In contrast, the settlement at X-ual-canil is quite varied. Unlike Zubin, the peripheral population surrounding X-ual-canil, at least on the ridge top, appears to have been far from dense. The predominance of solitary mounds is also interesting, as is the fact that some mounds are closely associated with large reservoirs. Seeing as these reservoirs are far too large to have been realistically constructed to sustain a solitary house mound, it seems plausible that the mounds housed individuals specifically involved in the controlled collection and diversion of stored water (this may explain the absence of extended family households). These reservoirs, in conjunction with the natural drainage networks and strategically placed check-dams, controlled water flow to the agricultural fields at the base of the ridge.

Reconnaissance in this area indicated the presence of some larger plazuela groups. It is telling that these settlement units do show the natural growth that would be expected of a residential group (when compared to the situation on the top of the hill). These larger groups also differ from those on the hilltop in that they were established much earlier, during the Terminal Preclassic/Early Classic. Considering the late appearance of X-ual-canil, it may be that during the Late Classic period a concerted effort was made to take control of the agricultural fields through the water management system administered from X-ual-canil. This scenario assumes that a more powerful social entity, such as Cahal Pech, may have been responsible for this take-over. The fact that X-ual-canil's peripheral population was relatively small and dispersed also indicates that the necessary labor force required to construct the impressive buildings within the site core may not have been readily available. Thus, the limited size of the overall population at X-ual-canil also attests to the fact that some kind of outside intervention by more established social entities would have been required to construct the site.

Discussion

The middle-level settlements of Zubin and X-ual-canil share certain qualities, particularly regarding overall size, timing, and duration of residential occupation (Late Classic) and the intermediate quality of both residential architecture and grave forms. The latter two criteria suggest that the principal inhabitants of the two sites shared a similar nonelite or subelite status. Beyond these basic similarities, however, Zubin and X-ual-canil constitute very different site types. Zubin appears to be a quintessential example of a residential corporate group (Hayden and Cannon 1982) or heterogeneous household (McAnany 1993). The residential and mortuary data suggest multiple statuses. In contrast, there are few indicators of specialization beyond basic agricultural pursuits. The importance given to ancestor veneration rituals, and the blending of these rituals with residential occupation, implies that kinship was a key integrative mechanism. It is important to note, however, that this lineage-based unit was established quite late in the use history of the Zubin locus. Ritual use of the site goes back to 850 BC, whereas residential occupation was established only during the Late Classic. I have argued elsewhere that this Late Classic occupation is reflective of a period of power sharing on behalf of Cahal Pech (Iannone 1996:433; similar arguments for power sharing have been made for Late Classic Copan [Fash 1991] and Palenque [Schele 1991]; see also Culbert 1991). Specifically, it seems plausible that the Zubin hilltop, which had formerly served as an important microregional shrine locus, was released to a nonelite (or at best subelite) lineage during the Late Classic as part of a microregional power-sharing strategy. This lineage, in turn, went to great lengths to establish this locus as its ancestral home through ancestor-related rituals. In doing so, the inhabitants transformed Zubin into a moderately restricted, internally differentiated, rural farmstead.

The corporate nature of Zubin is reaffirmed by the fact that the labor for construction and rituals was readily available in the immediate vicinity of the settlement. How this farmstead fit within the microregional hierarchy is less clear. There is little substantive evidence of either direct Cahal Pech control or total Zubin independence. As a result, Zubin may best be viewed as having had a heterarchical relationship with Cahal Pech. Importantly, regardless of whether it was sanctioned or not, Zubin's Late Classic ancestor veneration program, in and of itself, constitutes a denial of complete Cahal Pech control. Specifically, the rituals associated with claiming structure A1 as a localized ancestor shrine would have also de-emphasized the previous role this structure played as one of Cahal Pech's microregional shrines. This situation also implies that tensions and contradictions existed at the microregional scale during the Late Classic and that the Cahal Pech/Zubin relationship may have always been a fluctuating one characterized by constant negotiation.

X-ual-canil could not be more different from Zubin. The administrative and water control features at this site, combined with its sparse population, relatively late construction, and obvious agricultural potential (fields and terraces), suggests that X-ual-canil was built to integrate an already extant farming population (situated in the valley at the base of the hill) into a broader microregional alliance, possibly the one centered at Cahal Pech. The goal of this integration appears to have been primarily economic. Although this integration was partially achieved through administrative means, there was also a degree of ritual and ideological integration. Specifically, the two primary ritual features at the site, a stela/altar complex at the termini of a causeway and a ballcourt, are associated with the heads of two principal drainage channels. It seems plausible that fertility rituals were carried out in association with these features to promote integration of the extant farming populace. That some ballcourts may have served as the origin point for irrigation water (see Houston 1998:359) lends credence to this sacred landscape interpretation.

Overall, the aforementioned scenario corresponds quite closely with Scarborough's (1998) recent discussion of the role of Late Classic "water mountains." It is also consistent with similar administrative-type configurations in the Caracol periphery (Chase and Chase 1996a:807; see also chapter 10). Like X-ual-canil, the latter contexts have large administrative architecture, but there is a conspicuous absence of shrine features and ritual deposits. As with X-ual-canil, the Caracol groups have been interpreted as specialized economic centers that focused on the administration of agricultural production and redistribution (extensive terrace systems are associated with the Caracol groups).

In sum, how X-ual-canil fits into the microregional settlement hierarchy is less ambiguous. The site appears to have been a key managerial feature aimed at controlling the production and redistribution of agricultural surplus. That X-ual-canil was entrenched within the hierarchy to a greater degree than Zubin is also attested to by the fact that X-ual-canil would not have had access to the requisite labor pool to construct and maintain the site. This situation confirms that more established powers (probably Cahal Pech) enforced construction and maintenance. In addition, given that the status of X-ual-canil's principal inhabitants was moderate at best (nonelite or subelite, as suggested by grave elaboration and residential quality), it does not appear likely that these people administered from the vaulted range structures, orchestrated the rituals associated with the ballcourt, or led the processions along the causeway. Rather, it seems plausible that the inhabitants of X-ual-canil were full-time, or even part-time (rotating), site managers who were primarily responsible for the collection, storage, and redistribution of agricultural produce, and that the more courtly administrative and ritual tasks were conducted by elite authorities who did not inhabit the site. Specifically, it is possible that elite personages from Cahal Pech may have come to X-ual-canil at certain times to carry out administrative or ritual duties, after which they would return to Cahal Pech. If true, this scenario also explains why so few artifacts were found at the site (residential occupation was limited), why there was such a separation between kinship (residential) and kingship (administrative and ritual) features (the residential population at the site had little to do with the courtly administrative and ritual activities), why the site did not have to be materially sanctioned through ritual offerings (the X-ual-canil authority was sanctioned elsewhere), and why there was no need for either an ancestor shrine or ancestor-based rituals (the important courtly ancestors were buried elsewhere).

Broader Implications: Ancient Maya Sociopolitical and Socioeconomic Organization

For some time now there has been significant disagreement as to the nature of the Maya state. Proponents of decentralized, or segmentary-state, models argue that ancient Maya society was loosely integrated through ritual and kinship, and that there was little economic or administrative specialization (for example, Ball and Taschek 1991; Demarest 1992; Dunham 1990; Dunning and Kowalski 1994; J.W. Fox and Cook 1996; Houston 1993). In essence, the settlement continuum was based on redundant roles and functions, with larger sites being differentiated from smaller ones based primarily on degrees of elaboration and complexity. In contrast, advocates of more centralized, or unitary, frameworks argue for a high degree of political integration (through the centralizing apparatus of kingship) and the existence of economic and administrative specialization (for example, A.F. Chase and D.Z. Chase 1996a, 1996b; D.Z. Chase, A.F. Chase, and Haviland 1990; Culbert 1991; Folan 1992; Folan, Marcus, and Miller 1995; Martin and Grube 1995). Marcus (1992, 1993, 1998) quite aptly points out that this is not an either/or argument. Specifically, she has promoted a "dynamic model" in which the processes of centralization and decentralization were active on both the spatial and temporal scales (see also Demarest 1996; Haviland 1997; Sabloff 1996). This model seems to be both more fruitful and more probable.

Ultimately, research within the middle level of settlement lends support to Marcus' dynamic model. As the X-ual-canil example suggests, this site can in no way be viewed as a Cahal Pech writ small. In other words, X-ual-canil does not satisfy the redundancy in roles and functions that the decentralized model requires. Rather, X-ual-canil provides a strong case for economic and administrative specialization, as the unitary model implies. X-ual-canil is very much about centralized kingship. As indicated above, similar arguments can and have been made for comparable middle-level settlements in the vicinity of Caracol (see A.F. Chase and D.Z. Chase 1996a, 1996b; see also chapter 10). In contrast, much of what occurred at Zubin was tied to kinship-based rituals and agrarian/domestic activities. The Zubin data set therefore lends credence to some of the decentralist's assertions about nonspecialization and the importance of ritual.

In the end, the exploration of rural complexity suggests that sociopolitical and socioeconomic integration was much more sophisticated than previous models have assumed; this fits well with the dynamic model. It also implies, however, that things were much more complex than this model currently suggests. For instance, at the same time that Zubin appears to show evidence of Late Classic political decentralization (through the implementation of a power-sharing strategy), X-ual-canil seems to provide a good example of contemporaneous economic centralization. This example is consistent with observations made by de Montmollin (1989), when he notes that one can sometimes see economic centralization at the same time that political decentralization is occurring. In sum, research within complex rural settlements lends support to the dynamic model, but in doing so suggests that this framework needs to be applied in a multiscalar fashion to capture all the intricacies of ancient Maya socioeconomic and sociopolitical interaction.

Conclusions

It appears that the analysis of rural complexity can provide new and important insights into the character of ancient Maya social, economic, and political organization. The variability exhibited by sites of this size and complexity clearly attests to the diversity present within ancient Maya society. As more middle-level settlements are investigated, we should ultimately develop a better understanding of the range of variability these sites exhibited. Eventually, patterning will emerge from the chaos. As we begin to recognize this patterning, we will be in a better position to employ more theoretically powerful concepts, such as structure, agency, and the unifying notion of structuration. Until such a time as we develop more comprehensive knowledge of rural complexity, our characterizations of ancient Maya society will remain incomplete, and biased by a rather outdated urban/rural dichotomy.

Acknowledgments. The research at Zubin and X-ual-canil would not have been possible without the help of numerous individuals and funding agencies. The Zubin investigations were conducted with the help of funds from the Social Sciences and Humanities Research Council of Canada, the Commonwealth Scholarship Commission, the Gordon Childe Fund, and the University of London. The excavations at X-ual-canil were partially funded by the Social Sciences and Humanities Research Council of Canada, and Trent University. The hardworking people of the Department of Archaeology in Belize, and particularly John Morris, Allen Moore, Harriot Topsey, and Brian Woodeye, are thanked for the support and encouragement they provided over the period that these investigations were carried out. Jaime Awe has always been a pillar of support. He not only helped me get started in Maya archaeology but also spurred me to set out on my own when the time was right. The various field school students and staff members who helped out in the Zubin and X-ual-canil investigations are commended for the long hours they put into both the field and laboratory aspects of the two projects. A big thank you also goes to the numerous Belizeans who helped in various ways while we were working at Zubin and X-ual-canil. I must also graciously thank the many colleagues who took the time to discuss ideas and share information with me over the years. Finally, this chapter has benefited from the constructive comments provided by a number of anonymous reviewers, and both Edward Schortman and Patricia Urban.

4 Making Sense of Variability Among Minor Centers
The Ancient Maya of Chaa Creek, Belize

Samuel V. Connell

THIS VOLUME expands our understanding of ancient Maya social organization by highlighting activities at intermediate archaeological sites. These sites have most appropriately been labeled "minor centers" (Bullard 1960), though other names have been applied (Chase 1992; Haviland 1981; Iannone 1996; Puleston 1983; Willey 1965, 1981). Interpreting the social significance of these middle-level sites has become an important research issue, particularly the explanations of variability among these sites (A.F. Chase and D.Z. Chase 1996a; Marcus 1993). Based on ideas from site-planning studies and locational analysis, I propose that different, yet interrelated, activities were taking place among ancient Maya minor centers across rural landscapes. Although this proposition may explain some of the variability identified at minor centers, it also has substantial implications for our perspectives on ancient Maya rural integration. In this chapter, I examine the relationship among three distinct minor centers found at Chaa Creek, a 2 km^2 hinterland settlement zone 6 km to the east of the medium-size major center of Xunantunich in west central Belize (figure 4.1).

Site-planning Research

Site-planning research is "the deliberate self-conscious aspect of settlement patterning, at scales from individual structures through regional landscapes" (Ashmore 1989:272). Based on intra- and intersite comparisons of architectural blueprints and data gathered from accompanying excavations, investigations of site planning utilize various approaches (see de Montmollin 1989, 1995; Houk 1996 for thorough treatments) that are categorized very generally as either ideological or practical. Ideological investigations present architectural arrangements as microcosms of pervasive cosmologies from Mesoamerica and elsewhere (Ashmore 1991; Aveni 1977; Aveni and Hartung 1986;

Lathrap 1985; Schele and Freidel 1990). Practical approaches emphasize the functional reasons for various site arrangements in terms of socioeconomic, political, or natural (topographic) conditions (de Montmollin 1989, 1995; J.W. Fox 1987; Lewis 1995; Ringle and Bey 1992). Although an integrated approach has recently been called for (see Houk 1996; Hyslop 1990; Wells 2000), here I use the practical/functional approach.

Most site-planning investigations focus on architecture, such as public buildings, which is the least subtle at portraying social relationships (Ashmore 1991:199). Structure placement and the demarcation of space, as well as architectural alignments, are carefully planned to convey a sense of power and order. Not only can space be symbolically manipulated to reinforce power (Tuan 1977) but the activities taking place within these spaces also promote and sustain social integration. In the Maya area, archaeologists test inferences of site function and local activities based on interpretations of architectural plans supplemented by excavations of features and statistical analysis of artifacts in both civic/ceremonial (Ashmore 1991; Coggins 1980; Fash et. al 1992; Sanchez 1997) and private household contexts (de Montmollin 1989, 1995; Haviland 1988; Hendon 1987, 1991; Leventhal 1979; Leventhal and Baxter 1988; Tourtellot 1982).

The focus of this chapter is to determine the differences in activities among intermediate-level sites. I am proposing that different activities were taking place at different minor centers within regional groupings of minor centers. I want to understand the nature of this functional heterogeneity and examine whether it helped to promote and sustain integration across rural landscapes. The idea that social integration is defined by increasingly heterogeneous relationships among individuals or groups of individuals comes to us from sociology (Durkheim 1933). Archaeologically, the concept of functional primacy at sites is usually employed

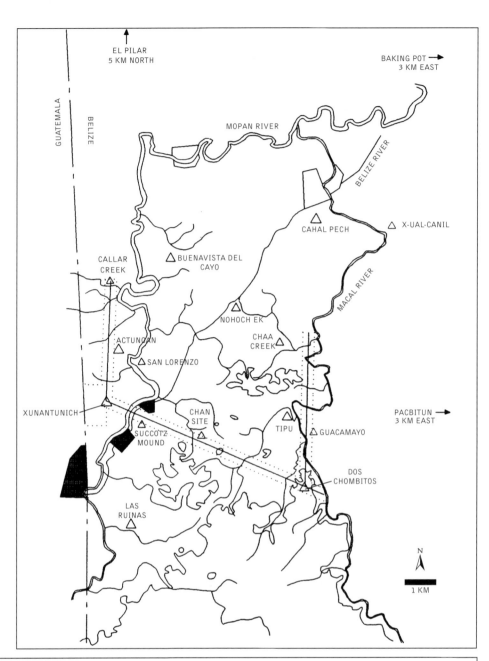

4.1 Upper Belize River Valley.
Based on a map (1993) by J. Yaeger

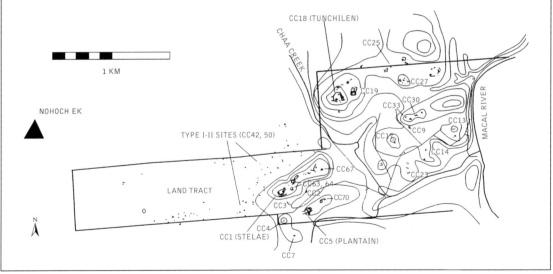

4.2 Chaa Creek settlement zone.
Note: Topographic lines are at approximately 15 m intervals

to make statements about regional social complexity in an economic (production centers) or military (fortresses) context. Moving beyond these single-factor explanations, I examine the functions of three Late Classic minor centers located in the same settlement area (figure 4.1). Then I discuss how different, yet functionally complementary, activities among minor centers are important for understanding locally vital integration across the ancient Maya countryside.

The Chaa Creek Investigations

Although earlier archaeologists working in the Belize River Valley had an interest in minor centers (for example, W.R. Coe and M.D. Coe 1956), research regarding ancient Maya rural complexity began in earnest with the work at Barton Ramie (Willey 1965). Many other research projects in the Belize River Valley pursued this line of investigation during the 1980s and 1990s (see various chapters in this volume; Awe 1993; Ball and Taschek 1990; Fedick 1988, 1989; Ford 1991; Ford and Fedick 1992; Garber and Glassman 1996; Iannone 1993a, 1994; Leventhal 1993, 1996, 1997; Leventhal and Ashmore 1994, 1995; and many others). This focus on rural settlement developed in the Belize River Valley partly by default due to a lack of primary centers. None of the major sites in the Belize River Valley can be rated in the highest category of Hammond's (1975) architectural site hierarchy.

Investigations in the Chaa Creek settlement zone began with reconnaissance and survey during short supplementary field seasons in 1992 to 1994 under the aegis of the Xunantunich Archaeological Project (XAP) (Carpenter et al. 1992; Connell 1993, 1994). Located 6 km east of the medium-size major center of Xunantunich, Chaa Creek settlement is found on and around a series of west-to-east–oriented limestone ridges intersected by deep seasonal creek beds, such as Chaa Creek, that drain into the Macal River (figure 4.2). The name "Chaa" derives from the Maya word *chak*, meaning red, and reflects a brownish red clay substrate that changes the color of the creek during the rainy season. Vegetation on the ridges is generally low forest, with dense brush in open and untended areas. Pastures and agricultural fields cover the lower flanks of every ridge.

Settlement at Chaa Creek is bounded on all sides: to the east by the Macal River; to the south by high, sparsely settled ridges; and to the north and west by a large level tract of agriculturally productive land. As it spreads across the landscape, the Chaa Creek settlement area, with its sixty-two recorded sites, is typical of hinterland settlement in the region. Large platform groups and smaller patio groups are arranged along ridge tops, and households flank these architectural foci on lower elevations. The three largest sites

are minor centers: Stela group (CC1), Plantain group (CC5), and Tunchilen group (CC18). Each has features distinguishing it from standard household groups, such as stelae, immense plazas, and 5-m–high temple mounds.

Interpretations derived from preliminary investigations suggested that the Chaa Creek zone, after experiencing a population surge during the Late Classic, was an economically and politically valuable area to the rulers of Xunantunich. Two variables connected with Chaa Creek's critical geographic location may have helped to increase the significance of the relationship between its residents and the elite at Xunantunich. First, a large fertile tract of land adjoins Chaa Creek to the west. This area, called El Chial Ranch, is a well-drained, agriculturally productive paleo-floodplain (Birchall and Jenkin 1979; Fedick 1989; Smith 1998). Today, El Chial Ranch is one of the most productive citrus, bean, and corn farms in the region. Second, Chaa Creek is positioned on the boundary between many larger centers: Xunantunich and Buenavista to the west, Cahal Pech to the north, and Pacbitun to the east (figure 4.1). This location suggests that it may have been an "interstitial" zone of settlement on the political borders of larger centers (Dunham, Jamison, and Leventhal 1989). Additionally, on the map provided by Ball and Taschek (1991:150), the settlement of Chaa Creek is situated at the intersection of three suggested political nodes: Buenavista, Pacbitun, and Las Ruinas. However one chooses to divvy up the upper Belize River Valley political nodes through time, Chaa Creek's potential boundary location is a significant factor to consider when piecing together the critical functional roles that minor centers played in maintaining stability in the region.

Excavations at Chaa Creek in 1995 and 1997 were designed to assess the nature of regional social integration vis-à-vis these potentially critical resources. A representative (30%) sample—nineteen of the sixty-two sites at Chaa Creek—was tested. The sites were chosen as a stratified sample of seven possible site types. This chapter focuses on describing and interpreting the results of excavations at the three largest platform groups. Preliminary architectural and artifact analysis of these minor centers shows the spatial dispersion of separate functions: Stela group exhibits primarily elements of ancestor veneration and divination; Plantain group exhibits primarily evidence for an elite residence; and Tunchilen group was primarily a feasting area.

STELA GROUP (SITE CC1):
ANCESTOR VENERATION AND DIVINATION
Stela group is located in the Chaa Creek west zone along the western end of the northern ridge (figure 4.2). The platform group is open to the north and has a 5-m–high temple-pyramid located on the east side (M1); a long, low-lying

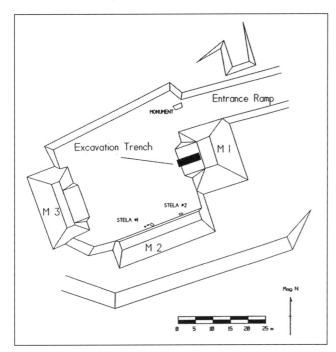

4.3 Stela groups (site CC1)

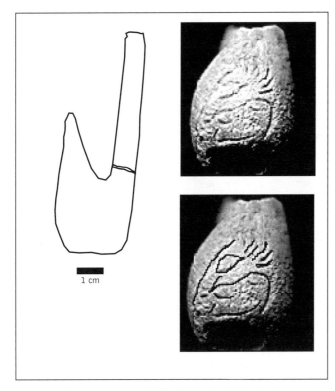

4.4 Carved human bone with glyph from burial #97-2 in crypt 2.
Illustration and photo (1999) by Brad Adams

platform to the south (M2); and a 3-m–high structure on the west (M3) (figure 4.3). Stela group is so named because two plain stelae are located in front of M2. Stela 1, in the center of M2, is remarkably well preserved and would have measured 2 m high based on a full reconstruction of the monument. In addition, a small sacbe-stela-entranceway complex leads toward two small patio groups to the east (CC63 and CC64). Entranceway complexes have been suggested to demarcate important sacred locations at access points; Keller (1995b, 1997) ties their significance to ritual processions. These features clearly support the initial conjecture that Stela group was ceremonial in nature.

During excavations, temple-pyramid M1 was trenched on its west face. Two crypts, dating to the Protoclassic (circa 75±25 BC to AD 400±20; see Brady et al. 1998) were discovered at the base of the 2-m–wide trench, deep below a series of earlier structures. Within each crypt, elderly males lay extended with few burial accoutrements (B. Adams 1998). In crypt 2, within the heart of M1, a single piece of jewelry carved from a human long bone was found next to the left hand of the articulated individual. Shaped like a pipe, the bone tube had a carved face on its largest surface (figure 4.4). A glyph depicting a human head in profile with flowing hair was incised on the front portion of the piece. In addition, cache 97-3 was discovered adjacent to the crypt just to the west along the building's centerline. This deposit of two small bowls was arranged lip to lip so that one was upside down. Called *finger bowls* because two human phalanges were placed inside them, the vessels were crudely made and poorly fired. Lip-to-lip cache vessels were an enduring Maya tradition and have been associated primarily with Protoclassic and Early Classic ritual activity in the Belize Valley and at Caracol (A.F. Chase and D.Z. Chase 1987, 1994b). These items were the entire extent of burial accoutrements found with Chaa Creek human remains. The discovery of even a few small items, however, indicates the high social significance of the remains in crypt 2. This find, coupled with the central location of the crypts within the heart of the main temple, suggests that both individuals were highly venerated ancestors of the community (see McAnany 1995).

Other finds symbolize the continued ceremonial significance of the site into the Late Classic (AD 600 to 900). Two patolli boards were exposed, located in a series of niches set into the stairs halfway up the front of the temple (figure 4.5). While the upper board, associated with the penultimate temple construction phase, had deteriorated, the lower board (2) was in good condition. This later board is unique because, although it appears to fit the standard pattern of a square board with an internal cross that has hatched spaces,

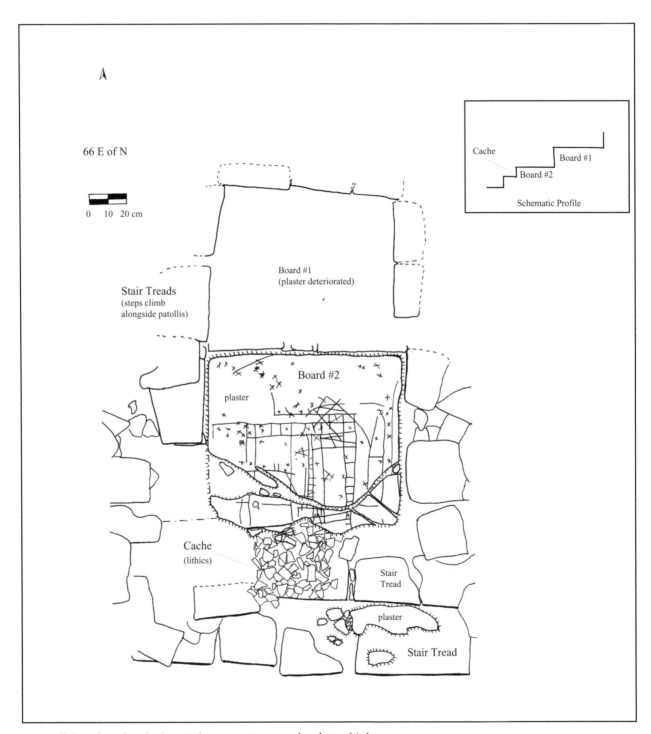

66 E of N

0 10 20 cm

Cache

Board #1

Board #2

Schematic Profile

Stair Treads
(steps climb
alongside patollis)

Board #1
(plaster deteriorated)

Board #2

plaster

Cache
(lithics)

Stair
Tread

plaster

Stair Tread

4.5 Patolli boards and cache from Stela groups M1-second and M1-third it is also covered with scattered incised Xs. The common pattern at Xunantunich has been to find these markings in prominent spaces within the board, such as at corners and midpoints (see MacKie 1985; Yaeger 1997), but these Xs are placed in curious alignments around the outside of the board. To the back of the board, a series of arching lines appears to connect groups of Xs. This unusual patterning, coupled with other work on patollis in Mesoamerica (A.L. Smith 1977), suggests that far from being just a game, patollis may be connected to the practice of divination. Corroborating evidence for the idea of divination was found in a cache placed to the fore of the board prior to it being sealed during a subsequent construction episode (figure 4.5). The cache contained 200 colored chert biface thinning flakes and 150 small colored river pebbles that appear to be game pieces or, rather, objects associated with the use of the board. In light of finding the incised Xs in alignments, the pieces were likely used for tracking celestial activity. This usage could be closely tied to, or may have been involved with, throwing stones and other shamanic practices.

In 1995, a dedicatory cache of 9 flint eccentrics was discovered at the base of the final phase staircase of M1. Interestingly one lunate eccentric was snapped in two in order to raise the total count of objects from eight to nine, which is a common number of eccentrics found in caches throughout the region and may be tied to the nine Lords of the Night. The objects were placed just under the deteriorated terminal-phase plaster floor. Each piece was knapped into peculiar, but familiar, forms. The cache contained three lunates, two scorpion forms, one serrated-edge chalcedony biface, and three other crudely anthropomorphic forms. The lunates were placed on top of the deposit, covering the scorpions that were placed in a cross at the base of the cache. Very similar caches have been found in the Xunantunich site core next to stelae and on top of temple A-1 (see Belize Department of Archaeology File Cards for Stewart and Schmidt labeled caches A, B, and C). The materials and forms are identical, but the Xunantunich caches have approximately two to three times more pieces. Flint eccentric caches have been documented at many lowland Maya sites and have been tied to royal elite dedicatory practice (Iannone 1992; Willey 1972).

ARTIFACTS AT STELA GROUP:
COMPARISONS OF POTTERY FORMS
The assertion that the Stela group was used primarily for ceremonial religious purposes is confirmed by an analysis of the distribution of artifacts found at the site. Although items of a specific ceremonial function were recovered, such as modeled effigy incensario fragments, it is also the overall lack of household materials, such as fragments of ground

stone, which argues for its ceremonial importance. An extensive test-pitting program circumscribing the site located only light concentrations of refuse. The almost complete lack of refuse deposits was striking and pointed to a less domestic and more ceremonial function.

Employing the research methods of Le Count (1996, 1999; Yaeger and LeCount 1995), the relative numbers of bowls to jars were compared to determine the degree of domestic activity at the site versus such other activities as feasting or ceremonial rites. Data were derived from two 1 x 2 m test units and from trenching and clearing excavations at the base of M1 and M2. Both bowls and jars are generally the largest part of a ceramic assemblage. When found in high concentrations, bowls, dishes, and plates are commonly associated with feasting because they are thought to be used more for preparation and serving. Jars are thought to be diagnostic of storage and cooking (LeCount 1996). In this analysis, I use the term *bowls* to represent all open forms, including plates, dishes, and bowls. Determinations of open-form subgroupings are usually based on the ratio of vessel height to width (P.M. Rice 1987a; Sabloff 1975). Rarely can the height of a vessel be measured, and as a result, all open forms are assigned to the bowl category. Closed forms are jars used to store water or staple goods; however, ollas with larger mouths are also used for cooking (LeCount 1996).

When comparing open to closed forms, both the frequency counts and density calculations (frequency/total weight of sample) of ceramics proved less statistically relevant than comparisons of the total weights of the rim samples. Bowl form rims can break into far more pieces than the rims of small-mouthed jar forms; therefore, bowls are over-represented in frequency counts and density measurements. Because the ratio value of the total weight of bowl rims to the total weight of jar rims is not affected by different patterns of breakage, the ratio value was used to compare activities at sites. The weight values of bowls and jars are presented as the calculated percentage of the total weight of the sample of sherds. For example, if the total sample of pottery from a site was 200 g and 20 g were bowl rims and 10 g were jar rims, the ratios would be presented as 10 and 5%. Assemblages used for this analysis came only from what were determined to be good contexts representative of Late Classic activities that took place at the site.

The relative percentage of bowls to jars at Stela group is higher than the overall Chaa Creek community average. For the whole of Chaa Creek, the ratio of the weight of rims from open-form bowls to the weight of rims from closed-form jars is 0.95:1, while for Stela group the bowls-to-jars ratio is 1.32:1 (table 4.1). The lower percentage of storage vessels at Stela group suggests more emphasis on preparation and presentation; however, it is not a significantly higher percentage of open forms. If anything, it suggests a low degree of serving activity in conjunction with religious activities.

Importantly, a surprising result occurred when this comparative technique was performed on data from Chaa Creek rural households isolated from the minor centers. At nonminor centers or commoner settlements, the bowls-to-jars ratio is a dramatic 1.60:1. Remarkably, domestic assemblages at Chaa Creek are, on the whole, characterized by food preparation and serving. Although scholars assert that high ratios of bowls to jars are indicative of feasting practices (LeCount 1999), I propose that, in this case, such ratios in rural domestic assemblages indicate less emphasis on storage. The low percentages of jars in domestic settlements suggests that there was either a lack of surplus goods at commoner houses or that surplus goods were being moved elsewhere for storage, possibly to minor centers. Although the data suggest that this was not happening at Stela group, other minor centers at Chaa Creek did have a higher capacity for storing surplus goods.

In sum, the relatively small trench into M1 recovered a series of interconnected features that demonstrate Stela group's devotion to ancestor veneration and divination. The placement of the later period cache of chert eccentrics in front of the final stairwell was likely tied to the earlier burials found within the stairs and, as such, is important evidence of the continued veneration of a single lineage. In addition, the patolli boards indicate the significance of divination at the site, especially in association with the ancestors. Further evidence is provided, most clearly, by the two stelae, which have been soundly tied to the importance of ancestor veneration at most Maya major centers. Though not treated in detail here, it is quite uncommon to find two, or for that matter any, stelae at minor centers (but see various chapters in this volume). This find further indicates the importance of ancestor veneration at Stela group, and may also be indicative of the important connections between Chaa Creek and Xunantunich.

An intense shovel test-pitting program in the area showed little evidence of domestic or feasting activities at Stela group. The analysis of pottery forms from Stela group also indicates a rather pedestrian distribution of bowls to jars, which is certainly not indicative of either intensive storage or feasting activity. Basically, activities involving high densities of pottery were not present. Instead, all evidence points, at least preliminarily, to the idea that Stela group was a high-intensity ritual locale for ancestor veneration and divination.

TUNCHILEN GROUP (CC18): FEASTING AREA

Located in the eastern part of the Chaa Creek settlement zone along the western edge of a long east-to-west trending

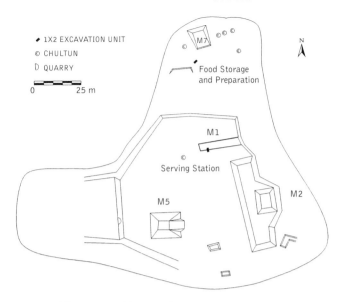

4.6 Tunchilen groups (site CC18)

Table 4.1 Comparisons of open forms (bowls) to closed forms (jars) of pottery at Chaa Creek

Contexts	Bowls (%)	Jars (%)	Ratio
All Chaa Creek	9.5	10.0	0.95
CC1 (Stela group)	8.7	6.6	1.32
Commoner Settlements	11.7	7.3	1.60
CC18 (Tunchilen group)	8.9	5.4	1.65
Op. 223 (CC18, M7)	8.2	3.8	2.16
Op. 217 (CC18, M1)	10.4	7.7	1.35
Op. 171A (CC5, M4)	11.9	9.4	1.27
Op. 161 (Plantain group)	6.7	13.7	0.49

ridge, Tunchilen is the largest and most imposing of the local minor centers (figure 4.2). It is noted primarily for its large open plaza (60 x 30 m) and adjoining subsidiary platform areas, all of which suggest social gathering and feasting (figure 4.6). Tunchilen group has a more open spatial arrangement and does not emit the same contained, controlled atmosphere as Stela group. The eastern building (M2) of the main group is an impressive 50-m–long winged platform with a structure perched along the central axis rising 5.5 m above the platform surface. Opposing this on the west side of the plaza is a 3-m–high structure (M5) offset at a slightly more northern angle. To the north is a low-lying building (M1) running to the northeastern edge of the platform. To the south are two more very low untested mound structures (M3 and M4). Large open hinterland plaza areas with low-lying structures widely spaced around their perimeters have been discovered elsewhere in the Xunantunich region. Dubbed *feasting platforms* (Yaeger and Connell 1993), these sites usually have evidence of storage facilities and dense amounts of serving wares, two of the main characteristics of Tunchilen group.

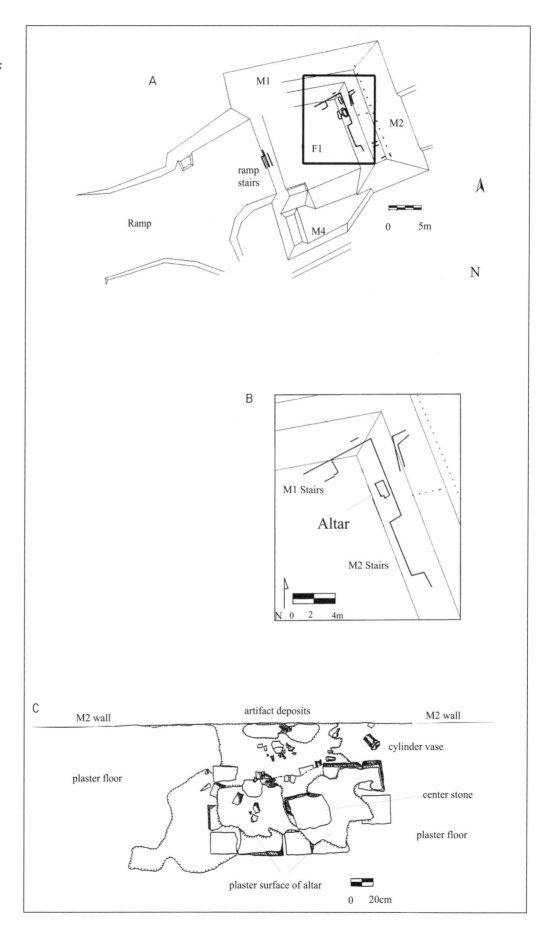

4.7 Plantain groups and associated excavations: a, Plantain groups (CC5); b, excavations (altar highlighted); c, Plantain groups altar, following removal of termination deposit. *Illustration by S. Connell and B. MacDougall*

Below the western and northern edges of the main platform are two ancillary activity areas (figure 4.6). The western area is most notable for its views of the Castillo at Xunantunich in the distance, the large tract of land below, and spectacular sunsets. The northern area contains two low-lying platforms surrounded by five chultuns. It is highly unusual for this many underground storage units to be located so near to one another. It is also important to consider that only collapsed chultuns were discovered and that others likely lie undetected, still capped by thick limestone covers. The survey evidence suggests that the northern area was an important location for collecting and storing large quantities of resources. According to our ideas about feasting locations, it is not surprising that this ancillary area exhibits the potential for the storage of goods needed to supply large community gatherings.

In addition, ancillary areas have also been tied to food preparation activities. For example, at Xunantunich an ancillary service area containing very high percentages of serving vessels (LeCount 1996:267–268) was discovered next to the royal compound (Jamison and Wolff 1997). To determine whether Tunchilen was used for feasting activities, test excavation units were placed in areas of refuse deposition, both in the northern ancillary platform in front of M7 and near M1 on the main platform. It is argued that higher percentages of bowl forms represent greater emphasis on presentation and formal consumption of items. The overall sample from Tunchilen does show an emphasis on serving vessels (1.65:1), particularly in the northern ancillary area, which has the highest bowl-to-jar ratio at Chaa Creek (2.16:1) (table 4.1). When compared to the overall Chaa Creek ratio (0.95:1), we see a strong emphasis on food preparation at Tunchilen group.

These data, coupled with the very open architectural plan, suggest an emphasis on social gathering. When compared to the other minor centers, Tunchilen also demonstrates this focus. For example, the entrance to the site is neither very formalized nor restrictive. It passes through the northern ancillary area where we suppose much of the preparatory activity took place. Other factors point to a far less religious role for Tunchilen group. Excavations deep into the most prominent structure (M2) produced no burials or caches, and no monuments were discovered.

PLANTAIN GROUP (SITE CC5): ELITE RESIDENCE
Plantain group is located on the western end of the middle of the three east-to-west running ridges in the western part of the Chaa Creek zone (figure 4.2). The primary feature of this site is an impressive 2-m–high platform with two long structures, each 2 to 3 m tall, arranged in an L-shape along the north and east sides of the platform (figure 4.7). Recov-

ered materials from the extensively excavated plaza area indicate that Plantain group served as an elite residence.

At Plantain group the interconnected structures of M1 (north building) and M2 (east building) wrap around the outside of a prominent plaza. Extensive clearing excavations exposed the plaster plaza floor and basal walls of the structures that were intact to more than 1.5 m. Excavations also cleared the main staircase of each building. The plaza floor excavations were aimed at finding artifact dumps and final occupation debris, as well as special deposits and evidence of subplatform features. XAP archaeologists routinely discovered in situ deposits of household debris on plaza floors (S.M. Chase 1993; Etheridge 1995; Yaeger 1994). Excavations at Plantain group focused on the interior part of the plaza (figure 4.7). Following removal of the collapse, clearing excavations were halted by an extremely hard-packed silty clay loam stratum that covered the well-preserved thick plaster plaza floor. This hard-packed matrix tapered off the edge of the structure as if it were the build-up of collapse debris or evidence of a deposit of materials strewn up against the basal wall of M2. Careful excavation exposed two strata in this deposit. The upper stratum was the first phase of collapse, consisting of plaster and stucco pieces that would have fallen off the superstructure before its architecture collapsed. In a sense, these would have "melted" off the building to create a hard-packed stratum. As moisture collected on the fallen matrix, the deposits of plaster and stucco deteriorated, forming a very hard-packed mortar. Fortunately, not all the stucco deteriorated. We managed to extract a few pieces of stucco sculpture from the collapse near the intersection of M1 and M2. In most cases, these pieces were limestone blocks containing two or more 15-cm–high tapered stucco columns appliquéd to the block facing. One larger piece with columns on two sides was probably originally on the corner of an architectural feature. In addition, one piece was formed differently, with diagonal stucco appliqué impressions. These pieces likely formed part of a superior molding or cornice that banded the roof of the vaulted superstructure. Blocks faced with stucco appliqué designs in the form of columns and diagonal bands also exist in another very significant place—the sky band at the top of the east frieze on the Castillo, the main temple at Xunantunich. This area on the frieze has been linked with the ancestral mythology behind royal power (Fields 1995). The use of similar symbols of power links residents of Plantain group to a regional elite ideological framework centered at Xunantunich.

The lowest stratum on the plaster plaza floor (F1) was not collapse material. The stratum contained an extremely dense ceramic and stone artifact deposit. The silty clay loam matrix had fewer calcite inclusions than the above collapse stratum, although it did have a large amount of charcoal. This artifact deposition took place at the end of the site's occupation and is indicative of a significant abandonment event at Chaa Creek. Many exotic and evidently valuable items were recovered during the excavations.

This dense deposit consisted of Late Classic and some Terminal Classic artifacts found both directly on the floor and in the matrix up to 10 cm above the floor. Aside from the great amount of smashed pottery wares, many other items related to domestic activity were recovered. On the main platform, 126 chert stone tools were recovered, 17.3% of the entire Chaa Creek assemblage. Of the sample, 25 are bifacial tools, 13.8% of the total assemblage. In this deposit, three of the five Pachuca green obsidian blades found in the Xunantunich region were recovered. The deposit also contained 45 ground-stone fragments (29.6% of the total assemblage) of mostly manos and metate forms but also finely ground celts. Furthermore, a high density of slate fragments was found. Fourteen artifacts found at the Plantain group, 40% of the total Chaa Creek sample, were marked as special items, including jade beads and pendants, as well as marine shell strombus (conch) pendants . Many of the special items were evidently placed or smashed as part of a ritual event. At the interface between the two collapse strata, for example, we found an intrusive special deposit that consisted of a smashed ceramic jar containing a piece of human cranium with a jade bead placed inside. This deposit was made after the general abandonment of Plantain group.

The deposit represents the domestic assemblage of a very wealthy group of people, perhaps the leading local lineage members. It is one of the richest artifact assemblages ever found in the Xunantunich region. The special deposit yields no stratigraphic evidence for different phases of deposition, other than distinct nodes of artifacts that appear to have been smashed or broken together. This single-phase deposition parallels other examples of what have come to be known as termination deposits (see Freidel 1999)—the ritual termination of living spaces. The circumstances surrounding these events are unclear. The deposit may represent the end result of a regional conflict and the sacking of Plantain group by victors or the peaceful ritual commemoration and closure of living spaces marking the cessation of veneration for locally important ancestors. Termination rituals were probably taking place simultaneously at elite residences elsewhere in the Xunantunich region during the end of the Late Classic and into the Terminal Classic periods, possibly in response to major political changes within the valley. Evidence of similar patterns of deposition was found at Actuncan (McGovern 1994), group D (Braswell 1994), and A-20 (L.S. Neff 1995).

Following the complete removal of the special termination deposit, we discovered a small platform feature at plaza level (figure 4.7). This unique feature appears to have been at the center of the entire termination event. It is a one course high 1.8 x 0.8 m platform constructed of limestone cut blocks that appear to have been moved from their original contexts. The blocks were either taken from architectural collapse or the altar was disassembled and then reassembled. This same architectural pattern is seen at Xunantunich (Leventhal et al. 1993; MacKie 1961; Schmidt 1974). Some of the blocks used for the small Chaa Creek altar were partially faced in plaster but not set into the plaster floor. Evidence suggests a hasty construction. The small feature was situated on top of an area of secondary fill where the platform's plaster floor had been cut into but was not replastered. In addition, this feature was not fully completed on the east side. Two blocks were found stacked on top of each other, not having been placed in their final destinations.

The plaster floor on top of the altar lips up to its central feature, which is an irregularly shaped, and rather ordinary looking, heavily charred limestone block. The top and sides of the block were burned as well as the plaster floor surrounding it. Evidence suggests that the burning took place over a long period of time and was quite intensive. A small probe into the central stone exposed a thick layer of carbonized material that had seeped into the pores of the limestone, disfiguring it. Remarkably, a well-preserved ball of copal incense that still retained its aroma was discovered. The block was called an altar not only because of its form and the evidence of burning on and around its central stone but also because it was covered with in situ artifact deposits. The entire deposit of heavily burned materials is centered on this feature. These are signs of an important ritual event having taken place during the abandonment.

The Plantain group seems to be a wealthy rural subelite lineage household. A locally important family abandoned most of its domestic possessions at the end of the Late Classic, most likely around AD 800. This cessation of activity may have been correlated with a breakdown of the formerly tight social connections between Xunantunich and Chaa Creek minor centers such as Plantain group. At the point when Xunantunich may have been losing regional power and influence, elites residing in minor centers throughout the region may have been forced to abandon the area. This possible abandonment might explain the devastatingly thorough termination event discovered at Plantain group. There are, however, many other possible circumstances under which a termination such as this could have taken place.

PLANTAIN GROUP (SITE CC5): POTTERY DISTRIBUTIONS
A test-pitting program was designed to locate refuse dumps around the perimeter of the site. A 1 x 2 m test unit was placed off the southwestern side of the lower ancillary platform just to the southeast of M4, in a location where refuse

would have been swept off the platform (figure 4.7). The test unit uncovered a dense mix of Late Classic ceramics, including Mount Maloney serving bowls. The analytical technique of comparing the ratios of bowls to jars was employed here. To determine the functional differentiation of activity areas at Plantain group, ceramic food preparation and serving vessels were again compared with those vessels used for storage. There was a higher frequency of bowls, dishes, and plates in the M4 ancillary area as compared to the rest of Plantain group. The bowl-to-jar ratio for test unit 171A is 1.27:1 (table 4.1), indicating a tendency for food preparation and serving in the M4 ancillary area. Likely, local subelites had retainers preparing their meals. On the other hand, excavations concentrated on the main platform next to the primary structures and within the termination deposit (operation 161) yielded a bowl-to-jar ratio of 0.49:1 (table 4.1). This ratio is the lowest at Chaa Creek and is indicative of a strong emphasis on storage jars. Although there are many variables for which we cannot account, the evidence of high storage capacity suggests that surplus resources were being funneled through the minor center during the Late Classic. Here, wealth could be accrued under the watchful eyes of local subelites. This interpretation would make sense, given that, on the basis of the excavation data, Plantain group was the residence of Chaa Creek's subelites. Also, because of the strong evidence of ties to Xunantunich, Plantain group subelites may have been sacrificing at least some degree of local community autonomy in the form of payments to royal elites at Xunantunich.

Discussion

The evidence presented above outlines, in broad strokes, functional variability among minor centers in the Chaa Creek region. Stela group was a ceremonial center, Tunchilen group an area for feasting, and Plantain group a residence for a rural subelite. What are we to make of this primacy of different activities at three minor centers located in the same settlement region? Is there a practical reason for this diversity and can it further our understanding of rural integration? These questions are best answered by considering in more detail the large volume of data regarding different kinds and scales of activities that took place at major Maya urban centers, which have been the basis for a series of popular site typologies (Hammond 1975; Sanders and Webster 1988; and see R.G. Fox 1977).

My research stems from a locally pertinent study that characterizes site plans of Maya centers in the upper Belize River Valley. In their consideration of central-place dynamics and the segmentary state model, Ball and Taschek (1991) cite investigations from sites of different sizes and complexity, including Xunantunich, to argue for "an essential re-

dundancy in functions performed and services provided by southern lowland centers of virtually all magnitudes" (Ball and Taschek 1991:157). They adopt Richard Fox's (1977) urban typology as a way to characterize the multifunctional attributes of Maya centers. Four categories of functionally interrelated space are found within Maya centers: elite residences; ceremonial loci for ancestor veneration and divination; administrative complexes; and demarcated arenas or public places for such civic activities as feasting or marketing. These functions are found in varying intensities at all sites—from a headman's residence (labeled a plazuela group) on up. They are most strongly represented at paramount cities, such as Tikal, or in this case Buenavista (labeled regal-ritual cities or centers, depending on their size; also see Sanders and Webster 1988 for a description of types of cities). As Ball and Taschek note, the precise functional emphasis may have varied from site to site, but the primary differences separating these centers involved the scale and frequency of the same restricted set of activities rather than any meaningful variations involving kinds or numbers of different activities occurring" (1991:157).

For example, the four site functions and services are clearly illustrated at the site of Buenavista, which is interpreted as the sole Late Classic "regal-ritual" center in the Belize River Valley. Other centers in the valley, however, display primacy of specific functions and therefore were not regal-ritual centers but instead something else representing the specific primary function or service. The sites of Xunantunich and Cahal Pech are modeled as restricted access citadels whose primary function was to serve as elite residences. Located on a hilltop, the location and site plan of Xunantunich may initially give the impression of a citadel cut off from the general populace; however, relatively recent survey and excavations at Xunantunich refute this "castle-on-the-hill" premise. Leventhal (1993) has described Xunantunich as a "full-service" valley center, providing all the necessary sacred and secular services to the surrounding communities. Despite the difference of opinion with regard to the multifunctionality of Xunantunich, this debate does bring to light the important issue of primacy of function across regional landscapes.

I am suggesting that at the intermediate site level, there is good evidence for groupings of minor centers in which each site strongly exhibits one of the four functions detailed by Ball and Taschek (1991). These functions, taken together, would reflect the panoply of ancient Maya social relationships that constitute the full range of segmentary state activities, or full service. Within the Chaa Creek settlement area there appear to be three of the four elements of full-service functioning: an ancestor veneration and divination node at Stela group; a ceremonial feasting zone at Tunchilen

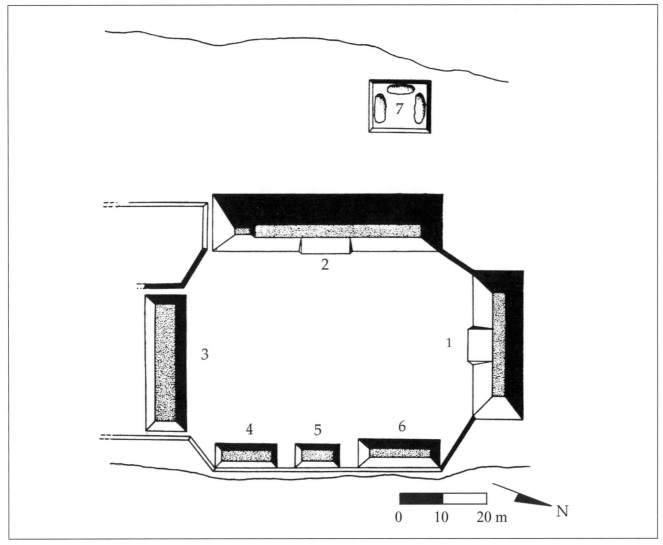

4.8 Nohoch Ek. After W.R. Coe and M.D. Coe 1956:371

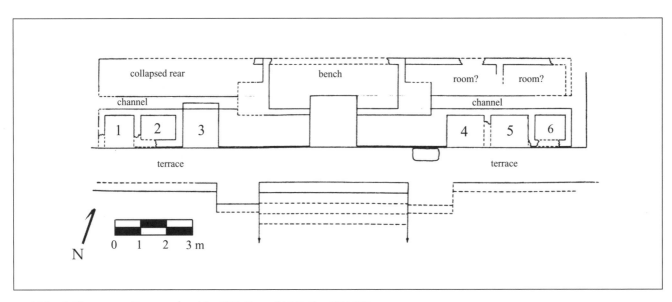

4.9 Nohoch Ek structure D, mound 1. After W.R. Coe and M.D. Coe 1956:374

group; and at least one elite, or subelite, residence at the Plantain group.

What is lacking within the survey area of Chaa Creek is a site displaying primarily administrative functions. That proposed missing link may lie to the west of the Chaa Creek zone at Nohoch Ek, situated on the west side of the large important land tract discussed above (figures 4.1 and 4.2). Nohoch Ek was described as a "common minor ceremonial center" at which local elite played a "religio-governmental role" (W.R. Coe and M.D. Coe 1956:380; see figure 4.8). Early survey and excavations at the site exposed an enclosed plaza group of six medium-size structures. Though no monuments, ballcourts, or caches were discovered, ties to Xunantunich in both architectural patterning and ceramic assemblages were recognized. These early excavations suggest that the site of Nohoch Ek was a "special-function" plaza group. Recent research at the site of X-ual-canil (chapter 3) and at Caracol causeway termini groups (A.F. Chase and D.Z. Chase 1996a; chapter 10) suggest that special-function administrative plazas are characterized by collections of low structures, a few narrow-range buildings on raised platforms, a lack of pyramidal temples, and low densities of both ritual and domestic items.

The Coe brothers' excavations into the northern mound 1 at Nohoch Ek uncovered a series of structures, the last two (structures C and D) dating to the Late Classic and into the Terminal Classic. In my view, the architectural plan of structure D suggests an administrative function (figure 4.9): It is a long, narrow platform topped by what William Coe and Michael Coe saw as a "problematic building of seemingly unique design" (1956:378). A central staircase climbs the substructure from the plaza floor to a thin staging terrace surrounding two groups of parallel range structures that flank a central stucco-covered bench. Running along the east-west axis of the platform is a small channel about 50 cm wide that divides the range structures into four separate masonry buildings. Each of the front, or southern, buildings contains three small cubicles (numbered 1 through 6 on the plan-view map of figure 4.9), while the rear buildings are too damaged to count the number of rooms. This specific architectural patterning of small room blocks is analogous to proposed administrative structures at Xunantunich and Caracol. Research at these sites uncovered range structures containing small rooms that may have been receiving rooms or storage compartments for sumptuary goods to be distributed in the political economy. This patterning has also been referred to in the literature as the architectural template for *audencias*, the equivalent of modern National Park visitor's centers (Taschek and Ball 1999). Overall, the architectural patterning at Nohoch Ek, coupled with a lack of household midden and ritual items,

suggests an administrative function. Admittedly, the above interpretation is based upon preliminary evidence from a limited data set, but recent research at Nohoch Ek as part of the Mopan/Macal Triangle Archaeological Project should provide further clarification.

The data from the Chaa Creek/Nohoch Ek settlement zone suggest the presence of all four elements of full-service site functions dispersed among separate minor centers. It is the contention of this study that the functional complementarity of these four elements provides more immediate and easy access to elite full-service functions in the hinterlands than would be the case if they were concentrated in one center.

Conclusion

Armed with data from four rural minor centers, all located in the vicinity of a large and likely very valuable agricultural resource, we see that the four functional elements expressed at full-service centers can be disentangled and distributed separately across the rural settlement landscape. While this pattern explains variability among minor centers, it also has implications for interpreting rural integration. Taken together, these minor centers may have comprised a heretofore undetected rural integrative unit equivalent in function to full-service regal-ritual centers discussed above, but spread among different sites. Obviously, because of the nature of the data, this claim should at best be construed as tentative; however, the implications of the identification of such social units are far reaching. If social units such as these did exist for the ancient lowland Maya, which I will call here rural full-service units, then we might be uncovering evidence of a nonhierarchical form of horizontal integration that possibly cross-cuts traditionally modeled units of regional integration. For example, the three types of territorial organization (types A, B, and C) proposed by the ethnohistorian Ralph Roys (1957) are most often employed by archaeologists modeling ancient Maya regional sociopolitical organization (Marcus 1993). Regional dynamic models point to the cyclical nature of integration as provinces segment and reintegrate over time. These newly identified rural full-service units very easily could, however, have spanned opposing *batabil* (provincial political units). On the basis of this supposition, again looking at the Roys and Marcus schematic, each hypothetical cluster of *chan cah* (small towns) located at the nexus of three batabiles may also have been an independent integrated unit (figure 4.10). These wholly different units of integration need to be taken into account to further understand ancient Maya regional integration.

The success of Maya polities may have hinged upon these separate and distinct rural integrative units, which would

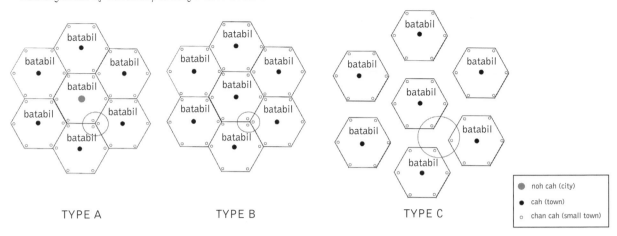

TYPE A   TYPE B   TYPE C

● noh cah (city)
● cah (town)
○ chan cah (small town)

4.10 Schematic representations of Roys's three types of provinces with proposed rural full service of minor centers encircled. Adapted from Marcus 1993:119

have been some of the most stable and enduring social entities. In fact, these units likely remained constant through time despite often turbulent lowland Maya regional sociopolitical dynamics. Returning to the example of Chaa Creek, I have already noted that its three minor centers with complementary primary functions were arranged along a critical interstitial zone between a collection of major centers which quite possibly were all vying for regional power. Taking the analysis a step further, I believe that it was precisely because of strong horizontally integrated rural zones, such as Chaa Creek, that the city and polity of Xunantunich was able to persevere during the tumultuous times surrounding the Late Classic/Terminal Classic transition.

Site-location studies used by geographers focusing on economic networks of production and distribution have long emphasized fluid and flexible scenarios of social integration that are largely dependent on particular sociohistorical events and natural or physical constraints (Haggett 1965; Losch 1954; Morrill 1974). Thus, it is not surprising that anthropologists working in the Maya area are borrowing models from social geography which make allowances for the coexistence of different types of social integration over landscapes (see Ball and Taschek 1991:157; Marcus 1976:24–25, 1993:116 for references to this phenomenon). Synthesized in the term *heterarchy*, Maya social organization can be viewed as unranked, or possessing the potential for being ranked in a variety of different ways, perhaps as a series of "counterpoised coalitions" (Crumley 1995).

It is precisely this variability we see in the archaeological record at the Maya middle level that helps to explain how the ancient Maya persevered despite the constant upheavals characterized by weakly integrated polities. While I do not dispute the importance of military conflict and factional competition in the machinations of Maya history and social organization (LeCount 1999; Pohl and Pohl 1994), I sug-

gest that the existence of communal corporate cognitive codes served also to unify hinterland areas (see Blanton et al. 1996). On local regional levels it is entirely possible that significant long-term community identities were forged among groups of minor centers. This communalism likely pervaded regional social organization to a much greater degree than previously assumed and operated hand in hand with competitive factional hierarchies (Saitta 1997). In these rural full-service communities, associated subelites, each not capable of performing all the functions needed to preserve a corporate group, formed mutual dependencies that likely led to strong horizontal ties across rural landscapes. Roys notes the existence of a middle-level Maya in the Yucatan who may have been at the center of such rural groupings:

> The bulk of the population consisted of commoners, or plebeians, who were the free workers of the country. Persons of this class were called *yalba uinic* ("small man"), *pizil cah* ("commoner")....There appears to have been an upper fringe of this class called *azmen uinic* ("medium man") and defined as "a man between principal and plebeian, of middling status." Roys (1957:5)

Although archaeologists have begun to emphasize the issue of rural complexity and demonstrate variability among minor centers, I want to call our attention to important patterns of similarity that I believe can be recognized at the regional scale of analysis. By examining functional interrelationships among minor centers, I found that the same complex sets of social interactions, which are now coming to be understood at major centers, were taking place among minor centers bound together as corporate units across regional settlement zones. The same multifunctionality inferred for major Maya centers also existed in all likelihood in the form of complementary groups of minor centers functioning as rural full-service units. This model for *rural full service* across settlement landscapes is not proposed to counter models of sociopolitical organization, such as the segmentary-state model. In fact, it should be made clear that I do not here dispute an essential redundancy of function at minor centers and only propose to extend the idea that other forms of integration may have coexisted within the lowland Maya social framework.

Acknowledgments. The archaeological investigations at Chaa Creek have been supported by an incredible group of people and funding agencies, including the National Science Foundation Dissertation Improvement Grant (SBR-9617566), Sigma Xi Grants-in-Aid, UCLA Latin American Center, UCLA Friends of Archaeology Research Grants, UCLA Department of Anthropology Research and Travel Grants, and the Xunantunich Archaeological Project. I appreciate the support and hope to return the favor in kind. At the center of this research have been Richard M. Leventhal and Wendy Ashmore, co-directors of the Xunantunich Archaeological Project, both excellent teachers and mentors.

In Belize, my work would not have been successful without the great support offered by the Department of Archaeology and its staff. Special thanks to the current and former Commissioners of Archaeology: George Thompson, Alan Moore, Brian Woodeye, John Morris, and Harriot Topsey. In addition, members of my excavation team deserve recognition for their contributions to this project above and beyond the call of duty. *Muchisimas gracias* to Gliss Penados, Miguel Medina, Ismael Chan, Marcos Godoy, Cruz "Doc" Puc, Miguel "Mac" Chan, Jose Louis Chan, and Wilfredo "Humina" Escalante. I particularly want to mention the Caracol 1992 team with whom this project was born, and Mick and Lucy Fleming and the entire staff of Chaa Creek on whose land I was fortunate to have been working. Without their support and friendship, this project would never have gotten off the ground. Finally, I must thank all colleagues who have provided excellent intellectual foils, including the anonymous reviewers and both Edward Schortman and Patricia Urban, who took the time to comment on and improve this chapter; nevertheless, any mistakes are my own.

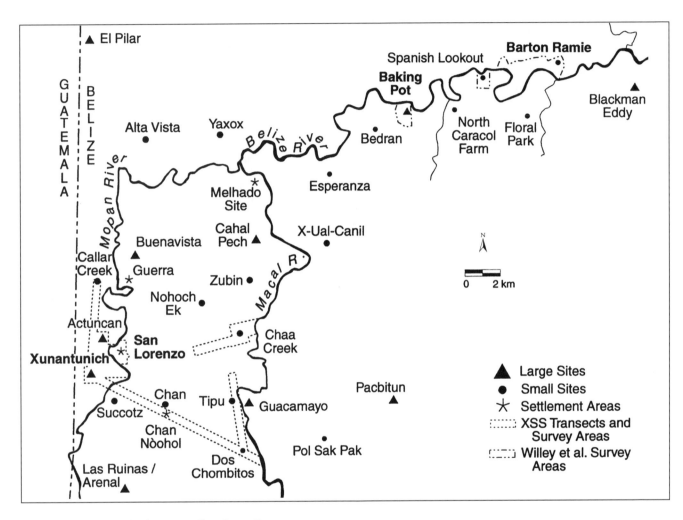

5.1 *Archaeological sites in the upper Belize River Valley*

5 Small Settlements in the Upper Belize River Valley
Local Complexity, Household Strategies of Affiliation, and the Changing Organization

Jason Yaeger

CHOLARS have for decades recognized the ubiquity of small settlements in the hinterlands of Classic period Maya polities (for example, Ashmore 1981a; Bullard 1964; de Montmollin 1988a; W.L. Fash 1983; Haviland 1968), but the top-down approaches that have historically dominated the study of Classic period Maya society have placed relatively little emphasis on studying such settlements (de Montmollin 1988b). Repeated calls to focus our analyses on smaller social scales (de Montmollin 1988b; Hayden and Cannon 1982; Tourtellot 1993: 235; Willey et al. 1965) have begun to bear fruit, however, in the form of a growing corpus of archaeological evidence that challenges simplistic views of small hinterland, or rural,[1] settlements and points us toward more complicated models of such settlements.

In this chapter, I present three kinds of complexity that characterize small settlements in the upper Belize River Valley and, it seems likely, throughout the lowland Maya area: heterarchical differences among sites, intrasite social heterogeneity, and diachronic complexity. I argue that the social and political relationships that linked individuals in a given settlement to individuals in other settlements, including large politically dominant centers, were key elements in structuring these complexities.

I illustrate my arguments with data from the Rancho San Lorenzo Survey Area and Barton Ramie, two settlement zones located in the upper Belize River Valley (figure 5.1). These two settlement zones would be classified together in many settlement typologies because they share four similarities. First, they are areas of roughly similar size and mound density (262 mounds in 2 km² at Barton Ramie and 74 groups within the 0.86 km² of the Rancho San Lorenzo Survey Area). Second, each settlement zone contains one group with specialized ritual architecture (BR-180 and SL-13). Third, each settlement zone is located

within 5 km of a major political center (Baking Pot and Xunantunich, respectively). Fourth, the settlement zones occupy the same ecological niche, the rich alluvial floodplain. Despite these similarities, excavation data from Barton Ramie (Willey et al. 1965) and San Lorenzo (Yaeger 2000a) demonstrate that these two settlement zones were quite distinct in several respects.

Many of the differences that exist between San Lorenzo and Barton Ramie constitute the first kind of settlement complexity: heterarchical differences among superficially similar settlements. Such differences are heterarchical because they do not consistently rank the settlements relative to one another, either because there are no rank differences among them or because they can be ranked in multiple ways, depending upon the criteria one chooses (Crumley 1987:158). This perspective sees each settlement as unique in a nontrivial way, characterized by its own local organization and particular history that can be understood only through intensive investigations at that site (also King and Potter 1994). Treating San Lorenzo and Barton Ramie as functional equivalents in a regional settlement system ignores this important fact, a point made by several chapters in this volume (6, 3. 8, among others).

The second type of complexity I examine is intra-settlement heterogeneity. Late Classic San Lorenzo and Early-to-Late Classic Barton Ramie demonstrate a surprising range of variability among households that is evident in domestic group size and morphology, construction techniques used in residential architecture, frequency of faunal remains, presence of items made of exotic materials, and burial practices. These data demonstrate that residents of these two areas had unequal access to labor and scarce goods, inequalities maintained in part through strategies of affiliation by which households created and represented their connections to people outside the community, especially the polity elite.

The final kind of complexity I discuss is diachronic. San Lorenzo and Barton Ramie were not timeless, static communities, but dynamic social bodies that experienced important changes in their internal organization over time. Although there are parallels in the changes at the two settlements, due in part to their participation in larger sociopolitical transformations and to similar choices of strategy by their members, the changes manifested themselves distinctly in each settlement zone because of particular local contexts. Following a presentation of the two case studies, I revisit these three kinds of complexity and discuss their implications for our understanding of Classic-period lowland Maya society. I present each case study historically to highlight parallel developments between the two sites.

San Lorenzo

The Xunantunich Archaeological Project (XAP) was a seven-year research project that sought to better understand the Xunantunich polity, especially its late founding date and rapid growth in the Late to Terminal Classic periods (Leventhal and LeCount 2001). One integral component of the XAP research design was the Xunantunich Settlement Survey (XSS), which systematically recorded all archaeological features along three 400-m–wide transects and in several opportunistic survey areas in the polity's hinterland (figure 5.1). A principal goal was to evaluate the degree of integration between hinterland settlements and the regional political authority seated at Xunantunich (Ashmore 1993; Ashmore, Yaeger, and Robin 2001).

One of the nontransect areas that the project studied was the Rancho San Lorenzo Survey Area. Jon Vanden Bosch (1992, 1993) and I (Yaeger 1992, 2000a) systematically surveyed this area, mapping 86 ha and recording over 100 cultural features (figure 5.2). Although some of these entities were terraces and others were human-modified cobble features, 74 were mound groups, most of which belong to one of six discrete settlement clusters that occupied distinct topographic zones. The Xunantunich Settlement Survey documented similar settlement clusters throughout the Xunantunich hinterland (Ashmore et al. 1994), and excavations have shown that despite gross similarities in scale and composition, these settlements cannot be considered functionally, historically, or socially redundant (Ashmore, Yaeger, and Robin 2001; Robin 1999; Yaeger 2000a; Yaeger and Robin N.D.).

In the Rancho San Lorenzo area, I concentrated my excavation efforts on the San Lorenzo settlement cluster (figure 5.3), a discrete aggregate of twenty mound groups, referred to hereafter simply as San Lorenzo. San Lorenzo

overlooks the Mopan river and its fertile floodplain, prime productive land favored by modern agriculturalists (Mazzarelli 1976; Muhs, Kautz, and MacKinnon 1985; Willey et al. 1965). Building on work by Sabrina M. Chase (1992, 1993), I directed research at San Lorenzo from 1994 to 1996 to investigate the development and internal organization of this small hinterland settlement, its relationship to larger social and political entities like the Xunantunich polity, and the transformations the settlement underwent in the Late Classic and Terminal Classic periods (Yaeger 2000a).

Based on group size and layout, and the domestic architecture and artifact assemblages recovered in excavations, I concluded that seventeen of the San Lorenzo mound groups were residential compounds. The settlement cluster also contains a chert quarry and three debitage mounds (labeled group SL-82[2]) and three very small platforms (<10 m^2 in area) that I judged not to be permanent habitations. The research design employed at San Lorenzo combined test excavations with extensive clearing of five of the settlement's domestic groups, sampling the three morphological types present there: multiple mound groups with patios, multiple mound groups lacking formal patio spaces, and individual mounds. We also conducted extensive investigations at SL-13, the only multipatio group in the survey area. Excavating 47 m^2 to 145 m^2 in each of these groups recovered hundreds of thousands of artifacts and ecofacts, including faunal and paleobotanical remains (Yaeger 2000a). To complement the extensive excavations, we placed 1 x 2 m test units adjacent to almost every other structure in San Lorenzo, excavating from 2 to 10 m^2 at each structure, and in the quarry and two of its debitage mounds.

The data from these excavations show that San Lorenzo was founded as early as the Ak'ab phase (AD 300 to 600; phases and dates from LeCount 1996 and LeCount et al. 2000), although the locale saw earlier sporadic occupations. The settlement grew rapidly during the Samal ceramic phase (AD 600 to 670), early in the Late Classic period, and expanded to its maximum size later in the Late Classic period during the Hats' Chaak phase (AD 670 to 780), when all seventeen domestic groups were occupied. Population dropped during the early facet of the Tsak' phase (AD 780 to 890), and the inhabitants of San Lorenzo abandoned the site completely sometime during the late facet of the Tsak' phase.

San Lorenzo is located 1.5 km from the Late-to-Terminal Classic capital of the region, Xunantunich, which sits on a high ridge on the opposite side of the Mopan River. Work by XAP has demonstrated that the center was founded in the Samal phase and that most of the monumental architecture dates to the Hats' Chaak phase (Jamison and Leventhal 1997; Leventhal 1996). The site's prosperity seems to have been short-lived, however. Beginning as early as the

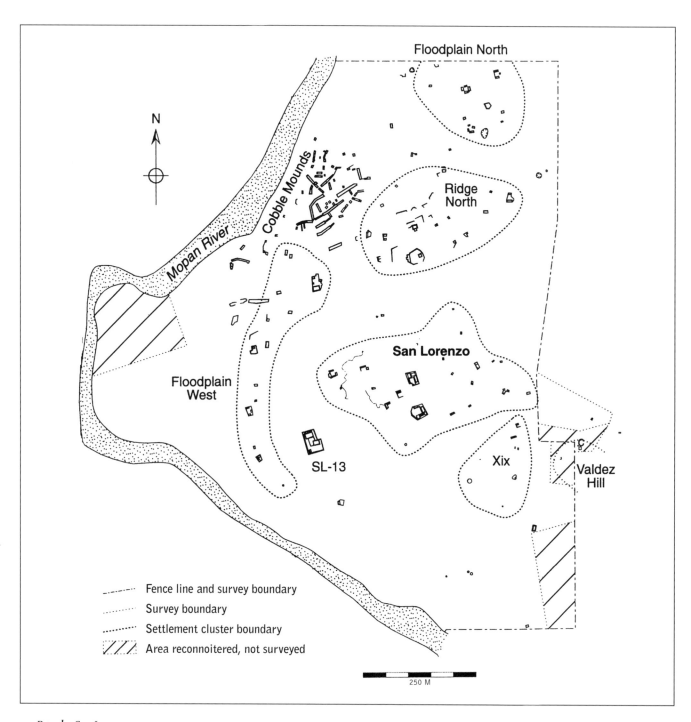

5.2 Rancho San Lorenzo survey area

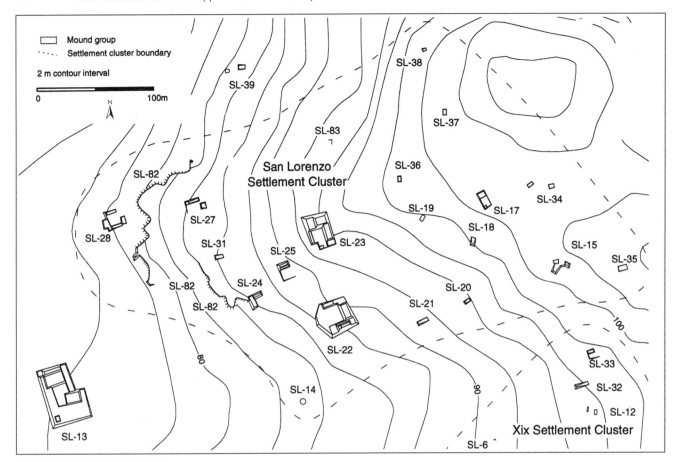

5.3 San Lorenzo settlement cluster

Hats' Chaak phase, people ceased using once important sectors of the site, culminating in the site's abandonment sometime in the Tsak' phase (Leventhal and LeCount 2001). Although San Lorenzo was founded prior to the Hats' Chaak phase florescence at Xunantunich, the parallel historical trajectories of rapid Samal phase growth to a Hats' Chaak maximum, followed by contraction in the Tsak' phase, suggest that the fortunes of the San Lorenzo residents were closely linked to those of the polity's rulers (Ashmore, Yaeger, and Robin 2001), a point to which I will return.

THE LATE LATE CLASSIC PERIOD (HATS' CHAAK PHASE)
The Hats' Chaak phase at San Lorenzo is one of marked differences among the settlement's households. The three different domestic layouts mentioned above arguably reflect, in part, compounds having been abandoned at different stages in a domestic developmental cycle (Yaeger 2000a; see also Fortes 1958; Haviland 1988; Tourtellot 1988a), but this cannot explain all the demonstrable differences among the households, including their ability to mobilize extra-household labor to build their houses and the architectural elements used in those houses, their ability to host feasts,

and their access to exotic goods. Because I have detailed the evidence for these differences elsewhere (Yaeger 2000a, 2000b), I only briefly summarize the data here.

One of the clearest manifestations of social difference at San Lorenzo is the amount of labor that households invested in domestic architecture. The architecture in most groups at San Lorenzo, including all but one of the nine isolated structures and two of the seven patio groups, consisted of low house platforms, generally less than 1 m high, topped by perishable wattle-and-daub buildings. The platforms were faced with cobblestones and the occasional small limestone block. Two additional patio groups also consisted of small platforms and perishable structures, but the platforms contained more limestone-block masonry. A third set of groups stands out as distinct from the previous two sets, however. This set, comprised of a single structure (SL-25; see figure 5.3) and three patio groups (SL-22, SL-23, SL-24) has markedly larger substructure platforms made of limestone blocks. Such blocks often supported buildings with masonry foundation walls. The labor invested in some of these buildings exceeded 1000 person-days, and a corbel-vaulted roof in one building may have required specialized masons (Yaeger 2000a). Elliot Abrams (1994) has argued that this scale of labor investment indicates that householders mobilized significant extra-household labor.

The households that could employ the labor of others made other architectural choices that showed their concern with differentiating themselves from their neighbors. At SL-22 and SL-24, houses incorporated architectural elements such as basal moldings and high interior benches that were not found elsewhere at San Lorenzo (figure 5.4) but were common in the monumental architecture at Xunantunich. In using such features, residents of these households created domestic settings that were visually more akin to elite residential compounds at Xunantunich than to the humbler houses of their neighbors.

The residents of San Lorenzo created and reinforced internal social differences through two other practices, the hosting of feasts and the wearing of exotic goods. Large quantities of animal bones were found only at the three largest patio groups (SL-22, SL-23, SL-24), and most groups had few or no faunal remains whatsoever. Given that bone-chemistry analysis at Barton Ramie indicates people in the Belize Valley in the Late Classic period ate similar amounts of meat (Gerry 1993), the uneven distribution of faunal remains at San Lorenzo presumably reflects the location of meat consumption, not the identities of the consumers. In places where it was scarce, meat was often consumed during special social events, and high frequencies of serving vessels in these same groups suggest that people ate meat at feasts.

A similarly limited group of households had access to important material symbols, specifically items of adornment made from exotic raw materials. Although marine shell ornaments were recovered from all the households we extensively excavated, the residents of the more modest houses had fewer marine ornaments, most of which were simple *Oliva* shell tinklers. More striking is the greenstone distribution. Only those families living in the largest compounds (SL-22, SL-24) possessed greenstone beads. While the residents of San Lorenzo presumably valued greenstone and marine shell for its exotic origins and cosmological significance, I have argued that they were also cognizant of the connections between exotic goods and the political realm and used these items to intentionally represent their relationships with the polity elite (Yaeger 2000b).

In examining these manifestations of heterogeneity at San Lorenzo, we find that there is considerable, albeit incomplete, overlap among those households that could marshal considerable labor for building their homes (SL-22 through SL-25), those that employed basal moldings and/or tall benches (SL-22, SL-24, SL-34)[3], those that hosted feasts (SL-22, SL-23, SL-24), and those that had access to greenstone (SL-22, SL-24).[4] A larger sample would probably confirm that these are overlapping rather than coterminous characteristics (Tourtellot 1988b, for example), but the correspondences remain. Why did only three households host feasts and why were those same households able to requisition the labor of others to help build their homes? Why did many of these same groups use distinctive architectural features in their houses and wear greenstone beads?

The descendents of the first settlers at Maya sites often controlled, Patricia McAnany has argued, the best local resources through the "principle of first occupancy" (1995:96–97). Given that two of the groups (SL-22, SL-23), where feasts were held in the Hats' Chaak phase, were also among the first to have been established at San Lorenzo, it seems plausible that the descendants of the settlement's founding families had privileged claims to land and other resources through their ancestors, whose veneration may have been the focus of some Hats' Chaak phase rituals and feasts (McAnany 1995; Tozzer 1941:92).

The feasts sponsored by these households brought the settlement's residents together to celebrate important occasions and share food and gifts, cementing the social ties that bound them together. Simultaneously, though, these feasts demonstrated that the economic and political resources needed to host them were unevenly distributed throughout the settlement. Although local social inequalities were facts of life in the Belize Valley as early as the Preclassic period, the rapid growth of Xunantunich and its rulers' polity-building strategies in the Hats' Chaak phase provided new symbolic and material resources, like items made of exotic materials, for creating and reinforcing these differences with special reference to the new polity's elite. Other practices that represented social distinctions in the community and created extra-community affiliations took place in SL-13, a ritual complex adjacent to San Lorenzo.

SL-13 is unique in the Rancho San Lorenzo Survey Area, as it is the largest group in height and volume and the only group with two connected patios. The closed North Patio of SL-13 and several unusual features of the buildings that flanked it, unlike any houses excavated at San Lorenzo, suggest that the group was nonresidential. An artifact assemblage with a high frequency of incensarios, serving vessels, and ornaments; a bone flute; and a large number of faunal remains suggests that the group was a venue for ritual celebrations.

Several lines of evidence suggest that the rulers of Xunantunich influenced, or even oversaw, the construction of SL-13, presumably as part of a strategy to integrate this

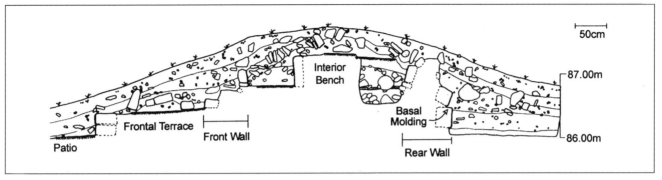

5.4 SL-24 Str 1: west section of axial trench

section of the Mopan River Valley into their polity. SL-13 is located in between the area's settlement clusters, and its construction involved more labor than any single settlement cluster could probably muster. Furthermore, SL-13's Str 3 is the only platform at San Lorenzo with two stairways, one facing the patio and the other looking west-southwest toward Xunantunich, plausibly providing an entryway for people coming from that center. Finally, the construction of the North Patio and its surrounding structures early in the Hats' Chaak phase coincided with the rising power of the Xunantunich elite. I have argued elsewhere that people created and represented various social alliances during the celebrations at SL-13. Those events that involved representatives from Xunantunich could have forged links between the ruler of Xunantunich and the local leaders of San Lorenzo and nearby settlements, a crucial task if the new rulers of Xunantunich were to routinize and institutionalize the flow of tribute and corvée labor from the countryside to their capital.

TERMINAL CLASSIC PERIOD (TSAK' PHASE)
Toward the end of the Hats' Chaak phase, the Xunantunich polity began to undergo significant changes (Leventhal and LeCount 2001). At the same time that the polity's rulers were making some of the most explicit visual statements of their power on three carved stelae, several important parts of the site, including the royal residential compound, fell into disuse (Keller 1995b; Yaeger 1997), and the polity witnessed a marked decline in population (Neff et al. 1995). At San Lorenzo, only five domestic groups showed significant evidence of occupation during the Tsak' phase, but three of these (SL-22, SL-23, SL-24) were the houses of the once powerful families discussed above. Just as the regional social and political context in which they lived had changed, so, too, had the internal organization of the settlement. The settlement was apparently much more homogeneous, and the social differences that did exist were no longer actively marked. For example, Tsak' phase architecture is generally

small in volume and is invariably made of roughly faced limestone rubble. Tsak' phase constructions also lacked the differentiating benches and moldings used in the Hats' Chaak phase, and remodeling in one building (SL-22 Str 3) obscured an interior bench. Such changes indicate that elite buildings had ceased to be a referent for San Lorenzo architecture.

Perhaps related to this, the SL-13 complex changed in function. In the early facet of the Tsak' phase, the collapse of several substructures covered parts of the two main venues for Hats' Chaak phase celebrations. Despite later, possibly residential, use of the complex, the architectural debris that covered these once important spaces was never cleaned up. Eventually, San Lorenzo, SL-13, and Xunantunich were abandoned, probably by the early eleventh century.

SUMMARY
The evidence presented for San Lorenzo demonstrates that the site was a complex and heterogeneous settlement, and that the nature and dimensions of this complexity changed through time. The data suggest that San Lorenzo's Hats' Chaak phase residents shared a community identity that was made explicit and reinforced in practices such as ritual feasts. These feasts and other common events, such as house construction, however, also required and reproduced inequalities within the community. Families that hosted feasts apparently sought to maintain or increase their privileged status through these practices and by using material symbols to represent connections, whether real or not, to the elite of Xunantunich (see also Schortman 1989; Schortman and Nakamura 1991). At the same time, the new rulers of Xunantunich were embarking on an ambitious building program requiring new levels of corvée labor and tribute from the local population.

For some hinterland residents, like the first families to settle San Lorenzo, such changes presented opportunities to enhance their local positions by serving as intermediaries between local settlements and the political and economic institutions of the emerging polity. The residents of the simpler houses at San Lorenzo also must have had reasons for participating in practices that legitimated local inequalities, perhaps to ensure access to land or chert resources, to improve the community's connections to the polity elite, or to satisfy familial obligations. For their part, the rulers of Xunantunich had to accommodate their strategies to the social and political structures presented by existing settlements like San Lorenzo, especially those that predated Xunantunich's founding.

Barton Ramie

One of the first projects dedicated to a comprehensive investigation of pre-Columbian lowland Maya households and their places in Maya society took place in the upper Belize River Valley. The goal of this groundbreaking research was to address the nature and function of hinterland settlements and their constituent features, their relationship to the natural environment, and their place within larger social and political systems (Willey et al. 1965: 15). To achieve this goal, Gordon Willey and his colleagues (Willey et al. 1965:30–34) spent three field seasons between 1954 and 1956 mapping and excavating house mounds and carrying out informal reconnaissance along the Belize River and its major tributaries, describing zones of settlement and larger sites with public architecture. The focus of their work was the Barton Ramie Estate on the north bank of the Belize River, 25 km below the confluence of its two tributaries, the Mopan and the Macal (figure 5.1).

Willey's project mapped 262 mounds in roughly 2 km^2 of cleared land (figure 5.5) and carried out excavations at a sample of those mounds. The boundaries of the settlement zone that Willey and his colleagues mapped were arbitrary, dictated by the area of ramie cultivation. Barton Ramie as a site, therefore, does not necessarily correspond to any past social entity, as the investigators point out (Willey et al 1965: 31). They do name several distinct zones within the site that are spatially isolated by topographic features, such as relic channels and swampy swales, many of which probably predate the settlement. Although the investigators were hesitant to equate the mounds that cluster in these zones with social groupings, it seems likely that these groups were socially meaningful in antiquity, although we currently lack data to test this possibility.

Willey and his co-investigators distinguished three formal types of mounds: the individual circular or oval mounds, which comprise the vast majority of the mounds at the site; *plazuela* mounds, consisting of multiple structures arranged around a patio; and one "temple" mound (BR-180), a 12-m–high pyramidal substructure associated

with an elevated plaza (Willey et al. 1965:34). Using axial trenches and clearing excavations, Willey and colleagues extensively excavated five mounds, four single mounds (BR-1, BR-123, BR-144, BR-194) and one large plazuela group (BR-147). They also tested sixty of the remaining mounds with 2 x 3 m units to bring the excavated sample up to just under 25%. Their testing included one unit in the plaza in front of the temple mound.

The investigators noted two problems with their mound typology that bear mentioning here. First, there are several double mounds that presumably consist of two structures facing each other across a low patio. Second, and more problematic, many of the single mounds are quite large, often exceeding 20 m in diameter, raising the possibility that they cover multiple structures arranged around a patio (Willey et al. 1965: 572). Two of the four single mounds that Willey and his colleagues trenched suggest this is indeed the case. The final two phases of BR-123, a single mound, consisted of a pair of masonry substructures on either side of a plastered patio (Willey et al. 1965: 126). BR-144, a 25 x 35 m single mound 1.5 m high, concealed a 10-m–wide elevated patio with a masonry platform at one end of the plastered surface. Although the single axial trench across the mound revealed no additional house platforms, it is quite likely that one or two platforms lie on the longer axis perpendicular to the excavation trench. This "masking" of multistructure groups is, I suspect, due, in part, to plowing of the cleared area (mentioned in Willey et al. 1965:72). The southernmost section of the Rancho San Lorenzo Survey Area had also been subject to mechanized cultivation, and the mounds there tend to be low in height and oval in shape. Regardless of the reasons, the strong probability that many of the single mounds at Barton Ramie conceal multistructure groups is of great significance because it means that single mounds at Barton Ramie, as a class, are not comparable with the single mounds at San Lorenzo.[5]

The excavations at Barton Ramie showed that the site had a long occupation history, having been founded in the Jenny Creek phase (c. 900–300 BC; phases and dates adapted with minor modifications from Gifford 1976[6]) and occupied for roughly two millennia. The Barton Ramie settlement data, summarized in table 5.1 and figure 5.6, show a population that grew gradually during the Jenny Creek, Barton Creek (300–100 BC), and Mount Hope (100 BC–AD 275) phases of the Preclassic period. A high frequency of mounds exhibiting diagnostic material of the Floral Park complex (AD 275) indicates a significant jump in population in the Protoclassic period.[7] The population remained stable during the Early Classic Hermitage phase (AD 275–600), growing again through the Late Classic Tiger Run (AD

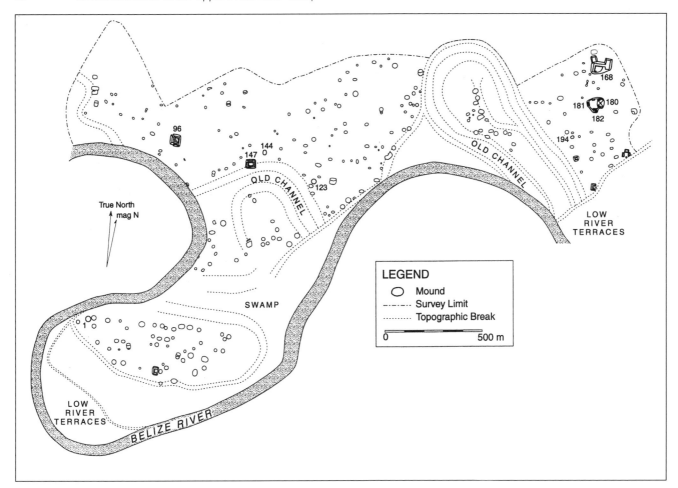

5.5 Barton Ramie Estate. *After Willey et al. 1965*

600–700) and Late-to-Terminal Classic Spanish Lookout (AD 700–900) phases before dropping slightly in the Postclassic New Town phase (AD 900–c. 1350).

The population history of Barton Ramie conforms broadly with those of other sites in the region (Ford 1990; Neff et al. 1995; see figure 5.6) with two exceptions. First, the settlement does not show the Early Classic decline recorded by most other surveys (discussed in Ford 1990). Second, the extremely high frequency of occupation in the Postclassic period is remarkable for this region, where most sites were abandoned during the Terminal Classic period, the late facet of the Spanish Lookout phase at Barton Ramie. The only well-documented exceptions are Baking Pot (Conlon 1999; Willey et al. 1965) and Tipu, which was occupied until the Spanish Crown forcibly moved its residents in 1707 (E.A. Graham, Jones, and Kautz 1985; G.D. Jones 1989).

Before ending this discussion of Barton Ramie's population history, I should note the caveat, expressed by Willey (Willey et al. 1965:157), that correlating excavation units with cultural stratigraphy is difficult. The relatively small exposure presented by 3 x 2 m test excavations prevented full understanding of the complex stratigraphy of most mounds, which consisted of interbedded refuse layers and fill, the latter a mix of clay and refuse. Close contextual analysis was further complicated by the practice of excavating 20-cm arbitrary levels, except where presented with clear stratigraphic breaks. Thus, although Willey and colleagues considered stratigraphic and contextual factors when determining whether a mound was occupied during a given phase, the overriding criterion was the frequency of sherds from that phase found in the mound (see especially Willey et al. 1965:158). Thus, they defined many mounds as being occupied during a given period on the basis of secondary and/or mixed contexts. One assumption implicit in this practice is that cultural materials in the fill of a structure were originally used at that same structure, an assumption that might not always be safe at Barton Ramie, where mounds are often less than 20 m from their nearest neighbor. Despite this potential problem, the population trajectory they present is accurate enough for the purposes of this chapter, and the criteria for dating construction events and features were more stringent.

PERIOD		CERAMIC CHRONOLOGY		POPULATION HISTORY		
		BARTON RAMIE (Gifford 1976)	XUNANTUNICH (LeCount et al. 2000)	XSS (Ehret 1995)	BRASS (Ford 1990)	BARTON RAMIE (Willey et al. 1965)
POSTCLASSIC	Late 1500 1400 1300 1200 1100 Early 1000 900	New Town	Yakunah	0%	21%	95%
CLASSIC	Terminal 800	Spanish Lookout	Tsak'	19%	48%	100%
	Late 700		Hats' Chaak	72%	98%	
	600	Tiger Run	Samal	59%		85%
	Early 500 400 300	Hermitage	Ak'ab	41%	49%	77%
PRECLASSIC	Protoclassic 200 100 AD/BC	Floral Park	Pek'kat	34%	91%	77%
	100	Mount Hope				37%
	Late 200 300	Barton Creek	Ok'inal	29%		23%
	Middle 400 500 600 700 800	Jenny Creek	Nohol	50%	51%	28%
	900 1000 1100 Early 1200 1300 1400	None defined by Gifford but see Awe 1992	Muyal	0%	0%	0%

5.6 *Xunantunich and Barton Ramie ceramic chronologies and settlement survey data*

Table 5.1 Frequencies of mound occupation and construction by ceramic phase at Barton Ramie

Ceramic Phase	Occupation (%)	Construction (%)
Jenny Creek	28	5
Barton Creek	23	6
Mount Hope	37	8
Floral Park	77	45
Hermitage	77	46
Tiger Run	84	77
Spanish Lookout	100	98
New Town	95	82

Source: Willey et al. 1965:Table 2

The largest center near Barton Ramie is Baking Pot, approximately 4 km west of the settlement area. The layout and architecture of Baking Pot, with three large plazas, three pyramids 13 m or more in height, a ballcourt, and a raised causeway, indicate that it was an important political center in the upper Belize River Valley. The construction history of Baking Pot is not well understood because the early investigations at the site by Oliver Ricketson (1931), A. H. Anderson, and William Bullard (1963; also Willey et al. 1965) were limited to excavating only a few structures, and later excavations in the 1990s by the Belize Valley Reconnaissance Project have concentrated on the final phases of occupation (see chapter 6). The available evidence suggests, however, a strong Tiger Run and Spanish Lookout occupation, with some subsequent use during the New Town phase. Structure M of group I and structures A and D in group II date entirely to the Late Classic phases, although the former shows some New Town use (Willey et al. 1965:304–305), and a probe into plaza I of group I found that the entire plaza fill episode dates to the Spanish Lookout phase (Willey et al. 1965:306).

The information available for Baking Pot thus suggests that the site did not serve as a political or ritual center for Preclassic and Early Classic Barton Ramie residents. That does not mean, however, that the residents of Barton Ramie were not affiliated with other sites, as there were several early centers of political power in the valley. The closest of these centers is Blackman Eddy, only 3 km east of Barton Ramie, where Str B-1 was adorned with stucco masks in the Preclassic period, and rulers commissioned a hieroglyphic monument in the Early Classic period (Brown and Garber 2000; Garber and Brown 2000).

PRECLASSIC PERIOD (JENNY CREEK, BARTON CREEK, AND MOUNT HOPE PHASES)

Barton Ramie's long Preclassic occupation history begins in the Middle Preclassic Jenny Creek phase. Despite considerable time depth, Preclassic Barton Ramie shows rela-

tively little evolving internal complexity (Willey et al. 1965:279–281). For centuries, houses were wattle-and-daub structures that sat on low clay platforms, sometimes with plaster floors. In the Mount Hope phase, some platforms were faced with rough limestone masonry (Willey et al. 1965:292), but they tended to be less than 50 cm high. During none of these phases does the size of domestic architecture, or the techniques used in its construction, imply any differential access to extra-household labor, although even rough estimates of architectural investment are complicated by the relatively limited excavation areas and the very small samples of exposed Preclassic architecture.

The Preclassic burials at Barton Ramie similarly suggest a lack of differential access to resources within the settlement. People were buried in simple pits, and most were interred without grave goods, although some graves contained ceramic vessels and one had a greenstone bead. Although Preclassic burial practices do not suggest social inequalities at Barton Ramie, a diversity of burial positions—prone, supine, and flexed burials, with heads to the north or the south (Willey et al. 1965:533)—suggests complexity of a different sort, perhaps heterarchical in nature, in which differences within the community were marked using apparently unranked burial practices.

PROTOCLASSIC AND EARLY CLASSIC PERIODS
(FLORAL PARK AND HERMITAGE PHASES)

Willey and his colleagues argue that Barton Ramie went through a marked cultural and demographic change in the Floral Park phase (Willey et al. 1965:564–566). The settlement's population nearly doubled or quintupled, depending upon whether one compares occupancy or construction figures, and we find the first evidence of clear internal hierarchical differences at Barton Ramie in this period, mainly evident in burial data.

The first elaborate burials—in which the deceased were accompanied by many objects, including pottery and artifacts of marine shell and greenstone, and their graves covered by limestone slabs—date to the Floral Park phase (Willey et al. 1965:531). It is very interesting that the establishment of stricter conventions of body positioning in interments coincides with this change. Beginning in this phase, individuals were almost always buried extended with their heads to the south or, rarely, seated. This standardization grows stronger over time, suggesting the establishment of an authoritative settlement-wide cannon that superseded or replaced an earlier diversity of practices. By the Spanish Lookout phase, people were no longer buried in a supine position (Willey et al. 1965:533–534).

The architectural techniques used during the Floral Park

phase of Barton Ramie show relatively little change from preceding phases, but two important classes of mounds are first occupied in this phase. There are three markedly larger plazuela groups at Barton Ramie (BR-96, BR-147, BR-168). Willey and his colleagues excavated BR-147 and tested BR-96, and they suggest that these loci were first inhabited in the Floral Park phase, although neither showed evidence of construction prior to the Tiger Run phase (Willey et al. 1965: Table 2). BR-168 is distinctly larger than the other two groups, and its size, coupled with its proximity to the BR-180–182 "temple group," led the investigators to compare it to a "palace" (Willey et al. 1965:572). Sherds collected from the surface of BR-168 and from bulldozer scars that revealed the mound's interior were predominately Tiger Run, Spanish Lookout, and New Town in date (constituting 20, 42, and 16% of the collection, respectively), with some Floral Park (10%), Hermitage (9%) and a smattering of earlier sherds (Willey et al. 1965: Chart 29). Given this, the investigators suggest tentatively that occupation began in the Floral Park phase and continued through the New Town phase (Willey et al. 1965:245).

The Floral Park founding dates for the largest plazuelas is mirrored at BR-180–182. A test unit into the 2-m-high plaza between BR-180 and two lower mounds, BR-181 and BR-182, revealed four plaster floors, one dating to the Floral Park phase, two of Floral Park to Hermitage date, and the fourth dating to the Spanish Look phase (Willey et al. 1965:251). It is not possible to correlate these floors with the mounds surrounding the plaza; so, some of them could be house-platform floors. The size of these fill episodes and their plaster capping hint, however, that they were part of a plazuela or ceremonial group.

That the three largest residential groups at Barton Ramie were not founded earlier in the settlement's history is an interesting contrast to the San Lorenzo case, where the settlement's largest groups were among the first to be established at the site. Furthermore, the establishment of the area's ceremonial focus, BR-180–182, predates the known public architecture of Baking Pot, again contrasting with the correlation between the construction of SL-13 and the growth of Xunantunich. I discuss this interesting difference between the two case studies and the possible role of Blackman Eddy in more depth below.

LATE AND TERMINAL CLASSIC PERIODS
(TIGER RUN AND SPANISH LOOKOUT PHASES)
The Late-to-Terminal Classic at Barton Ramie shows the most marked level of internal heterogeneity at the site in terms of both mortuary practices and architecture. The Tiger Run phase, especially the Tiger Run–Spanish Lookout transition, is the period for which Willey and his colleagues found the greatest disparity in grave offerings, with some burials including more than 20 ceramic vessels and many nonceramic artifacts, while others lacked grave goods altogether. Simultaneously, the head-to-south prone position predominates, with few exceptions (Willey et al. 1965:532). This position suggests that the political climate in the Tiger Run phase emphasized settlement-wide conformity and standardization in some practices, such as burial positioning, as well as displays that reinforced internal differences. The Spanish Lookout phase burials continue in this pattern, although the richest graves contain fewer items than those of the Tiger Run–Spanish Lookout transition (Willey et al. 1965:534).

Tiger Run phase architecture shows two important developments that distinguish it from that of previous periods. First, some households built relatively large house platforms, up to 0.8 m high, faced with limestone masonry and sometimes plastered, suggesting an ability to invest significant labor in domestic architecture. Second, the first masonry bench and masonry foundation wall date to the Tiger Run–Spanish Lookout transition (Willey et al. 1965:289, 142). I argued above that these two features were used by higher status households at San Lorenzo to intentionally represent connections with the polity's elite. These features arguably played the same role at Barton Ramie, although a larger excavated sample that includes the smallest mounds at the site is needed to ascertain more fully the distribution of these features and evaluate this possibility.

Finally, the first identified construction at the two large plazuela mounds that were tested date to the Tiger Run phase, although Willey and colleagues used sherd counts from these groups to suggest they were occupied as early as the Floral Park phase. The initial Tiger Run buildings are of minimal height, even in the case of the extensively excavated BR-147, and it is the Spanish Lookout construction episodes that make the greatest contribution to the volume and elaboration of both groups. Somewhat surprisingly, the BR-180 temple group was apparently not used at all in the Tiger Run phase. It did undergo a renovation of undetermined scale in the Spanish Lookout phase, but the addition to the plaza is surprisingly small, consisting of 10 to 15 cm of fill placed on top of some 1.75 m of Floral Park–Hermitage construction (Willey et al. 1965:249–251).

POSTCLASSIC PERIOD (NEW TOWN PHASE)
The New Town phase shows a marked decrease in material heterogeneity from the Spanish Lookout phase. The excavators found no evidence of limestone masonry, and the volume of individual construction efforts, where they could

be identified, was quite low. Overall, architectural invest- ment seems to have been minimal (Willey et al. 1965:291). It should be pointed out, though, that disturbance of New Town architecture, especially by modern plowing, might have destroyed some masonry.

Burial position remained relatively standardized, with all but one burial extended with the head to the south and prone in those cases where preservation allowed observa- tion of this characteristic; the single exception was a seated burial. But the differences in interment architecture and grave goods nearly disappeared. In all the burials except the seated example, bodies were placed in simple pits without any stone architecture. Furthermore, fewer people were ac- companied by grave goods, and those goods tended to be modest items of personal adornment; no pottery was placed in graves (Willey et al. 1965:533).

The three large plazuela groups show continued occu- pation into the New Town phase, and BR-96 witnessed ad- ditional construction at this time. The BR-180 ceremonial group has so few New Town sherds, however, that Willey and colleagues do not even designate it as having been oc- cupied during this phase (Willey et al. 1965: Table 2).

SUMMARY
Like San Lorenzo, Barton Ramie was a complex settlement that underwent significant changes over the course of its history. Although we lack evidence for some of the inte- grating practices found at San Lorenzo, notably feasting, the material markers of inequality are significant. These markers appear in the Floral Park phase, contemporaneous with the first occupation of the largest plazuelas, groups that would be homes to households that controlled signifi- cant extra-household labor by the Tiger Run phase and might have had other privileges like those inferred for some residents of San Lorenzo. The Floral Park phase also wit- nessed three construction phases in the BR-180 group, which apparently created the first architectural space dedicated to settlement-wide ritual use. The lack of monumental archi- tecture at Baking Pot at this time suggests that this innova- tion was not related to events at that site but rather arose through local social processes. Some role for the rulers of Blackman Eddy remains possible, given that the mask-bear- ing platform there reached a height of 4 m by the end of the Preclassic period. This platform was the cumulative prod- uct of nine construction efforts over the span of many cen- turies, none of which represented a labor investment on the scale of later Xunantunich or Baking Pot.

There are, however, several major changes at Barton Ramie contemporary with the first monumental architec- ture at Baking Pot in the Tiger Run phase. The first con-

struction at the larger plazuela groups occurs late in the Tiger Run phase, and this time period sees an increase in local inequalities, as reflected in grave goods. Some Tiger Run phase residents of Barton Ramie also used architec- tural symbols that displayed an affiliation with the regional elite, who probably lived at Baking Pot. This correlation between plazuela construction and strategies of elite affili- ation suggests that some Barton Ramie residents success- fully pursued a strategy in which displaying their connec- tions with the polity rulers bolstered their local positions of prominence, while their local authority made them tar- gets of those rulers' political strategies.

The BR-180 complex was apparently neither modified nor even used during this period. Could this also be a sign of interference in local matters by the Baking Pot rulers, who transplanted socially significant celebrations from this lo- cal autonomous ritual venue to the newly built pyramids and plazas at Baking Pot? One could envision a process by which the rulers kept strict control of public ritual celebra- tions until polity-wide loyalties were well established. At Barton Ramie, BR-180 would again become a site for local ritual during the Spanish Lookout phase.

The high population of the New Town phase suggests that any weakening in political authority at Baking Pot, where monumental construction was much reduced, did not affect Barton Ramie as severely as it did Tsak' phase Xunantunich and San Lorenzo. But some of the local hier- archical differences, such as the architectural investment described for the Late Classic period, disappeared prior to the New Town phase, suggesting a leveling of household inequalities at Barton Ramie. Interestingly, the BR-180 group was apparently not used in this phase, suggesting that most ritual activity occurred in household contexts.

Discussion
The data from Barton Ramie and San Lorenzo amply dem- onstrate the complexity inherent in small settlements in the upper Belize River Valley. To structure the discussion of this complexity and its implications, I would like to return to the three dimensions of difference that I outlined in the introduction to this chapter: differences among settlements, differences among households within settlements, and changes within settlements over time.

HETERARCHICAL COMPLEXITY: DIFFERENCES BETWEEN
SAN LORENZO AND BARTON RAMIE
I was first drawn to compare the Rancho San Lorenzo Sur- vey Area and the Barton Ramie Estate because of their simi- larities: the comparable size and density of settlement, the presence of a specialized ritual complex at each site, their

relative proximity to a large political center, and their eco-logical locations in alluvial settings. In addition, the mounds at both sites encompass the same range of morphological variability, from small single mounds to large multistructure patio groups. Despite these similarities, the excavation data show the two settlements are significantly different. This fact underlines the danger of using a formalist, typological approach to study Maya rural complexity, a point made more broadly by the other chapters in this volume.

First, the sites have markedly different population histories. Following initial settlement in the Middle Preclassic period, Barton Ramie grew until the New Town phase, with very few mounds showing occupational hiatuses (see Willey et al. 1965: Table 2). At San Lorenzo, several mounds show evidence of Middle and Late Preclassic occupation, but there was then a decline so strong as to suggest widespread abandonment in the Protoclassic and Early Classic (Yaeger 2000a). The new settlement that was founded just prior to the Samal phase was relatively short-lived, and it was abandoned sometime during the Terminal Classic Tsak' phase, contrasting with the strong Postclassic occupation at Barton Ramie.

Second, although each site has an associated specialized ritual complex, SL-13 lacks a pyramidal structure like that at BR-180. Studies have shown that large pyramids often served as funerary monuments and ancestral shrines (Freidel and Schele 1989; Ruz Lhuillier 1954), and smaller pyramidal structures at hinterland Belize Valley sites like Zubin may have been analogous (Iannone 1996; chapter 3). The absence of a pyramidal structure at San Lorenzo indicates a significant difference in ritual practice. Although it is possible that other architectural forms provided a venue for similar ritual observances at San Lorenzo, they would have occurred in a built environment that would have structured these rituals very differently from those at Barton Ramie.

Third, San Lorenzo and Barton Ramie show distinct patterns in the founding dates for the groups that would become the largest plazuela residences during the Late Classic period. As described above, two of the three largest groups at San Lorenzo were the first to be founded at the settlement. At Barton Ramie, however, the three largest plazuelas show their first evidence of occupation after Barton Ramie had been occupied for nearly a millennium. The principle of first occupancy may not have played as strong a role in legitimating the privileged position of the occupants of the largest groups at Late Classic Barton Ramie.

Finally, there are differences in the material cultures of the inhabitants of the sites, most apparent in the Late-to-Terminal Classic ceramic assemblages. At Barton Ramie, the

Garbutt Creek and Vaca Falls ceramic groups, dominated by red-slipped restricted jars and large bowls, comprise nearly 16% of the assemblage (frequencies are calculated from sherd counts in Gifford 1976; also see the frequencies for the Atalaya Group near Baking Pot, described in chapter 6). The black-slipped Mount Maloney ceramic group, which forms less than 2% of the assemblage, contains analogous forms. In contrast, these red wares, especially the Garbutt Creek ceramic group, are very rare in the Xunantunich region, where the incurving bowls and jars of the Mount Maloney Black ceramic group dominate, comprising almost 30% of the Hats' Chaak and Tsak' pottery assemblages (LeCount 1996:391). These notable differences indicate that the two settlements participated in different pottery distribution networks. Furthermore, the contrast between the black-slipped Mount Maloney group at Xunantunich and the red wares at Barton Ramie may have been intentional, perhaps reflecting an effort by the newly founded Xunantunich polity to distinguish itself from other polities in the valley, where red-ware bowls were a long-standing tradition (illustrated in Gifford 1976: Fig. 214; thanks to Angela Keller for bringing this contrast to my attention. Connell [2000] finds that a similar pattern corresponds with significant political shifts within the hinterland of Xunantunich).

These important differences between San Lorenzo and Barton Ramie caution us against treating sites as equivalent settlement units on the basis of similarities in surface morphology and layout. Few of the differences outlined above can be discerned from maps of the two sites, underscoring the fact that many complexities of hinterland settlements and households cannot be elucidated from survey data alone. In making this point, however, I do not wish to detract from the importance of the morphological, spatial, and ecological factors that led me initially to classify San Lorenzo and Barton Ramie together. These criteria are "superficial" insofar as they can be identified without excavation, but it would be erroneous to imply that they were trivial or unimportant. There is no doubt that a site's size and composition, its place within a regional settlement system, and its local ecological setting all reflect and structure its social organization and thus provide valuable information for understanding past society. But relying only on such data inherently limits our understanding of a settlement, its inhabitants, and their places in society, reifying a hierarchical view of settlement systems at the expense of complementary heterarchical perspectives that see the differences between sites as being as meaningful as their similarities (Haviland 1981; Hendon 1992; King and Potter 1994). As I note below, it seems that the two settlements discussed here both underwent similar processes that integrated them into larger polities, but their differences played an important role in structuring that process distinctly at each settlement.

INTRASETTLEMENT COMPLEXITY: INTERNAL
HETEROGENEITY AT SAN LORENZO AND BARTON RAMIE

Changing our scale of analysis, we find that both San Lorenzo and Barton Ramie were notably heterogeneous internally. There were important differences among households in these two settlements, some hierarchical and others unranked or heterarchical. As noted in the discussion of Barton Ramie, differences in the mound typologies and excavation strategies used at the sites prevent direct comparisons of the data, but the available information does suggest some important similarities between the two sites.

Much of the local heterogeneity involves differential access to resources. At San Lorenzo in the Hats' Chaak phase and at Barton Ramie beginning in the Tiger Run phase, some households built their homes using construction techniques that required much more labor than the low cobble platforms that had predominated at Barton Ramie in earlier phases and continued to be common at both sites. Estimates suggest that extra-household labor was involved in the construction of some of these structures at San Lorenzo (Yaeger 2000a; also Abrams 1994), and the Spanish Lookout architecture at BR-147 probably required extra-household labor as well.

At San Lorenzo, some of these same households bolstered and maintained local inequalities in the Hats' Chaak phase through affiliations with polity elite, expressed by incorporating certain architectural elements to their houses and by wearing items fashioned of exotic raw materials. At Barton Ramie, Tiger Run, and Spanish Lookout, household architecture incorporates the same differentiating features as seen at San Lorenzo. Furthermore, the frequency of marine shell rises in the Hermitage phase, suggesting that such items became increasingly important in similar displays of affiliation. Although these data suggest the existence of social inequalities at Barton Ramie like those identified at San Lorenzo, they do not permit me to examine whether the various markers of social inequality correlate as they do at San Lorenzo.

The burial data from Barton Ramie show an interesting trend in which an increasing standardization in burial positioning is paralleled by an increasing variation in the quantity of grave goods and the elaboration of grave pit architecture. This trend presumably marks a divergence in household resources that could be deposited in graves, but it also reflects a changing social climate in which these acts of conspicuous consumption served a household's strate-

gic ends. This trend begins in the Floral Park phase, and the standard body position continues into the New Town phase despite a marked drop in the variation in grave goods and grave elaboration. Unfortunately, the very small sample of three burials at San Lorenzo, two of which were in SL-13, precludes comparing mortuary data from the two sites.

The internal heterogeneity evinced by the excavation data from San Lorenzo and Barton Ramie leads to another important conclusion about Classic-period lowland Maya society. These two small settlements, and probably most others of the Classic period, simply do not conform to the "little community" (Redfield 1955) and the closed corporate community (Wolf 1957) models that still influence archaeological interpretations (Schwartz and Falconer 1994a). The archaeological data show that the homogeneity, conservatism, and closed nature of these ideal constructs do not pertain to our two archaeological cases, where internal inequalities were strong and local differences were created and reinforced through dynamic interaction between a settlement's residents and individuals and groups outside the settlement.

DIACHRONIC COMPLEXITY: THE CREATION OF INTERNAL
INEQUALITIES AT SAN LORENZO AND BARTON RAMIE

The final kind of complexity demonstrated by these two settlements is diachronic. The internal complexity just described was not a static characteristic intrinsic to the settlements, but was something that changed over time. Some aspects of this process of change seem to pertain to both sites, while other aspects do not. At both sites, residents of some groups used material symbols in what I argue was an intentional effort to represent affiliations between themselves and regional or polity elite. In both cases, these practices of affiliation coincide with periods of growth and expansion at the two nearest large political centers.

At San Lorenzo, the households that most aggressively represent links to the polity elite were those with privileged access to the labor of people outside their domestic unit and those who could acquire exotic goods that were arguably controlled by the polity's rulers. It seems likely that these households were intentionally trying to bolster their local position, and that the polity's leaders were complicit in this, looking for ways to ensure the flow of tribute to the polity capital. This stance may have led to the construction of SL-13 as well. Another local ideological resource that these San Lorenzo households used to negotiate and legitimate their authority was the principle of first occupancy.

The history of Barton Ramie differs; here the founding of the groups that would become the largest residential compounds occurred nearly a millennium after the settlement's initial establishment. These groups became architecturally prominent during the Tiger Run phase, a period during which Baking Pot began to grow and its rulers started to commission monumental architecture. As at San Lorenzo, the growth of Baking Pot is coeval, with increasing evidence at Barton Ramie for social inequality, including disparities in burial practices and the first use of architectural symbols that represent connections to the polity's rulers. Polity elite, many of them living at Baking Pot, were apparently an important source of affiliation by which some Barton Ramie residents created identities that extended beyond the local community.

The Barton Ramie leaders apparently did not rely as heavily on local sources of legitimacy. For example, they did not have the precedence of occupancy that their San Lorenzo counterparts possessed. Furthermore, their apparent rise to power in the Tiger Run phase corresponded with the abandonment of the BR-180 temple complex. The first construction phases in the BR-180 group predate Baking Pot and were probably the product of local initiatives. This ritual venue, however, was neither used nor modified during the phase when Baking Pot began its growth, perhaps reflecting efforts by the Baking Pot elite to extend their influence over the settlement and relocate ritual practices to their capital. Such a transferral would have overridden local rituals that bolstered, and perhaps sacralized, local identities. The renewed use of the BR-180 group in the Spanish Lookout phase could indicate reestablishment of local control over ritual practices subsequent to the successful establishment of a polity-wide identity. The latter could be one factor accounting for the continuity in population at Barton Ramie and the use of Baking Pot into the New Town phase, contrasting with the Tsak' phase abandonment of Xunantunich and San Lorenzo.

Conclusion

I conclude by briefly stating three of the more general theoretical and methodological implications that follow from the comparative study carried out here. First, the constitution of lowland Maya polities was a flexible processes that did not result in any typical pattern of political integration, even within the upper Belize River Valley. People in different places and at different times employed distinct strategies to create the political relationships that constituted the polities in which they lived. The economic, social, and symbolic resources that households could employ in their efforts varied, however, influencing the nature of integration among households and the structure of hinterland settlements and polities alike.

Second, lowland Maya sociopolitical integration is best understood by taking a comparative approach. Although Barton Ramie and San Lorenzo each had complex histories, a comprehensive view of the positions of these small settlements and their members in their larger societies must neither neglect each settlement's particular history nor dismiss the broad social processes that affected each settlement in similar ways. Comparative investigations of Maya "settlement" must complement particularistic studies of Maya "settlements," and the inherent tension between these two approaches can be a productive one.

Finally, rural settlements like San Lorenzo and Barton Ramie and their relationship to larger social and political institutions are best understood by employing a middle-level approach (de Montmollin 1988b; Iannone 1996; Yaeger 2000a; Yaeger and Canuto 2000). Household-level excavations provide detailed data regarding the settlements' past inhabitants, but a middle-level perspective provides the analytical framework needed to understand the dialectical relationships between larger political and material structures that influenced the settlement and the larger polity, settlement-level political and social institutions, and strategies of individuals both within the settlement and beyond its boundaries.

Acknowledgments. I thank the Belize Department of Archaeology and its Commissioners, the late Harriot Topsey, John Morris, Allan Moore, and Brian Woodeye, for their support of the San Lorenzo research. Rudy Juan, Dorrell Biddle, and Mel Xix generously gave permission to work on their properties despite the inconveniences this work sometimes posed, and the Juan and Penados families were always gracious and cordial hosts in Belize. I also thank all my colleagues on the XAP for the intellectually stimulating and supportive environment they created, with special thanks to project directors Richard M. Leventhal and Wendy Ashmore, and to Sabrina Chase, Sam Connell, Jennifer Ehret, Lisa LeCount, Ted Neff, Aimee Preziosi, Cynthia Robin, Jon Vanden Bosch, and Laura Villamil. My analysis has benefited from a stimulating exchange of data and ideas with other archaeologists working in the Belize Valley, notably Jaime Awe, James Conlon, James Garber, Gyles Iannone, and Terry Powis, although I remain responsible for any shortcomings in the interpretations presented here. Thanks are also due to Florentin Penados and the XAP crew members from San José Succotz and Benque Viejo del Carmen, whose careful work laid the empirical foundation for my study of San Lorenzo. Generous funds supporting the San Lorenzo research came from the National Science Foundation, the Fulbright/II-E Program, the University of Pennsylvania's Graduate School of Arts and Sciences and the Department of Anthropology, and Sigma-Xi. I wrote much of this chapter while a Junior Fellow at Dumbarton Oaks. Finally, I extend my appreciation to Gyles Iannone and Sam Connell for their gracious invitation to contribute to this exciting volume.

NOTES

1. I avoid the use of the term *rural* because it is often seen as the opposite of urban, implying a dichotomous settlement typology of questionable value (Yaeger 2001; chapter 8). Empirically, population distributions in many Maya polities do not conform to the urban-rural pattern of a nucleated and densely populated urban center surrounded by a more sparsely populated countryside (Drennan 1988; Marcus 1983a; Sanders and Webster 1988), although some regions are clear exceptions (D.Z. Chase, A.F. Chase, and Haviland 1990). Instead of rural, I describe settlements as "small" to refer to their size and as "hinterland" to indicate their distance from a polity's political center.

2. Group labels at San Lorenzo bear the prefix SL but should not be confused with groups similarly designated by Willey et al. (1965) at the site of Spanish Lookout.

3. The lack of evidence of these features in SL-23 and SL-25 may reflect the limited testing we undertook at those groups rather than the absence of these architectural elements.

4. Again, because of limited testing at SL-23 and SL-25, the absence of rare items, such as like greenstone, is probably owing to the small artifact samples from those groups.

5. Willey and colleagues' selection of mounds for testing at Barton Ramie further limits the comparability of single mounds at Barton Ramie with single mounds at San Lorenzo. The smallest mound that Willey and colleagues excavated was BR-120, measuring roughly 79 m², and only eight of the sixty-five tested groups measured less than 150 m². At San Lorenzo, all but one of the single mounds was less than 79 m² in area, and several of the smaller patio groups fell within the 79 to 150 m² range.

Therefore, it's likely that even some of the smallest mounds tested by the Barton Ramie project were multistructure groups, and that very few of the single mounds they tested represent single structures. This is not to say that there were no single-structure mounds; I estimate from the site map that some 15% of the mounds at Barton Ramie are smaller than the single-structure BR-120, but they have not been tested. Beyond the implications for comparing Barton Ramie and San Lorenzo, the clear lack of correspondence at Barton Ramie between a mound's shape and the number of contemporaneous structures buried therein has clear implications for how we use mound counts to estimate a settlement's past population and mound morphology for inferring patterns of household composition and social organization.

6. The ceramic typologies developed by Gifford (1976; also in Willey et al. 1965) for Barton Ramie and by Lisa LeCount (1996) for Xunantunich use many of the same diagnostic modes and types, and the ceramic complexes are very similar in composition. The discrepancies in the dates that they assign to the Late and Terminal Classic complexes (figure 5.6) is an artifact of the near absence of radiocarbon dates at Barton Ramie (Willey et al. 1965:29). The Late and Terminal Classic complexes at Xunantunich are dated by a robust set of over twenty radiocarbon dates (LeCount et al. 2000).

7. Gifford (in Willey et al. 1965) originally defined the Floral Park complex as an intrusive complex that was partially contemporaneous with the Mount Hope complex. Joseph Ballís exhaustive study of ceramic material excavated at Cahal Pech, Buenavista, and Las Ruinas de Arenal refutes the site-intrusion hypothesis, demonstrating that the diagnostic ceramic groups that Gifford used to define the Floral Park complex postdate those he used to constitute the Mount Hope complex (Brady et al. 1998:26–27). Consequently, I treat Floral Park as a phase that postdates Mount Hope.

6 Identifying Urban and Rural Settlement Components

An Examination of Classic Period Plazuela Group Function at the Ancient Maya Site of Baking Pot, Belize

James M. Conlon and Allan F. Moore

THE INABILITY to correlate consistently and reliably an architectural grouping's size with the wealth and status of its occupants has repercussions for assessing intrasite organization. For some time now it has been recognized that "structures of similar size, architecture, and arrangement could serve quite different purposes" (Haviland 1981:117). Conversely, it is no less inconceivable that structures of different sizes, styles, and arrangements could serve quite similar purposes. The implication for studying "middle-level settlements" (see Iannone 1993a) is that comparatively diminutive groups of settlement can be included in our analyses, particularly those that may conceal their potentially significant roles within site-level organization, such as formal plazuelas (see Ashmore 1981a:47). When dealing with groups of this size and complexity, it must be recognized that the exercise of initial settlement typological classification may be less productive than understanding the role(s) various mound groups played in intrasite definition, interaction, and integration (Ashmore and Wilk 1988:3; Pendergast 1979:25).

Group analysis and site intrarelationships have long been championed as the basis for settlement pattern studies (Willey 1956b:107), and investigations of this type are particularly important in elucidating the reasons for the distribution of a population over the landscape, particularly at the site level. Here, the term *site* equates with the epicenter of the major centers of the Belize Valley and their associated contiguous settlement. An intrasite study involves the comparison of settlement components characteristics, from large to small, within a site. To assess intrasite community structure in the vicinity of Baking Pot, a predominantly Late Classic (AD 600 to 900) Belize Valley major center, a general group-focus strategy is employed. A group-focus strategy is preferred over a more complex classification typology because settlement typologies constructed from surface morphological characteristics recorded during survey programs do not always accurately reflect the results garnered from excavation data (Hendon 1992:35).

An attractive aspect of group-focused analysis is the ability to identify and extract smaller archaeological units (units larger than single housemounds but not recognizably minor centers) from the larger settlement continuum. The main benefit of investigating groups of mounds is one of acuteness, since groups may have been the emic units of the Maya (Becker 1982:112; A.F. Chase and D.Z, Chase 1987:54), and at this level of settlement research, bridging arguments may be more readily constructed (see de Montmollin 1988a:165). Furthermore, analysis of intrasite differentiation, "is probably most reliably made at the level of corporate groups rather than at the level of the household" (Hayden and Cannon 1982:140–141). The generality of such a settlement typology allows greater concentration on collecting data that will serve as the basis for empirically based examinations of the archaeological record (Iannone 1994:15).

Members of the Belize Valley Archaeological Reconnaissance Project (BVAR) have been investigating ancient Maya community organization in the upper Belize Valley for over twelve years now (for example, Awe and Brisbin 1993; Awe, Campbell, and Conlon 1991; Conlon 1995; Conlon and Moore 1998; Conlon, Powis, and Hohmann 1994; Golden and Conlon 1996). The investigative strategy employed by BVAR investigators includes varying scales of study (for example, Cheetham et al. 1993; Goldsmith 1992; Iannone 1994; Powis 1994), but the ability to discern definable groups and clusters of mounds allows the BVAR project to use a group-focus research strategy to investigate intrasite variability.

At the same time, without at least a general understanding of site-specific settlement morphology, discerning functional relationships becomes haphazard and tenuous. It remains incumbent upon the archaeologist, then, to determine the site limits of major centers as the first step in examining intrasite variability and therefore constructing understandings of rural complexity. Our understanding of rural complexity at Baking Pot is defined by its site limits using the basic settlement distribution data and incorporating a group-focus strategy as the unit of analysis. The group-focus methodological framework is utilized to investigate of two plazuela groups at the major center of Baking Pot. The excavation data from pottery types, architecture, burials, and caches are used to compare and contrast the specific group functions of the Atalaya and Bedran Groups. Results are discussed first within each individual plazuela group (intragroup), then between the two plazuelas (intergroup), and also with regard to their overall setting of greater Baking Pot (intrasite). Their assigned functions are explored in conjunction with the settlement distribution data to answer questions concerning the probable roles these groups played within the ancient community of Baking Pot during the Spanish Lookout phase of the Late Classic period (AD 700 to 900).

Urban and Rural Settlement at Baking Pot

One of the original considerations of this volume is the question of rural complexity and how it is exemplified at ancient lowland Maya sites. Thus, it is worthwhile to define what we, the authors, understand rural to mean from a site-level perspective. The analysis presented here compares estimates of population density with agrarian potential and consumption requirements generated from the Baking Pot settlement data. These data help discern and define site limits and delineate urban and rural settlement zones at Baking Pot (Conlon 1997). This analysis further assists in determining the specific social and economic segments of society associated with the Bedran and Atalaya plazuelas.

The ancient Maya site of Baking Pot (Bullard and Ricketson-Bullard 1965; Ricketson 1931; Willey et al. 1965) is located in the Cayo District of western Belize, roughly equidistant between the major centers of Cahal Pech on the west and Blackman Eddy to the east (figure 6.1). The most recent settlement survey of Baking Pot has expanded the known mound count for the area to 320 (figure 6.2). Generally, settlement patterns fluctuated according to subtleties in relief, as well as with increased distance from the site core (Conlon 1995:92). Mound density follows a general pattern of diminishing numbers with increased distance, declining rapidly 500 m from the epicenter (the monumental architecture of groups I and II) and finally leveling out beyond 1000 m. The drop in mound frequency represents the extent of site core settlement limits. As our concern here is

with groupings of mounds, a more detailed description of their distribution is warranted. The distribution of singular versus grouped mounds shows that grouped mounds occur more frequently nearer the epicenter, however, grouped mounds occur at all distances from the epicenter, albeit sporadically, with increased distance from the epicenter (figure 6.3).

The surveyed area of Baking Pot has been divided into a number of zones (see for example, Bullard 1960:367–370), designated A through F, to facilitate identifying urban and rural areas (figure 6.2). These zones are defined by the creeks and ridges that bound these waters, as well as old (that is, dry) river channels. All six zones together generate a total settlement database for the surveyed portion of Baking Pot (table 6.1). Total mound counts in all zones were utilized to generate both mound density and population estimates. We have not taken issues of nonresidential functions or the noncontemporaneity of occupation into account in these calculations. The issues of estimating ancient populations for the Maya area are complicated and involve lengthy debates in themselves. We have undertaken to present as simple and broad a potential picture of ancient population totals at Baking Pot as possible without convoluting the picture with our own factor preferences for adjusted estimates. To this end, although estimates of ancient Maya household members are commonly considered to range from 4 to 5.6 people (D.S. Rice and Culbert 1990:18), for simplicity's sake a single factor of 5 persons per mound is employed in generating population estimates at Baking Pot.

Pursuant to our understanding of site limits and variability at Baking Pot, the zonal breakdown shows that zone A possesses the highest number of mounds (105) and the second highest mound density (1.75 mounds/ha; see figure 6.2 and table 6.1). Zone A, together with zone B (140 mounds), forms a large core settlement segment, maintaining a high mound density (averaging 1.77 mounds/ha). This high mound density, and the proximity of zones A and B to the epicenter defined by groups I and II, are suggestive of an urban settlement component at Baking Pot (Conlon and Awe 1995a:72). Zone C, at 1.12 mounds/ha, more closely approximates the average mound density for the total surveyed extent of Baking Pot (0.92 mounds/ha). Zone D, in comparison, displays a below average mound density (0.78 mounds/ha), representing the limit in the areal extent of the site core settlement and the transition to a more rural settlement component. Mound densities fall to roughly half the site average at the farthest extent of our survey in zones E and F. Based on reconnaissance beyond the present survey limits, this is as near a complete picture of Baking Pot proper as will likely prevail.

Mound densities and population estimates provide pri-

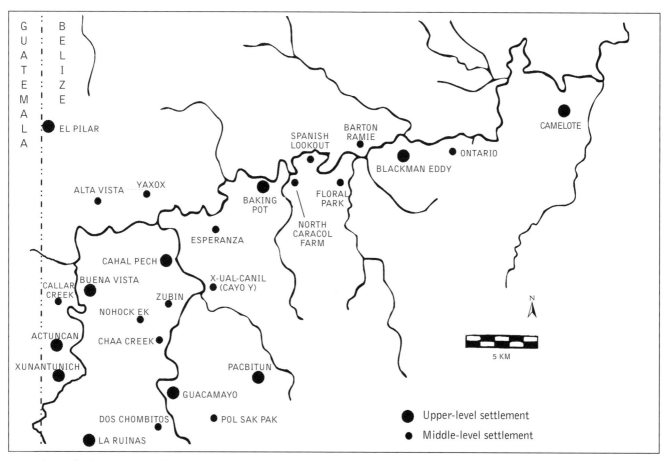

6.1 *Major and minor centers of the Belize Valley. Illustration by Gyles Iannone*

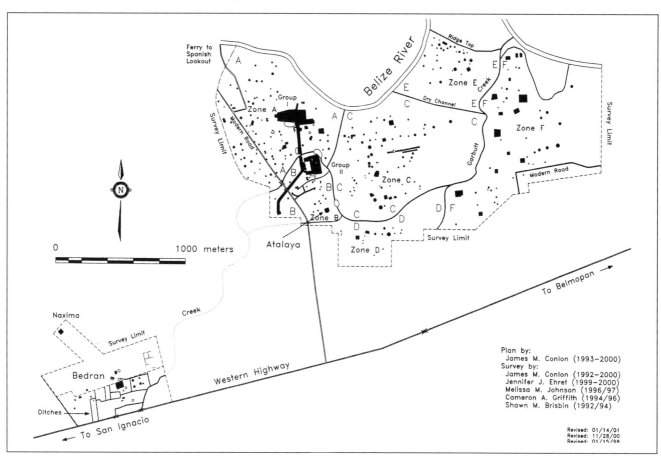

6.2 *Settlement and zone designation of Baking Pot, Belize, with Bedran group and Atalaya group. Illustration by James M. Conlon*

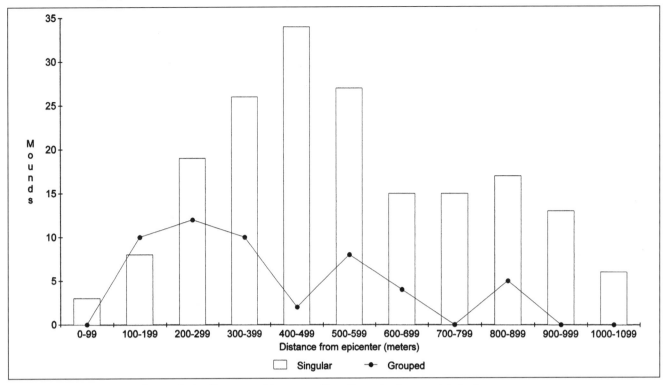

6.3 Singular versus grouped mounds, by distance, Baking Pot, Belize. Illustration by James M. Conlon

mary data that can prove useful for preliminary comparisons among sites (intersite) within the Belize Valley. Our goal, however, is to test our observations concerning the urban and rural zones at Baking Pot suggested by the available settlement data from Baking Pot alone (that is, an intrasite analysis). The estimation of agrarian potential and sustenance requirements provides further evidence to examine the ability of any group of people (that is, those living in a defined zone) to provide for themselves as a measure of self-sufficiency and to cross-check population estimates based on mound counts themselves. This comparison enables us to define clearly what we mean by urban (presumed net consumers) and rural (presumed net producers) zones at Baking Pot.

As with the population estimates discussed above, no adjustment has been made for factors that may affect estimates of both agricultural production and food requirements. Ideally, estimations of ancient agricultural production are enhanced by the identification of both suitable arable lands, as indicated by soil analysis (for example, Fedick 1995), and hillside modifications, as indicated by terracing or leveling of slopes (for example, Healy et al. 1983). Factors affecting availability of arable land relate most often to accessibility and include physical and cultural barriers, such as proximity and ownership, respectively.

To maintain simplicity and for the purposes of this study, the total areal extent of all zones at Baking Pot is considered as potentially arable for growing maize only, including lands occupied by mounds. Two agricultural production estimates, the Kirkby and Roosevelt productivity estimates employed by Spencer, Redmond, and Rinaldi (1994), are applied in the analysis presented here. The Roosevelt factor of 1800 kg/ha represents a maximum production potential, hereafter referred to as yield B. This factor is based on both modern observations of milpa maize production and similar size maize cobs of the La Betania phase (AD 650 to 1200) recovered from archaeological investigations in Venezuela (Spencer, Redmond, and Rinaldi 1994:135). The Kirkby factor, a minimum production estimate (yield A), accounts for the potentially smaller (37%) maize cobs grown during the Late Classic period in the Valley of Oaxaca (Kirkby 1973:126; Spencer, Redmond, and Rinaldi 1994:135; also see Flannery 1976:94–95). These production values are multiplied by the area of each zone defined at Baking Pot to generate potential yields for one crop of maize in one year.

Factors affecting estimates of sustenance requirements, like population estimates, can also be quite involved. The effect of a mixed farming strategy (such as that likely employed at Baking Pot) on estimates of consumption is not as well understood (for example, Spencer et al. 1994:122), neither are the potential contributions of hunting, fishing, and gathering to ancient diets (Healy et al. 1990:170). The maize consumption of individuals is, however, better understood, and, as employed in the analysis presented here, corresponds to roughly 220 kg of maize per person per year (Spencer, Redmond, and Rinaldi 1994:135; see also M.D. Coe and Diehl 1980:78; Flannery 1976:106). Estimates of supportable population are generated by dividing consumption estimates (220 kg per person/year) into the agricultural production potential (yield A and yield B), yielding populations A and B, respectively. These results are compared with the original population estimates based on the settlement data from the survey to reveal net consumers of maize (urban areas) and net producers of crops (rural areas).

The results indicate, using conservative production figures (yield A), that zones A and B could support only 410 people a year through maize cultivation alone, well short of the total estimated survey population of 700 inhabitants for these zones (table 6.2). The immediate core population closest to the epicenter could not be sustained by farming in this zone alone, and as net consumers of maize, can be considered representative of a highly populated, urban zone. Zone C also had more people (385 by survey) than could be fed by farming in its zone (maize for 355 people), though it was not as severely stressed as the immediate urban population of zones A and B. To this end, zone C can be classified as suburban. Only zone D is potentially capable of sustaining its estimated inhabitants (100 by survey), with the ability to produce maize for 132. Zone D is apparently on the margin of greater Baking Pot and likely represents, as indicated earlier in the description of settlement density, a population transitional between suburban and rural. Both zones E and F represent major net producers of maize and are thus designated as rural in nature.

Maximum production potential (yield B) paints a much different picture of Baking Pot. The estimated population of the previously identified urban zone (zones A and B) would seem to be nearly manageable at maximum production (produce enough maize for 650 people compared with an estimated 700 inhabitants by survey), indicating a more suburban type of settlement. Even in this light, as a net consumer of agricultural produce, it is still reasonable to identify zones A and B as an urban settlement component. Overall for Baking Pot, it appears that the totality of land surveyed could easily support the total estimated population (1600 by survey) at maximum production levels (maize for 2855 inhabitants). Even at minimum maize production (enough for 1799 inhabitants versus the survey estimate of 1600 people), it appears Baking Pot would have been self-sufficient agriculturally, based on the extent of our survey.

Using this comparison of surveyed settlement, agrarian production potential, and subsistence requirements, we have defined urban and rural zones for Baking Pot. At minimum agricultural production levels, the core population would

Table 6.1 Mound and population densities for Bedran and Baking Pot, Belize

Zone	Area	Mounds	Population	Density	
				Mound	Population
A	60.09	105	525	1.75	8.74
B	19.33	35	175	1.81	9.05
C	68.80	77	385	1.12	5.50
D	25.59	20	100	0.78	3.91
E	75.86	32	160	0.42	2.11
F	99.33	51	255	0.51	2.57
BP Total	349.00	320	1,600	0.92	4.58
Bedran	39.79	21	105	0.53	2.64

Area = hectares; Population = number of mounds x 5 people; Mound density = mounds/area; Population density = population/area

Table 6.2 Estimates of potential agricultural yield and sustainable population for Baking Pot and Bedran, Belize

Zone	Area	Yield A	Yield B	Population		
				A	B	(surveyed)
A	60.09	68,142	108,162	310	492	525
B	19.33	21,920	34,794	100	158	175
C	68.80	78,019	123,840	355	563	385
D	25.59	29,019	46,062	132	209	100
E	75.86	86,025	136,548	391	621	160
F	99.33	112,640	178,794	512	813	255
BP total	349.00	395,766	628,200	1,799	2,855	1,600
Bedran total	39.79	45,122	71,622	205	326	105

Area = hectares; Yield A = area x 1,134 kg (Flannery 1976:94–95; Kirby 1973:126; Spencer et al. 1994:135); Yield B = area x 1,800 kg (Spencer et al. 1994:135); Population A = Yield A/220 kg (Coe and Diehl 1980:78; Flannery 1976:106; Spencer et al. 1994:135); Population B = Yield B/220 kg; Population (surveyed) = number of mounds x 5

have been heavily dependent on the rural outliers at the limits of the survey area for their maize requirements, and there would be no surplus for storage. In a maximum agricultural production mode, the former inhabitants of Baking Pot appear to easily exceed their sustenance requirements for maize. The Atalaya plazuela group, as part of the core population nearest the epicenter (zone B), is in a suburban, if not urban, area of Baking Pot. The Bedran plazuela group, over 2 km distant from the epicenter, is in a rural setting similar to the high net producing zones E and F. With these settlement parameters defined, we can begin to look closer at the two plazuela groups in question to discern their roles within the settlement system of Baking Pot.

"Rural" Bedran Group

The Bedran group is located approximately 2.27 km southwest of the Baking Pot epicenter (figure 6.2). The plazuela covers roughly 660 m², and the mounds encompassing the plazuela approximate configurations known as Plaza Plan

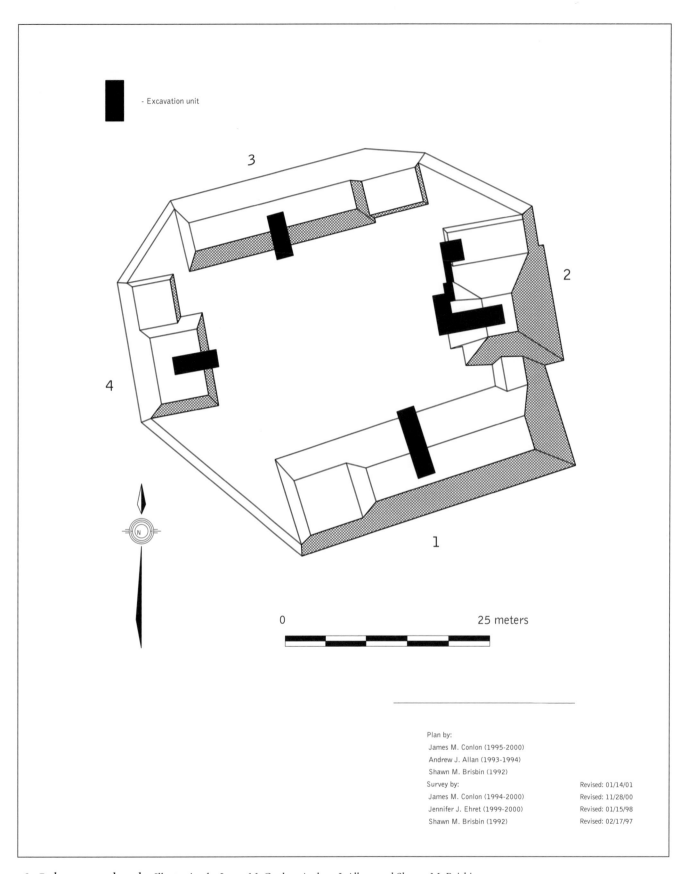

- Excavation unit

3

2

4

N

1

0   25 meters

Plan by:
    James M. Conlon (1995-2000)
    Andrew J. Allan (1993-1994)
    Shawn M. Brisbin (1992)
Survey by: Revised: 01/14/01
    James M. Conlon (1994-2000)   Revised: 11/28/00
    Jennifer J. Ehret (1999-2000)   Revised: 01/15/98
    Shawn M. Brisbin (1992)   Revised: 02/17/97

6.4 Bedran group plazuela. Illustration by James M. Conlon, Andrew J. Allan, and Shawn M. Brisbin

II from Tikal (Becker 1983:169) and the East-Structure Focus-Groups from Caracol (figure 6.4; A.F. Chase and D.Z. Chase 1987:55).

As a further introduction to the Bedran group, a brief review of its chronological development is warranted. Initial settlement at the Bedran group, late in the Early Classic period (circa AD 500), consisted of structure 2-1st, a 1.5-m–high circular platform on the east side of a small patio, and structure 1-1st, a 15-cm–high platform on the south. By AD 600, structure 1-3rd had reached a height comparable to that of structure 2-2nd on the east. At approximately the same time structure 3-1st on the north was added, as was the first plazuela platform. Sometime shortly after AD 700, structure 4-1st was added to the west end of the plazuela, and all other structures underwent further modification or construction. Also around this time, the small floor ballast that occurred in most of the early phase constructions was replaced by dense orange alluvial clay, identical to soil underlying the general humus layer (approximately 20-cm deep) in the field surrounding the Bedran plazuela. This is also the first period for which evidence of settlement outside the Bedran group plazuela has been recorded. It is also in the Spanish Lookout phase (AD 700 to 900) that structure 2-3rd, the terminal architectural phase, became an important locus of burials and caches. By the end of the Spanish Lookout phase the group had been abandoned. Only one early facet New Town phase (AD 900 to 1200) sherd (Daylight Orange type) was recovered from structure 4, and it likely represents an ephemeral reoccupation of the group sometime in the Postclassic period (Conlon and Awe 1995b).

If size is "the feature that consistently distinguishes the elite" (Wilk 1988:146), then Bedran would barely register on the elite scale in the Belize Valley. The areal extent of the plazuela is relatively large; yet, the structures defining it are comparatively unimpressive. The plazuela group's morphology, though, does bear out important comparisons. The shrine "niche" of structure 2-2nd is similar in configuration and placement to "rooms" in group II of the epicenter at Baking Pot (see Bullard and Bullard-Ricketson 1965). This replication of core architecture in the Bedran group is significant for its use of a "standard grammar" to express status differentiation (Ashmore 1992:173). The eastern shrine is indicative of a ritual focus for the group (Powis 1993:220), likely for a powerful local lineage head. The largest mound volumetrically, structure 1 on the south, may also bear significant symbolic weight. It has been suggested that the southern position is representative of the underworld, and that anyone who occupies such a locale "controls access to supernaturals," and similarly a "deliberate reiteration by the sovereign of his authority" (Ashmore 1992:178, 179). The

physical attachment of structure 1 to the eastern shrine is a likely indicator that the group's lineage leader was the resident of structure 1.

It is not possible to present here all the excavation data from the Bedran group here. Therefore, structure 2, on the eastern side of the plazuela, a favored location for shrines in the Maya lowlands, is the focus of attention. Twelve burials and twenty-four caches were recovered from this locale, some of which warrant special mention (figure 6.5). Among the more significant finds is cache 3, a large concentration of forty-eight chert and obsidian eccentrics, eight whole (but fragmented) Spanish Lookout phase vessels, and one mano fragment. Eccentrics were not only considered to be representative of gods, ancestors, and the ruling bloodline, but were also used by lowland Maya elite to justify and reaffirm their own position among one another (Iannone and Conlon 1993:82).

Thus, the occurrence of cached eccentrics in peripheral groups indicates that the residents of these groups may have been included in an upper stratum of ancient lowland Maya society. Conversely, in contexts such as the Bedran group, peripheral to major centers, it has been noted that eccentrics cached in these instances more likely represent interaction of a vertical nature, linking ruling elite with a subordinate social stratum, such as a local kin-based group (Iannone 1993b:233).

Cache 16 is an effigy censer fragment found directly in front of the inset shrine feature. Similar offerings of effigy censers from Postclassic Santa Rita Corozal of northern Belize are frequently found within high-status groups (D.Z. Chase 1992:123), effectively unifying and integrating segments of the larger community (D.Z. Chase and A.F. Chase 1988:71, 75).

The inclusion in burial 11 of parts of the lower arm from the adolescent of burial 9, and the bloodletting paraphernalia that separates these two coeval burials (Cache 18), may be the best indicators that inhabitants of the Bedran group fully participated in such typically elite associative behavior as human sacrifice. The accompaniment of sacrificial victims is characteristic of site-center tomb-interment behavior (Haviland 1981:105). The ability to conduct ritualistic human sacrifice may be the strongest indicator of the elite authority and entrenchment exhibited by the Bedran group residents. The quantity and quality of the Bedran group's burial and cache assemblages demonstrate a high degree of sophistication in the use of epicentral ritual (Conlon and Awe 1995b).

As a spatially distinct settlement cluster, the Bedran group's occupants had access to both land and labor. The presence of ditched fields within its settlement cluster zone

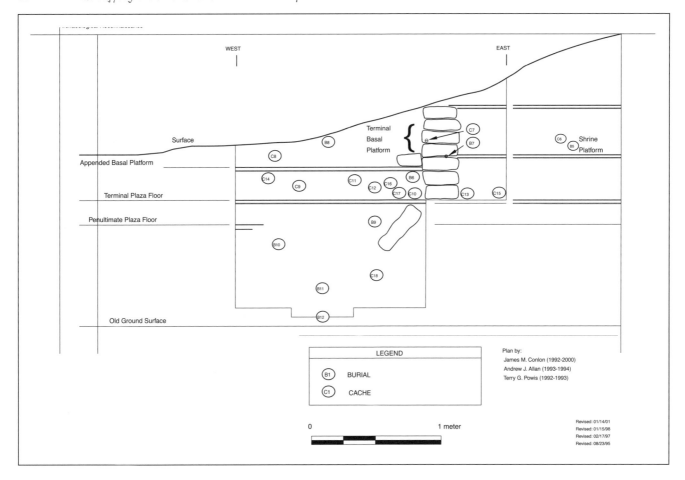

6.5 Shrine inset, structure 2, Bedran group, Baking Pot, Belize. Illustration by James M. Conlon, Andrew J. Allan, and Terry G. Powis

(see figure 6.2) indicates that managing intensive agricultural surplus crop production was the main function of the Bedran group lineage leaders (Conlon and Awe 1995a, 1995b). The Bedran group inhabitants were able to generate economic prosperity as active producers of important foodstuffs for trade and/or tribute. Identification of typically epicentral associated architectural conventions, and the elaborateness and diversity of grave goods and ritual deposits at the Bedran group, indicate the trade link was epicenter focused, rather than market driven by individual consumers (Conlon and Awe 1995a:74–75). Access to ceremonially significant differentiators can be considered suggestive of a social integrative function. Based upon a surplus mode of production, however, the Bedran group inhabitants may have enjoyed a degree of subsistence (that is, economic) autonomy (for example, Freidel and Scarborough 1982:149). In a situation of economic independence, integration may be more aptly considered as interactive rather than subsuming, based on a patron-client relationship of economic status inclusivity that does not necessarily translate into social inclusivity. In this manner, the Bedran group may have remained an autonomous kin-based unit tied only economically to the epicentral elite of Baking Pot.

"Urban" Atalaya Group

The Atalaya group is located approximately 275 m south of group II at Baking Pot (figure 6.2). The plazuela covers roughly 235 m² (35% of the Bedran plazuela) and the four mounds encompassing the group approximate configurations known as patio groups (Ashmore 1981a:49) and South-Structure Focus-Groups from Caracol (A.F. Chase and D.Z. Chase 1987:55; figure 6.6).

The chronological development of the Atalaya group spans a shorter sequence than Bedran's, making it more difficult to discern trends or transitions (A.F. Moore 1998). While Tiger Run phase (AD 600 to 700) and some Hermitage phase (AD 300 to 600) ceramics occur, they were all recovered from within later Late Classic Spanish Lookout phase construction contexts (AD 700 to 900). Thus, the inception of the group is not much earlier than the beginning of the Spanish Lookout phase (circa AD 650 to 700).

Only three early facet Postclassic New Town phase (AD 900 to 1200) sherds were recovered, all from operations at structure 164 (see figure 6.6). This paltry sample of New Town ceramics at Atalaya, coupled with a similar lone instance for Bedran's structure 4, is suggestive of an ephemeral Postclassic period occupation, inconsequential to the subsequent intergroup comparison of Atalaya and Bedran presented here.

While Atalaya and Bedran both grew and prospered within the Spanish Lookout phase of the Late Classic period (AD 700 to 900), they display contrasting levels of development. Only two caches were recovered in the numerous excavations at Atalaya. One, from under the terminal phase platform atop structure M161, consists of an inverted red-ware bowl; another from the back of structure M162 is made up of one large plate and one gourd-like vessel with a Belize Red–type slip. Only two burials were recovered, both from along the central axis of structure M164. These simple interments, extended on a north-south axis, contained no grave goods.

The paucity of burials and caches recovered from the Atalaya group, as compared to Bedran, necessitated a closer look at the ceramic assemblage of Atalaya in a comparison with the ceramic data from Barton Ramie (see Gifford 1976) to discern residential and ritual locales within the plazuela group. We used Barton Ramie as the basis for comparison because of its large sample size (65 mounds), potentially varied database (arguably a "housemound," or primarily domestic in nature), and availability of ceramic frequencies from sites within the immediate Belize Valley. General trends observed in the ceramic data, coupled with the knowledge of concentrations of the different ceramic groups within the different structures at Atalaya, help to define potential structure function (table 6.3).

Structure M161 is, by its pyramidal configuration and dominant height within the group, readily recognizable as the focus for the plazuela group and is likely nonresidential in function. Its significance within the group is bolstered, in part, by the recovery here of one of the two aforementioned caches from this group. Structure M162 seems, by all accounts to be residential. The occurrence here of the only other cache retrieved from Atalaya, coupled with the comparatively high frequency and concentration of black-slipped Achote–type sherds (table 6.3), suggest that it was a focus of heightened ritual activity within the group. We have designated this structure as one potential residence for the lineage leader of the Atalaya group. An overabundance of unslipped, typically utilitarian pottery (predominantly large jar forms of the Cayo ceramic group) was recovered from structure M163, indicating that is was a primary locale for

some form of domestic activities within the group, and perhaps even a storage area. Structure M164's location on the east side of the plazuela and the placement of two interments here suggest that there might be a shrine focus. Its identification as a shrine locale is further supported by the high frequency of Palmar group polychrome ceramics recovered from this locale (table 6.3). Structure M164's rectilinear shape, though, indicates that it could also have functioned as a residence, a possible alternative to structure M162 for the lineage head's residence.

Atalaya shows none of the settlement cluster focus, distinctiveness, or status markers of the Bedran group. The southern pyramidal structure M161 may indicate the presence of some sort of local lineage leader, but the lack of symbolic power features recovered from excavations of this structure, and the entire group, may be the result of a diminished exploitable resource base (for example, Hayden and Cannon 1982:149). The relatively high frequency of unslipped pottery types, in comparison to Barton Ramie frequencies, particularly the large number of jar forms represented at structure M163, suggests one possible role for the Atalaya group residents could have entailed collecting and storing crops destined for the Baking Pot epicenter (compare Freidel and Scarborough 1982:149; Harrison 1990:110; Spencer, Redmond, and Rinaldi 1994:137). Local scions, in the role of passive, nonproductive administrators, were not only unable to control their own land and muster a labor force, but may have been destined for this bureaucratic role from the inception of the group. In this situation, they were unable to participate in the reciprocal economic production partnerships that garnered the investment in ritual, or ritual items, of wealth and status that more distantly located, and possibly more socially marginal, locally based kin-groups, such as Bedran, required for integration at Baking Pot (A.F. Moore 1997).

Conclusion

The pattern revealed at Baking Pot of restricted epicentral influence, within 500 m of the center, and more dispersed nodes of intermediary settlement requires a more integrative social construct than divisive hierarchical models tend to imply. It forces Mayanists to reconsider various modes of interaction between both vertically and horizontally tied individuals or groups within the social hierarchy of a site, as defined by its settlement morphology. It is becoming more apparent that the inhabitants of minor centers, and similarly plazuela groups, were beginning to play a larger role throughout this region during the Late Classic, both within (intrasite) and among (intersite) neighboring epicenters of the Belize Valley.

6.6 Atalaya group plazuela. *Illustration by James M. Conlon*

Table 6.3. Atalaya and Barton Ramie ceramic type and group summary for the Spanish Lookout complex

Type	Type Sherd Ct	Ceramic Gr	Gr Sherd Ct	Gr (%)			Type/Group (%)		
				A	BR	A/BR	A	BR	A/BR
Dolphin Head Red	229						99.57	99.50	100.07
Silver Creek Impressed	1	Dolphin Head	230	3.51	4.75	73.89	0.43	0.50	86.00
Belize Red	2994						98.42	81.50	120.76
Platon Punctated-incised	17						0.56	11.40	4.91
Martins Incised	1						0.04	0.80	5.00
McRae Impressed	22						0.72	4.90	14.69
Gallinero Fluted	8	Belize	3042	46.45	40.12	115.78	0.26	0.40	65.00
Garbutt Creek Red	140						79.55	85.00	93.59
Rubber Camp Brown	36	Garbutt Creek	176	2.69	7.97	33.75	20.45	15.00	136.33
Roaring Creek Red	42						30.66	28.40	107.96
Vaca Falls Red	85						62.04	56.70	109.42
Kaway Impressed	10	Vaca Falls	137	2.09	7.59	27.54	7.30	14.90	48.99
Yaha Creek Cream	12	Yaha Creek	12	0.18	2.14	8.41	100.00	100.00	100.00
Mount Maloney Black	80	Mount Maloney	80	1.22	1.31	93.13	100.00	100.00	100.00
Meditation Black	13	Meditation	13	0.20	1.07	18.69	100.00	100.00	100.00
Achote Black	20						80.00	85.20	93.90
Cubeta Incised	5	Achote	25	0.38	0.04	950.00	20.00	14.80	135.14
Yalbac Smudged-brown	37	Yalbac	37	0.57	2.82	20.21	100.00	100.00	100.00
Benque Viejo Polychrome	245						83.33	99.40	83.83
Xunantunich Black-on-orange	35						11.91	0.40	2,977.50
Chunhuitz Orange	14	Chunhuitz	294	4.49	4.21	106.65	4.76	0.20	2,380.00
Palmar Orange-polychrome	40						55.55	58.65	94.71
Zacatel Cream-polychrome	19						26.39	4.81	548.65
Paixban Buff-polychrome	1						1.39	4.81	28.90
Yuhactal Black-on-red	1						1.39	12.50	11.12
Tunich Red-on-orange	4						5.56	6.73	82.62
Tialipa Brown*	7	Palmar	72	1.10	0.11	1,000.00	9.72	6.73	144.43
Tu-Tu Camp Striated	65	Tu-Tu Camp	65	0.99	5.55	17.84	100.00	100.00	100.00
Alexanders Unslipped	515						21.77	36.80	59.16
Cayo Unslipped	1851	Cayo	2366	36.13	22.32	161.87	78.23	63.20	123.78
TOTAL	6549		6549	100.00	100.00				

A = Atalaya; BR = Barton Ramie
* included in Palmar rather than Tialipa Ceramic group (see Gifford 1976:53)

In a scenario of centralized bureaucracy, territorial control is seen as removed from the hands of "local kin based groups" (D.Z. Chase and A.F. Chase 1992:309; see also Haviland 1981:117; Tourtellot, Sabloff, and Carmean 1992:80). In a decentralized or loosely organized state, however, kin groups could be important for maintaining site and regional organization. In a loosely defined organizational system, smaller and smaller units of settlement would have operated to integrate various aspects of social, political, and economic spheres within, and across, various levels of both intra- and intersite settlement. The Bedran group data suggest that its inhabitants did not enjoy total status inclusivity until circa AD 700 when they became economically important to the ancient community of Baking Pot as net producers of agricultural products. The integration of the Bedran group within the Baking Pot polity late in its

development may be representative of a local kin-based group that eventually acquired increased economic inclusivity through its advantageous location for producing agricultural surpluses. In contrast, the Atalaya group may have been destined for mediocrity from its inception with the nonproductive role of administrator.

The view from Baking Pot suggests the interrelationship between epicenters and their associated rural groups in the Belize Valley of the Late Classic period was more an interactive and integrative affiliation than one of subjugation by the sovereign. Epicentral rulers forged alliances, rather than fostered competition, by defining "status inclusivity" (for example, D.Z. Chase, A.F. Chase, and Haviland 1990:501; Lincoln 1985:75; Sanders 1992:280). Integrating more distant zones of settlement meant investing greater resources in groups such as Bedran because of their economic importance and role in territorial definition. A focus on integrating important settlement nodes by epicentral authorities enabled autonomous rural kin groups, with local control of their lands and labor, to accrue greater power, access prestige items, and perform high ritual. Mutual interdependence more often worked to suppress and surpass class/strata divisions to the point where members of different social ranks were partners in political and religious matters, but more importantly, equal participants in economic endeavors necessary for sustaining the epicentral and core populations.

Acknowledgments. The authors would like to express their gratitude to all the members of the Belize Department of Archaeology, past and present, and especially Commissioners John Morris, Brian Woodeye, and the late Harriot Topsey. The Department of Archaeology staff not only permitted investigations at Baking Pot but also supported our endeavors. We are pleased to recognize the guidance of our principal investigator, Jaime Awe, whose enthusiasm for fostering and supporting our individual research goals often do not translate to a direct benefit for him. His immense capacity for streamlining logistical difficulties and his unselfishness make him a respected colleague and revered friend.

Over the course of several years of research at Baking Pot (1992–2000), many others also made various contributions, both directly and indirectly, as well as knowingly and unknowingly, to the BVAR enterprise. We would like to thank them all, and so, although the following appears to be more of a laundry list, please be assured we are grateful for having been able to collaborate with so many of you, including Andrew Allan, Mark August, Carlos Ayala, Grant Aylesworth, Adib Bejos, Sr., Adib Bejos, Jr., Abdala Bedran, Shawn Brisbin, Joseph Dantona, David Driver, Matt Edmunds, Jennifer Ehret, Scott Fedick, Kerri Finlayson, James Garber, David Glassman, Charles Golden, Cameron Griffith, Paul Healy, Bobbi Hohmann, Stephen Houston, Gyles Iannone, Dito Juan, Angela Keller, Lisa LeCount, Richard Leventhal, Effrain Martinez, Marcos Martinez, Frances Norris, Jennifer Piehl, Terry Powis, Daniel Silva, Rhan-Ju Song, Norbert Stanchly, David Valencio, Gabriel Wrobel, and Henry Young.

We are further indebted to the editors of this volume for their considerations and patience. This chapter has benefited from the comments of several anonymous reviewers who helped to shape its final form, for which we are grateful. In the end, though, the authors take full responsibility for errors, omissions, or any misrepresentations contained within this chapter.

7 Wetlands, Rivers, and Caves
Agricultural and Ritual Practice in Two Lowland Maya Landscapes

Patricia A. McAnany, Kimberly A. Berry, and Ben S. Thomas

WHILE TRAVELING across the Petén on muleback in the 1950s, William Bullard (1960) noted a rural sector of ancient settlement and mused that small settlement clusters might have been composed of lineages of related extended families. With the establishment of settlement studies, archaeologists working in Mesoamerica began to survey systematically beyond the boundaries of the large urban centers. In this process, the remains of substantial rural settlements were documented (for example, Ford 1986). Based on artifactual and locational patterns, the inhabitants of this rural sector were practitioners of agriculture, craft production, and domestic ritual, and often were involved in both local and long-distance trade. While the recognition of interstitial settlement is not novel, the implications of this pattern for political and economic integration of the rural with the urban sector have been explored less frequently. Likewise, variability among rural settlements remains an underdeveloped realm of inquiry. Does one collection of housemounds look just like the next? Is it really necessary to survey and excavate every rural settlement that existed? Are our limited resources better spent in documenting seats of power and authority in ancient Maya society?

As this volume shows, the diversity among rural settlements and their internal complexity emphatically demonstrate that all rural locales are not alike. In this chapter, we try to clarify this diversity by comparing two settlement locales situated in contrastive landscapes: the wetland-riverine landscape of the New River and the riverine-karstic terrain of the Sibun River. Central to this analysis is the notion that diversity in the rural sector emerged from the interpenetration of society and landscape. As Ashmore and Knapp (1999) have observed, traditional studies of settlement treated the landscape as a passive and malleable backdrop. More recent studies recognize that a landscape is an entity that exists "by virtue of its being perceived, experienced, and contextualized by people" (Ashmore and Knapp 1999:1). Ancient lowland Maya rural societies were embedded within local landscapes that fashioned society and were fashioned by it. This relationship with landscape contributes, in large part, to the diversity of settlement types, artifact assemblages, and ritual practices documented for locales at a distance from large political capitals.

Landscapes Contextualized

Close attention to the nuances of the local landscape may account for the longevity of pre-Hispanic lowland Maya society, as well as the regional variations archaeologists have detected. The latter are examined here from the perspective of place-making in the sense described by Feld and Basso as the ways in which people "encounter places, perceive them, and invest them with significance" (1996:8). The focus is not on place-making at political capitals but rather at the interstices. Without knowledge of cultural landscapes outside major seats of power, we will never be able to comprehend fine-grained variations in social textures, agricultural production strategies, and ritual practices of lowland Maya society. A contribution toward this identification and understanding of rural complexity in the Maya lowlands is offered here by examining two very different landscapes and the manner in which populations settled in them ritually, agriculturally, and politically. Throughout this analysis, the referential dimension of place is interwoven with the temporal dimension of settlement depth.

The two landscapes under discussion include the wetland-riverine environment of northern Belize and the riverine-karstic region of the Sibun Valley of central Belize (figure 7.1). A single place, K'axob, illustrates the manner in which Maya farmers utilized wetland landscapes. In contrast, several karst- and river-related places are examined in the Sibun Valley (figure 7.2). These two regions are separated by only 85 km, yet their built environments display distinct characteristics, particularly in settlement signature, historical depth, and ritual expression related to ancestors and fertility.

The landscape of the north is more thoroughly domesticated. Landscape modification is writ large on the archaeological record of K'axob. With a long-term and seemingly stable growth trajectory, the settlement of K'axob was vitally linked with wetlands exploitation. The wetlands provided a buffer against devastating droughts, while ancestors interred under house floors guaranteed usufruct rights to upland and wetland fields. As shown below, this pattern contrasts markedly with the Sibun Valley, where settlement does not appear to predate the Classic period (AD 250– 850) and farmers sought protection from the devastating effects of annual flooding through frequent pilgrimage to nearby caves. The flooding regime, however, deposited soils suitable for cacao production that could be successful only if the Sibun Valley landscape was maintained in a semi-domesticated state. As a supplier of a key item of the luxury economy, inhabitants of the Sibun Valley were closely linked with the Classic lowland Maya political economy. In short, both locales were occupied by farmers with similar goals: to maintain productivity in their fields and orchards, to thwart the profound effects of natural disasters, and to reproduce socially and biologically. The materialization of these desires, particularly in ritual and agricultural practice, yielded highly contrastive signatures.

Information for this comparison comes from six seasons of excavation at K'axob and two seasons of regional survey and test excavations in the Sibun River Valley. Due to the disproportionate amount of fieldwork conducted within the two contrastive landscapes, interpretations offered here must be considered preliminary and subject to verification (or falsification) as field research continues in the Sibun River Valley.

Wetlands and Ancestors of K'axob

The landscape surrounding K'axob is relatively flat. The primary relief is formed by northeast-trending fault lines that provide secure pathways for rivers and long, linear wetland complexes. The interfluves, predictably, were the locales of ancient Maya settlement and today contain thousands of acres of monocrop sugarcane. The real armature of this landscape, however, is the wetlands. The wetlands played host to various species of plants and animals that provided the region's human inhabitants with a tremendous diversity of resources. Exploitation took the form of hunting such game as deer and turtle, gathering edible plants, culling trees suitable for construction, and harvesting fish and mollusks (Pohl 1985).

At some point during the Formative period (2100 BC– AD 250), Maya farmers began to modify the wetlands actively, probably to expand the diversity of edaphic locales available for agricultural production and thus reduce the risk of crop failure (McAnany and Berry 1999; Turner and Harrison 1983). Domestication of the wetlands further expanded the resource value of these watery places. Small wonder, then, that some of the earliest recognizably Maya populations settled in northern Belize at such places as Colha, Lamanai, Cuello, and K'axob. Two key features of Maya occupation of northern Belize are the longevity of settlement (with locales such as Lamanai evincing continuous settlement from the Middle Formative through Colonial times) and, concomitantly, the profound environmental impact of these populations. Pollen and macrobotanical studies throughout northern Belize show a trajectory of steeply diminishing rain forest that commenced in the second millennium BC and continued through the Classic period (Hammond and Micsicek 1981; Pohl et al. 1996).

K'axob, which sits on a low rise framed by the southern arm of Pulltrouser Swamp and the New River (figure 7.3), was settled between 800 and 600 BC. The site appears to have been continuously occupied until the Terminal Classic (see McAnany and López Varela [1999] for an extended discussion of the settlement history). The presence of Mayapan-style incensarios in the two pyramid plazas further mark K'axob as a place of ritual activity and possible residence through the Postclassic period (AD 950 to 1520).

One of the early Middle Formative (800 to 400 BC) rituals to occur at K'axob involved the burial of an adult male who was interred with more than two thousand shell beads and two pottery vessels—one a faux resist (figure 7.4; see also Isaza and McAnany 1999:Table 4; McAnany, Storey, and Lockard 1999: Fig. 9). This early burial uncovered in operation 1 marks the onset of construction at this locale. Shortly thereafter, an apsidal structure with a white packed-marl floor was built, initiating a thousand-year–long cycle of construction, ritual burial interment, structure renovation, and expansion that would ultimately culminate in the construction of a Classic-period pyramid. Metaphorically, this burial served as a "foundation" for the construction that occurred over the next thousand years.

While the timing and tempo of this cyclic construction pattern varies across the household and civic structures of K'axob, the pattern is a very strong characteristic of "place-making" at the site. Other examples include the foundation burial found in operation 16, as well as the modification of a domestic structure into a civic building in operation 21.

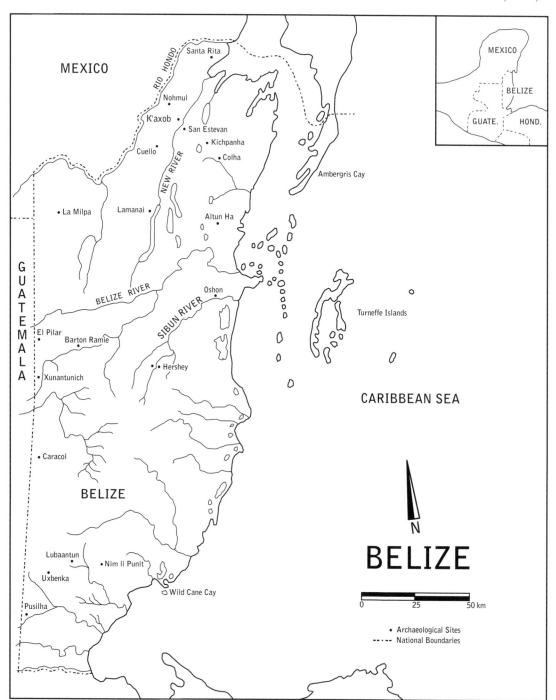

McAnany (1995:64–110) has discussed this pattern in terms of the establishment of a genealogy of place, and Shipton (1994:360–364) has referred to it as an "ideology of attachment." Both terms refer to the ritual expression of place-making behaviors, specifically those through which a group maps onto a landscape and, in so doing, not only effects a claim but also grapples with both the challenges and opportunities that a particular place affords. When this ideology is materialized in ritual paraphernalia, architectural sequences, and settlement an-

tiquity, we are granted a rare glimpse into cognitive processes not often visible to archaeologists.

The long duration of settlement at K'axob is complemented by the emergence of distinct community-based pottery styles during the Late Formative period, 400 BC to AD 250 (Bartlett and McAnany 2000). At K'axob, community identity was expressed through specific use of the quadripartite motif, which was painted on the bases of large flat-bottomed bowls, classified as Society Hall Red, and small cache bowls modeled with horizontal ribbing (López Varela

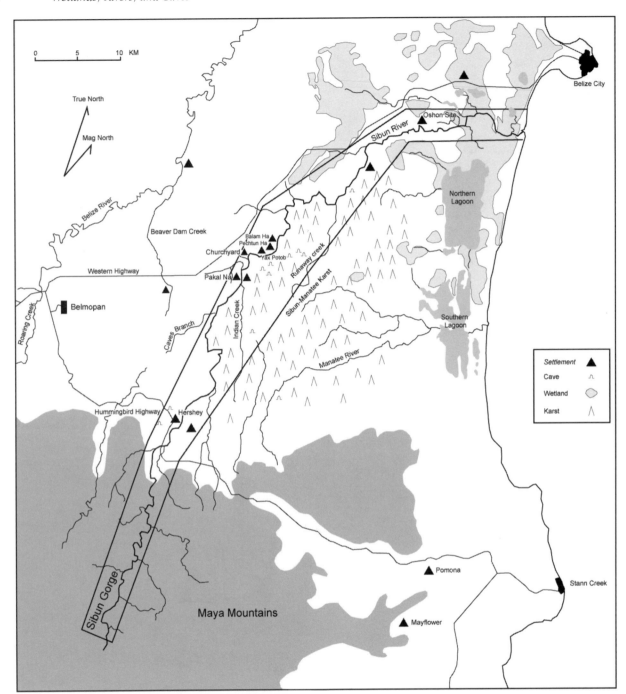

7.2 Sibun River Valley, showing significant physiographic features and selected sites. Map by Ben Thomas

1996). This expression is matched by increasingly localized patterns of clay acquisition, as determined by mineralogical and chemical analysis of local clays and pottery fabric (Angelini 1998).

The persistence of settlement at K'axob through the Classic period may be attributable, once again, to the adjacent wetlands that exhibit a complex pattern of canals and island fields. An intensive program of excavation throughout this patterned ground has yielded stratigraphic and artifactual data supportive of Classic-period construction,

complete with the ritual caching of marine shell and chipped-stone tools (McAnany and Berry 1999). Such modifications generated new planting surfaces, facilitated a longer growing season, and provided an edaphic locale for growing crops during prolonged droughts. The key importance of such a resource was illustrated during the drought of 1995 when many of the wetland canals of the adjacent Pulltrouser Swamp retained a significant amount of water. Because of the continued humidity afforded by the wetland environs, the landowner of K'axob, Señor Concepción

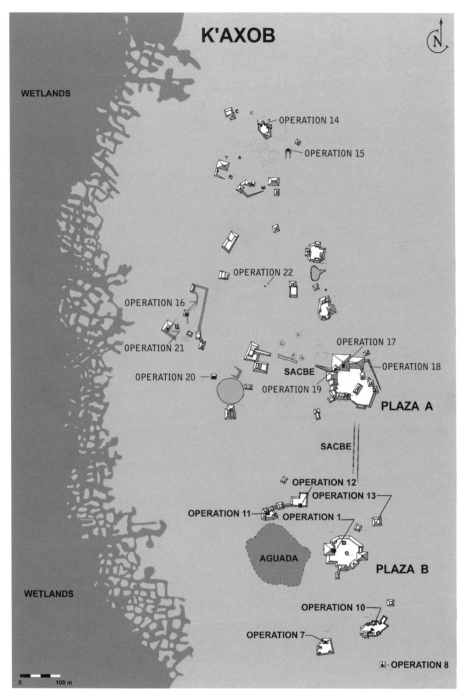

*7.3 Settlement of K'axob with principal
structures and excavation units
(operations) indicated.*
Note band of wetland fields
along the western border of K'axob.
Map by Kimberly Berry

Campos, reaped a successful harvest of sugarcane from the high ground of K'axob.

It is doubtful that the resilience of this landscape was lost on ancient Maya farmers who displayed an intense interest in tracking cycles of drought and in using their well-supplied arsenal of rituals to mitigate the effects of such meteorological disasters. Cycles of drought are discussed and depicted in the Farmer's Almanac of the Codex Dresden. Folio 45c, for example, pictures Chak, the deity of rain and storms, brandishing hot torches instead of his usual "thunderbolt" ax. He sits astride a deer dead from dehydration, its tongue swollen and distended. Chak both delivers and withholds waters that are key to agricultural fertility and renewal. In codices of northern Yucatecan origin, Chak is often shown standing on, in, or near a cenote or an opening to a cave (figure 7.5). Ritual deposits recovered from cenotes and caves may refer to the propitiation of Chak, but in the flat wetland-riverine landscape of northern Belize

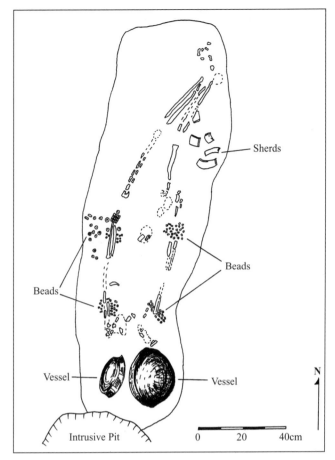

7.4 *Foundation burial from the Middle Formative village of K'axob, operation 1, burial 43.* Illustration by Ben Thomas, Kimberly Berry, and Eleanor Harrison

7.5 *Chak, seated above the opening of a cenote.* Adapted from Codex Dresden, Folio 39c

cenotes are rare and caves scarcer. To examine the materialization of Chak-related ritual, we turn south to the Sibun-Manatee karst system of the Sibun River Valley.

Sacred Landscape and Settlement of the Sibun River Valley

While the rivers of northern Belize flow leisurely through predetermined fault lines to join the salt water of the Bay of Chetumal, the Sibun River runs through a narrow granite gorge in the Maya Mountains. After dropping more than 400 m in elevation, the river begins to carve through deep alluvium on its way to the Caribbean Sea. Tributaries disgorging from underground limestone caverns, such as Caves Branch and Indian Creek, join the main channel in its middle reaches. Torrential rainfall in the Maya Mountains, as well as localized tropical storms within this complex and partially subterranean tributary net, renders the middle section of the river prone to sudden flooding (often five to eight floods per year) and produces catastrophic shifts in the river's meander pattern (decadal shifts are observable on older topographic maps). The hydrological regimes of the middle reaches of the Sibun River are exacerbated by the fact that this 35-km–long section of the river (between Caves Branch and Cedar Bank) is sandwiched between an agriculturally infertile sandy pine "ridge" and the ruggedly dissected landscape of the Sibun-Manatee karst. Toward the sea, the cone-karst falls away, and mangrove swamp begins to frame the river channel. Near this transition point, putative evidence of Archaic-period occupation has been reported (MacNeish, Wilkerson, and Nelken-Terner 1980:34, Fig. 14).

Despite the formidable challenges posed by this landscape, the area was settled by the Classic period, if not earlier. Possibly, the risks were perceived to be outweighed by the opportunities provided. As with the Nile and the Mississippi, frequent flooding events deposit rich alluvium, creating a natural system of sustained fertility. Moreover, cacao, a crop highly desired by Maya elites, thrives in just this type of soil, as does the river fig tree. Judging from the frequency of bark beaters in the collections of farmers living along the Sibun today, the fig tree appears to have been harvested for paper production. Unfortunately, artifactual or ecofactual evidence substantiating ancient cacao production has proved more elusive. Reports from the time of Spanish colonization indicate that the Xibun Maya (using the Colonial-period spelling of the river) were involved in cacao production (G.D. Jones 1989:18–19). Originally an understory tree from high canopy Amazon rain forests, domesticated cacao is still dependent upon rain forest ecology for shading and successful pollination (Young 1994).

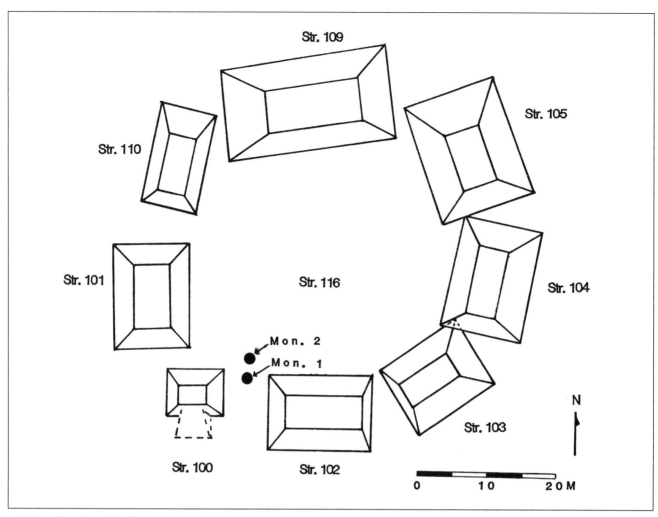

7.6 Central portion of Pechtun Ha. Map by Kimberly Berry

Given the success of cacao in the Maya lowlands, it is likely that it was cultivated in small orchards in proximity to intact rain-forest habitats (Young 1994:167). If this were the case along the Sibun, then it is likely that the landscape of the Sibun Valley was not as thoroughly domesticated as that of the wetland landscape to the north around K'axob. Future pollen studies will examine this proposition.

Test excavations in the lower and middle sections of the valley have failed to yield evidence of significant occupation either before or after the Late/Terminal Classic period. The active hydrological regime of the river could have buried earlier sites under a mantle of alluvium. Or, because of the high risk of devastating floods in the middle reaches of the Sibun, Maya farmers such as those who colonized K'axob may not have been attracted to the Sibun Valley until the demand for cacao among Classic-period elites created a strong impetus for colonization. Surveyed settlements are typically located on the highest terraces above the river, suggesting a concern for, and close knowledge of, the flooding regime of the river. Once significant populations moved into the middle valley, however, a three-tiered settlement hierarchy was immediately established. The lowest tier is represented by low, single platforms that line the terrace edge like green beads on a necklace (thus, the name Yax P'otob for one of these arrangements). This pattern is punctuated by large plaza complexes situated on impressive terrace edges behind oxbows or abandoned meander bends.

Several examples of these middle-tier settlements have been survey and tested. Pechtun Ha (figures 7.2 and 7.6) is notable for its two stone monuments and a water shrine surfaced with speleothems (Str. 100). Another large plaza complex probably existed at a site called Churchyard (figure 7.2), eradicated by bulldozer activity so that little is left other than a collection of eccentrics and bark beaters held by the landowner. A third site, Pakal Na, is larger than both Pechtun Ha and Churchyard and represents the upper range of the middle tier. The largest structure at this site has yielded

7.7 Cave vessels from Pottery Cave. Photograph by Patricia A. McAnany

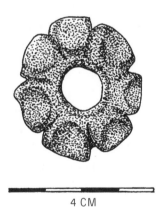

4 CM

7.8 Marine shell, carved into the shape of a flower, excavated from wetland fields adjacent to K'axob. Illustration by Ben Thomas

evidence of a Terminal Classic axial burial, as well as a possible cacao-drying surface. The entire settlement of the valley is anchored by two larger centers that occupy the top of the site hierarchy: the Oshon site, a gateway center located at the lower end of the valley, and the Hershey site, which is situated upriver at the base of the gorge.

To the south of the Sibun floodplain lies a vast system of karst, a sacred landscape of caves. Our survey of these caverns has yielded a wide array of artifacts that were cached, offered, and/or ritually destroyed during the course of ritual activities. Complete vessels, sherds, chert and obsidian tools, pine torches, figurines, musical instruments, freshwater gastropods, and worked marine shell constitute the majority of materials left inside the cave chambers. Pottery vessels tend to be Late and Terminal Classic types (figure 7.7), although sherds of Early Classic types, such as Actuncan polychrome, have also been identified. As noted above, caves often are associated with the rain deity, Chak, because they are also perceived as a source of water. In the Sibun watershed, this association takes on a very literal meaning as tributaries of the river flow out of underground caverns. Often, the discharge from these subterranean tributaries causes the flooding and frequent (and also disastrous) shifts in the meander bends of the river.

Given the relatively late settlement of this region, the density of pottery in the Sibun cone-karst indicates that this rugged area was frequently visited, probably through local pilgrimage. It also seems significant that in external profile the cone-karst appears as a forest of pyramids. Within the valley itself, few pyramids were constructed, although substantial labor was invested in the large plaza complexes. Taken together, these observations suggest that the artifacts deposited in the caves may be a materialization of Chak-related cave rituals; that is, the signature of a dynamic and ritually complex series of negotiations for the advantageous renewal properties of floods and ample rainfall without the disadvantages of severe flooding. Because floods were inevitable, petitioners sought to minimize their ill effects, desiring floods that would recede quickly without rotting the roots of the trees and crops, and gentle floods that would not reconfigure the meander pattern of the river, washing away fields and orchards. On the Sibun, there was much to gain through propitiations to Chak and much to lose by ignoring him.

Comparison of Wetland with Karstic-Riverine Landscape

The wetland and karstic-riverine landscapes exhibit contrastive settlement and ritual histories. These differences testify to the complexity of rural Maya place-making. Maya populations in each area adapted their agricultural and ritual practices to their local environment, thus creating a landscape that would forever bear the signature of their presence. Keen local differences are counterbalanced by similarities in underlying cosmological armatures and agriculturalists' general concerns of rain and drought.

Politically, both landscapes discussed here supported settlement hierarchies, thus providing a strong indication of the pyramidal structure of Maya political organization in the rural sector. In the wetland environment, the two pyramid plazas of K'axob probably were secondary to larger regional centers such as San Estevan or Nohmul. The latter boasts massive platform construction during the Late Formative (Hammond et al. 1988). Along the Sibun River, the two large centers of Oshon and Hershey occupy the upper tier of the settlement hierarchy. Remaining settlements are situated geographically between these two major centers and hierarchically beneath them. Given the data at hand, the exact nature and antiquity of the Sibun Valley hierarchy is not clear, but it is apparent that the hierarchies of the northern wetlands are grounded in the Formative period in a manner not apparent in the Sibun Valley.

Deep stratigraphic sequences from excavations at K'axob indicate the longevity of settlement at this locale (McAnany and López Varela 1999). This longevity is expressed in the accretional development of civic and household structures, the modification and utilization of the wetlands, and the importance attached to mortuary ritual (see McAnany, Storey, and Lockard 1999). Conversely, test excavations conducted at Pechtun Ha, Yax P'otob, Pakal Na, and the Oshon site indicate that construction was nearly uni-episodal, with limited stratigraphic separation within platform fill. All the Sibun settlements examined thus far can be placed firmly within the Late to Terminal Classic period and do not exhibit the accretional development of structures that is evident at K'axob.

At Pechtun Ha, the rapidity of plaza construction suggests the transplantation of a social hierarchy or the creation of an administrative node, perhaps to develop cacao orchards along this section of the river. As Grant Jones (1989) has documented, the Sibun Valley supported a cacao-producing *encomienda* (hacienda) during Colonial times; even today it is actively farmed for cacao and citrus. K'axob, on the other hand, contains a record of sustained growth of a farming community around a core of Classic-period pyramidal architecture. K'axob farmers seem not to have relied exclusively on a certain crop but, over time and through careful planning and earth-working projects, created a diversified agricultural base, which they exploited for subsistence and local trade (McAnany and Berry 1999). Nonetheless, the magnitude of landscape modification in the wetland region appears to have far outweighed that of the riverine-karst zone. This contrast is further bolstered by the

7.9 Stone monuments of Pechtun Ha: top, stela; bottom, altar. Photographs by Patricia A. McAnany

fact that cacao thrives primarily within environments that successfully mimic rain-forest ecology. A premium may have been placed on reducing landscape domestication in the Sibun River Valley.

Archaeologically, the shorter occupation history of sites along the Sibun River may explain the scarcity of artifacts in the construction fill and on the surface of settlements. This point of contrast with K'axob, where extended occupation has led to the accumulation of occupational debris around and within mounds, reinforces the domesticated nature of the wetland landscape. Plowing of the sugarcane fields has brought many artifacts to the surface, further highlighting the prevalence of occupational loci. At sites along the Sibun River, equivalent sheet middens in contemporary citrus and cacao orchards have not been discovered, and there is a notable lack of surface debris near platforms. Seasonal flooding might contribute to this perceived sterility, but the shorter duration of occupation certainly plays a part in the light scatter of occupational debris. The scarcity of surface artifacts in the settlements stands in striking contrast to the abundance of material in the region's caves, which were utilized coincident with occupation of the valley. Despite the high artifact densities within the caves, there is no evidence that the caves were occupied. Artifacts tend to be located in inaccessible parts of the cave, reaffirming the notion that caverns were used for ritual practice.

Ritual space was created within both landscapes. Such creations were, however, greatly affected by local influences. At K'axob, burials, particularly those of ancestors, created sacred space that was the basis for further construction activity within the settlement proper. These important foci of ritual activities at K'axob linked ancestor interments with the explicitly built environment of the residential compound. The perceived extent of this built environment encompassed a larger area than simply that of upland platforms and pyramids, however. Excavations in the adjacent wetlands have revealed ritual deposits of worked shell and lithics that attest to the inclusion of these areas in the ritual cosmology of the K'axob Maya. In the Sibun Valley, on the other hand, ritual practice involved pilgrimage or procession to the caverns on the south side of the river. The vast ritual landscape of the Sibun-Manatee karst contains numerous portals to the underworld. Within these caves, objects were deposited as offerings or left as debris from ritual performance. Speleothems were removed from the caves and transported to surface settlements, such as Pechtun Ha. While the exact nature of the ritual activities undertaken inside these portals to the underworld is not clear, some type of dialogue with deities, perhaps including revered ancestors, certainly transpired. Given the associations between water and caves, it is not unreasonable to suspect that some of the rituals were focused on the rain deity, Chak.

The importance of Chak to the Xibun Maya may derive from the local severity of flooding which, in the Sibun River Valley, could be as devastating as drought at K'axob. On the other hand, flooding enriches the soil and the alluvium deposited by each flooding event provided natural fertilizer for crops. In the wetland landscape to the north, rains are confined to the wet season and drought is not unusual. This factor favors settlement near wetlands that provide a stable water source, even during periods of drought. Within excavations in the wetland fields adjacent to K'axob, fifteen intricately carved worked shell objects have been recovered (for one example, see figure 7.8). Such offerings, heretofore, had not been documented by excavations in island fields. These ritually cached objects indicate that an offering to the watery underworld repeatedly took place on the wetland island fields of K'axob. In some respects, these deposits are analogous to the Chak offerings the Xibun Maya left in caves.

Ritual space was further designated at K'axob by the creation of two large pyramid plazas. Excavations at both plazas A and B (see figure 7.3) have yielded stratigraphic sequences, indicating that the pyramids were also constructed accretionally over many years. The lack of pyramids in the middle and lower sections of the Sibun Valley may be owing to the proximity of natural conical mountains and caves. Insofar as Maya pyramids were conceived as culturally constructed *wits* (hills) and their apical temples as artificial caves, there may not have been a need to create artificial examples of mountains and caves that were, in actuality, only a short distance away.

Another dramatic difference between the settlements in the two locales relates to the presence of stone monuments. A stela and altar pair was discovered at Pechtun Ha (see figure 7.9), and two additional stelae were located at the Oshon site. Despite its vibrant Late Classic population, stone monuments were not found at K'axob. Their absence may be due to the paucity of hard stone in the wetland landscape, or there may have been very fundamental differences between the two regions regarding the manner in which power was expressed.

Finally, the location of the Sibun Valley sites, near the banks of the river, indicates that these settlements were involved in trading activities along the length of the river. From preliminary observations, such exotic materials as obsidian were much more accessible in the Sibun Valley than at K'axob. Although the New River flows less than a kilometer from K'axob, this more northerly site seems to have concentrated its trading efforts on the local acquisition of chert tools from the production center of Colha. Furthermore, the highly desirable cacao produced by the farmers of the Sibun Valley may have positioned the Xibun Maya in a more visible role in the luxury economy and long-distance trading spheres of the Late Classic.

Conclusion

Investigation of Maya settlements in two contrastive landscapes of Belize—one wetland-riverine and the other karstic-riverine—indicates the profound complexity of the rural experiences of the ancient Maya. Removed from the political capitals of divine rulers, K'axob and Xibun Maya concerned themselves with agricultural and ritual practices that were fine-tuned to their ambient landscape. In the two landscapes, early settlers reacted to local influences in the planning and locating of their sites. While common threads unite the sites under discussion, farming strategies and ritual practice differed dramatically between the two regions.

The sites along the Sibun were linked closely to the extensive trade and movement of goods that were part of the Late Classic Maya world. Possible specialization in cacao production may explain the rapid construction of the Sibun Valley sites during the Late Classic period and the relatively short duration of occupation. Their ritual practice was focused on the landscape of caves located a short distance away. In contrast, K'axob shows the longevity of settlement and the accretional development of a site geared primarily to what appears to have been subsistence farming and localized trading. Ritual expression was focused on ancestor interments and, to a lesser extent, the watery world of the adjacent wetlands.

Contrasts in ritual practice between K'axob and the Sibun sites are profound. The use of caves in the Sibun Valley is not directly paralleled at K'axob, although ritual caching within the wetlands does appear to be linked with water concerns. By emphasizing the possible role of Chak in cave rituals of the Sibun Valley, we are not suggesting that the rain deity was not also important to farmers further north at K'axob, only that their ritual propitiations are not so visible to us. The primary ritual practice observable at K'axob relates to the long chain of progenitors. Ancestor interments within the settlement of K'axob sharply contrast with the artifact-rich caverns of the Sibun-Manatee karst. In effect, the contrastive place-making activities of lowland Maya societies resulted in a highly textured landscape that encoded many vital concerns and challenges negotiated through ritual and agricultural practice.

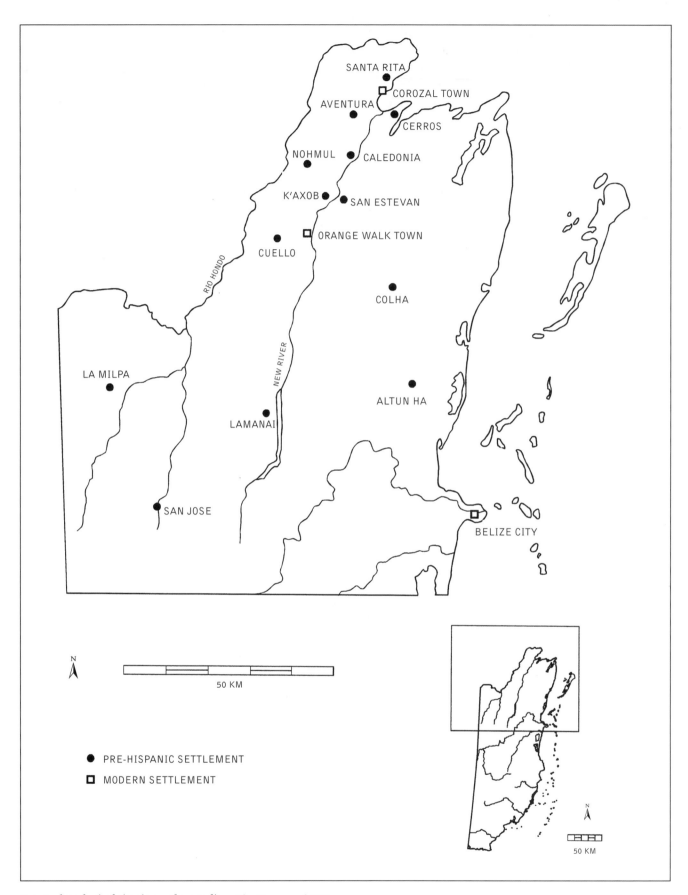

SANTA RITA

COROZAL TOWN

AVENTURA

CERROS

NOHMUL

CALEDONIA

K'AXOB

SAN ESTEVAN

ORANGE WALK TOWN

CUELLO

RIO HONDO

NEW RIVER

COLHA

LA MILPA

ALTUN HA

LAMANAI

SAN JOSE

BELIZE CITY

N

50 KM

● PRE-HISPANIC SETTLEMENT

□ MODERN SETTLEMENT

N

50 KM

8.1 Archaeological sites in northern Belize. After Hammond 1981

8 Space and the Limits to Community

Laura J. Levi

THIS CHAPTER WEIGHS the merits of assessing settlement variation in the Maya lowlands according to the social and evolutionary dimensions implied by the term, *rural complexity*. The evaluation is based upon a preliminary comparison of residential distributions at three archaeological sites in northeastern Belize: Nohmul, Pulltrouser Swamp, and San Estevan. Together, these sites span a continuous territory that extends from the Rio Hondo on the west to a series of large seasonal wetlands lying a few kilometers east of the New River. Unlike the arguments presented by a number of contributors to this volume, the distributional patterns found across the study area do not mesh well with prevailing ideas about the nature of rural and urban forms, nor do they lend their support to notions of rural complexity. This lack of fit suggests the need to consider the sources of our convictions about rural and urban settlement, the implications of conjoining the terms rural and complexity, and our prospects for finding theoretical frameworks that give clearer voice to settlement pattern data.

Rural and Urban, Simple and Complex: A Legacy of Social Evolutionism

There is a deceptive clarity to the term *rural complexity* that conceals a lengthy history of thought and a tangled bundling of meanings, both scholarly and conventional. It is, perhaps, our conventional understanding of the terminology that makes the phrase so appealing, so patently accessible. Yet that very same conventional knowledge is also what makes rural complexity so dangerous when used as an analytical or explanatory construct. Convention is notoriously resistant to direct frontal attack, and so I will make my case for the intellectual pitfalls of rural complexity more circuitously, briefly examining changes in scholarly usages of the

term during the late nineteenth and twentieth centuries. Over the course of this time span, rural complexity moved from theoretical impossibility to index of evolutionary process. Throughout, notions of the rural and the complex remain irrevocably tied to their binary opposites, the urban and the simple. Moreover, the entire suite of terms gains meaning only within the context of the evolutionism that emerged so prominently in nineteenth-century social theory and that persists to the present day.

There has never been a single brand of social evolutionary theory, some pure form, which was not subsequently and inevitably diluted by the march of time and the shifting of agendas. Social evolutionary theory had multiple nineteenth-century inspirations, from the burgeoning sciences of geology and naturalism (Eiseley 1975) to the social philosophies arising from political and moral commentary on industrialization and an expanding capitalist sector. Often differing on the basis of analytical methods, issues of causality, and the details of evolutionary progression (for example, see Durkheim's (1938[1895]:99–112) critique of Spencer), the diverse brands of early social evolutionary theory shared only the most general of themes—themes that gained currency and resonance in relation to the ongoing reorganization of Europe's social landscape. In all, the history of human societies was perceived to mirror the history of the natural world only obliquely and in part. Human social history was one of change and not stasis; of primitive or simple forms ceding to more modern, complex ones; of the gradual generation of social variation and differentiation. But as seemingly testified by events in Europe, that gradually expanding variation ultimately spawned convulsive change—a dramatic transformation thought to mark the transition from natural to political economy (Rosebury 1989:198–206). The transformation was credited with both social and spatial consequences. The older, natural economy had been born of the "natural" landscape of the countryside (Olwig 1993). It was perceived to be embedded in the narrowly circumscribed needs of household and community and was characterized by the presumed productive self-sufficiency and shared values of country people or peasants. Political economy, in contrast, was variously conceived as the social and/or economic structures and policies necessitated by industrial capitalism with its elaborate productive processes and divisions of labor (J.H. Moore 1993). It was an artificial state (in the dual senses of this term), arising in response to the organizational needs of a socioeconomic differentiation that unnaturally concentrated people and activities into densely packed cities.

In Americanist anthropology, this intermingling of ideas about the rural and urban, the simple and complex, was first and most impressively codified in the influential works of Robert Redfield (1930, 1941, 1953, 1955, 1960). To Redfield, the rural denoted pockets of social homogeneity and moral order, small bastions of tradition and kin-based self-sufficiency harkening back to an earlier, simpler age. Complexity, on the other hand, was the hallmark of modern urban society: spaces defined by broad socioeconomic heterogeneity, an organic complementarity, and the transcendence of secular authority at the expense of the sacred. Through the curious twists of this social evolutionary logic, the terms rural and urban, simple and complex, conflated issues of social space and evolutionary time. Within that logic, a premodern rural complexity could not exist.

Social evolutionary theory is no less complicit in more recent scholarship, but different processes are emphasized and meanings have shifted subtly. Rural and urban have been redefined "expedientially" and functionally (Wheatley 1972:620). Expedientially, the terms are used to indicate differentials in population size, socioeconomic activity, and political control. Functionally, they are argued to be flip sides of the same coin, with the process of urbanization demanding a corresponding ruralization (Yoffee 1993). Rural hinterlands are thought to be produced by the very same forces of specialization and centralization that aggregate people and activities into cities. The socioeconomic homogeneity attributed to rural spaces by earlier scholars is now understood as an extreme and enforced specialization underwriting urban diversity. In like fashion, the traditionalism presumed to characterize rural populations is reconceived as a culture of poverty or as resistance to the hegemonic orders lodged in urban spaces (for example, Foster 1965; Scott 1985; Wolf 1966, 1969). In this second formulation, should we find something in the real world that calls to mind rural complexity, labeling it so would imply that here the forces of specialization and centralization have short-circuited. The

urban has failed to differentiate itself from its surroundings because sufficient power to structure the social landscape does not exist or cannot be consolidated. Our real-world case might even be used as an example of how the ineluctable march toward complex society sometimes falters.

There are sound empirical and epistemological reasons for not pursuing this discourse. Empirically, social life appears to possess its own fractal geometry: wherever we choose to situate our analysis, whatever the scale, we can always find heterogeneity. Historically, anthropology's tendency to homogenize its subject matter (Gupta and Ferguson 1992) has never gone completely unchallenged, and the literature is rife with observations of diversity and variation. So-called primitive society did not disappear simply as a result of colonial interference and capitalist penetration, but through anthropology's inability to adequately model the range and variety of socioeconomic and political forms glossed by the term (Douglas 1967; Flanagan 1989; Kuper 1982). Similarly, the ideal of a self-sustaining and undifferentiated rural peasantry has been undermined by a growing awareness of the fractious domestic politics of age and gender (Donham 1981; Hart 1992) and of the variation and inequalities endemic among farming households (for example, Boserup 1965; Cancian 1972; Hill 1986; G.D. Stone, Netting and Stone 1990). Longtime intellectual bulwarks of the countryside, these idealized models and social types are either obsolete or in imminent danger of becoming so. Rural complexity is empirically unremarkable archaeologically and ethnohistorically, as well as ethnographically (for example, see Brumfiel 1987; Falconer and Savage 1995; Smith and Heath-Smith 1994). It becomes notable only within the context of social evolutionary theory.

It is social evolutionary theory that informs the notion of rural complexity, and it is the tenacity of social evolutionism that brings us full circle to question our bases for understanding the rural and the complex. Mary Douglas (1986) provides one possible explanation for such tenacity in her examination of "how institutions think." Observing the entrenchment of linguistic codes and categories of thought in academic disciplines, she argues that conventional means of expression and ways of thinking are some of the most effective strategies institutions possess to communicate their legitimacy, to assign rights of membership, and to signal inclusion. The longstanding pervasiveness of social evolutionary thought, both across academic disciplines and outside academe, suggests, however, that its legitimacy springs from some deeper well (Rowlands 1989:35). In fact, social evolutionism only masquerades as theory. As Adam Kuper (1988) demonstrates, it has proven immune to the Kuhnian paradigm shifts that routinely torpedo mundane scientific theories. No amount of empirical ammunition seems capable of destroying it. Instead, social evolutionism has undergone successive structural transformations, always emerging gloriously and essentially intact. Accordingly, Lévi-Strauss and not Kuhn offers the more appropriate understanding (Kuper 1988:11–13). Social evolutionism is not theory, but one of the most enduring origin myths of western civilization (Rowlands 1989; Stahl 1993). It has epistemological status. It is our way of knowing ourselves.

The dangers attending a notion of rural complexity thus arise from the epistemological system that gives meaning to the term. Because the terminology has such historically specific epistemological roots, there is every reason to suppose that the outcome of pursuing rural complexity in the Maya lowlands may illuminate little about the Maya. The question of whether the Maya organized themselves into social spaces that correspond to our ideas about rural and urban landscapes clearly presupposes articles of faith about our own history, our own world. What we are really asking is whether the Maya distributed themselves in the way we believe we do, and for the same reasons. Answering this question simply reaffirms what we believe about ourselves without ever truly revealing the way we are. How can we expect the answers to reveal anything about the Maya? My inclination, therefore, is to suggest at the outset that lowland Maya settlement cannot be adequately understood through the terms rural and urban, simple and complex. This response might allow greater latitude to explore the landscapes of the lowland Maya in their own terms.

Spatial Architecture of Community

In geography, issues of landscape formation currently fall within the domain of spatiality, a term used to convey the idea that social space is simultaneously the "mediator and outcome" of social practice (Soja 1985). Spatiality implies that space is constituted by ideational, organizational, and material processes that emerge in historically particular contexts. The concept has its origins in geography's critique of its own preoccupation with the urban-rural dichotomy and with the narrow social and spatial contrasts this dichotomy afforded. Minimally, spatiality points to the inherent unity of social, spatial, and historical processes. The larger message, however, is that space is differently constituted from one context to the next. Space must, therefore, be empirically discovered rather than assumed a priori.

Spatiality remains an elusive concept in the absence of particular examples that demonstrate how space can be variously systematized and made organizationally concrete within particular historical circumstances. Here I offer one such example derived from an ongoing comparison of resi-

dential distributions at the Belizean sites of San Estevan, Pulltrouser, and Nohmul. The settlement area defined by these three sites extends from the Rio Hondo east past the New River to the seasonal wetlands joining northern Belize's flat coastal plain (figure 8.1). This is a large and archaeologically well-explored area, with data available in the form of site maps produced by the San Estevan (Levi 1993), Pulltrouser (Harrison and Fry 2000; Turner and Harrison 1983), and Nohmul projects (Hammond et al. 1988). Adding significant detail are Stanley Walling's (1993) study of residential groups in the northern half of Pulltrouser, Patricia McAnany's (1995) work at K'axob in the central Pulltrouser zone, and Anne Pyburn's (1989) investigation of Nohmul's residential settlement.

FINDING THE SPATIALITY OF SETTLEMENT
AT SAN ESTEVAN

The impetus to inspect this broad area of settlement in northeastern Belize arose from an analysis of residential distributions I conducted at San Estevan (Levi 1993). My research was designed to demonstrate how residential diversity at the site implicated variation in the organizational and productive strategies of San Estevan's pre-Hispanic households (Levi 1996). In the process of my analysis, I stumbled across the unexpected finding that there was an underlying spatial scheme to San Estevan's social landscape.

At the outset of this research, I anticipated that San Estevan's pre-Hispanic community spanned between 30 and 35 km², with its boundaries drawn along natural topographic features: the New River to the west and the seasonal wetlands to the north, south, and east (figure 8.2). Within this area, residential settlement had been distributed across three separate ridges that bordered the perennial wetland, Long Swamp. Each ridge also housed a node of monumental architecture, and the principal monumental precincts of the community, the largest and most functionally complex node, were located at the center of the large western ridge.[1] Modern cane cultivation has lent an unparalleled visibility to San Estevan's small-structure architecture. Archaeological fieldwork in the defined site area documented diverse residential forms by means of a sample of twenty survey blocks measuring 250 m on a side. All architectural remains in survey blocks were transit mapped and surface collected, and selected residential groups were test excavated. Additionally, residential units in several other areas of the site were mapped, collected, and tested opportunistically as they were cleared of cane.

The analysis of San Estevan's residential architecture proceeded from the identification of recurring residential arrangements which, through differences in structure number and mechanisms of structure incorporation, seemed

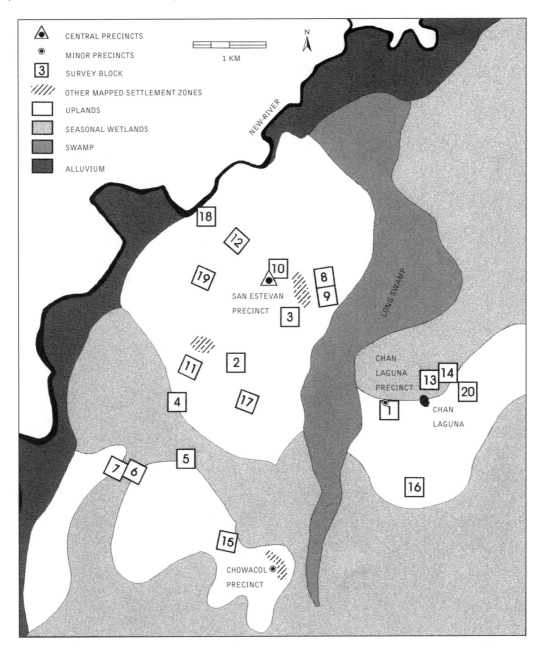

8.2 San Estevan Project's research area

indicative of different kinds of domestic organization (Levi 2000). Four of San Estevan's most important (and numerically prevalent) residential group classes are briefly described: isolates, paired platform groups, basal platform groups, and large composite groups. Test excavations showed that each class possessed slightly differing developmental trajectories through the lengthy occupational history of the settlement. All, however, were well represented during San Estevan's Late Classic period; on the basis of both excavations and systematic surface collections, I estimated that 80% of the site's small-structure architecture possessed a Late Classic component (Levi 1993:123).

Isolates. San Estevan's simplest class of residential architecture consisted entirely of single-structure platforms (figure 8.3a, b). Lacking any obvious clues to domestic group composition and organization, the isolates found at lowland Maya sites seem highly susceptible to conflicting interpretations (Freidel and Sabloff 1984:111; Marcus 1982; Tourtellot 1988a:114–116). There is the possibility that a number of San Estevan's isolates did not possess a residential function. On the other hand, excavations in some of these units yielded dedicatory caches similar to those found

ISOLATES

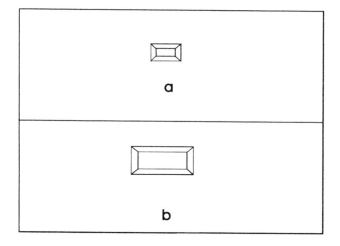

PLAZA FOCUSED GROUPS

PAIRED PLATFORM GROUPS

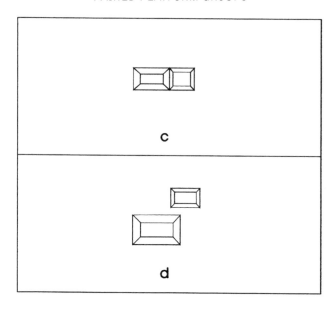

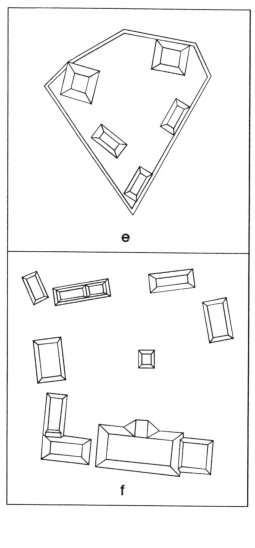

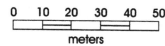

8.3 Four classes of residential architecture at San Estevan: a, b, isolates; c, d, paired platform groups; e, basal platform groups; f, large composite groups

in multistructure groups (Levi 1993:210, 296, 300–301). Additionally, San Estevan's isolates occurred in greatest frequency wherever multistructure units were absent and, therefore, cannot readily be dismissed as mere adjuncts to larger, plaza-focused residential groups.

Paired platform groups. Another of San Estevan's frequently occurring residential arrangements possessed two structure platforms (figure 8.3c,d). The integrity of paired platforms was expressed through either abutment or spatial proximity, and these groups tended to lack well-defined plazas.

Basal platform groups. As the name would suggest, membership in basal platform groups (BPG) this class was determined by the presence of a basal platform supporting three or more structures arranged around a central plaza (figure 8.3e). Basal platform groups consistently showed intricately stratified occupation histories, and they comprised San Estevan's most enduring residential loci.

Large composite groups. These residential groups were distinguished by the profusion of mechanisms to incorporate buildings into vast multistructure units (figure 8.3f). Although plazas were an important integrating mechanism,

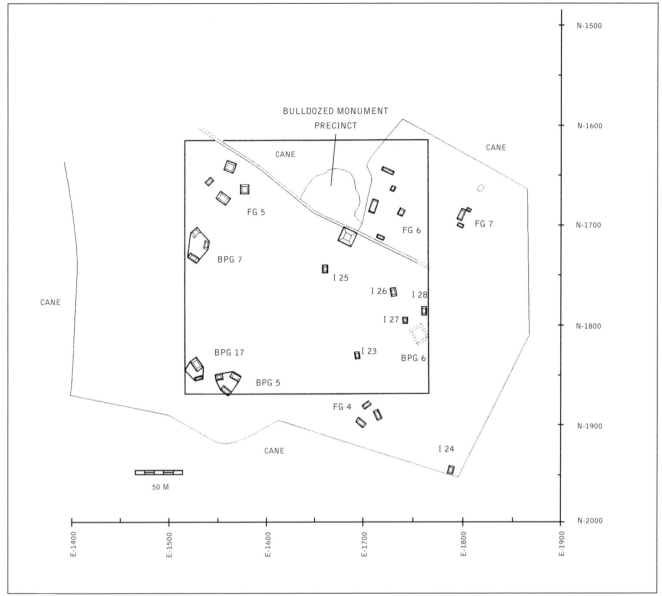

8.4 *Residential locality at San Estevan showing a preponderance of basal platform groups.* Drawn by Eric M. Levi and Jeffrey Jones

other types of linkages or discrete activities probably tied groups of individual structures together into subunits within each group. Despite their size and spatial intricacy, however, large composite groups (LCOMP) were constructed and abandoned all within the Late Classic period.

This classification of San Estevan's domestic architecture proved very useful, first helping to define distinctive kinds of localities within the settlement and, subsequently, helping to reveal how the pre-Hispanic community had been spatially constituted as a whole. With regard to the former, an examination of the frequency distributions of San Estevan's residential classes (weighted by mean class volume) showed important differences in the composition of residential assemblages across the site (Levi 1993:234–239). Certain localities were dominated by basal platform groups

(BPG) (figure 8.4), others by large composite groups (LCOMP) (figure 8.5), and still others by a combination of paired platform groups and isolates (PP/I) (figure 8.6). A final set was marked by wide diversity, with no one residential form dominant (NONE). The variable distributions of these different kinds of residential localities proved most evocative, suggesting that San Estevan's pre-Hispanic community had achieved a distinctive spatial coherence (figure 8.7). Areas dominated by basal platform groups never appeared farther than 0.5 km from any one of the site's three monumental precincts. Areas characterized by high diversity and the absence of a dominant residential form occurred only within a 0.75 km radius of these precincts. Beyond that point, and extending for roughly 0.5 km, the landscape was marked both by a loss of diversity and the preponderance

8.5 Residential locality at San Estevan showing a preponderance of large composite groups. Drawn by Eric M. Levi and Jeffrey Jones

of paired platforms and isolates. Moving even farther away, there was yet another dramatic shift, with large composite groups eclipsing all other residential forms (figure 8.7; see chapter 6, for a comparative analysis of the distances of settlement to site centers).

Out of the distributions of San Estevan's residential and monumental architecture there emerged another kind of architecture—quite literally an architecture of space. The surprising concreteness of this phenomenon is expressed in figure 8.8 where distance intervals from monumental precincts have been examined according to their aggregate residential assemblages rather than by the assemblages characterizing specific survey blocks. But did all lowland Maya communities possess their own distinctive spatial architectures? A positive demonstration of this phenomenon would

establish the comparative framework needed to investigate the particular forces through which pre-Hispanic lowland Maya spatialities had been forged. The logical first step was to determine whether San Estevan could be distinguished from adjoining areas, not on the basis of topography, but by the way in which the community had been spatially constituted. This question prompted my examination of residence at Pulltrouser and Nohmul, San Estevan's nearest neighbors.

LIMITS TO COMMUNITY

Described below are the early findings of a comparison of residential distributions at San Estevan, Pulltrouser, and Nohmul. Both Nohmul and San Estevan had been substantial pre-Hispanic Maya centers, ranking in the first and

8.6 Residential locality at San Estevan showing a preponderance of paired platform groups and isolates.
Drawn by Eric M. Levi and Jeffrey Jones

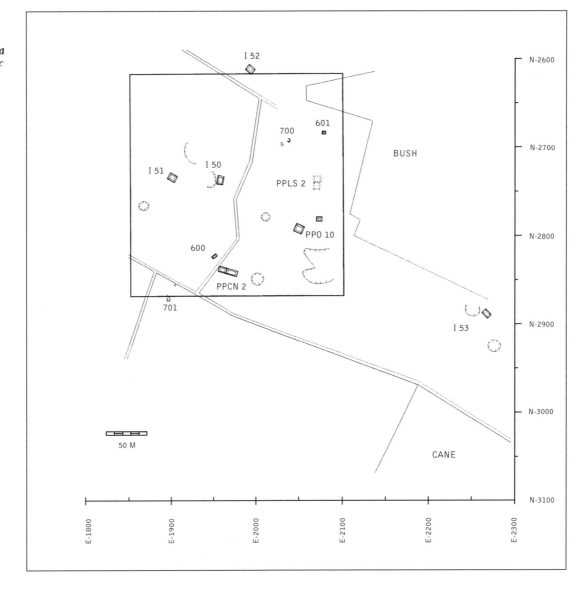

second tiers, respectively, of Hammond's (1981) hierarchy of northern Belize sites. The Pulltrouser settlement area, lying immediately to the west of San Estevan (figure 8.9) across the narrow banks of the New River, occupied the middle ground between San Estevan and Nohmul. Possessing a few small nodes of monumental architecture, Pulltrouser has been variously interpreted as a patchwork of "autonomous" or "semi-autonomous units" (McAnany 1995:154–155) and as a locus of rural cultivators (Walling 1993:9–12, 238). The settlement spanning San Estevan, Pulltrouser, and Nohmul, therefore, provided a promising setting within which to explore the limits of a pre-Hispanic Maya community. The analysis of Pulltrouser's residential distributions has been completed, and the brief presentation of research results that follows will focus upon settlement in this area. The analysis of the Nohmul data has just begun, and Nohmul's settlement patterns are addressed only

in relation to readily apparent departures from San Estevan.

Since the San Estevan residential analysis formed the baseline for comparisons with Pulltrouser, I first applied San Estevan's residential classification to the Pulltrouser area and then assessed whether Pulltrouser settlement deviated in any way from the distributional patterns identified at San Estevan. Fortunately, only minimal tampering with the San Estevan classification was needed to accommodate Pulltrouser's residential remains. The next step, inspection of the spatial parameters associated with Pulltrouser's residential localities, called for an examination of the composition of residential assemblages around Pulltrouser's monumental precincts according to the distance intervals established at San Estevan. This assessment could be readily made for half the Pulltrouser area. Pulltrouser has three principal zones of settlement with substantial Late Classic occupation. Two of these, Kokeal and K'axob, possessed small precincts of monumental architecture. Residential settlement around the Kokeal precinct extended along the southern arm of the swamp, while the K'axob precinct and its settlement were more centrally situated along the swamp's eastern margins.

Pulltrouser's third settlement zone, Tibaat, posed something of a problem, however. Tibaat is located in the northern half of Pullutrouser, between the west and east arms of the swamp. From a San Estevan perspective, settlement in the area just looked all wrong. First, as Walling (1993:194) observed, there appeared to have been no abiding locus of monumental architecture. Walling did suggest that a node may have begun to coalesce by the end of the Classic period in the central sector of the zone, but its monumentality was quite dubious (Walling 1993:195, 237). Second, basal platform groups achieved a wide areal distribution at Tibaat, while at San Estevan they never occurred more than 700 or 800 m from monumental precincts. To confound things even further, Tibaat possessed several nonplatform dwellings dated to the Classic period. At San Estevan these residential forms were extremely rare, their occurrence restricted to a few Late Preclassic examples.

The Tibaat zone was sufficiently distinct to warrant inspection apart from Kokeal and K'axob. Anchoring San Estevan's spatial parameters to Tibaat's Terminal Classic focal point, the residential landscape there offered a striking contrast to San Estevan (figure 8.10). Basal platform groups predominated for a radius of almost 1 km. Beyond that point, the landscape was characterized by great residential diversity. The combined consideration of residential distributions at Kokeal and K'axob (figure 8.11), on the other hand, highlighted important spatial differences between these areas and Tibaat. More significantly, settlement at Kokeal and K'axob mimicked the distributional patterns found at San Estevan almost to the last detail (compare figure 8.11 with figure 8.8). The same distance intervals were marked by the same kinds of residential assemblages: basal platform groups, followed by a diversity of residential forms, followed by paired platforms and isolates, and culminating in large composite groups.

Discussion: The "Production of Space"

During the Classic period, there appears to have been a boundary running through Pulltrouser Swamp, etched by differences in the organization of space. Pulltrouser's southern and central zones shared the same spatial architecture that characterized San Estevan. I would like to suggest, therefore, that the area delimited by Kokeal, K'axob, and the three San Estevan ridges constituted a single socioeconomic and political entity for at least some portion of its occupational history. For want of a better term, I think we must call the

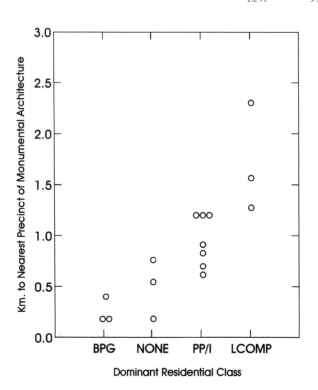

8.7 Distribution of survey localities in relation to monumental precincts at San Estevan. Localities are grouped according to dominant residential class.

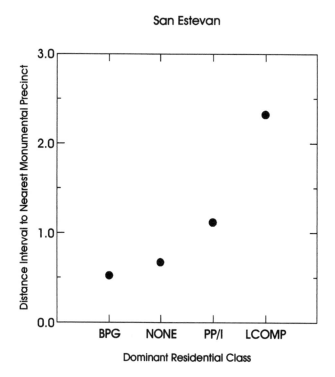

8.8 The architecture of space at San Estevan: dominant residential classes characterizing radial distance intervals around monumental precincts

8.9 The Pulltrouser Swamp settlement zones in relation to San Estevan. Drawn by Bruce Moses

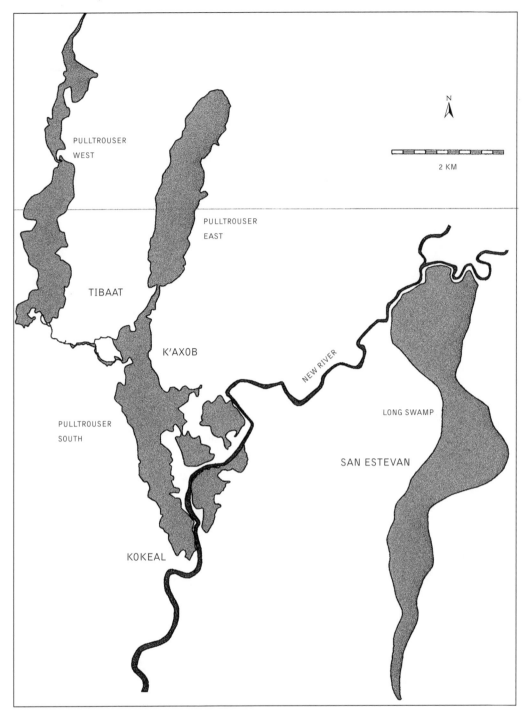

area a community. Centered upon San Estevan's large monumental precinct, this community dismissed as insignificant the topographic impediments posed by Long Swamp, the New River, and Pulltrouser Swamp, and strategically marshaled settlement in relation to arable swamp lands.

If my suspicions are borne out, Pulltrouser's Tibaat settlement zone will prove to have been part of the Nohmul com-

munity. Tibaat was situated a little less than 4 km east of Nohmul's acropolis, a radial distance that Anne Pyburn (1989) used to define the perimeters of the Nohmul settlement system. Unlike the San Estevan-K'axob-Kokeal community, but in keeping with Tibaat, Nohmul lacked clear subsidiary monumental precincts. As was true of Tibaat, Nohmul's basal platform groups achieved a wide areal distribution. In the same vein, the relatively high incidence of

Classic period nonplatform dwellings at Tibaat was mirrored in the settlement along Nohmul's northern perimeters. These observations only hint at what was probably a vastly different spatiality for the Nohmul community.

To return to my point of departure, such terms as *rural* and *urban* seem to find no purchase in this particular corner of the Maya lowlands. They are, quite literally, out of place. What we encounter, instead, are large communities carved from the terrain by a history of human relationships and their attendant economic, political, and ideological motivations. These communities, in turn, through their internal differentiation and external boundaries, served as organizational benchmarks for individual activity and institutional action (Levi 2000). In a very real sense, then, the spatial architecture of community, and the spatiality it implies, arise from what Henri Lefebvre calls the "social production of space" (1991 [1974]). At this point in my research, it would be premature to attempt to explain exactly how space can be so differently produced. I venture to suggest, however, that for the San Estevan-K'axob-Kokeal community, ecology, institutional relationships defining labor and its products, and cultural expressions of these institutions through the medium of architecture were all involved in the process. To begin to detect diversity among these spatial productions, such as that between San Estevan and Nohmul, is to begin to gain real insight into the organizational amplitude—the complexity—of lowland Maya civilization.

Acknowledgments. Grants from the National Science Foundation (BNS8910970) and the Wenner Gren Foundation for Anthropological Research funded the investigations at San Estevan discussed in this chapter. Many thanks to Bruce Moses for his efforts to standardize and digitize the San Estevan illustrations. Once again, I extend my gratitude to the many individuals associated with the San Estevan Project: Dionicio Pech, Alfredo Pech, Noel Pech, Argelia Martinez, Ovel Martinez, Vildo Gonzalez, Amir Gonzalez, Omar Vasquez, Armando Ya, Nellie Donaldson, Julian Pat, Daniel Pat, Jeffrey Jones, Daniela Triadan, Stacey Ruetter, Jeff Baker, John Rose, Kevin Kuykendall, Marianna Wetters, Cynthia Robin, Colleen Gleason, Norman Hammond, T. Patrick Culbert, and Eric and Madelaine Levi.

NOTES

1. In the last decade, bulldozing for road fill has stripped San Estevan of most all of its monumental architecture.

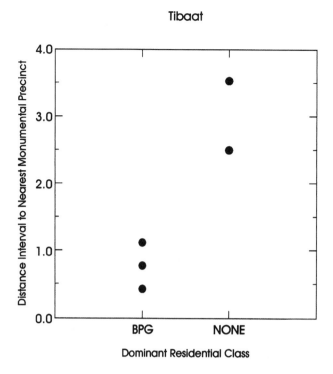

8.10 Tibaat: dominant residential classes characterizing radial distance intervals around monumental precincts

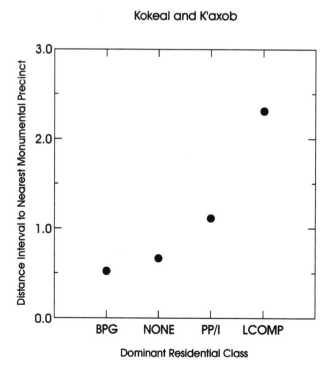

8.11 Kokeal and K'axob: dominant residential classes characterizing radial distance intervals around monumental precincts

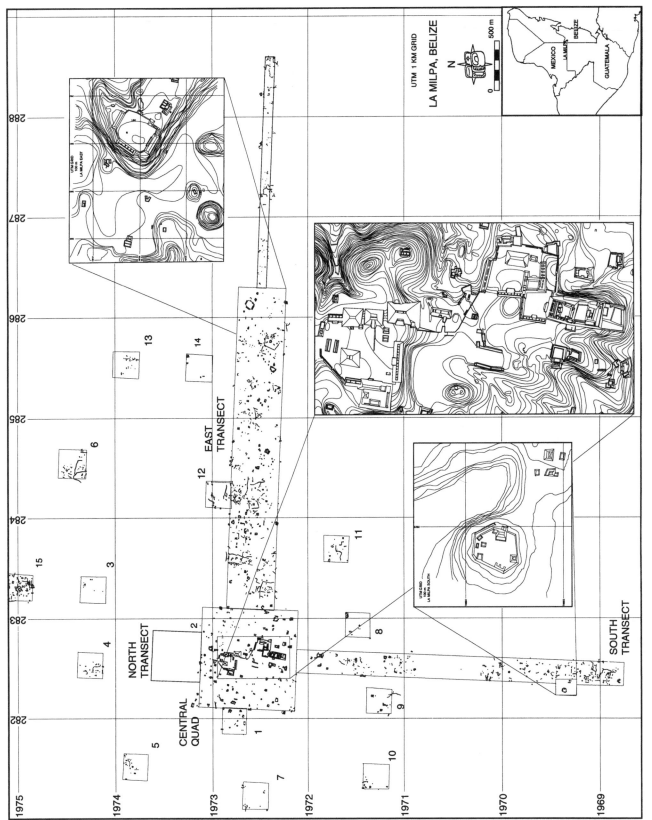

9.1 *La Milpa, Belize: mapped center, transects, and survey blocks. Maps by Gair Tourtellot, GIS by Francisco Estrada Belli*

9 Suburban Organization
Minor Centers at La Milpa, Belize

Gair Tourtellot, Gloria Everson, and Norman Hammond

INVESTIGATIONS beyond the major center of La Milpa have yielded evidence of several types and levels of middle-level sites within this ancient community. Here we focus on new data concerning upper middle-level sites, or "minor ceremonial centers," dating to La Milpa's Late/Terminal Classic apogee, and propose how these sites might have been articulated within local and regional organizational frameworks.

La Milpa lies in northwestern Belize, close to the borders with Mexico and Guatemala, on the eastern edge of the Petén uplands, and in an ecological preserve owned by Programme for Belize (figure 9.1, upper right inset). Boston University has conducted five seasons of work there since 1992 (Hammond 1991; Hammond and Bobo 1994; Hammond et al. 1996, 1998; Schultz, González, and Hammond 1994; Tourtellot, Clarke, and Hammond 1993; Tourtellot, Hammond, and Plank 1997; Tourtellot et al. 1994; Tourtellot, Rose, and Hammond 1996). La Milpa is the largest known site between Lamanai on the east and Rio Azul on the west, and appears to be rather precisely centered within a community 10 km across. The internal organization of such a large and populous site is of great interest.

The site core, or La Milpa Centre (figure 9.1, middle inset), lies in an upland semitropical forest 180 m above sea level on a limestone ridge with a steep eastern scarp. The Great Plaza (plaza A) terrace at the northern end covers some 18,000 m², one of the largest open spaces laid out by the Classic lowland Maya. The plaza has four major temple pyramids, as well as two ballcourts: the visible architecture dates to the Late/Terminal Classic period (AD 750 to 900).[1] Structures of the Early Classic and Late Preclassic periods have been encountered only in excavations and almost exclusively in this part of the site. Plaza A also holds sixteen of the nineteen known stelae, the highest total for any site in this region. Their style dates fall into an earlier group

(AD 350–500) and a later group (AD 750–850), corresponding to the two occupations of La Milpa; only stela 7 has a fully legible inscription, dated 9.17.10.0.0. (AD 780).

The southern group in La Milpa Centre, reached via a short *sacbe* (formal walkway), includes two large ground-level plazas defined by long-range buildings and only one (incomplete) pyramid. South of Plaza C is the Tzaman Acropolis with a succession of elevated courts and throne rooms (Hammond et al. 1998). Unlike the northern area, the southern group dates exclusively to the Late/Terminal Classic, a period when La Milpa underwent a truly dramatic expansion in population size, area, and density, prior to an equally dramatic decline. Beyond La Milpa Centre is a vast suburban zone of houses, gardens, fields, and engineered landscapes of terraces and earthworks. The 78 km² of terrain that our survey established as the community territory of ancient La Milpa largely comprises rugged upland landscapes spotted with numerous small *bajos* (marshy areas). The current count of mapped structures and features exceeds 3200, most of which were Late/Terminal Classic. La Milpa had many people to organize at that time and several ranks of middle-level centers to assist in that endeavor.

Hypotheses

We argue that the middle-level sites around La Milpa are organized in a concentric and cardinally aligned cosmogram and explore their meaning for city planning. Then, we examine the evidence that supports these contentions, how we identified the middle-level sites, and how we think they functioned.

We propose an arrangement of middle-level centers, of which La Milpa East and La Milpa South are examples, in a possible ring configuration 3.5 km within the La Milpa community (figure 9.2). This putative ring is consistent with the somewhat fuller evidence of another concentric ring at twice that distance from La Milpa Centre, about 7.5 km, and apparently outside the contiguous, high-density, residential suburbs of La Milpa. Two of the three centers in the outer ring, Las Abejas and El Guijarral, lie halfway to the next major sites, and Ma'ax Na may prove to lie in a similar position. It is possible that middle-level sites in such transitional positions served as intermediaries handling cross-border transactions, as well as serving as local control centers in their own right.

It may be possible to find measurable proxies for the radii of easily projected power at lowland Maya sites. Indeed, rings of secondary centers (or at least modes of distances at approximately 3, 7, and 10 km) can be inferred from work at Tikal (Puleston 1983:25, Table 1), Ek Balam (Bey et al. 1998), or perhaps Caracol (A.F. Chase and D.Z. Chase 1987, this volume). The putative La Milpa circles we propose here also echo on a grand scale the network of numerous tertiary, or lower middle-level, sites with little pyramids like those encircling Seibal (very minor centers; Tourtellot 1988b: 277, 291, 376, 381, 396, 402, Fig. 216), although many may be Preclassic in origin. In contrast to La Milpa, their territories average only 0.3 km² (see also Becker 1971). An alternative perspective would be to construe middle-level centers like La Milpa East and South at 3.5 km on the one hand, or Guijarral, Las Abejas, Bedrock, and perhaps Ma'ax Na out some 7.5 km on the other, as just so many cells in a quilt of segmentary units subdividing and organizing the entire landscape. Such a construction of the landscape would privilege an historical discourse among volatile centers at all levels, flexibly agglomerating smaller cells for different purposes or shifting allegiances to different major centers as their dynastic rulers experienced success in trade, war, or kinship manipulations and wrote the sole surviving texts (compare Lucero 1999). At the moment, however, we do not have a time depth at La Milpa that requires (or allows us to see) more than a single static outcome developed during the Late/Terminal Classic.

More general yet, the two tentatively reconstructed concentric rings of middle-level sites bear an uncanny resemblance to the emic view of the world the lowland Maya depicted in their *pepet tsibil* (native maps) from the time of the Spanish conquest. These maps show their mundane world as a circle, top to the east and capital city in the center, with dependencies and provinces arrayed around them in four quarters, the whole bordered by a double circle that may contain regularly spaced sites (Marcus 1993; Roys 1972). We know the Classic lowland Maya were familiar with exactly the same design, for we have the same image of a cross inscribed within two concentric circles pecked into plaster or stone at several Classic-period sites (for examples see A.L. Smith 1950: Figs. 15a, 60, 1982:51) and possibly used as sur-

vey benchmarks or actual maps, among other things (Aveni, Hartung, and Buckingham 1978; Coggins 1980; Tourtellot 1988b:282). Figure 9.2 suggests that the city planners of La Milpa may indeed have constructed in their minds, and embodied in their community, what our perceptions now only hint at, and that this design penetrated down to and controlled the inner workings of individual cities well beyond the small compass of their central plaza groups.

General Administrative Patterns

We first briefly look at the organizational features of the site center and then turn to the evidence for two concentric rings of middle-level centers beyond the major La Milpa Centre. La Milpa Centre consists of two plaza groups linked by a sacbe on its high hill (figure 9.1, central quad). Appended to the southern group is a Late/Terminal Classic royal acropolis palace. Another acropolis off plaza A is possibly the remnant of another high elite residence.

Pairs of long buildings (30 to 80 m in length) are repeated four times around the three main plazas. These largely uninvestigated pairs may be office, warehouse, or ritual buildings. One long building is associated with an axially placed stela, and three of the buildings could be oriented on temple pyramids across the plazas. These structures may be ancillary to the central government or religion, or even another layer of government (perhaps the headquarters for quadripartite divisions of the site, a potential arrangement of the community as described below).

Flanking the southern acropolis are five basal platform groups of notable height and size, exhibiting varied layouts, including masonry buildings, some of them vaulted. These groups might represent the in-town houses of many powerful clans or high officials attached to the ruler's court. Their disparate designs suggest many different functions in support of the palace establishment. Alternatively, they might have been embassies from many other polities. Courtyard group 69 is known to contain a reception room with a throne bench (of the same design as thrones in the acropolis palace), another group has a late Yukatekan-style pillared shrine building facing onto a galleried court (not a Chichén Itzá–style gallery patio). All have patios (200 to 500 m²) screened from the public; excavations in four yielded only Late/Terminal Classic materials (Hammond et al. 1996, 1998).

Other basal platforms of lesser magnificence are more widely scattered around the plaza groups of La Milpa Centre, and single- and double-courtyard groups are found here and there throughout the community. Additionally, numerous ordinary residential units (some with masonry buildings) and two extraordinary groups extend along the main hill. The house groups close about the center appear to be finer than the average farmer's house, as monitored by the

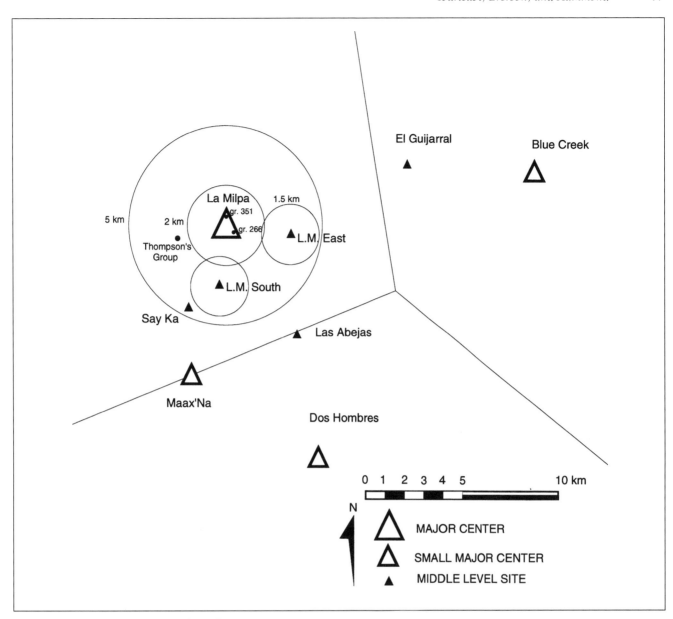

9.2 Hierarchy, space, and territory around La Milpa. Illustration by Francisco Estrada Belli

height of the ruins, the amount of plaster and obsidian in the test pits, and the better preservation of identifiable slipped pottery. Occupation density here is identical to the site average (an estimated 736 persons per km² but is greater when adjusted for an excess of uninhabitabe steep or public terrain).

Elements of site organization—plaza groups, acropoleis, and grand basal platforms—occur together on the main high ridge at La Milpa and were arguably involved in top-level and external affairs. Along with many ordinary house groups (the lower-level sites), these elements cover about 1.5 km² at an estimated population density of 736 persons per km², or about 1100 people total. This number represents about 2% of the estimated total population of La Milpa at its peak around AD 800.

Off the main hill, we have hints of two possible concentric rings of administrative loci.[2] As background to understanding the hierarchical and geographic position of the middle-level sites inside La Milpa, let us review the hints of administrative units possibly forming an outer ring outside La Milpa. Between 7 to 8 km out from La Milpa, beyond what we think is the residential (suburban) area, 5 km in radius and subject to La Milpa, lie three medium-size sites, each with one or two plazas and a temple (figure 9.2). These are, first, Ma'ax Na (RB-49), sited on a high ridge 7 km south across a bajo from La Milpa Centre (Shaw and King 1997; Shaw, King, and Moses 1999). Ma'ax Na has a plaza with a ballcourt and unlooted vaulted range structures, a set of elite compounds, a sacbe, and at least one temple pyramid and two stelae. Still under investigation, it is potentially a major center rather than a middle-level site. Yet it is far too close to La Milpa to be an independent capital, unless its apogee corresponds to a different time period, such as the seventh century (Tepeu I). The second site is Las Abejas (RB-5), about 6.9 km southeast of La Milpa (Sullivan 1997). Las Abejas has two informal Late Classic plazas in a valley, with a single small temple or feasting house. The third site in this putative ring is El Guijarral (RB-18), some 8 km to the northeast (studied by Paul Hughbanks of Tulane University). It is an agricultural settlement on the shoulder of a high ridge visible from La Milpa Centre. One assemblage consists of a small plaza group with a pyramid and range structures located alongside a bajo.

These three sites fall at a distance equivalent to halfway between La Milpa and its next largest neighboring centers, which are Blue Creek 15 km to the northeast and Dos Hombres 12 km to the southeast at a lower elevation across the Rio Bravo (Houk 1996; Jon Hageman of Southern Illinois is investigating a complete transect between the two major sites of La Milpa and Dos Hombres). Thus, with the three sites of Ma'ax Na, Las Abejas, and El Guijarral, we have about one-third of a potential ring of middle-level sites some 7.5 km out from La Milpa Centre. Their location outside La Milpa's 5-km radius, but well short of the neighboring major centers, suggests potential independence and some degree of local autonomy. Las Abejas lies just over halfway from La Milpa to Dos Hombres farther to the southeast, and El Guijarral is just over half way to Blue Creek. If this relationship also holds for Ma'ax Na, then the pattern predicts that a still unknown major site should be found in the trackless area southwest about 6 km beyond Ma'ax Na (that is, halfway from La Milpa to Kinal in Guatemala) and perhaps also 12 km west from Dos Hombres. If the pattern is correctly reconstructed, then the middle-level sites in this ring may have served as intermediaries between neighboring major centers, perhaps located on the provincial frontiers between potentially competing polities (there is currently no indication that these three middle-level sites are more, or less, fortified than any other centers in the area; all are relatively open).

A cautionary note should be entered here: what looks like three sites on a curved path inferred to be circular might instead be the fortuitous by-product of the particular spacing of the three major centers. No major sites are known west or north of La Milpa in Belize, perhaps because of the large bajos (including Bajo Santa Fe and Dumb-bell Bajo) and the broad valley of the Rio Azul (Blue Creek) lying in those quadrants. Three middling sites are now reported to exist in that direction: Bedrock, Gray Fox, and X'noha (Guderjan 1997), all of them probably more than 7 km from La Milpa.

What about middle-level centers closer to La Milpa? Within its residential radius of 5 km, we have had, until recently, only two hints of a secondary level of administrative centers. In 1994 Hugh Robichaux located a single-temple group he named Thompson's Group, in honor of the late Sir Eric Thompson, the original recorder of La Milpa in 1938 (Hammond 1991; Robichaux 1995a). Thompson's Group is located 2.8 km west by southwest of La Milpa Centre. This group is very similar in layout, components, and scale to other elaborated house groups found on hills or adjacent to good farmland throughout the environs of La Milpa. These comparable groups also have a small pyramid mound, 2 to 5 m tall, on the court, usually on the east side, as is the case in Thompson's Group (and also Las Abejas and El Guijarral).

A more likely candidate for a secondary minor center within La Milpa is the lost site of Say Ka. In 1991, Tom Guderjan reported a hilltop site with large buildings up to 12 m high, one or two temple pyramids on a 1250 m² plaza, and a reservoir still retaining water (Guderjan et al. 1991:73). Say Ka was reputedly located 4 km southwest of La Milpa, but all subsequent efforts to relocate it have failed. Most recently, we explored the tall hill under its alleged UTM coordinates, 2.5 km southwest of La Milpa Centre, and found nothing notable. Based on new information (generously provided by T.H. Guderjan in March, 1998), we now think Say Ka is instead somewhere east (probably southeast) of La Milpa Centre, perhaps on one of the 160+ m high hills shown on regional maps. Say Ka is a prime candidate for a secondary administrative center subject to La Milpa. It appears to be contemporary with both Early and Late Classic La Milpa. It falls well within the 5 km residential radius for La Milpa, and it might be located at about half the distance to Las Abejas. To the glimmer of a system of minor centers hinted at by the existence of Thompson's Group and elusive Say Ka, our recent discoveries of La Milpa East and La Milpa South add fixed data points and new perspectives.

La Milpa East: A Minor Center

La Milpa East is a full-fledged minor plaza center located 3.5 km east of La Milpa Centre, within our eastern survey transect (figure 9.3). Continuous residential occupation between the two shows only a single break, at 2.2 km from the Centre. La Milpa East is located on the leveled summit of a steep rock-girt hill, an imposing promontory with natural stair-step rock terracing along much of it. La Milpa East includes (table 9.1) a large square plaza that is the third largest public space at La Milpa, eclipsing in size plaza C within La Milpa Centre. The large plaza of this minor center would do credit to many famous Maya sites elsewhere in the low-

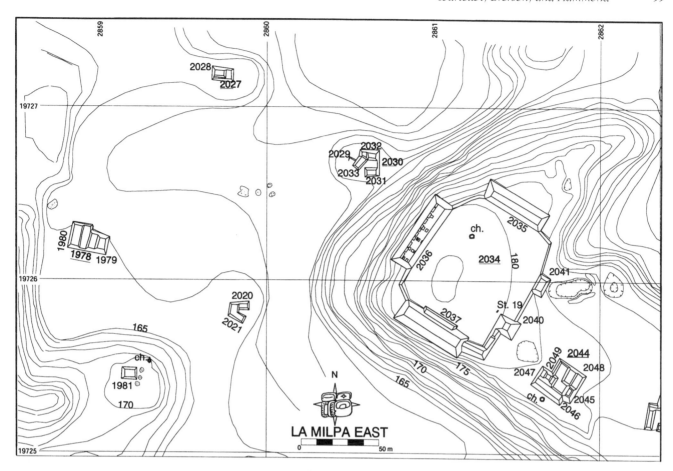

9.3 Plan of La Milpa East and environs. Map by Gair Tourtellot; GIS by Francisco Estrada Belli

lands, but its size is typical of the exaggerated plazas of northwestern Belize, as documented by Houk (1996). The plaza at La Milpa East appears to be leveled with rock fill behind the terrace edges that connect the five structures around the plaza (figure 9.3). Most unusually, its four corners, rather than its four sides, are more closely oriented to the cardinal, than to the intercardinal, points of the compass.

Three sides of the plaza are defined by collapsed multiroom range structures, now 3.5 m high by some 35 m long (structures 2035 to 2037), abutting the plaza from low terraced plinths. Similarities in size, height, plan, siting, and alignment among the range structures suggest that all three were built contemporaneously and pursuant to a unified plan. It is likely all three served the same purpose, but their size, formality, redundancy, and great separation suggest the purpose was not domestic. Instead, it is tempting to see them as presentation or feasting halls dedicated to a more public use commensurate with the size and prominent location of the group.

Two structures are found along the fourth (southeastern) side of the plaza. The irregular positions of these two structures may indicate that they are the earliest compo-

Table 9.1 Basic data on some middle-level groups at La Milpa

Group	Distance	Plaza (M2)	Hgt	Axis	Main str.	Stelae
East	3.5	5000	5	300	5	1
South	3.5	1500	3	270	4	?
266	0.6	2000	3	285	6	0
351	0.2	1050	2	245	5	0

*Distance = km from pyramid 1 in La Milpa Centre
Hgt = pyramid height; Axis = pyramid axis (in °);
Main str. = # of main structures

nents present. The northern building, structure 2041 at the easternmost point of the plaza, is the smallest structure. It appears to have been a simple rectangular platform, now gutted by a looter's hole exposing not only a crude rubble fill but also the opening to an older *chultun* (underground chamber) below the center of the platform. We speculate that this rubble platform, close to the eastern corner of the plaza, sealed and commemorated the contents of this buried chultun, whether it was equivalent to a sacred cave, a source of precious water, or the final resting place of someone special. At least one other chultun lies in the open plaza, its intact lid displaced alongside. A plaza is a strange place for a storage chultun (two also occur near range structures on

*9.4 Section of La Milpa East
Plaza through stela 19, Op. G22.*
Drawing by Jan Morrison

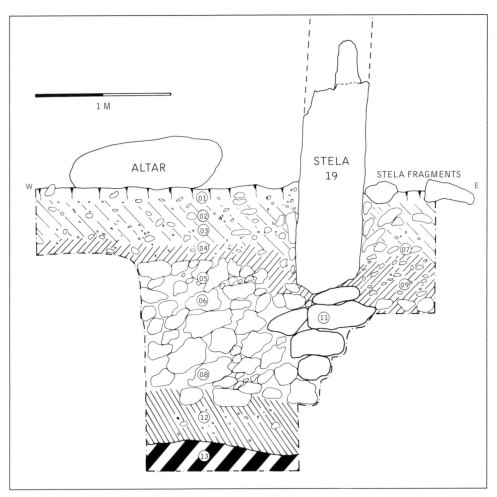

9.4 Section of La Milpa East Plaza through stela 19, Op. G22.
Drawing by Jan Morrison

plaza A at La Milpa Centre); perhaps they were involved in rituals or feasting (see Dahlin and Litzinger's hypothesis [1986] that chultuns were used to prepare fermented beverages).

The other building on the southeast side of the plaza is structure 2040, the sole temple pyramid at La Milpa East. A collapsed looter's trench defaces the higher rear side and reveals rubble fill without clear walls or floor levels, or a looted tomb. This pyramid, which lies well off-axis in the group, is the only principal structure that intrudes onto the plaza. The pyramid has a low side platform to the south that projects toward a similar side platform, or collapsed building, projecting from the southwest range structure 2037. These projections close the south corner of the plaza, the only corner that is not wholly open. A looter's tunnel through one of these side extensions exposes three floors representing at least two refurbishments.

Gloria Everson discovered stela 19 and its altar, placed off one corner of the small pyramid. Both are plain, but the presence of a stela of any sort does rather take La Milpa East out of the middle-level ordinary group category and places it firmly in the minor ceremonial center category (Bullard 1960). Excavation showed that both monuments

are in their original settings (figure 9.4). The stela is socketed in clean jagged rubble and chocked with unusual tabular pieces of finely laminated limestone. The meter of loose rubble fill that levels the plaza under the stela is a unitary deposit overlying the original soil horizon on bedrock.

Ceramics from several test pits clearly dated the patently single period of plaza construction for La Milpa East as Late/Terminal Classic (provided by Laura Kosakowsky in March, 1998). All ceramics excavated just beneath and around the altar and stela are censer pieces. The censers, with their hourglass forms, rather vertical walls, pierced windows, and appliqued ridges, are very late Tepeu II/III. The old soil horizon below the plaza fill, exposed in Op. 22 (figure 9.4), also contains only Late/Terminal Classic pottery, but of the usual non-censer forms. Ceramics from other excavations at La Milpa East and in nearby house units show the usual predominance of Late to Terminal Classic types. The only earlier pottery at La Milpa East is Early Classic Z-angle bowl sherds mixed in Late Classic contexts on high bedrock under the west side of the plaza. Thus there is no identified locus of occupation before the Late Classic, although subsequent excavation in group 1978 in the valley west of La

Milpa East (figure 9.3) revealed that the basal platform below structure 1979 appears to be Early Classic in construction. As one of the very rare pre-eighth century construction contexts found outside La Milpa Centre, this basal platform suggests a settlement locus that might have attracted later settlement to this spot, or it may merely signify especially good soils or moisture obvious to any farmer.

The Late/Terminal Classic date for La Milpa East is important because it is consistent with the evidence that earlier periods of occupation at La Milpa, going back to the Late Preclassic, were tightly restricted to the area immediately surrounding the present La Milpa Centre (Tourtellot, Hammond, and Rose, N.D.). The needs La Milpa East served late in the Classic period probably did not exist earlier. The late date, and apparently single episode of construction, are also consistent with our developing appreciation that the Late/Terminal Classic occupation at La Milpa was massive, extensive, rapid, and perhaps short. Suburban La Milpa lacked Tepeu I ceramics, middens were often thin, burials were shallow, and construction was generally unitary with few rebuildings and little replastering.

The peculiar orientation of the La Milpa East group, 30° off the cardinal points, may relate to the geographical and astronomical position of La Milpa East and also to its field of view or viewshed. La Milpa East is located 3.5 km directly (magnetic) east of the central plaza at La Milpa Centre (figure 9.1): One possibility is that the exact site for La Milpa East was chosen because it lay due east of the largest pyramids in La Milpa Centre, on the highest point where it could serve as an eastern horizon marker or sunrise shrine, the seat of a lord of the eastern sector of the city.

Topographic surveys along the east transect and in two sample survey blocks just to the north, where hill summits top out at 170 m (figure 9.1), suggest that one could look from the pyramids on plaza A in La Milpa Centre, at over 200 m altitude above sea level, directly across to La Milpa East, at over 181 m altitude. One hill immediately east of the central pyramids crests at 197 m, just below the line of sight. Maintaining a free sightline to La Milpa East may explain why nothing was ever built on this summit despite its attractive location.[3] We must assume that the contemporary forest was nearly clear-cut on the densely occupied hilly terrain between La Milpa Centre and La Milpa East—as it may well have been during intense landscape engineering at the peak of occupation about AD 800. To obtain a view of the plaza A pyramids from the La Milpa East plaza, it was necessary to leave open the western side of the La Milpa East plaza. A simple rotation of 30° accomplished this, while still providing for structures on all sides. Viewshed analysis of the intervening topography by Francisco Estrada Belli (Boston University) confirms that the corner of temple 2040,

where stela 19 stands, is just visible from pyramid 1 on plaza A, whose top is the highest, potentially most visible, point in all of La Milpa. If stela 19 had been placed axially on pyramid 2040, it would have been screened from view by range structure 2037. The shape and size of the hilltop forced no particular configuration on the builders.

What sort of place, then, was La Milpa East? Current evidence suggests that, minimally, it was a locus of temple and stela-altar ritual. Its position on the horizon due east of La Milpa Centre emphasizes its sacred potential, being positioned under the rising sun. The large size and openness of the plaza implies it was not a domestic unit. If the large size of the La Milpa East plaza is an indication, then events here could have accommodated mass audiences of up to about 5000 people. The range structures are likely logistical support structures; they are too similar to be the result of accretion during the growth of a family group. Each structure appears to consist of a single row of rooms, and there is no surface evidence of the simple domestic ancillary structures beside or behind them, as would be expected if they were domestic. Nor is there a palatial group (closed-corner courtyard) either linked or in the vicinity. Nevertheless, it is possible that the range structures on the plaza were maintained not only as depots for ritual equipment or tribute, but as temporary living quarters for visiting dignitaries and their entourages, people who traveled here to use the permanent ritual facilities on the east side of the plaza. Eastern platform 2041 and temple pyramid 2040 may be places of important burials or other special deposits whose significance was celebrated with commemorative rituals. The looters certainly thought so, but whether they proved it in the buried chultun under structure 2041 or the deep tunnel into structure 2040 remains unknown. The presence of a stela and altar certainly marks the sacred use of this space, and it suggests the very direct interest of La Milpa's rulers, for monuments were a highly restricted class of politically significant items. Possibly, La Milpa East was part of a politico-religious circuit used in boundary maintenance for the central La Milpa polity. While La Milpa East lies close to the edge of denser settlement at La Milpa, it is still 1.5 km from the beginning of the rural intersite area.

La Milpa East does not appear to have been involved in water management or control, as Scarborough and his associates (Scarborough et al. 1995) have proposed in explaining the growth and power of La Milpa Centre. Control of water storage in a riverless upland, with an annual season of drought, would be a powerful coercive tool for any administrator (Lucero 1999; see also chapter 3). We have seen no evidence that the large plaza surface served as a collection area for an associated reservoir or distributor. Given the large size of plastered plazas in northwestern Belize—

9.5 Plan of La Milpa South. Map by Marc Wolf; GIS by Francisco Estrada Belli

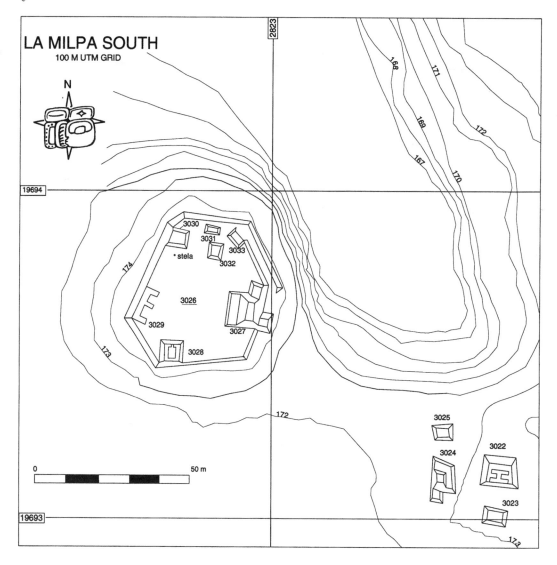

9.5 Plan of La Milpa South. Map by Marc Wolf; GIS by Francisco Estrada Belli

possibly serving as rainfall catchments where permanent water sources are very rare—the lack of evidence for water storage here is perhaps surprising. The edges of the plaza surface lack parapets, except at the south end, and surface flow would be out the eastern corner of the plaza, bypassing two quarry holes perhaps convertible into water tanks, with no hint of a channel or other reservoir. A shallow quarry basin behind the little temple pyramid shows no means of ingress and lies off the one closed corner of the plaza. We are not even sure the plaza had been plastered; there was no plaster in our two test pits, and bedrock outcrops poke through the surface in several spots. We did find a chultun in the plaza, but the intact lid beside it is a solid stone disk, as used for a dry storage pit, instead of the perforated disks familiar from indubitable water cisterns in, for example, the Puuc region of Yucatán. An absence of water storage here suggests that occupation was either nondomestic or of a transient nature. Unfortunately, the

same could be said for most houses around La Milpa, which also lack a visible means of water storage.

Northwest of La Milpa East, north of group 2030 (figure 9.3), is a patch of low ground that may flood during the wet season, forming a small bajo, while another wet area lies at the foot of the cliff on the eastern side of the La Milpa East hill. Although these are potential reservoirs draining broad valleys, we saw no attempts at artificial improvement during our mapping. The nearest known bodies of standing water to La Milpa East are two *aguadas* (perennial ponds) at least 1 km away, well outside our survey transect. We do not think it likely that there is a large bajo any closer. Water control, as expressed in special facilities or physical proximity, is not yet in evidence at La Milpa East.

Although the La Milpa East hilltop is naturally defensible, owing to its many steeply terraced sides, we do not see evidence of making it so. Three of the plaza corners are open, and natural ramps give access onto the hilltop itself on the northeast and southeast. Buildings are not crowded onto the hill as for a refuge, nor are earthworks (walls or ditches) in evidence. Numerous property walls occur only on neighboring hills to the west. La Milpa East appears to lack evidence for coercive mechanisms, such as exclusive reservoirs or artificial fortifications.

The La Milpa East hilltop is also the site of quarries and a small residential area east of the plaza. Two of the four widely spaced house groups on the hill include at least low masonry buildings erected around small patios. These two groups are also the highest and closest to the plaza (figure 9.3). Perhaps significantly, the closest house unit, group 2044, shares the same unusual 30° orientation as the plaza group (as the three more distant domestic groups on the hill do not). Judging from its compact size, yet tall mounds (probably collapsed masonry buildings) and courtyard screen, we speculate that group 2044 might have been the house of a resident caretaker or ritual specialist attached to the plaza group; the house seems too modest to be the home or independent power base of a lord. Although it includes the tallest ordinary house structure on the hill, this building is dwarfed by buildings in larger house groups on adjacent hills.

Five excavations in house units in the vicinity of La Milpa East have not yet been analyzed to establish the possible effects of La Milpa East on local lifestyles. We will look for peak values in masonry, plaster, architectural styles, obsidian, stone-tool-to-debitage ratio, burials, and pottery that may enable us to judge just how "disembedded," or not involved in local affairs, La Milpa East really was, since we do not recognize a clear residential component. At present, La Milpa East does not appear to have been the seat of a resident leader, for example, the head of a local conical clan. The three range structures on the plaza are nearly identical, none of which is singled out as the residence. Several large residential patio groups and a single courtyard group are found within 400 m but off the hill. The single courtyard group is surrounded by its own property walls, a rare occurrence (see walls southwest of La Milpa East; figure 9.1). Dozens of ordinary patio groups are in the vicinity, along with an unusual concentration of chultuns. If La Milpa East really is the seat of local power, despite appearances, then the power holders may be so embedded in their social, residential, and agricultural matrix, somewhere nearby, that they are invisible to us. Such a degree of invisibility could be caused either by frequent rotation of different people through temporary roles enacted on the plaza (for an ethnographic analogy, see Vogt 1983b), thus spreading status markers widely, or such severe extraction of local tribute by paramounts at La Milpa Centre that local people literally could not construct personal material representations of their nominal power.

La Milpa South

Late in the 1998 season, we found another middle-level site, group 3026, near the end of the south transect (figure 9.5). Gratifyingly, it is located 3.2 km from La Milpa Centre, as was predicted from the distance to La Milpa East alone.

Basal platform 3026 is the largest single artificial construction surface mapped along the south transect (table 9.1). An apparent ramp access is visible on one side (an unusual feature for the southern lowlands, although occasionally seen in the northern lowlands). Unlike La Milpa East, all structures intrude onto the plaza surface. Structure 3027, on the east side of the plaza, is the tallest and likely conceals a small pyramid or vaulted masonry building. To its south is a large shapeless platform. On the west is a long structure composed of two rooms. On the north side of the plaza is a collection of four small mounds of uncertain conformation (they are too broad to be wall stubs for a single building); a possible stela stone protrudes from the earth on the south side of the larger west mound.

What we know of its environs suggests that La Milpa South is situated near ordinary house groups and removed from nearby agricultural or drainage works such as terraces and berms. One of the larger of these house groups is located a short distance to the southeast (figure 9.5). Group 3022 is a middle-size domestic unit with two masonry buildings suitable for a caretaker's residence, but we know little of what lies undiscovered in the other directions from La Milpa South, for the 200-m–wide south transect passing here crosses only a small portion of a long ridge. La Milpa South's hilltop location and site plan do not suggest that it was fortified, although it is possible that the hill falls toward a large bajo over a kilometer to the west. No permanent source of water, in which its residents might have had a management role, is yet known nearby.

The knoll on which La Milpa South rests is an unimpressive gentle knob on the ridge, but it is one of the highest spots along the south transect. Viewshed analysis by Francisco Estrada Belli suggests that this plaza, too, was visible from atop pyramid 1 on plaza A in La Milpa Centre, in this case exactly 3.5 km away, as was La Milpa East. He finds that a nearly perfect 90° angle is formed by the sightlines from La Milpa West and La Milpa East, as they converge on pyramid 1 at the northeast corner of La Milpa Centre (figure 9.1). Again, this conclusion requires that the forest be cleared.

La Milpa South is significantly smaller than La Milpa East in any dimension of comparison. The sizes of its structures are typically those of domestic groups, but the spaces between them are large. While gratifying that La Milpa South was located close to the predicted 3.5 km distance from the center, its identification may be fortuitous and somewhat self-fulfilling. It certainly is not a copy of La Milpa East and equally is not an ordinary house group due to the large size of the plaza, the arrangement of the widely spaced structures, the presence of a probable eastern temple, and the possible stela. At least, it is an unusual plazuela-type group that bears an intriguing resemblance to La Milpa East and to the two central groups discussed next. All four of these groups can be classified as exhibiting Plaza Plan 2 layouts, recognized as a pyramid sited on the east side of a plaza defined by several long structures (Becker 1971).

Other Candidates

Two other groups, 266 and 351, located in a very different context, share many of the features of La Milpa East and South. They are found on the main hill just outside La Milpa Centre (just visible in figure 9.1 as hollow squares to the east and north of the inner rectangle marking La Milpa Centre). They cannot be part of the same putative 3.5-km–radius ring as La Milpa East and South but might signify that the same local and secondary organizing principle was actually carried out "right under" the major elite center, displacing La Milpa Centre from having to oversee its local people.

Group 266 lies on a ridge 250 m east of the southern plazas. Unique among the middle-level sites discussed here, it does not crown its local hill but lies some 9 m below an ordinary house group and a solitary 5-m–tall pyramid. Unexcavated group 266 is second in size only to La Milpa East among the middle-level groups considered here (table 9.1). The tall mound on the east was looted and yielded only a plain vessel from a sacked burial. A long building on the west has six rooms and a largely perishable superstructure. One chultun penetrates the plaza surface.

The approach to this group is easy on all but the eastern side. While there are ravines nearby, there is no permanent source of water and not much space for gardening. Group 266 would have had clear views of the south group and the pyramids on the Great Plaza if foliage were removed.

Platform group 351 is located off the northeast corner of plaza A in La Milpa Centre. Its elements are familiar: the small (looted) structure 53 pyramid on the east, a long building facing it on the west, and two or three structures on the north and south sides of a generous central space that barely qualify it for the plaza category, but it is certainly far larger than commoner house patios in the 200 to 700 m² range.

A distinguishing characteristic of group 351 is that it is situated at 199 m, the highest natural elevation known at La Milpa and 7 m higher than the nearby Great Plaza. Like group 266, it is right on an escarpment. The knoll beneath group 351 is only large enough for this group, which probably accounts for the placement of the main plazas on flatter and broader, albeit slightly lower, ground to the south.

Neither of these groups is associated with property or agricultural features, such as the terraces, stony berms, property walls, or rock piles associated with groups a few hundred meters below the main hill. Nor are there linear features close around any of the other middle-level candidates discussed.

A caveat is that groups 266 and 351 are only 700 m apart on the main La Milpa hill, rather than the much longer distances that separate the other middle-level groups. Speculatively, their proximity has to do with uniquely rugged canyon terrain between them. Another possibility is that they are not centrally located in their territories (as supposed for the 3.5 km ring of groups) because of the powerfully distorting attraction of the hilltop plazas that drew them to one side of territories extending well off the hill to the northeast for group 351 and to the southeast for group 266.

On the other hand, if these two groups really are centrally located inside their territories (as well as properly identified), we can construct an intriguing alternative that their territories extended "under" the main plazas and out to the west (where the closest known competition is Thompson's Group nearly 3 km distant).

The proximity of groups 266 and 351 to La Milpa Centre thus raises some provocative questions about how local territory was managed. Conceivably, the royal and elite residents of La Milpa Centre (residing in the acropoleis and nearby elite groups) were not directly involved in working the land around them, but only in community-wide and foreign affairs. It is certainly the case, both here and across the Maya lowlands, that palaces do not sit atop the extra-broad parcels of "empty" terrain that would be required to grow food for their many people. If the top elites were "floating" on the land (as well as skimming off its produce), then local administration was delegated to middle-level "islands" that dotted the seas of household gardeners.

With the suggested addition of groups 266 and 351 near La Milpa Centre, and Say Ka perhaps close by, the previously proposed inner ring of middle-level centers at 3.5 km is evolving toward a network of sites, as intimated by Bullard (1960, 1962) and Hammond (1975). The actual situation was probably more complicated still, because of the existence of other types of middle-level sites not discussed here, such as the six smaller but elegant double courtyard groups, the dozens of single courtyards, or the smaller patio groups with tall eastern mounds (which happen to be particularly common halfway between La Milpa Centre and La Milpa East).

In sum, the four middle-level La Milpa groups of La Milpa East and South, and groups 266 and 351 are intermediate in size between the largest plaza groups at La Milpa and large ordinary domestic groups. More significantly, they share fundamentally similar plans that distinguish them collectively and individually from all other suburban groups. All are sited on hilltops (usually the highest point in their vicinity) at a long distance from one another. They are erected on a basal platform terrace that supports an open-cornered and generous central space (versus the many tight house groups). Each exhibits structures on all four sides of the central space, multiple structures on one or two sides of this space, the chief pyramidal mound placed to the east, and a long structure with multiple rooms to the west. None seems to have a central shrine or altar, but two may have plain stelae. Thus, they have some of the elements and scale of the major plazas but share less with house groups. Of course, these are superficial characteristics only; none of the groups has been extensively excavated. While their basal platforms might conceal earlier materials, as at La Milpa East, we have no reason to suspect that any of these middle-level groups acquired their special function and layout before the Late/Terminal Classic period.

Completing the Ring

Having indicated why the arrangement of large middle-level sites may be rather more complex than a ring, let us return to the simpler question of the 3.5 km La Milpa ring on the west and north (figure 9.2). Thompson's Group, which appears to be an elaborate house group with an eastern shrine mound, is located only 2.8 km westward of La Milpa Centre. It is located on sloping high ground below 180 m, but viewshed analysis suggests its eastern shrine may have had a clear view of La Milpa Centre. It is on a slope among neighboring house groups rather than standing in splendid isolation and has a cramped patio only some 400 m² in area within the domestic range. We should classify it as a very minor center or Plaza Plan 2 (Becker 1971). The potential availability of a better site, as yet unexplored, 3.3 km west of La Milpa Centre and across the Far West Bajo, is another reason for currently disallowing Thompson's Group as the western participant in the putative 3.5 km ring.

In his discussion of Thompson's Group, Robichaux (1995b) claims that it and Say Ka were situated so as to oversee extensive tracts of bajo lying within a kilometer of each. Acknowledging that La Milpa Centre is not positioned next to a (major) bajo but is located centrally some 3 km distant from five such depressions, he suggests that "minor centers are the specific loci of oversight and management activities for intensive agriculture production efforts in the bajo zones" (Robichaux 1995b:22). This oversight would be un-

der the major center, another reasonable explanation of the function served by people using these middle-level groups. The problem is not that the location of Say Ka is currently unknown and its association with a bajo unproven; rather, the claim that a middle-level site within a kilometer of a bajo was therefore involved in managing the bajo, is dubious. Any part of the La Milpa community is likely to lie within a kilometer or so of some bajo terrain (or, equally, of a seasonal stream, an *aguada* (reservoir), a tall hill, chert outcropping, or a zone of earthworks). La Milpa South is centered between fingers of a bajo 500 m to the north and south, and within a kilometer or two of the vast Thompson Creek Bajo between La Milpa and Ma'ax Na. La Milpa East overlooks two little bajos.

Furthermore, we cannot accept a more specific argument for central control of Thompson's Group out of La Milpa Centre based on Scarborough's proposal that the Far West Bajo was flooded from a reservoir next to Great Plaza A by means of an irrigation canal and a 3-km–long gorge (Robichaux 1995a:210, 295–298; Scarborough et al. 1992; Scarborough et al. 1995) until this relationship is proved feasible. Nor would we accept the related notion that La Milpa Centre physically controlled all its people in a seasonally parched landscape, because it alone had artificial reservoirs. Even if La Milpa Centre had three reservoirs and little pools behind a dozen checkdams in its adjacent ravines, we doubt that enough water could be stored to meet the needs of the some fifty thousand people estimated to be present by the Late/Terminal Classic period (although it might have done so for the small concentrated population at its founding in the Late Preclassic). Although difficult to prove, we suspect that every household looked out for its own water provision and stored it in quarry holes, chultuns, casks, rubberized bags, or pottery jars. We have not yet identified a water-management role for the residents of middle-level sites. To the contrary, we have noticed that suburban aguadas are not directly associated even with large domestic groups.

To complete a ring of middle-level sites at 3.5 km, what about a site north from La Milpa? Coincidentally, the next patches of high ground (more than 160 m) around the vicinity of Thompson's Group in the west do not occur until 2 and 3.5 km due north of La Milpa Centre. The 2 km distance is on the hill sampled by survey block 15 (with its high density of stony berms; see figure 9.1), while the hillock at 3.5 km is north of that along the west flank of the large Dumb-bell Bajo. Elsewhere within the circumference of La Milpa, most other high spots lie south of La Milpa Centre, where the land gradually rises toward the distant crest of the La Lucha Escarpment above 200 m. Plots of high land appear to us to have been suitable for constructing at least six well-spaced minor centers, thus completing a ring of such locales situated approximately 3.5 km out from La Milpa.

Conclusion

Middle-level centers are recognized by a congeries of familiar elite components writ small (Hammond 1975). At least the upper ranks of middle-level centers, like minor centers, include some combination of prominent location, large open spaces (plazas rather than patios or courts), temple pyramids, range structures, and monuments. Ballcourts appear at the transition from middle-level to major sites, as may be the case with Ma'ax Na south of La Milpa. So far, only major sites in northwestern Belize possess causeways, that is, at least two separate architectural assemblages requiring such formal links.

The community of La Milpa exhibits material traces of numerous potential levels of sociopolitical expression, control, or organization, only the highest of which we discuss here. At La Milpa we discovered several plaza groups outside La Milpa Centre. La Milpa East is complementary and secondary to La Milpa Centre, having been built too late to constitute an abortive earlier developmental alternative. Current evidence does not support the conclusion that La Milpa East was anything more than a periodically used ceremonial precinct.

We suggest that middle-level centers together may trace potentially coherent or regular geopolitical or georeligious patterns on the physical and conceptual landscape (figure 9.2). La Milpa East and South may be parts of a ring of middle-level centers encircling La Milpa Centre at a radius of some 3 to 4 km, each commanding a radius of approximately 1.5 km (approximately 7 km²), a radius derived from the approximate distance by which they fall short of the La Milpa community border. Analysis by Gloria Everson of the frequency distributions of mounds and artifact ratios along the east transect suggests that the actual border occurs 2.2 km from La Milpa Centre and 1.3 km from La Milpa East, although this point corresponds to no natural break in settlement. Towards La Milpa South, this distance falls in a broad finger of bajo. To the extent they were involved in local social and resource management, such outlying minor sites imply that direct control over land or intervention in the affairs of people stemming from the major center extended only over a radius of some 2.2 km, or 15.2 km². Beyond this radius, supplemental secondary (or middle-level) administrative centers located some 3.5 km out, with an area of 5.3 km², were found useful or necessary to interact with the densely dispersed population. Together, the major and minor centers would oversee the total La Milpa suburban community (some 50,000 people).

Heuristically converting these areal figures into population estimates for the major and minor centers, La Milpa Centre directed some 12,000 people (at 791 people per km², projected from the central quad and near east transect). Each satellite, like La Milpa East or South, would have drawn upon the reproductive and labor powers of more than 3,000 people (at 572 people per km² within the range of La Milpa East on the east transect). Note that the large size of the La Milpa East plaza could have simultaneously accommodated all of the local population within 1.3 km, or nearly all, totaling 2,600, if they were seated.[4] This size audience, if realized, greatly exceeds the number of people in basic social units such as families or lineages. If the satellite centers represent any single type of sociopolitical unit, then it was far larger, perhaps a super-clan, and commensurate with a territorial scope of many square kilometers, a virtual mini-province.

If each minor center had a radius of control of 1.3 km, then there is room for eight of them in a circle 3.5 km from La Milpa Centre. At present, we have only two outlying plaza groups with known locations, one directly east and the other directly south of La Milpa Centre. We have mapped only about 6% of the whole city, Say Ka is not yet pinned down, and Thompson's Group appears to belong instead to a class of smaller middle-level Plaza Plan 2 groups scattered throughout the community.

If celestial orientation toward the cardinal points was the operative cause for the location of middle-level plaza groups, rather than the demographic service areas we have been considering, we would expect a total of four (not eight) middle-level plaza groups, one in each of the cardinal directions. The axes from pyramid 1 to La Milpa East and La Milpa South happen to be precisely 90° apart, and almost exactly oriented to the true (rather than magnetic) cardinal points. The larger size of La Milpa East relative to La Milpa South would materialize the prime importance of the eastern axis. If cardinally placed minor centers are the only consideration, then it seems more likely they are creatures of the central administration, or more purely ritual foci, because they seem too small in comparison to La Milpa Centre to have efficiently administered the number of people living in the outer belt between them.

A cardinal arrangement would also suggest a quadripartition of the community, resulting in four much larger "territories" up to 19.5 km² apiece, with some 13,500 persons in each. Any scheme of quadripartition reminds us of the four pairs of range-type structures defining the three main plazas of La Milpa Centre. It is pure speculation that the large middle-level sites, whether cardinal or simply circular in arrangement, served as terminals for activities connected directly to many long structures in the main center (for example, as tribute collection versus central storage points, or as ritual versus regalia-storage points); there are no causeways like those of Cobá or Caracol to improve this likelihood.

It is difficult to believe the ancient Milperos could pick their spots and design a city so precisely. If the forest were already cleared at the height of the Late Classic when these centers appear to have been built, then direct views from pyramid 1 were possible in order to project lines along certain directions over great distances. In a bowl-shaped landscape filled with dozens of karstic hills of every shape and height, rising to the horizon some 10 km distant and still visible today over the forest from atop pyramid 1, perhaps it was easier to spot just the right hilltops that happened to be there to fulfill a cosmic layout reflecting their quincuncial vision of the world.

This study of middle-level sites around La Milpa has raised provocative ideas about the internal spatial organization of major communities, and the areas and means of effective influence exerted by different-size centers nested within a single community. The alleged patterns or cosmograms on which these interpretations are based will be fairly easy to test with new explorations and spatial data. We have also raised questions about systematically differing roles for centers located at varying distances from major centers rather than simple nesting, and suggested that perhaps roles depended on different geopolitical situations. We have also yet to prove that La Milpa East or the other candidates actually had an administrative or "centralizing" role rather than a merely ceremonial function. Questions of function will require much larger and longer programs of excavation before we can truly understand how intermediate levels within ancient La Milpa were organized within the diverse Maya universe.

Acknowledgments. Permission to work at La Milpa was graciously granted by the Government of Belize (through John Morris, Archaeological Commissioner, and his predecessors) and by the landowner, the Programme for Belize, which also provided logistic help through Joy Grant, Bart Romero, and Ramon Pacheco. Funding was generously provided by the National Geographic Society, Boston University, Raymond and Beverly Sackler, and an anonymous donor. We have enjoyed the assistance of numerous graduate and professional supervisors from the Old World and North America, many undergraduate apprentices, and our skilled crew of local assistants. Kerry Sagebiel (University of Arizona) and Laura Kosakowsky (Boston University) analyzed the pottery. We are gratified that such an international group would come together to contribute their diverse skills and help us complete five productive seasons. We are also grateful to our on-site colleagues Nick Dunning, Vernon Scarborough, Fred Valdez, Jr., and their knowledgeable associates for diverse help, many courtesies, and collegiality.

NOTES

1. We have not yet satisfactorily distinguished Late Classic (Tepeu II equivalent) ceramics from Terminal Classic (Tepeu III) ceramics, a continuing analytical problem for the region (Kosakowsky et al. 1997). Accordingly, what may be two phases have to be treated for now as one, approximately AD 830 ± 100, obviating studies of late community development apart from local stratigraphies.

2. Future work may show they form part of a broader network of middle-level sites reaching into the center. Here, we depend largely on the vagaries of survey coverage that is still far short of total. Our project has mapped La Milpa Centre; radial transects to the north, east, and south; and fifteen randomly scattered spot sample blocks around the community (figure 9.1), aggregating 6% of the 78 km^2 that we project was La Milpa's direct territory. Additionally, the University of Texas regional projects under R. E. W. Adams and Fred Valdez, Jr., have followed up Tom Guderjan's initial inventory of sites in northwest Belize (Guderjan 1991) and ongoing investigation to the north, and together they provide information concerning minor sites lying beyond the 5-km radius deduced for La Milpa proper (see R.E.W. Adams and Valdez 1995; Guderjan 1997; and Houk 1996). There seem to be a number of objectively different levels of architectural assemblages, based on considerations of size and the readily visible surface elements present. Our proposed pattern recognitions are tentative, however, because our surveys are incomplete, excavation is absent or spotty, and the number of examples for each level is still tiny. Initial distinctions made on the basis of these samples also may be exaggerated because of the myriad ways in which the same cosmological, religious, and iconographical elements, among others, seem to pervade all levels of Maya society.

3. Another argument for a late date for La Milpa East is it would have been visible across this hill only from the last stages of pyramids 1 and 2 on the Great Plaza.

4. That is 5000 m^2 at 1 m^2/standing person = 5000 people, or at 2 m^2/seated person = 2500 people.

10 Minor Centers, Complexity, and Scale in Lowland Maya Settlement Archaeology

Arlen F. Chase and Diane Z. Chase

Problems exist in dealing with lowland Maya settlement considerations on a regional scale. These difficulties exist at both methodological and theoretical levels. Practical considerations, such as the difficulty of surveying in heavy overgrowth or the expense of large-scale excavation, may lead to partial and potentially problematic samples. Residential groups may be sampled by test pits, but may not be intensively dug. Settlement survey may focus on specific centers, on specific parts of an outlying settlement system, or on long, narrow transects used to position samples within a broader settlement universe. Within this kind of methodology, however, the utility of Maya settlement data is often limited to questions concerning local chronology, artifact distribution, and/or population trajectories. While such data are relevant to considerations of the structure of ancient Maya society, they do not readily lend themselves directly to the creation or discussion of ancient social, economic, or political models.

In spite of the fact that settlement data are well suited to discussions of relationships within and among sites, settlement archaeology is not usually the major source of data for models that explain Maya political organization or regional integration. Instead, settlement archaeology has often been overlooked in favor of models derived from other data sets, such as those based on ethnographic, ethnohistoric, or hieroglyphic interpretation (for amplification, see A.F. Chase and D.Z. Chase 1992, 1998a). A focus, however, on Classic-period political organization, using primarily epigraphic history, easily relegates centers without or with only a few hieroglyphs—even major ones—to lesser status within any site or regional hierarchy.

In addition, single finds can dramatically change the perceived totality of the political landscape viewed through an epigraphic lens. For instance, the discovery of Caracol altar 21, recording a star-war at Tikal in AD 562 (Houston 1987, 1991), dramatically altered our perception of lowland Maya political history and, ultimately, site organization and hierarchy (A.F. Chase 1991; A.F. Chase and D.Z. Chase 1987:58–62; Schele and Freidel 1990). A new reading of a single "agency" glyph resulted in the complete epigraphic re-interpretation of Classic-era Maya political structure and alliances (Martin and Grube 1995). The discovery of a broken eighth cycle monument at Caracol (Grube 1994) changed the perceived importance of political development in northern Guatemala and southern Mexico (compare Pincemin et al. 1998). Incomplete sampling may even lead those sites with hieroglyphs to be prematurely written out of a part of Maya history in which they may have played key roles, as has been the case for Terminal Classic Caracol (see, for example, Mathews 1985:Fig. 14 in comparison to A.F. Chase, Grube, and D.Z. Chase 1991). "Minor centers," which are usually bereft of hieroglyphs, may be completely ignored within epigraphically based and conceptually simple "city-state" or "regal-ritual" models of Maya political organization (Mathews 1991; Webster 1997). Yet, it may be precisely these kinds (and level) of settlement data that allow a regional understanding of ancient Maya political, social, and economic organization, permitting a more accurate and useful definition of Classic Maya polity size and integration.

In its most basic form, *minor center* (Bullard 1960) designates small nodes of architectural concentration. Such nodes are often identified by the presence of vaulted buildings, pyramidal structures, stelae, causeways, and/or ballcourts. The term has been applied, however, to a variety of architectural forms, ranging from distinctive non-residential architecture to elaborate residential groups to clusters of housemounds. The very use of the minor-center concept implies the existence of major centers and establishes a contrastive set that suggests a superordinate and subordinate status within a settlement hierarchy. There are other considerations, however, and the overall settlement context of minor centers is important to understanding their development and function. When no major center is immediately present, such as in the Belize Valley (Garber and Leventhal N.D.), debates can rage over what the designated minor centers represent. They may be portrayed as politically independent units that formed hegemonies of small centers, as segmentary states, or as border areas variously included in larger centralized states. There also may be developmental considerations, for a minor center can become a major center over time. Yet another point is the isolation of minor centers. Because minor centers often exist at some distance from major centers, their architectural plazas may be mapped, but they may not be contextualized within broad, areal, block-mapped settlement matrices. Thus, minor centers sometimes may be given a conceptual independence that they may not always deserve, and large-scale, regional, integrative patterning may be completely missed.

Settlement data from Caracol, Belize, demonstrate that at least some minor centers are not necessarily separate entities but are instead functional, though spatially distinct, parts of major centers. These same data reveal the internal organization of a large Maya city and suggest Caracol's position within an even larger regional hierarchy. Most important from the standpoint of this chapter, the Caracol settlement data lend themselves to social and economic models that cannot be derived from the epigraphic database alone.

Settlement of Caracol, Belize

Caracol, Belize, was a "primate center," a major regional capital that monopolized its immediate region (what we refer to as the city of Caracol) and occupied the summit of an extensive settlement hierarchy that presumably controlled a spatial area greater than 12,000 km² by AD 650 (A.F. Chase and D.Z. Chase 1996a:808, 1998a:17). In the case of Caracol, its immediate region (about 7 km in radius, representing an estimated 177 km²) appears to have been subsumed into a single metropolitan city during the Late Classic period when the site's population peaked at between 115,000 and 145,000 people (A.F. Chase and D.Z. Chase 1994c:5). For this reason, the University of Central Florida Caracol Archaeological Project, of necessity, has been concerned with defining a large settlement matrix, one that could be used conjunctively with other bodies of data, such as the hieroglyphic history.

At the start of the Caracol project in 1985, Caracol's ruling dynasty had been tentatively outlined and defined by Beetz and Satterthwaite (1981) and A. Stone, Reents, and Coffman (1985). Stephen Houston (1987, 1991) and Nikolai Grube (1994 N.D.) have since further refined this history. While this epigraphic record served as a starting point for interpreting the political fortunes of Caracol (A.F. Chase 1991, 1992; A.F. Chase and D.Z. Chase 1987:58–62), it has been conjunctively utilized with extensive settlement and archaeological data to gain a much broader understanding of Caracol as a city, a polity, and an ethnic identity (A.F. Chase and D.Z. Chase 1994a, 1994c, 1996a, 1996c, 1998a; D.Z. Chase and A.F. Chase 1998).

Site population and construction history can be compared with monument erection to show increased unity following sixth- and seventh-century warfare and decreased unity following late eighth- and early ninth-century warfare (D.Z. Chase and A.F. Chase 2000). Thus, there are sometimes different archaeological manifestations for somewhat similar historic statements. In addition, the epigraphic record and settlement history sometimes show contrasting curves. For example, excavations show that Caracol was exceedingly large, prosperous, and populated during the later part of the Late Classic era (post AD 650), a time when relatively few known stone monuments were erected within the site core. While the dearth of monuments has been taken by epigraphers to reflect the site's relative unimportance at this time, the archaeological data demonstrate continued prosperity. We believe that Late Classic political organization at Caracol was not based solely on dynastic kingship and, therefore, would not necessarily be reflected in the hieroglyphic record found on stone monuments (A.F. Chase and D.Z. Chase 1996c).

In studying the settlement of Caracol, our concern has been to sample as much as possible of Caracol's settlement area and not just to map a single large square area surrounding the epicenter. As a result of settlement work, the area sampled at Caracol by means of mapped transects and causeways measures 13 km north to south by 14 km east to west. We have also attempted to survey large "blocks" of settlement throughout the core of the site and have to date block-mapped approximately 21 km² of Caracol (figure 10.1), estimated at approximately 12% of its total area. Settlement is continuous and quite dense throughout this area (especially as compared with other Maya centers such as those examined below) but is slightly more concentrated in the area immediately about the site's epicenter (see A.F. Chase and D.Z. Chase 1994c:4–5 for detailed population estimates). The mapping program has also intensively recorded broad areas of agricultural terraces, attempting to present these areas in km² blocks. Three of these km² blocks have been illustrated (A.F. Chase and D.Z. Chase 1996a, 1998b) and help to provide needed information concerning how Caracol's population sustained itself. The expansive spread of residential settlement and agricultural ter-

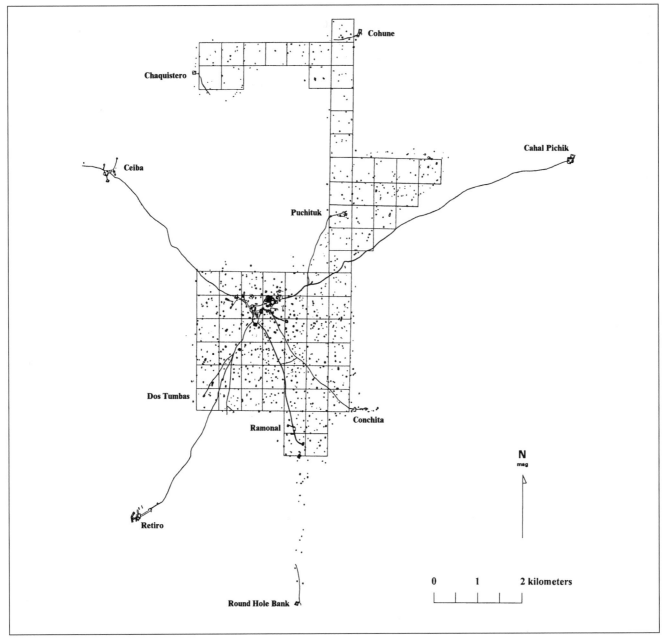

10.1 Settlement map of Caracol, Belize, current as of March, 1999. Diagonal lines represent causeways; named termini are shown. Each square measures 500 m by 500 m. For ease of comparison, this settlement map of Caracol is at the same scale as that illustrated for Tikal (figure 10.5), Calakmul (figure 10.6), and Coba (figure 10.7)

races was integrated by means of an extensive radial causeway system that connected the site's epicentral groups with strategically placed minor centers, most of which were also termini located at the ends of the causeways (figure 10.1).

Caracol has a large number of rather lengthy causeways (*sacbeob*). Over 30 km of Caracol's roads have been mapped and ground-checked. These causeways and *vias* are readily visible during on-the-ground survey (A.F. Chase and D.Z. Chase 1996b); their widths range from 2.5 to 12 m, and their known lengths range from less than 50 m to approximately 7.6 km. These roads are of two kinds: formal *sacbes* con-

necting the site epicenter with embedded architectural nodes, and less formal *vias* (Hellmuth 1971) connecting residential groups to larger *sacbes*, plazas, or other groups. Twenty-eight different groups at Caracol are associated with *sacbes* or *vias*. One *via* runs approximately 500 m and connects two causeways 1.5 km from the epicenter. In many cases, the less lengthy *vias* are as formally constructed as the longer *sacbes*.

Most Caracol causeways are linked directly to the site epicenter and end in formal architectural groupings arranged around plazas that are on the same order of scale as those found in the site epicenter. These formal architectural nodes are referred to as termini at Caracol, because they comprise formal causeway endings. Based on the block-mapping undertaken at Caracol, there is generally continuous settlement between the epicenter and architectural concentrations at the ends of causeways; the site's termini are fully embedded within the site's expansive settlement system and are integrated with the site epicenter as a cohesive urban whole. If Hatzcap Ceel, connected to Cahal Pichik by a 12-*m*–wide causeway, can be considered part of Late Classic period Caracol, then the radial causeway distance for the urban system would be on the order of 9.6 km. On this same scale, remote sensing indicates that a causeway links the site of Caballo, some 9.2 km north of the Caracol epicenter, to epicentral Caracol LANDSAT images indicate that even longer roads connect Caracol with other sites to the southeast and northwest (A.F. Chase and D.Z. Chase 1996a: Figure 1).

There are three main kinds of Caracol causeway termini: special-function administrative plazas, engulfed preexisting centers, and residential groups. Eight of Caracol's nonresidential termini and five stand-alone residential termini have been mapped (figure 10.1). Significantly, at least ten of the known Caracol causeway termini would have qualified for the label *minor center* had they not been tied to the site epicenter by causeways and situated within Caracol's continuous settlement matrix. In fact, J.E.S. Thompson (1931) had previously identified Hatzcap Ceel and Cahal Pichik as distinct centers. Yet, by the Late Classic period (if not earlier), Cahal Pichik had been subsumed within urban Caracol, because the one carved monument at Cahal Pichik honors a late Caracol lord (Grube N.D.).

Caracol's termini are spatially distributed in two rings. The first ring of formal nonresidential termini occurs approximately 3 km from the site epicenter. Three of these architectural concentrations are known (for example, Conchita, figure 10.2); all constitute special-function administrative termini consisting of large plaza areas, as large as the epicentral ones, surrounded by low-range buildings that are occasionally elevated. An administrative function has been ascribed to these termini (A.F. Chase 1998; A.F. Chase and D.Z. Chase 1994c, 1996a) because of a lack of residential and ceremonial deposits and debris in these plazas and their associated buildings. Archaeological work indicates that these administrative termini (A.F. Chase 1998; A.F. Chase and D.Z. Chase 1996a) were purposefully located within the Caracol settlement matrix at the beginning of the Late Classic era (circa AD 550).

Large residential complexes, some with palaces, are directly linked to these nonresidential termini by means of their own spur causeways. Isolated residential groups are attached by causeway directly with the Caracol epicenter. While many of these groups are attached by short causeways no more than 500 m long, in one case a residential terminus is located 2.2 km distant from the epicenter. Again, these residential termini are formal parts of the Caracol epicenter.

Archaeologically, the creation of this road and plaza system, both residential and nonresidential, dates to the early part of the Late Classic era, or after AD 550. This causeway and termini system sometimes bypassed large-scale architecture of an earlier date. The block-mapped Caracol settlement extends out and includes three of the known nearer nonresidential termini (Conchita, Ramonal, and Puchituk), conclusively demonstrating that even though 3 km distant, all these architectural nodes are an integrated part of central Caracol.

The second ring of the Caracol causeway termini consists of preexisting, but engulfed, centers (for example, Retiro, see figure 10.3) and extremely large elite compounds (for example, Round Hole Bank, see figure 10.4) that are linked by causeway to the site epicenter. These termini range in distance from 4.6 to 7.6 (and possibly 9.2 to 9.6) km from the site epicenter. Archaeological data indicate that these Caracol termini were engulfed by the expanding urban center of Caracol during the Late Classic period (AD 550 to 800). In several cases, these engulfed centers (Retiro, Ceiba, and Hatzcap Ceel) witnessed the purposeful addition of a special-function administrative plaza to their architectural landscapes. At Ceiba it was placed adjacent to a larger preexisting plaza and ballcourt; at Retiro (figure 10.3) it was placed northwest and exterior to the preexisting plazas; and at Hatzcap Ceel it was placed west of the major architecture and reservoir.

Settlement transects additionally join two other termini (Cohune and Round Hole Bank) to the formal map; their associated causeways have not yet been completely tied into the Caracol road system through ground-checking. Residential settlement is continuous, however, within the mapped transects. In an effort to examine Caracol's urban boundaries relative to engulfed architectural nodes, as well as to examine internal differences in agricultural fields and practices, a settlement area approximately 5.5 km due north of the Caracol epicenter is currently being block-mapped by Timothy Murtha (Pennsylvania State; see figure 10.1).

We believe that causeways served an important function within Caracol. They did not merely join elite residences to the epicenter. The more numerous special-function plazas, bounded with low-range buildings that served as termini, are thought to have also functioned as embedded Caracol administrative nodes that were fully contextualized within a continuous settlement matrix. The positioning of the dis-

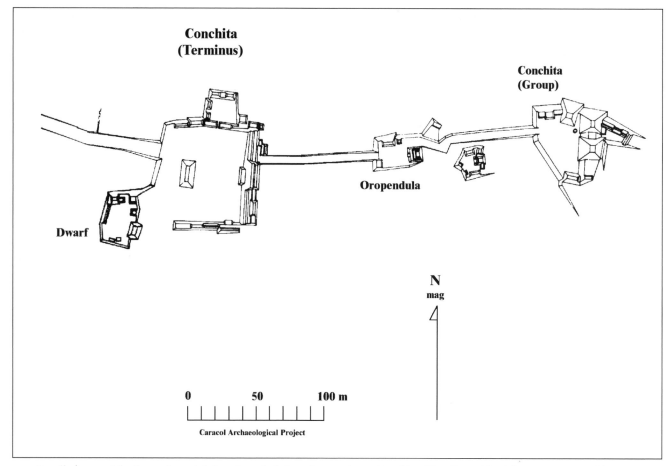

10.2 Detailed map of the Caracol special-function administrative terminus, Conchita. Two elite residential groups are east of the terminus plaza and are linked by causeway to it.

tinctive range-building plazas at the junction of engulfed centers and causeways bolsters the idea of Caracol administrative control. In sum, the causeway system unified the termini, site core, and site epicenter. The Maya of Caracol could make a round-trip from one terminus to another (within the 5 to 10 km radius) within a single day, thus facilitating communication, transportation, and distribution of goods.

Late Classic Caracol has a distinct and relatively uniform identity (A.F. Chase and D.Z. Chase 1996c). Over 60% of Caracol's residential groups are east-structure focused (A.F. Chase and D.Z. Chase 1987, 1996c). Most residential groups contain formal tombs and special ceramic cache vessels decorated with modeled faces (A.F. Chase and D.Z. Chase 1994a). Compared to other sites, a sizable proportion of Caracol's population, over 20%, exhibited inlaid teeth (D.Z. Chase 1994, 1998). Most residential groups at Caracol had access to shell ornamentation and polychrome ceramics (DZ. Chase 1998). Epicentral Caracol, the Caracol termini, and household groups located several kilometers from the epicenter all participated in the same ritual activities (D.Z.

Chase and A.F. Chase 1998). These activities unified the inhabitants and distinguished them from their neighbors.

While there was unity in ritual activity at Caracol, there was diversity in the production of items, at least on a household level (for example, A.F. Chase and D.Z. Chase 1994c; Pope 1994). Individual households at Caracol appear to have been the major units of production for a wide variety of items made from lithics, shell, and perishable materials (probably wood). The distribution of goods was facilitated and administered, however, through the causeways and termini. The overall pattern of the Caracol causeway termini fits a central place, K-7 model of an administered landscape, believed to be reflective of monopolistic control of a market system (C.A. Smith 1974, 1976; see also Santley 1994). Elsewhere, we (A.F. Chase 1998) have more clearly presented the argument that the Caracol special-function plazas served as market locales in a centrally controlled administrative economy. Briefly stated, C. A. Smith (1976:334) argued that in situations of high population density, large urban-size markets must develop to efficiently distribute needed items. Caracol exhibits both the required size and density; within

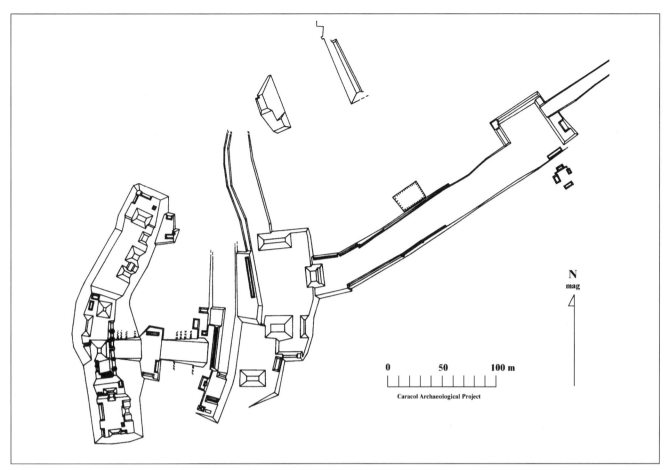

10.3 Detail map of the engulfed Retiro terminus showing the siting of a special-function plaza before entry to the preexisting site and its settlement

its urban landscape the only nodes that could have functioned as control points or markets are the special-function plazas that are regularly embedded within the site's settlement matrix and are all directly linked to the site epicenter.

In summary, block mapping and intensive survey at Caracol have demonstrated that several minor centers, some of which were initially presumed to be discrete sites and all of which are located some 3 to 10 km distant from the epicenter, were fully embedded in a large, expansive, and integrated settlement matrix by the middle of the Late Classic period. The minor centers or termini are identifiable, but integral, parts of Caracol's urban core. The causeways, termini, and distinctive ritual activities at Caracol both exemplify Marcus' (1983a) comments on the way in which the ancient Maya combined contemporary concepts of urban and rural and contradict implications of dichotomy between center and sustaining area (see also A.F. Chase and D.Z. Chase 1998b). It is suspected that Caracol integrated other, even more distant, centers, such as La Rejolla, Ucanal, and Naranjo (all in Guatemala), into even larger and more complex settlement and political matrices during the Late Classic period.

Settlement at Other Sites: Tikal, Calakmul, and Coba

Were such large integrated systems, like the one at Caracol, at work elsewhere in the lowland Maya area? We believe so. They may not be as easily identifiable as the one at Caracol because of the lack of clear-cut field systems and causeways, but we are certain that many minor centers located in proximity to major centers were actually functional parts of those major centers rather than separate hierarchical units. While settlement archaeology has been a focus of a number of large-scale archaeological projects (for example: Dzibilchaltun, see Kurjack 1974; Quirigua, see Ashmore 1981b, and Schortman 1984; and Seibal, see Tourtellot 1988b), the current comparative discussion is limited to three lowland sites with a scale most comparable to Caracol: Tikal, Calakmul, and Coba.

TIKAL

Tikal, Guatemala, is traditionally cited as one of the largest and most important Mesoamerican cities (W.R. Coe and Haviland 1982). It is spread over 120 km², with an estimated

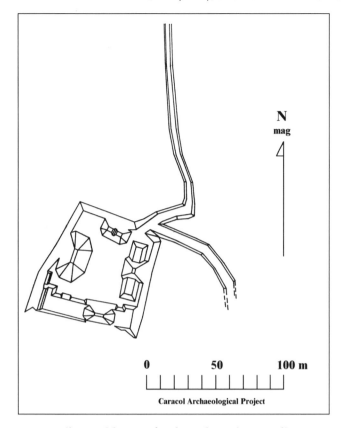

10.4 Detail map of the Round Hole Bank terminus, an elite compound

urban population of approximately 62,000 people; accounting for a rural population 10 to 12 km distant from the site epicenter raises this total to between 92,000 and 120,000 persons. More than 425,000 people are believed to have occupied Tikal's "realm," which has been estimated at 1963 km² (Culbert et al. 1990:117), a spatial figure we believe is too small for such a significant political unit (A.F. Chase and D.Z. Chase 1998a).

Settlement work at Tikal focused first on mapping a square extending out 2 km in each direction from Tikal's central plaza (Carr and Hazard 1961). Following the recording of this central 16 km², four cardinally oriented 500-*m*– wide settlement transects were assayed beyond the central portion of Tikal (figure 10.5). Eventually, the northern transect was extended to Uaxactun, some 19 km distant from Tikal's central plaza (Puleston 1983:24). All these transects were used to establish the limits of the city of Tikal through a demonstration of settlement drop-off. Puleston (1974, 1983:2, 23–24) showed specifically that cultural features and settlement density could be used to identify the limits of the city. On his northern transect, he encountered a wall 4.6 km from Tikal's central plaza. Inside the wall he was able to document 112 structures per km²; outside the wall he found only 39 structures per km².

Tikal presents a very different site and settlement pat-

tern than does Caracol. It has causeways, but they are very broad, ranging from 39 to 60 m in width, and tie together only a small portion of the overall site. The maximum causeway length is only 1 km. Tikal's mapped causeways apparently do not serve the same integrative function as those at Caracol; rather than tying the outlying population and economy together, the Tikal causeways integrate centrally located ritual architecture.

Does this mean that Tikal did not have an integrated marketing system like the one postulated for Caracol? Not necessarily; it means only that formal roads probably did not tie the system together. Where Caracol has two recognizable rings of outlying termini embedded in its settlement, all of which are centrally linked by direct roads, Tikal appears to have a single ring of definable nodes and features at a distance of approximately 4.5 km from its Great Plaza. To the north of Tikal at the 4.5 km distance is an east-west wall and ditch (Puleston and Callender 1967) that marks the urban boundary of Tikal in this direction. Due west and south at 4.5 km distances are the minor centers of Chikin Tikal and Bobal (Puleston 1983: Figs. 14, 16). Both sites exhibit similar plans. They either represent earlier centers that were engulfed within the urban boundaries of Late Classic Tikal or nodes that were purposefully located in the Tikal urban landscape in the Early Classic era (as suggested by excavation data from Chikin Tikal) when Tikal was at its height. The massive Bajo de Santa Fe effectively bounded Tikal on the east. Other minor centers are known from the Tikal urban zone, and at least two of these, Tintal and Mixta Xuc (Puleston 1983: Figs. 13a, 15), both located in the southwestern portion of the site, reflect the form of the Caracol administrative/market nodes with their large plazas and low-range buildings. At least to us, this scenario suggests that further settlement work at Tikal may yet define an embedded economic system similar to Caracol's but without the causeways.

CALAKMUL

Calakmul, Mexico, has come into prominence in the last decade as a result of both extensive archaeological work (Folan et al. 1995) and extrapolated hieroglyphic history (Martin and Grube 1995) that identifies this site as the almost mythological Site Q, a Maya city known primarily from its prominence in hieroglyphic texts at other known sites and in looted nonprovenienced carved monuments (Marcus 1976, but see A.F. Chase and D.Z. Chase 1998a:20–21 and Schuster 1997). Regardless of whether Calakmul may be identified with Site Q, it is a large, major site minimally estimated to have encompassed some 70 km² and to have had a population of 50,000 people; it is believed to have controlled a polity of approximately 8000 km² (Folan et al.

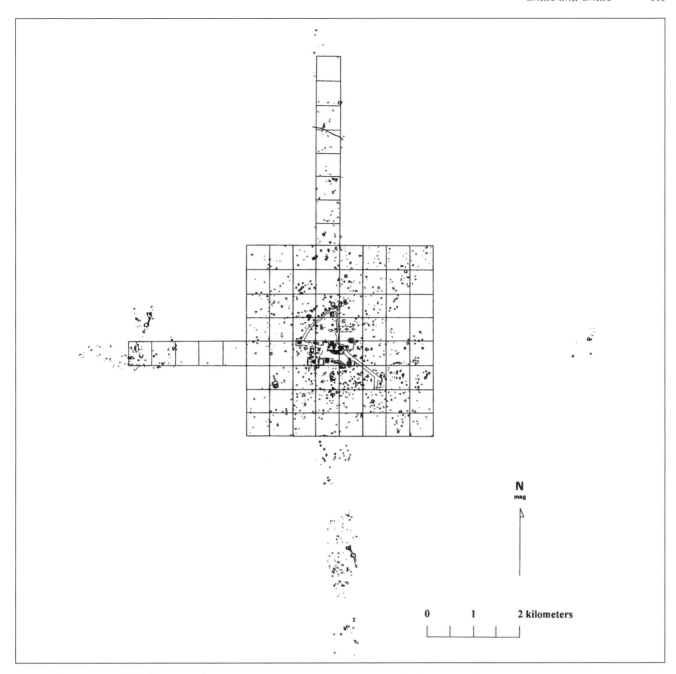

10.5 Settlement map of Tikal, Guatemala. *Map combines the settlement and central maps into a single unit.*

1995:310). Some 30 km² of Calakmul have been mapped (figure 10.6), with the mapped area extending out 3 km north-south by 2.5 km east-west from that site's epicenter. Yet, despite having mapped a large area, no obvious embedded matrices, such as those known from Tikal and Caracol, have been located. In spite of the large scale of the map, it may be that the Calakmul mapping effort did not extend far enough laterally to have discovered embedded settlement matrices; alternatively, none exist.

Calakmul's settlement differs substantially from that found at Tikal and Caracol. Two small internal causeways measuring 450 x 70 m in length exist within Calakmul's mapped area (Folan et al. 1995:313). Five other causeways have been defined either visually or through remote sensing (Folan, Marcus, and Miller 1995), but none have been ground-checked. Calakmul's causeways do not appear to integrate the site in the way that Caracol's do. Rather, the majority of Calakmul's causeways appear to focus on long-distance linkages with other centers that are 8 to 38.25 km distant (Folan et al. 1995:313). If the long-distance causeways of Calakmul can be verified on the ground, they would appear to conform with the previously known long-distance

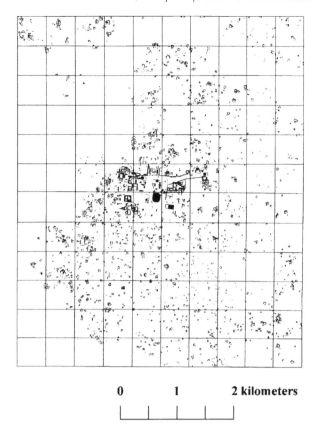

10.6 Settlement map of Calakmul, Mexico. North is to the top of the page. Each square measures 500 x 500 m

system that centers on Mirador (I. Graham 1967), 38.25 km south of Calakmul (and joined to Calakmul by a causeway). Settlement drop-off is also evident within the area mapped at Calakmul, especially to the southwest and northeast (figure 10.6). The southwestern portion of Calakmul is dominated by an area of bajo, but no such claim can be made for the northeastern section of the site.

While Calakmul can be placed into a very broad regional frame because of its externally oriented causeways, the internal organization of the site does not lend itself easily to comment. Calakmul is not tightly organized internally like Caracol, and its urban area is not bounded by walls like Tikal. Because no minor centers have been identified within the urban boundaries of Calakmul, unlike Tikal and Caracol, there is currently no evidence of a similar embedded economic and administrative system.

COBA

Coba, Mexico, dominated the eastern part of the Northern lowlands during the Late Classic period. Its population has been estimated between 42,870 and 62,652 persons within a 63 km² area (Folan et al. 1983:197–202). Based on its causeway linkages, Coba's polity size may have exceeded that of

Caracol, Calakmul, and Tikal. Two of Coba's causeways were long distance and joined distinct centers, specifically Ixil, 24 km away, and Yaxuna, 101 km distant. Like Caracol, however, the vast majority of Coba's causeways linked internal parts of the site (figure 10.7). Like Caracol, Coba's causeways clearly served an internal integrative function (Benavides Castillo 1981).

Extensive settlement work has been undertaken at Coba. Under the auspices of the Carnegie Institution of Washington at the beginning of the twentieth century, Thompson, Pollock, and Charlot (1932) first presented a map of downtown Coba, while Villa Rojas (1934) documented the Yaxuna-Coba causeway. Extensive downtown settlement plans for Coba were first published by Folan, Kintz, and Fletcher (1983). A cruciform settlement survey, mimicking that of Tikal, was carefully documented by Garduno Argueta (1979). Garduno's detailed mapping clearly shows a substantial settlement decrease as one leaves the urban area of Coba, as defined by its causeways and termini.

It is suspected that at least some of the causeways so evident at Coba (Benavides C. 1981; Folan et al. 1983) may be representative of an administered economy similar to that proposed for Caracol. Coba's causeway system is not as centralized as the one found at Caracol, but it does have two rings of embedded nodes, the first 2 to 3 km from the middle of the site and the second 4 to 5 km from downtown Coba (figure 10.7). Folan suggests that the intrasite causeways primarily served as "high-status links between the central core of Coba and its peripheral zones," but he also notes they served political and administrative purposes (1983:55). Based on the Caracol data, it is likely that some causeway termini at Coba may also have served market functions.

Conclusion

The extant settlement data in the Maya area demonstrates the striking variability of scale and emphasis that occurs within the lowland Maya landscape. Some of this variation is indicative of differing degrees of political centralization. Some of the diverse interpretations of settlement data are, however, also related to strikingly different concepts of polity size that are held by different investigators (for a review, see A.F. Chase and D.Z. Chase 1998a). Thus, there may well have been situations within the Maya lowlands where loosely organized polities existed, such as in the Puuc area of the Yucatan peninsula (Dunning et al. 1994) or where centers 3 to 10 km apart were conceivably independent rivals, as has been suggested for the Petexbatun area (Demarest 1997). In these instances, however, conceptualizations of small Maya polity size are often based on interpretations of geographic or other spatial models, such as nearest neighbor analysis or thiessen polygons, rather than on detailed settlement work. Other, more complex organizations clearly existed in the Classic Maya lowlands, such as at Late Classic Caracol and Late Classic Coba, where all occupation within a 3 to 10 km radius of the site epicenter was incorporated into a single functional city. In these instances, detailed settlement work has led investigators to record the on-the-ground, large-scale integration of single urban centers, and the massive size of such centers is usually considered to reflect the existence of large centralized polities during the Classic period.

Not only is there variation in settlement scale and intensity within the different regions that comprise the Maya lowlands, there is also great variation in the size, composition, and layout of most Maya sites. Even the largest Maya cities are composed differently. They may be inwardly focused and less spatially integrated like Tikal and Calakmul, or outwardly expanded and highly integrated, like Caracol and Coba. Minor centers at Caracol have these characteristics: They were located 3 to 8 km from that site's epicenter; they were connected to the epicenter by an extensive web of causeways; they were embedded within Caracol's urban matrix and growth; and, importantly, they appear to have served as key nodes in Caracol's administered economy. It has been suggested that a similar situation may have existed at Tikal, but without the radiating causeway system. While all four of these centers have recognizable central areas and are clearly hierarchically scaled above other centers in their respective extended regions and polities, the distinctiveness of this settlement signature does not necessarily hold for the entire Maya region. Until more regional projects record contiguous large-scale settlement matrices (such as exists for Caracol, Tikal, Calakmul, and Coba), however, we will be unable fully to characterize and contextualize Maya settlement.

The interpretation of ancient Maya settlement patterns and their various components will remain a somewhat quixotic practice until problems of scale and focus are resolved. In particular, there is a need for more long-term block-mapping of any given regional settlement matrix in conjunction with the mapping of architectural concentrations and narrow settlement transects. Such block-mapping is extremely labor intensive, often adding only a small slice to an already existing map. But, if one wishes to interpret Maya settlement, contextualize minor centers, and understand ancient social complexity, then "large-scale regional survey employing systematic sampling procedures" (Fowler 1997:207 paraphrasing Marcus 1983a) that go beyond the regional epicenter is the appropriate approach. Otherwise, like Don Quixote, we will continue to tilt with windmills in interpreting ancient Maya sociopolitical and economic organization.

Acknowledgements. Throughout its sixteen-year history, the Caracol Archaeological Project has been supported by the University of Central Florida, the Government of Belize, and private donors. In addition, funding has been obtained from the National Science Foundation (1987 [BNS-8619996], 1994–1996 [SBR-9311773], 1997 [SBR-9708637]), the Harry Frank Guggenheim Foundation (1988, 1989), the Agency for International Development (1989–1992), the Dart Foundation (1996), the Stans Foundation (1997–2000), the Kislak Foundation (1998), and the Ahau Foundation (1998–2000). An earlier version of this essay, entitled "Tilting with Windmills," was presented at the 63rd Annual Meeting of the Society for American Archaeology in Seattle, 1998; this version has benefited from the suggestions of two anonymous reviewers and one anonymous copy editor.

11 Laguna de On and Caye Coco

Economic Differentiation at Two Postclassic Island Communities in Northern Belize

Marilyn A. Masson

THE EVIDENCE for variation in production activities among rural Postclassic communities of northern Belize is examined here by comparing the material assemblages from two island settlements, Laguna de On and Caye Coco (figure 11.1). Though these communities are contemporary and share inland lagoon island settings, they are quite different when surface features are compared (figures 11.2, 11.3). Laguna de On is about one-quarter the size of Caye Coco, and it lacks mound architecture and carved stone monuments. Laguna de On Island, measuring 200 x 60 m, was a contemporary settlement of about 1 km along the shore of the lagoon. Caye Coco has seventeen mound structures, six stone altars, and one carved stone lintel (Barnhart 1998; Hare, Campbell, and Durivage 1999). Caye Coco Island, extending 600 x 400 m, was also contemporary with shore settlements along the banks of the lagoon. All but two of the mounds at Caye Coco were built during the latter portion of the Postclassic period (AD 1250–1500), as dated by ceramics found in architectural fill (Barrett 1999; Rosenswig 1999; West 1999). All the structures at this site, regardless of the date of their inner cores, exhibit a final Late Postclassic construction phase, indicating they were modified and used during this period. These features clearly suggest that Caye Coco was more politically significant than Laguna de On and that comparisons of economic systems from these sites show contrasting communities with very different roles in regional political interaction.

Although Caye Coco's large Postclassic architecture was built during the later centuries of the Postclassic occupation (Rosenswig 1999), off-mound testing indicates that this site was a thriving community from at least the eleventh century. Laguna de On was also occupied from the eleventh century, with a notable acceleration in public works projects (a ballcourt, shrines, and terraces) documented after AD 1250 (Masson N.D.). These sites thus represent contemporary communities. At each, clear breaks are not observed in features or artifact inventories between AD 1050 and 1500, and a continuum of occupation is inferred at both locations. At both sites, surface feature construction of a public nature increased over time.

Laguna de On and Caye Coco are located along the Freshwater Creek drainage, a south-to-north running waterway and inland lagoon system that extends from the interior of northern Belize near Laguna de On to the Caribbean Sea (figure 11.1). It is one of three parallel north-running drainages in northern Belize. The other two drainages include the New River and the Rio Hondo, both of which are located west of Freshwater Creek and have deeper, more navigable channels. The lack of extremely large monumental centers, by Belize region standards (R.E.W. Adams 1982), along the Freshwater Creek drainage from any time period suggests that this zone was a rural agrarian setting during all pre-Columbian periods.

This volume seeks to evaluate "middle-range" communities that occupied social positions between large urban centers and agrarian hamlets. Due to a lack of systematic survey of Postclassic settlement in northern Belize, it is difficult to know the full distribution of site sizes of this period in northern Belize and the relative position of Laguna de On and Caye Coco within this continuum. Numerous Postclassic sites have been located in this region (Sidrys 1983: Table 1, Map 2), which suggests that northern Belize was home to thriving populations from at least AD 1050 until the arrival of the Spanish by AD 1517. Previous investigations have identified political centers at the sites of Lamanai (Pendergast 1981, 1985, 1986) and Santa Rita (Gann 1918; Sidrys 1983; D.Z. Chase 1982; D.Z. Chase and A.F. Chase 1988). Other sites of substantial magnitude, such as Shipstern, Aventura, Bandera, Sarteneja (Sidrys 1983: Table 1, Map 2), and Caye Coco, may represent additional centers

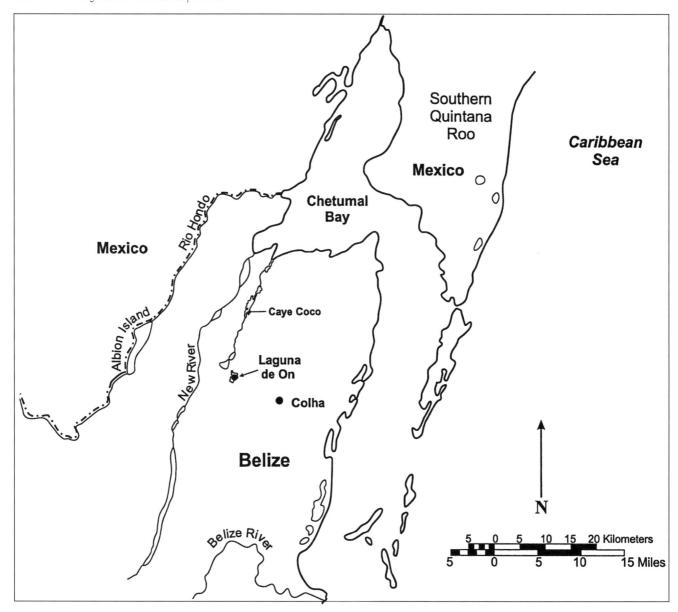

11.1 Location of Laguna de On and Caye Coco in Belize

(Sidrys 1983: Table 1; Masson N.D.). Postclassic settlements smaller than Laguna de On have been located, such as the Postclassic component of Colha (Michaels 1987, 1994; Michaels and Shafer 1994) and numerous additional small sites identified by Sidrys (1983: Table 1, Map 2). This evidence suggests that Laguna de On lies within the middle range of settlement sizes for Postclassic northern Belize. Caye Coco may be just one of several contemporary centers in this region and lies toward the upper end of the site size continuum.

It is clear that middle-range settlements are defined relatively for each time period. During the Classic period, Caye Coco's architecture and monuments would have resulted in its classification as a "minor ceremonial center," as defined by

R.E.W. Adams (1982). Because of the reduction in scale of monumental construction that characterizes the Postclassic period (Masson N.D.) Caye Coco is of a size that suggests it was an important subsidiary center to the regional capital of Chetumal (identified by D.Z. Chase and A.F. Chase [1988] as the site of Santa Rita). Caye Coco may have briefly served as the primary capital of the Chetumal territory during Colonial times (Masson and Rosenswig 1998).

Measures of Complexity at Classic and Postclassic Settlements

The reduction in scale of Postclassic lowland Maya monumental works does not imply a reduction in political complexity. All the trappings of civilization, such as writing, stelae erection, mural painting, mound construction, well-developed crafts production, trade, and aspects of calendrics and astronomy, persisted through the Postclassic period until the arrival of the Spanish. As Rathje and Sabloff have noted (Rathje 1975; Sabloff and Rathje 1975), the expression of power during the Postclassic period underwent a fundamental transformation from the Classic period, and a mercantile economic focus emerged as a new source for the investment of social energies. Accelerated trading and economic production during the Postclassic led to greater overall affluence among regional populations, but this trend also deflated settlement and social hierarchies compared to earlier times. Concurrently, conventions of power-sharing replaced the stringent, apical, hierarchical political institutions of the preceding period (Schele and Freidel 1990:348).

Appropriate criteria by which middle-range settlements may be identified are thus different for the Postclassic than for the Classic period. Beyond site size, features such as monumental architecture, stelae, altars, and ballcourts are used to identify politically significant settlements for the Classic period and to differentiate them from sites of similar size that lack these symbols of authority or ritual practice (for examples, see R.E.W. Adams 1982; Mathews and Willey 1991: Table 3.1). In the case of Caye Coco, symbols of authority include large residential mounds and stone altars. Residents of other Postclassic centers expressed their power using different symbols of authority. For example, Santa Rita is a dispersed coastal settlement distinguished by its murals and elaborate caches (D.Z. Chase 1986, 1988; D.Z. Chase and A.F. Chase 1988) rather than by the large mound architecture of Postclassic date, stelae, or altars. The nearby center of Ichpaatun in Quintana Roo, Mexico, also did not have large monumental architecture, but a well-fortified wall was built around the site and several re-erected stela were found there (Escalona Ramos 1946). At Lamanai, construction focused on the modification of an earlier monumental structure (Loten 1985; Pendergast 1981, 1985), and elaborate burials also attest to the site's significance (Pendergast 1981).

Conspicuous surface features attest to the political aspirations of an individual or sets of individuals at a given site during an event or several events in a site's history (Blanton et al. 1996; Demarest 1992; Proskouriakoff 1960; Schele and Freidel 1990). An alternative and perhaps more valid measure of a polity's success may lie, however, in assessing the duration, economic stability, and affluence of the community. This type of information cannot be determined from surface features but is provided through settlement excavations and analysis of recovered materials. If Rathje's suggestion that the true basis of social power in Postclassic com-

munities lay in their economic affluence, then the examination of surface features, such as art and architecture, may reveal little about the economic differentiation of settlements within a regional system. An examination of variation in patterns of production and exchange provides a useful basis for evaluating forms of community variability that are distinct from elite signatures of power.

Economic Patterns as an Appropriate Measure for Assessing Community Heterogeneity

The relationship between political and economic power has yet to be clearly determined for pre-Columbian Maya society. Recent examinations suggest that dispersed utilitarian craft workers and subsistence producers, who occupied the rural landscape away from major political centers, even during the height of Classic-period political hierarchies, held a high degree of autonomy (Fry 1980; Hester and Shafer 1984; King and Potter 1994; McAnany 1993; Rands and Bishop 1980; P.M. Rice 1987b). Evidence also suggests that some degree of community-level specialization in utilitarian craft production may have occurred during the Preclassic, Classic (Rands and Bishop 1980; Fry 1980; Shafer and Hester 1983), and Postclassic periods (D.Z. Chase and A.F. Chase 1988:78; E.A. Graham and Pendergast 1989:11; ; Michaels 1987, 1994; Michaels and Shafer 1994;P.M. Rice 1980; Shafer and Hester 1983, 1988). It has been suggested that land-holding lineages maintained the enduring economic affluence and social power of the Classic period through controlled access to resources critical to the maintenance of society on relatively autonomous terms (McAnany 1995:65, 75–77).

It is probable that the level of economic autonomy and differentiation of Postclassic communities would be equivalent to, or more pronounced than, that proposed for communities of the Classic period. If we accept the acceleration of emphasis on mercantile activities that Sabloff and Rathje propose for Postclassic society, then the examination of domestic artifact assemblages to determine economic variability is useful in evaluating the differentiation of various size Postclassic settlements (Rathje 1983). Comparisons are offered below concerning the economic production and exchange systems of Laguna de On and Caye Coco, as reflected in artifact assemblage inventories from these sites.

Comparisons of Economic Production and Exchange at Two Communities

The comparisons of assemblages from Laguna de On and Caye Coco are presented by artifact class, including ceramics, local chipped-stone tools, spindle whorls, net weights, faunal bone, ground stone, obsidian, marine shell, and exotic

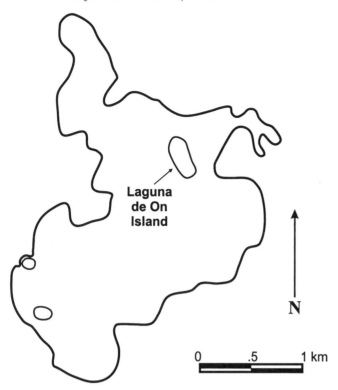

11.2 Laguna de On and Laguna de On Island. Illustration by Pamela Headrick

Table 11.1 Ceramics at Laguna de On and Caye Coco

	R/S Plain	R/S Incised	Unslipped	Eroded	Total
Laguna	34.8%	0.2%	53.87%	11.13%	12,961
Coco	36.0%	0.8%	51.9%	10.3%	20,440

Note: R/S = red-slipped. Percentages are calculated from the total number of sherds for each site (ceramics from Laguna de On classified in the field by Shirley Boteler Mock; ceramics from Caye Coco classified by the author, Georgia West, Janel Orsi, Alex Mullen, Monica Reed, and Jennifer Meanwell).

objects. At Laguna de On, artifacts come from domestic structures, courtyards, middens, and ritual shrine structures (Masson and Rosenswig 1998, 1999). At Caye Coco, most artifacts are from off-mound domestic zones, although materials from one elite residential mound and one public structure are also included (Masson and Rosenswig 1999). These artifacts represent a variety of economic activities and contexts at each community. They also represent local resources and commodities obtained or produced directly by each community, local resources acquired through intercommunity exchange, and long-distance resources secured directly or indirectly through maritime traders who operated along the nearby Caribbean coast. Ceramic and lithic types at each community are evaluated below, followed by an examination of the proportions of the full range of materials found during excavations. These data suggest patterns of community-based specialization and indicate

differential access to local and long-distance resources. Important commonalities in community production are also indicated, showing that pronounced economic differentiation is not observed among sites of different regional political status.

CERAMICS

The three major categories of ceramics identified at Laguna de On and Caye Coco are slipped wares, unslipped wares, and censer wares. The first two categories represent primarily utilitarian serving and storage vessels found in all contexts at the sites. Slipped vessels include small and large jars and bowls, small ollas, and footed "sag-bottom" bowls or dishes classified primarily as Payil Red and Rita Red (Mock 1997, 1998; following D.Z. Chase 1982; Mock 1994; Walker 1990). These slipped wares can be plain or engraved near the rim. Unslipped vessels primarily include large folded-rim ollas, as well as bowls. Censer wares represent a number of unslipped ritual ceramic types that have a limited distribution at each site (Masson 1999; Mullen 1999). The relative percentages of censer ceramics are not compared in this examination, because sampling strategy can greatly affect their recovery. Considerable overlap occurs in the types of utilitarian ceramics found in elite, nonelite, and ritual contexts at each site, though evidence derived from analyses performed at Laguna de On suggests that elite and ritual contexts have slightly higher percentages of red-slipped wares and decorated wares (Masson N.D., 1999).

Differences in the relative social position of communities may be reflected by the percent of slipped wares or decorated wares relative to unslipped wares, as the former are more finely made. The comparison of these broad ceramic groups provides a basis for assessing functional differentiation in ceramic production and use within these communities. While it is probable that varieties of regionally similar slipped and unslipped ceramic types were manufactured at each site (Mock 1998; Masson N.D.), the meaning and function of these types are not expected to change from settlement to settlement. Red-slipped ceramics may represent a finer category of serving vessel, with some forms perhaps used for storage; unslipped ceramics may represent a coarser form of vessel used primarily for storage. Forms of slipped and unslipped wares overlap, suggesting that some of these ceramic types were functionally interchangeable.

Table 11.1 presents the proportions of these general categories for each site. Laguna de On exhibits a lower ratio of slipped to unslipped ceramics (0.65) than Caye Coco (0.71). Caye Coco also has higher proportions of incised wares (0.8%) compared to Laguna de On (0.2%). The higher inferred social position of the Caye Coco community is probably reflected in the greater abundance of slipped and incised wares at this site. It is important to note, however, that the magnitude of these differences is not great and that substantial quantities of slipped ceramic wares were used at Laguna de On. These slipped wares were broadly distributed among all sectors of society during the Postclassic period and are probably not the most useful indicator of social status.

CHIPPED-STONE TOOLS OF LOCAL RAW MATERIALS
Local chipped-stone tool industries were well developed in northern Belize during the Postclassic period, partly owing to the fine chert and chalcedony beds available for exploitation (Oland 1998, 1999a, 1999b; Shafer and Hester 1983; Wright et al. 1959). Laguna de On and Caye Coco inhabitants obtained formal lithic tools from the site of Colha, where resident craft specialists produced items such as lenticular bifaces, triangular bifaces, and stemmed bifacial projectile points for local and long-distance exchange (Hester and Shafer 1991; Masson 1997; Michaels 1987, 1994; Michaels and Shafer 1994; Oland 1998, 1999a, ; Shafer and Hester 1988). Expedient tools at these sites were made on recycled tools scavenged from earlier occupations and on lower quality cherts, chalcedonies, or other materials available in their immediate vicinities (Masson 1997; Oland 1998, 1999a, 1999b).

Preliminary examinations of lithic raw materials available to these sites, as reflected in their expedient tool and debitage assemblages, suggest that Laguna de On was in a more advantageous location. Chalcedonies located within a day's walk of this site are of reasonable quality, and abundant tools and debris derived from these materials are found at the settlement (Oland 1998, 1999a). In contrast, lithic debris at Caye Coco is less abundant, and manufacturing detritus often consists of low-grade, heavily weathered, brittle surface cherts found in small pebble form at Progresso Lagoon where the site is located. Surveys of Progresso Lagoon conducted by Oland (1999b) failed to locate outcrops of chert or chalcedony of quality comparable to those found near Laguna de On. Raw materials available at both sites pale, however, in comparison to the world-class superior-grade cherts at the site of Colha (Shafer and Hester 1983). It thus appears that lithic resources are highly variable on a local level at Colha, Laguna de On, and Caye Coco. This condition is conducive to the intercommunity exchange of such resources.

If political position influenced these exchange relationships, occupants of higher ranked sites, like Caye Coco, might be expected to have greater access to top-grade formal Colha tool products. Residents of lower ranked sites like Laguna de On, might be expected to have fewer Colha formal tools and to possess greater numbers of expedient

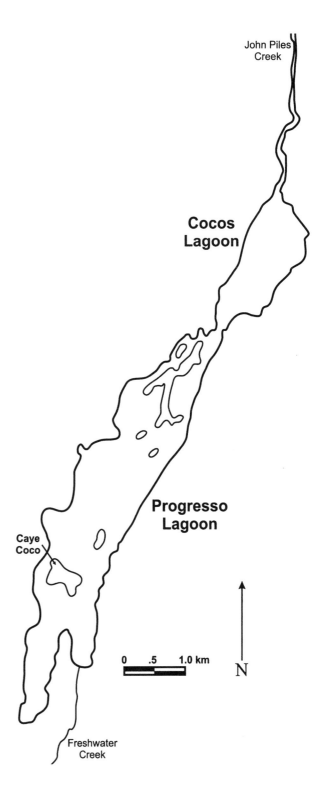

*11.3 Progresso Lagoon and the Island of Caye Coco. I
llustration by Pamela Headrick*

Table 11.2 Formal Classic, Formal Postclassic, and expedient local chipped-stone tools from Laguna de On and Caye Coco

	Form. Classic*	Form. Post.	Expedient	Total
Laguna	76 (14.7%)	54 (10.5%)	386 (74.8%)	516 (100)
Coco	50 (14)	18 (5.1)	288 (80.9)	356 (100)
				*(46 of sample)

* probably recycled earlier tools

Note: Calculated from Masson N.D.:Table 5.8 and Oland 1999:Table 4

Table 11.3 Raw materials of local chipped-stone tools from Laguna de On and Caye Coco

	Colha	Chalcedony	C/Q	Local	Coarse	Unident.	Total
Laguna	151	104	25	132	44	60	516
	29.3%	20.2	4.8	25.6	8.5	11.6	100
Coco	91	79	53	43	20	70	356
	25.6%	22.2	14.9	12.1	5.6	19.7	100

Note: Colha= Colha chert; C/Q = chalcedony/quartz; Local = local chert; Coarse = coarse chert; Unident. = unidentiable.

Derived from Masson N.D.:Table 5.9 and Oland 1999:2

tools manufactured on locally available materials. In reality, intercommunity exchange appears to have been complex and varied in northern Belize (Freidel 1981; McAnany 1993), and the patterns described below do not indicate that the Caye Coco settlement had "preferred" access to Colha products. A more open exchange system is implied, wherein Caye Coco's residents probably obtained chalcedony products or raw materials from Laguna de On merchants and finer tools (of chalcedony and chert) from Colha flintknappers. Resource distribution may have encouraged Laguna de On residents to specialize in lithic raw material extraction and Colha artisans to manufacture finished products. This distribution may have cultivated dependency of Caye Coco's occupants on its more lithic-rich neighbors to the south. Presumably, Caye Coco would have developed other industries, capitalizing on its own assets to generate commodities for local and long-distance exchange.

Table 11.2 presents the proportions of formal and expedient tools found at Laguna de On and Caye Coco based on analyses performed by Oland (1998, 1999a, 1999b) and Masson (1997, N.D.). The percentages of raw materials represented in the tools analyzed for each site are presented in table 11.3. Formal tools listed in table 11.2 include those classified as recycled Classic-period oval bifaces, tranchet tools, blades, and general utility bifaces. Postclassic formal tool forms include lenticular bifaces, triangular bifaces, laurel-leaf bifaces, parallel-sided bifaces, miscellaneous knives or other thin bifaces, and projectile points (Masson 1997; Oland 1998, 1999a, 1999b). Expedient tools in table 11.2 include those classified as utilized flakes, notched flakes, thick or irregular bifaces or choppers, unifaces, utilized cores, hammerstones, and nonutilized cores (Masson 1997; Oland

1998, 1999a, 1999b). While cores represent debris rather than tools, they are an important part of on-site expedient industries (reflecting the manufacture of flake tools and so are included here). The Laguna de On tools represent 100% of the site's assemblage, and the Caye Coco sample represents 46% of the 1998 sample of 766 nonobsidian tools analyzed thus far by Oland (1999b).

According to these data, Laguna de On and Caye Coco share equivalent proportions of recycled formal Classic period tools. Laguna de On exhibits double the proportions of Postclassic-period formal tools (10.5%) compared to Caye Coco (5.1%). Caye Coco thus exhibits around 6% more expedient tools in its assemblage than Laguna de On. These data suggest that Laguna de On residents had greater access to formal tools through regional exchange, perhaps because of their proximity to the site of Colha where tools were manufactured (Michaels 1987; Shafer and Hester 1983). Caye Coco, despite its greater political status, did not obtain a greater amount of Colha Postclassic-period formal tools than Laguna de On. Caye Coco is farther from Colha than Laguna de On, and the quantity of Postclassic-period formal tools at this site suggests that a "distance decay" principle (Renfrew 1975) is in effect for these communities, with the relative number of Colha products decreasing with distance from the source. The amount of recycled Colha tools at each site does not adhere to this principle because the availability of these materials is affected by economic systems of the Classic period (or earlier) and perhaps scavenging activities. Colha tools were abundantly distributed in earlier periods (Gibson 1986; Shafer and Hester 1983), and these resources are generally available at earlier sites located in close proximity to each community. The greater proportions of expedient tools observed in the Caye Coco assemblage is not correlated with the greater availability of local raw materials suitable for lithic industries. As stated above, chert outcrops at Caye Coco and along the shores of the lagoon were of a poor quality compared to those noted elsewhere, yielding few nodules of a size appropriate for tool manufacture.

The lithic raw materials at Laguna de On and Caye Coco, as documented by Masson (1997) and Oland (1998, 1999a, 1999b), exhibit patterns similar to those described in the preceding tool type comparisons. Laguna de On has 4% more tools made of Colha chert than Caye Coco, but this difference is not major. The sites exhibit similar proportions of chalcedony and coarse materials, but Caye Coco has more chalcedony/quartz blends and fewer local cherts than Laguna de On (table 11.3). These patterns imply that Caye Coco's residents relied more heavily on a source of chalcedony with quartz impurities or quartzite, or they relied on an exchange relationship with a community that exploited such a source. As the percentage of this category of material is low at Laguna de On, it does not appear that this site provided these materials to Caye Coco. Quartz blend chalcedonies and other comparable quartz-like materials have been previously noted to occur in small numbers at Laguna de On (Masson 1993, 1997; Oland 1998, 1999a), and the source for this material has yet to be identified. As Caye Coco has percentages of chalcedonies comparable to Laguna de On, and Laguna de On is noted to be quite close to several chalcedony outcrops (Oland 1998, 1999a), it is likely that Caye Coco was exchanging with Laguna de On for chalcedonies and with Colha for formal tools made of chert and chalcedony (Michaels 1987). Low percentages of local poor-grade cherts underscore the paucity of quality materials at Progresso Lagoon. Caye Coco has fewer pieces overall of flakes and shatter (lithic debris lacking striking platforms) than Laguna de On, with 6,785 pieces tallied for Caye Coco (Oland 1999b) and 19,315 pieces collected from Laguna de On. Ratios of platform-bearing flakes to shatter are higher for Caye Coco (1.28) than for Laguna de On (0.71). Flakes represent 41.6% of the flake and shatter sample from Laguna de On, and 56.3% of the Caye Coco assemblage. This difference suggests that more primary manufacturing activities, such as core preparation, which results in more irregular debris and shatter than controlled late-stage thinning (B.A. Bradley 1975), occurred at Laguna de On. The greater proportion of platform-bearing flakes at Caye Coco reflects more finely controlled resharpening and thinning activities at this site.

Obsidian artifacts at Laguna de On include 1,209 blades and 11 projectile points. At Caye Coco, 1,121 obsidian blades and 8 projectile points have been found. As obsidian points appear confined to specific locations associated with ritual at each site (Masson N.D.; West 1999), their representation may be related to sampling issues. The local lithic tool/obsidian-blade ratio of Laguna de On is 2.46 (516/1209), four times the ratio of Caye Coco, .68 (766/1121). It is clear from these ratios that Laguna de On's occupants relied more extensively on local raw materials than their Caye Coco counterparts.

Despite the differences outlined above indicating that Caye Coco may have engaged in fewer primary production activities (suggested by shatter proportions) and had more expedient tools than formal tools in its assemblage compared to Laguna de On, Caye Coco is not poor in lithic resources. In fact, its total number of expedient and formal tools of local materials (766, including analyzed and unanalyzed) exceeds the number of tools from Laguna de On (516).

When the number of lithic tools relative to the number of ceramic sherds is compared (table 11.4), Caye Coco and Laguna de On share very similar sherd/tool ratios. These data suggest that Caye Coco was not "poor" in either local or long-distance lithic resources, despite the lack of fine materials available in its immediate vicinity. This community probably obtained much of its local resources through exchange or extraction of tribute. The abundant quantity of obsidian indicates that Caye Coco had easy access to this material, perhaps to a privileged degree beyond that experienced by Laguna de On. Greater proportions of obsidian relative to lithic tools at Caye Coco reflect greater reliance on obsidian, and this trend would have reduced the need of Caye Coco consumers for local lithic products.

A "distance decay" principle may also be in effect for obsidian distribution among these communities. Obsidian is thought to have come from trading sites along the coast of Belize, where merchants brokered the importation of exotic commodities brought by circum-Yucatecan maritime traders for exchange with products from inland lowland Maya communities. This economic relationship had begun by at least the end of the Classic period and became more fully developed during the Postclassic (Guderjan and Garber 1995; McKillop 1996; McKillop and Healy 1989; Mock 1994; Sabloff and Rathje 1975; Thompson 1970). As Caye Coco is located closer to the coast along the Freshwater Creek drainage than Laguna de On, it may have had easier access to commodities such as obsidian available from coastal trading.

COLLECTIVE INDUSTRIES AT LAGUNA DE ON
AND CAYE COCO

The relative quantities of lithics, ceramics, and other materials in the entire site assemblages at Laguna de On and Caye Coco provide a basis for comparing local production industries and long-distance exchange relationships at these sites. Table 11.4 provides frequency data for spindle whorls, net weights, faunal bone, ground stone, marine shell, lithic tools, lithic flakes, obsidian, and adornments made of exotic materials; the quantities of these materials are standardized by dividing them into the total number of sherds at each site (following M.E. Smith 1994). Figures 11.4 through 11.7 illustrate the relative proportions of these materials at each site. Two sets of data are charted in these figures. The first set (figures 11.4, 11.5) compares categories of materials that are numerically abundant at each site (>1000), including ceramic sherds, lithic debris (flakes and shatter), obsidian, and faunal bone. The second set of (figures 11.6 and 11.7) compares the frequencies of materials present in smaller quantities at each site (<1000), including lithic tools, spindle whorls, net weights, ground stone, marine shell, and exotic ornaments. This arbitrary division based on abundance is useful especially for comparing scarcer items whose proportions are difficult to assess when

Table 11.4 Frequencies of other artifacts from Laguna de On and Caye Coco and ratios of total sherds to each material

	Spindle whorls	Net weights	Faunal bone	Ground stone	Marine shell/coral	Exotic ornaments	Obsidian	Lithic tools	Lithic flakes
Laguna(N)	55	396	10231	18	46	12	1209	516	19315
ratio*	235.7	32.7	1.3	720.1	281.8	1080.1	10.7	25.1	0.7
Caye Coco	29	396	7879	17	657	14	1121	766	6785
ratio	704.8	51.6	2.6	1202.4	31.1	1460.0	18.2	26.7	3.0

* Sherd/material ratio; total sherds = 12,961 for Laguna de On and 20,440 for Caye Coco

the quantities are examined as a percentage of much larger artifact totals.

Figures 11.4 and 11.5 indicate that ceramics form a greater proportion of the Caye Coco assemblage (56% of the abundant materials at the site) than at Laguna de On (30%). Lithic debris, in contrast, forms a much smaller proportion of the Caye Coco sample (19%) than in the Laguna de On sample (44%). These data suggest that lithic industries were more developed at Laguna de On. The greater relative abundance of artifact debris (such as ceramic sherds) is one indicator of craft production localities within a site (Costin 1991:20–21), and the same may be true for community-level production patterns. The data provide preliminary indications of possible community production emphases at Laguna de On and Caye Coco. It is difficult to interpret the significance of greater proportions of ceramics at Caye Coco. This pattern may simply reflect the smaller amount of other types of materials, or it may signal different kinds of activities at this site. Little is known of community specialization in ceramic production during the Postclassic period, although potting hearths have tentatively been identified at Laguna de On (Masson N.D., following the criteria in Deal 1988). It is likely that many communities made their own ceramics, though a high level of regional standardization is noted for this period (Sabloff and Rathje 1975).

Obsidian tools are equally represented at each community in this sample according to figures 11.4 and 11.5, but they are present in relatively low numbers compared to other artifacts (table 11.4); the significance of obsidian is thus dwarfed by comparison. Lower sherd/obsidian ratios (table 11.4) imply that Laguna de On had more relative obsidian than Caye Coco. The ratios of local lithic tools to obsidian blades presented previously, however, probably serve as the better means of evaluating the relative abundance of this imported material at each community, as obsidian blades and lithic tools overlap functionally for many activities (Masson 1997). These measures, as discussed above, indicate that Caye Coco had advantageous access to obsidian. The sherd/obsidian ratios given in table 11.4 reflect the fact that obsidian was also abundant at the Laguna de On settlement.

Terrestrial and aquatic game were abundantly available to each community, as indicated by the recovery of 7,879 pieces of faunal bone at Caye Coco and 10,231 pieces of bone at Laguna de On (table 11.4). Figures 11.4 and 11.5 indicate that the proportions of faunal bone within the sample of abundant materials at each site are almost exactly equivalent. The sherd/faunal bone ratio (table 11.4) implies that fauna was more abundant at Laguna de On, but it is clear that both communities had plentiful access to animal resources, which were probably extracted primarily for community use rather than as a form of specialized industry.

Figures 11.6 and 11.7 compare the proportions of artifacts present in lower quantities at each site. Lithic tools are shown in these charts to be slightly more abundant at Laguna de On (50%) than at Caye Coco (40%), but the sherd/tool ratio shows these quantities to be more equivalent (table 11.4). A more vast discrepancy is shown for lithic manufacturing debris (figures 11.4, 11.5), and this trend is also observed in the sherd/flake ratios (table 11.4). These patterns support the interpretation that as compared to the situation at Laguna de On, Caye Coco was gaining more of its tools through intercommunity exchange than through on-site manufacture.

Ceramic spindle whorls are one remnant of an important industry for Postclassic Maya communities: the production of cotton textiles. While the production of this commodity in southern lowlands provinces is well documented in the ethnohistoric records (Pina Chan 1978), little material evidence, other than the whorls themselves, reflects this activity. A total of 55 whorls was recovered from Laguna de On (Murray 1998), with a total of 29 spindle whorls discovered at Caye Coco. Figures 11.6 and 11.7 indicate that spindle whorls were relatively more abundant at Laguna de On (5%) than at Caye Coco (2%), and this trend is also reflected in the sherd/whorl ratios (table 11.4). Cotton cultivation and textile production may have been more important at Laguna de On, although such activities were also conducted at Caye Coco.

Notched ceramic net weights indicate the significance of fishing and turtling industries in these communities. The same number of notched net weights, 396, was recovered

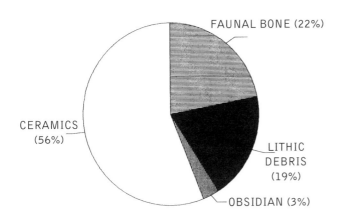

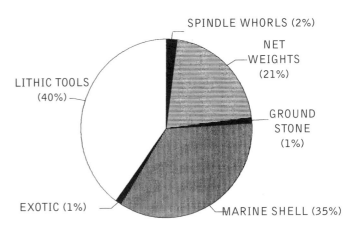

11.4 *Proportions of artifact and ecofact categories that occur in high numbers (> 1000) at Caye Coco. See table 11.4.*

11.6 *Proportions of artifact categories that occur in low numbers (< 1000) at Caye Coco. See table 11.4.*

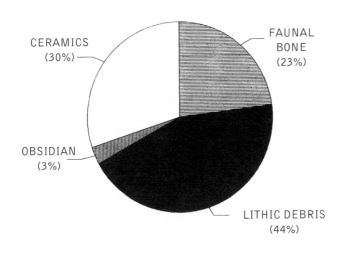

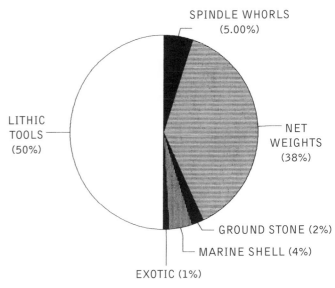

11.5 *Proportions of artifact and ecofact categories that occur in high numbers (> 1000) at Laguna de On. See table 11.4.*

11.7 *Proportions of artifact categories that occur in low numbers (< 1000) at Laguna de On. See table 11.4.*

from each site (table 11.4). The relative proportion of this artifact category at each site (figures 11.6, 11.7), as well as the sherd/net weight ratios (table 11.4), suggest that fishing and turtling were more important to the Laguna de On community (38%) than to Caye Coco (21%), but that members of both settlements engaged in this activity. As the environments of these two lagoons and other aquatic bodies accessible from these sites are very similar, there is little reason to believe that differences in aquatic resource availability in the immediate catchment zones of Laguna de On and Caye Coco were a factor in the amount of fishing that took place.

Ground-stone metates and manos represent a class of utilitarian artifacts that can be made from local or exotic materials. Exotic materials were often transported a considerable distance from areas such as the Maya Mountains in southern Belize. Their bulky size and weight imply that the effort required to transport these materials (or finished products made from them) would have contributed to the value and cost of such objects. The use of "exotic" materials to furbish grinding stones, a basic household utilitarian item, may have represented a symbol of prestige employed by upper-status members of society. Eleven manos and 8 metates were recovered at Laguna de On. Almost all pieces of ground stone were made of local limestone, except for one basalt metate fragment (Masson N.D.). At Caye Coco, 17 pieces of ground stone were found. At least one-third of all ground stone was made of basalt (according to Lisa Spillett), which would have been transported to this location from a distant mountain source. This pattern suggests that Caye Coco had increased access to exotic ground-stone materials, probably obtained through maritime trade. Ground stone forms a small percentage of each assemblage (1 to 2%) and significant differences in the quantities of this tool category are not apparent between the two sites. The sherd/ground-stone ratios (table 11.4) imply that ground stone was more abundant at Laguna de On.

Forty-three pieces of marine shell and 3 pieces of coral were recovered from Laguna de On (Masson N.D.). Much of this assemblage consists of debitage resulting from marine-conch and whelk-shell ornament manufacture (Masson N.D.). At Caye Coco, 595 pieces of marine shell and 62 pieces of coral have been recovered (table 11.4). It is clear from these numbers alone that the marine shell–working industry was much more developed at Caye Coco. Figures 11.6 and 11.7 also illustrate this pattern, with marine shell and coral representing a far greater proportion of the Caye Coco artifacts (35%) than of the Laguna de On sample (4%). The sherd/shell and coral ratios also reflect this trend (table 11.4). Many whole conch shells are found at Caye Coco, both as burial offerings (Barrett 1999) and lying on the surface. It is possible that this site's residents specialized in provisioning marine shell raw materials to other sites such as Laguna de On. Residents of both sites also fabricated finished products from shell, as indicated by fragments of worked debris, cups, and beads made of this material.

Nine stone beads of exotic material were recovered from Laguna de On, along with 2 greenstone celts and 1 fleck of gold (Masson N.D.). These artifacts comprise the "exotic ornament" category in table 11.4. At Caye Coco, 7 greenstone celts and 7 stone beads of exotic materials were found. Such exotic materials were not frequently recovered at either site, forming less than 1% of the artifact sample, as shown by the lower numbers in figures 11.6 and 11.7. The sherd/exotic ornament ratio (table 11.4) implies that Laguna de On may have had more relative quantities of such items than Caye Coco. Caye Coco's inferred higher political position suggests that individuals of higher social status would have occupied this site. Signifiers of social status, such as adornments made of exotic materials, might thus be expected to occur in greater numbers at Caye Coco; this, however, does not appear to be the case. These items may have circulated in Postclassic society in ways that caused them to be more generally distributed among communities of varying political rank, as in an open-market system (M.E. Smith 1998:11, 1999). Alternatively, they may not have been assigned

the social "value" that is generally implied in the distribution of rare, long-distance commodities in Mesoamerica (Clark 1987; Clark and Blake 1994). Based on the current data from these two sites, it is not possible to use these materials to discuss heterogeneity in community economies or to identify differences in status among members of each settlement.

Summary

Comparisons of artifact and ecofact assemblages from Laguna de On and Caye Coco provide new information concerning the variation in production and exchange during the Postclassic period in northern Belize. These settlements evidence a degree of community-level specialization in the extraction of local resources and the production of commodities from these resources for local and long-distance exchange. Laguna de On's population engaged in substantially more lithic tool production than the people at Caye Coco. This pattern coincides with Caye Coco's proximity to a number of chalcedony outcrops, which are thought to have facilitated development of an expedient tool industry here. Both settlements obtained formal tools from craft specialists at the site of Colha (Hester and Shafer 1991; Michaels 1987, 1994; Michaels and Shafer 1994). A range of expedient tools made of poorer quality materials at each site supplemented these Colha commodities. Caye Coco residents gained more of their tools through local exchange than is observed for Laguna de On, where more manufacturing debris is found. Laguna de On residents may have also been involved in more fishing and weaving activities than Caye Coco's.

Caye Coco's assemblage has a much greater proportion of ceramics than that of Laguna de On. This site's inhabitants may have more ceramics relative to lithics for their own consumption and perhaps for local exchange. This trend is difficult to interpret as little evidence of ceramic production has been found at Caye Coco. The greater abundance of ceramics at this site affects the sherd/material ratios in table 11.4, as all but two categories of items (lithic tools and shell/coral) are indicated as proportionately more abundant at Laguna de On. Percentage comparisons that do not take sherds into account (figures 11.6, 11.7) show more equivalent proportions of ground stone and exotic ornaments at the two sites, and these percentages confirm the sherd ratio indications that Laguna de On had greater proportions of spindle whorls, net weights, and lithic flakes than Caye Coco. Caye Coco's occupants specialized in the procurement of marine shell and the manufacture of marine shell ornaments, and they relied more on obsidian than on local lithic tools. Although it is not a coastal site, Caye Coco is located within a half day's canoe trip up the Freshwater Creek drainage (through John Piles Creek, Cocos Lagoon, and Laguna Seca to Lowry's Bight) to the coast (figure 11.1). This proximity would have allowed members of the Caye Coco community to obtain marine shells directly from the shallows inside the Caribbean reef or to have obtained them more easily from coastal communities. This access to the coast could also have increased opportunities to obtain obsidian from coastal merchants.

These data suggest that community commodity production varied at Postclassic northern Belize sites. Specialization in local resource extraction probably encouraged local intercommunity exchange and was conducive to the integration of regional polities. There is evidence of both down-the-line forms of intercommunity exchange and the existence of regional markets. The amount of obsidian relative to local lithic tools is less at Laguna de On than at Caye Coco. The latter is located nearer to trading sites on the Belize coast, and the former is nearer to Colha chert beds and sits on its own chalcedony outcrops. Caye Coco also possessed a greater proportion of ground-stone artifacts made of exotic materials, which presumably arrived through maritime trade contacts. The amounts of Colha chert and formal Colha tools are slightly less at Caye Coco than at Laguna de On, which may be the result of Caye Coco's greater distance from Colha in intercommunity exchange networks. The presence of abundant quantities of obsidian at Laguna de On suggests that access to this material was not highly restricted. The presence of open-market systems is suggested by the comparable proportions of exotic ornaments recovered at each site and may also be inferred from the lack of evidence of restricted access to all long-distance items, as suggested for highland Mesoamerican commodity distributions (M.E. Smith 1998, 1999).

Conclusions

Economic specialization at Laguna de On and Caye Coco appears to have existed in degrees and does not seem to have been exclusive in nature. Craft specialization may be most closely related to variations in resources available to each community. Northern Belize is a mosaic of microenvironments with variable raw materials, which Maya populations exploited since the first Formative villages (Rathje 1971). This comparison of two Postclassic communities of markedly different size and political scale suggests that a community's political rank was not closely tied to economic production or exchange privileges. While the site of Caye Coco has slightly higher frequencies of certain commodities that are perhaps indicative of status, such as slipped or incised ceramics and obsidian blades, these items are also present at Laguna de On in abundance, and the difference appears to be one of small degree. Caye Coco's residents

engaged in the production and extraction of their own agricultural and wild food resources and in the manufacture of essential commodities such as textiles. Laguna de On's inhabitants also farmed, fished, and turtled for local sustenance. Spinning and local lithic technologies were more important at this site. Both sites made shell ornaments, although this industry was far more prevalent at Caye Coco.

A comparison of the artifacts at Caye Coco with those at Laguna de On thus suggests that both communities were avidly engaged in localized production activities, and both enjoyed access to long-distance commodities obtained through maritime trade. Community exchange was probably symbiotic because of differences in production emphasis which were influenced by access to variable local resources and proximity to the coast. Vast disparities are not observed in the essential components of these sites' economies on a scale analogous to the differences in magnitude inferred from their size and surface architecture. These observations suggest that political power was not strongly rooted in economic control. Processes of state formation documented for the Maya area were elastic and exhibited regular cycles of fissioning and fusion (J.W. Fox 1987; G.D. Jones 1989). Nonetheless, evidence of long-term economic stability is observed in the duration of the Postclassic ceramic sequence (A.F. Chase and D.Z. Chase 1985), which spans approximately 500 years in northern Belize and an even longer period in the Petén (A.F. Chase and D.Z. Chase 1985: Figs. 2, 3).

The enduring nature of attributes of ceramic manufacture during this period suggests the periodic collapse of local fiefdoms did not disrupt ceramic producers (Masson N.D.). The dispersion and autonomy of Maya producers during the Classic period, who operated in rural precincts located away from urban political centers, has been described (Freidel 1981; King and Potter 1994; McAnany 1995; P.M. Rice 1987b:77). It is apparent that this mode of organization was conducive to economic stability during the Classic period, and it continued during the Postclassic as an effective balance to cyclical political dynamics that were much reduced in scale compared to earlier times. This examination of the assemblages at Laguna de On and Caye Coco illustrates just how "undifferentiated" the economy of one political center was in comparison to a middle-size settlement during the Postclassic. The artifact signatures of these sites suggest they were very similar, consisting of two industrious villages, one exhibiting the vestments of political clout and one lacking such symbols. According to this analysis, the political "bite" of Caye Coco did not penetrate far into the local Postclassic economy. This is not to say that political centers did not play key roles in mediating exchange with long-distance merchants or in organizing local markets or "market fairs," as Freidel (1981) has suggested. In Maya Postclassic political systems, however, it was probable that the organizing and mediating role of a particular center might easily be fulfilled by its local successor, with business proceeding as usual at the production end of society.

This volume examines the evidence for rural complexity in the southern Maya lowlands. Postclassic settlement data collected to date (Sidrys 1983) suggest that most communities of this period were "rural," or at least represented dispersed, autonomous polities that did not exhibit dramatic centralization tendencies. While some settlements may have been nucleated (as notably exemplified by Mayapan), there is no evidence to date that their distribution across the landscape was anything but dispersed (Andrews 1977; Andrews and Vail 1990; Sidrys 1983). In this sense, it is difficult to define rural contexts in the absence of urban ones. Perhaps the settlement mode of regionally dispersed small centers of the Classic period that characterizes much of northern and central Belize, the topic examined in most of the contributions to this volume, was a prelude to the Postclassic pattern with its truncation of large regional centers. Certainly, this pattern appears to be conducive to long-term economic stability and a high degree of affluence and autonomy for each community, as suggested by the prosperous attributes of Belizean settlements documented for all time periods (Freidel 1981; McAnany

1995:155). Further systematic survey of Postclassic settlements is needed, however, to document fully sizes of sites, distributions of sites, and duration of occupation. Continued research will, we hope, refine our understanding of variation in community production in the Postclassic southern lowlands and the relationship between political power and economic stability.

Acknowledgments. Research at Laguna de On and Caye Coco has been supported by the Center for Field Research: Earthwatch, the National Science Foundation, the Foundation for the Advancement of Mesoamerican Studies, the Wenner Gren Foundation, and the Departments of Anthropology at The University of Texas, Pacific Lutheran University, and (currently) The University at Albany-SUNY. This research is conducted with the gracious cooperation and permission of the Department of Archaeology, Belmopan, Belize, and I appreciate the assistance of Archaeological Commissioners Bryan Woodye, John Morris, and (currently) Allan Moore, and Caye Coco landowners Fabian and Deodoro Perez. I am very grateful to members of the Belize Postclassic Project staff, whose analysis of artifacts in the field laboratory has made the comparisons in this chapter possible, including Maxine Oland's work on project lithics and a team of ceramicists, including Dr. Shirley Mock, Dr. George Bey, Georgia West, Janel Orsi, Alex Mullen, Monica Reed, and Jennifer Meanwell.

12 Coping with Diversity

Edward M. Schortman and Patricia A. Urban

THE CHAPTERS IN THIS VOLUME illustrate important changes in how pre-Hispanic lowland Maya society is conceptualized. Traditionally, lowland Maya polities of all periods, but especially those of the Classic era (AD 200 to 900), were viewed through models that stressed stability. Bounded polities were thought to have been divided into distinct, internally homogenous, hierarchically arranged social strata. Members of each tier were charged with carrying out functions integral to preserving equilibrium. Social units, and the tasks they performed, were physically linked to sites of different sizes, organized into hierarchies with clearly delimited levels. Settlement dimensions were, therefore, equated with functional complexity and social status. Paramount elites monopolized performance of ritual and administrative behaviors through which entire polities were unified, these actions taking place within special-purpose facilities concentrated at regional centers. Each progressively smaller site in the hierarchy sheltered a proportionately less powerful cadre of officials offering an ever diminishing subset of identical services to ever smaller sustaining hinterlands. Numerically preponderant hamlets, in turn, were homes to a culturally and socially homogenous peasantry who dutifully contributed labor to, and derived benefits from, the hierarchy of centers to which they were subordinate.

This model parallels and, to some extent, was inspired by Christaller's Central Place formulation in human geography (Haggett 1965:118–125). Both are idealized representations of how activities conducted at different scales should be distributed across a uniform landscape to maximize efficiency. Adoption of the above perspective was also encouraged by an enduring dichotomy in western thought between internally heterogenous modern industrial states and the homogeneity imputed to even the most complex prehistoric agrarian polities.

Such viewpoints are coming under increased scrutiny throughout archaeology (for example, Schwartz and Falconer 1994a). An emphasis on the role of competition among individuals and factions in shaping society is creating a political archaeology at odds with earlier models that stressed cooperation in the fashioning of enduring social and economic structures (Bourdieu 1977; Brumfiel and Fox, eds. 1994; Giddens 1985; Kohl 1981; Paynter 1989; Roscoe 1993). Even more fundamental is the growing recognition that neat functional correlations among a site's size and the status and activities of its occupants may more accurately reflect our own wishful thinking than ancient reality (see chapters 4, 3, and 8). Earlier categorical reasoning, and the resultant site typologies that elided function and size, obscured more than they revealed. In leveling such criticisms it is easy to lose sight of the earlier model's utility as a research guide. Following its precepts, knowledge of ancient lowland Maya behavior and material patterns was greatly enriched. That these investigations ultimately revealed shortcomings in the over-arching conceptual scheme only confirms the framework's usefulness.

Constructing a Replacement: Describing Diversity

Pointing out problems in an old theory is relatively easy; cobbling together an alternative is much harder. Taking up the challenge requires that we develop concepts that encourage recognition and description of functional, cultural, and social variety occurring along the entire settlement continuum; identify relations among variables that explain the observed differential distribution of activities, identities, and statuses; and to learn better to distinguish divisions within the landscape that conform to ancient political/cultural units rather than our preconceptions of them (see chapters 2, 8, 7, and 9). None of these tasks is easy.

The first step, stressing recognition and description, has already been taken by all the volume contributors. Rigid, functionally defined hierarchies rooted in site-size differences have been eschewed in favor of more fluid conceptualizations in which settlement dimensions are not mechanically correlated with the activities performed within their boundaries or the identities and statuses of their occupants. Who lived within a site and what they did are matters to be determined through direct observation and not to be assumed on a priori principles. This is not an invitation to wallow in rampant empiricism, delaying theory building until all the "facts" are in. Rather, we have to create concepts appropriate to describing the newly perceived complexity with which we are confronted. These intellectual tools will certainly be developed within specific theoretical contexts, shaped to some extent by their generative environments. Nevertheless, comparative studies and fruitful conversations crucial to understanding rural complexity will occur only if our descriptive concepts are clearly defined in terms we can all grasp.

Practitioners of human geography faced a similar situation about four decades earlier. Here, efforts have long been under way to bring Christaller's idealized depiction of functional relations among settlements more in line with reality. Losch, for example, modeled the urban landscape as a flexible settlement hierarchy in which the functions and locations of villages, towns, and cities varied in complex ways (Haggett 1965:124; Losch 1954). The simple urban-rural dichotomy in western industrialized societies was, therefore, reconceptualized as a behavioral continuum. Like most geographic models, Losch's formulation is based on economic principles of cost and efficiency appropriate to capitalist settings and cannot be applied wholesale to prehistoric contexts. Nevertheless, insofar as understandings of the past are informed by perceived relations in the present, shifting views on modern urban-rural patterning alert us to the possibility of similar continuities in the remote past (see chapters 3 and 8).

Heterarchy, as Iannone (chapter 3), Yaeger (chapter 5), and Conlon and Moore (chapter 6) explicitly observe, may be useful in modeling rural complexity, as well as urban-rural interconnections (Ehrenreich, Crumley, and Levy 1995). This concept refers to relations among variables that are ordered, but not hierarchically so, or have the potential for being ranked in several different ways (Crumley 1995:3). Connell points to a situation in the Chaa Creek settlement zone where unranked activities, such as elite residence, ancestor worship, administration, and public feasting, were distributed among functionally specific centers. Heterarchy in this and other cases offers a means of transcending the strictures of hierarchical thinking, encouraging us to imagine different, not necessarily ranked, ways in which activities and other variables might be distributed across societies and the landscapes they occupy.

Consideration of heterarchy, however, brings up the important issue of scale. For example, middle-level sites within the communities described by Connell may have been venues for the performance of functionally complementary, unranked activities. As such, relations among their residents and the behaviors in which they engaged might fruitfully be described as heterarchical. Nevertheless, occupants of these intermediate settlements were subordinate to the Xunantunich lords. The same general situation pertains to the intermediate sites described in chapters 10, 3, 9, and 5. The behavioral and developmental heterogeneity that assaults our senses and undermines cherished models, therefore, results, in part, from the intersection of hierarchical and heterarchical processes operating with variable force across entire settlement systems.

But what is it that is distributed in ranked and unranked formats over ancient landscapes? Heterarchy and hierarchy describe relations; what is ordered in these divergent ways must still be specified. We have tended in the past to describe societies by charting the spatial and temporal distribution of such conceptual entities as complexity, status, and elite-level functions as though these represented unitary constructs composed of mutually interdependent, virtually inseparable elements. This thinking is based on assumptions of such absolute functional interdependence among components of, say, complexity, that one aspect, political centralization, for example, could reliably stand for other such constituents as wealth, socioeconomic differentiation, and inequality (de Montmollin 1989; McGuire 1983; Roscoe 1993; see chapter 2). What is so troubling now is the recognition that these elements do not coincide as expected, nor do they change in lock-step. Functional links among variables comprising omnibus categories are not as strong as we guessed. This realization is encouraged, as Ashmore and Iannone note, by a growing awareness that culture is not a package of values and behaviors that all members accept equally. Instead, it is increasingly seen as the product of individual, mutually adjusted decisions and actions guided by varying goals pursued through different strategies (Bourdieu 1977; Ortner 1984; see also chapter 1). Accepting the latter view alerts us to the existence of behavioral and material heterogeneity, just as subscribing to the earlier position encouraged identification of homogenous cultures in the archaeological record.

This is not to say that all is chaos. It will take much more work, however, before we can articulate the conditions under which aspects of such broad concepts as complexity are related in predictable ways. As Ashmore and Levi remark, successful achievement of this vital objective requires breaking down complex variables into their constituent parts and studying the spatial and temporal distributions of each as continua of variation (de Montmollin 1989; Feinman and Neitzel 1984; McGuire 1983; Roscoe 1993). Allowing for diverse interconnections among factors, rather than assuming correlations from the start, is part of what Ashmore refers to as the "conceptual fluidity" needed to advance lowland Maya studies.

The task before us, therefore, is to reexamine basic concepts, teasing out their components; name those elements in ways that facilitate comparison; specify archaeological measures of these abstract entities; and chart their heterarchical and/or hierarchical relations across space and time. This formidable challenge must be addressed before we can satisfactorily describe ancient settlement systems.

Happily, the chapters in this collection indicate that considerable progress has already been made toward achieving these objectives. Concepts employed in these descriptive efforts include site size; function; and the wealth, power, identities, and autonomy of the people residing in middle-range settlements. The activities pursued at intermediate centers are given the greatest amount of attention by the volume's contributors. All the authors eschew the simplistic proposition that site size accurately indicates the range and scales of behaviors pursued at a settlement. The Chases, Conlon and Moore, Connell, Iannone, Yaeger, along with Tourtellot and his colleagues, effectively point out that "minor centers" are not functionally homogenous, replicating on a small scale all those services provided at the hierarchy's apex. Instead, they suggest that administrative, ritual, and economic institutions and their facilities may be physically disassociated and dispersed to different locales within a realm. The Chases, Connell, and Tourtellot et al. even go so far as to suggest that we should think of intermediate and paramount centers as functionally related components of single, large communities, no element of which can be understood in isolation. Commonalities in the spacing of middle-level sites around major centers noted by the Chases and Tourtellot et al. reinforce this notion and hold open the possibility of inter-areal regularities in the distribution of activities associated with elites. The above points reiterate Ashmore's position that connections among sites are at least as important as the sites themselves.

The chapter by McAnany and her co-authors takes the argument two major steps further by: reminding us that indigenous perceptions of the natural and constructed landscape played major roles in determining the significance of those features in the operation of ancient societies; activities important in that operation may well have taken place in areas outside traditionally defined settlements, such as in caves. As Ashmore noted, contextualizing sites with visible architecture requires paying attention to the broader cognized landscape of which these settlements were crucial parts.

The elements of site function that enjoy the greatest attention in these essays are those related to administration and ritual (though the Chases raise the possibility that some middle-level sites were nodes in ancient marketing networks). This bias may well reflect an enduring tendency to view lowland Maya societies as composed of economically self-sufficient and redundant entities united under the supernaturally sanctioned rule of priest-kings (for example, Thompson 1966). Such a position finds recent expression in the regal-ritual model advanced to describe Classic period lowland Maya political organization (Ball and Taschek 1991; Marcus 1983a, 1993; Sanders and Webster 1988). Masson diverges from this trend by pointing out that not only was there community-based economic specialization in the Late Postclassic eastern lowlands but that variations in production and political rank did not correlate. More work along these lines is needed to evaluate the significance of economic variables in the creation of rural landscapes during all periods.

The observed distribution of administrative, economic, and ritual activities charted in the above contributions calls to mind the Dispersed Cities Model from economic geography (Haggett 1965; Morrill 1974). In this case, the need to integrate large far-flung populations under conditions of poor transportation encouraged the spreading of functions that would otherwise have been concentrated at one or a few major centers (Haggett 1965; Morrill 1974). Whether this was also the case among the lowland Maya, and what other factors might have played roles in creating the noted patterns, remain questions in need of answers.

Related to, but more challenging than, the study of functional variation among sites is the analysis of rural social, economic, and cultural heterogeneity. Here, we confront such concepts as status and cultural identity, unpacking their components and struggling to identify their material signatures. Conlon and Moore, Connell, Iannone, and Yaeger grapple with these issues, pointing out in the process that wealth, power, identity, and autonomy are variably expressed within, as well as across, settlements and do not necessarily coincide in expected ways within any particular social unit.

We have been pursuing similar questions in our research within the Naco Valley, northwestern Honduras. Specifically, we have been impressed by the degree to which two components of social status—wealth and power—diverge within the rural hinterland of the valley's Late Classic (AD 600– 950) regional capital, La Sierra (a discrepancy also noted in chapter 11). Power, defined as the ability to direct the actions of others, is estimated from the sizes of residences and associated buildings that individual families could commission. Wealth, on the other hand, denotes the success with which social units could amass valuable items (measured by the proportions of imported and locally made, elaborately decorated ceramics found within the terminal debris assemblages of different domestic groups [Smith 1987]). Power and wealth are concentrated at La Sierra but the relationship falls apart outside the center. Here we find sites with monumental constructions (platforms at least 1.5 m high) that yield wealth measures half the magnitude of those derived from settlements lacking impressive architecture. Comparing the average percentage of elaborately decorated and imported ceramics between monumental and nonmonumental rural sites reveals a near identity (4.1 versus 3.7, respectively). Observed differences cannot be accounted for by variable sampling, comparable amounts of the sites in question having been excavated and proportions of recovered ceramics studied. Rather, it appears that material success and power were disassociated from each other to some degree among those residing outside the capital. Wealth, it seems, could not buy happiness or political clout. Wealth and power, therefore, were acquired by different, not necessarily related, means in rural portions of the Late Classic Naco Valley.

Heterogeneity, whether organized heterarchically or hierarchically, might best be understood, therefore, as the variable intersection of diverse domains. The behavior and material patterns at any particular site can be described at a specific moment in time by reference to such vectors as administrative function, economic production, wealth, and power that converge at the locus. Rather than assuming correlations among such variables, we must identify what values for each of these continua pertain in particular cases and then determine how they might be related under specific conditions. Culture-change processes could then be reconstructed by charting temporal shifts in the measures of these different factors. But what forces produce the observed distributions of descriptive variables?

Explaining Heterogeneity

The contributors to this volume offer a wide array of processes to account for the differential distribution of behaviors across middle-level settlements. These approaches grow out of broad, over-arching archaeological perspectives variably stressing structure or agency, adaptation, or political machinations in accounting for human behavior.

Traditionally, it has been argued that variations in such factors as the activities performed at different sites are rooted in the adaptive responses of populations to ecological challenges. Cultural form and change, in this view, are products of ongoing human struggles to secure a living from the physical environment. Though far from faceless automatons, people see it in their best interests to cooperate in this essential endeavor, eventually achieving a balance with their surroundings that benefits all. Within this perspective, intermediate settlements are essential linchpins in an armature designed to promote unity within environments more conducive to fragmentation. Variations in their forms and functions result from the different roles resident elites play in forging social integration, these roles being partly determined by the ecological settings in which these notables operated. Though paramount individuals benefit from this arrangement, their subordinates derive some advantage from the services provided at minor centers, including redistribution of food and exotics.

Opposing this perspective is a more avowedly political viewpoint that sees culture as a product of competitions for power among factions whose members are united in pursuit of specific objectives that may well conflict with the aims espoused by other blocs (see chapter 2). Adherents of this Marxist-inspired view of history do not imagine an anarchic free-for-all with victory going to the most obnoxious. Instead, blocs operate within inherited structures composed of social, political, economic, and ideological elements that most actors treat as given and immutable. Working within these parameters, however, change invariably occurs if only because the long-term consequences of factional strategies are very different from what their initiators intended. Concepts of equilibrium and balance are replaced as explanatory variables by competition and conflict.

Political perspectives are rapidly gaining acceptance in archaeology, the excitement surrounding their advent accounting in part for the large number of the volume's contributors who espouse them. Iannone and Yaeger offer some of the most explicit statements of the roles played by competition in shaping the forms and functions of middle-level settlements, their position seconded by Connell, and Conlon and Moore. Especially prominent in these formulations is the significance of alliances forged among people of different ranks in search of clients and patronage. At widely varying scales, reaching from the hinterlands of major centers down to areas encompassed by particular sites, alliance-formation processes fragment what had previously been seen as a relatively stable, culturally homogenous landscape. In this model, the fortunes of any social group depend partly upon the success their allies enjoyed. Since that success is conditioned by a wide range of factors, each of which is subject to change, shifts in the power, wealth, and autonomy of actors are always imminent. Consequently, the archaeological landscape is littered with the juxtaposed material remains of winners and losers in factional contests. It is this heterogeneity that undermined earlier models of cultural homogeneity and the social harmony that was thought to have encouraged it.

Yaeger introduces the important issue of social identity into this equation. How people define themselves vis-à-vis others within their society is central to understanding the ways in which cultures are structured at any moment and change through time. This important element of an individual's social persona is strongly affected by, and affects, those with whom one associates and makes common cause. Though difficult to recognize archaeologically, social affiliations comprise an important continuum of variation in prehistoric and modern settings, and deserve more attention in our studies of the past. Material signifiers of varied identities, such as the architectural features discussed by Connell and by Conlon and Moore, most likely contribute to the complex patterning of archaeological remains found in the hinterlands of major centers (Beaudry, Cook, and Mrozowski 1991; Larick 1991; Schortman 1989; Wiessner 1983; Wobst 1977).

Following from these considerations, cultures are seen as highly volatile structures wherein wealth, power, identity, and autonomy may well vary markedly across small spatial distances and temporal spans. This emphasis on alliance formation as a cause of material and behavioral heterogeneity has proven fruitful, as the essays in this collection clearly indicate. It is important to keep in mind, however, that other processes can contribute to the diversity recognized in all settlements. Among these is specialized craft production.

Masson, for example, notes that variations in artisanal activity among sites are sometimes related to the distribution of locally available resources. We would like to take this valuable insight a couple of steps further by referring, again, to wealth and power differences within the Late Classic Naco Valley. In this case, heterogeneity seems to derive in part from unresolved contests in which social units deployed resources at their disposal to accumulate valuables and capture labor while protecting the results of their own productive efforts from acquisition by others. Craft production, we argue, was one of the assets used in these struggles. Households that could draw on the widest array of raw materials from the immediate vicinities of their settlements, and controlled the requisite skills, engaged in an extensive suite of manufacturing processes, yielding items with which to meet their own needs and to exchange with those employed in complementary economic pursuits. Less fortunately situated social groups pursued fewer crafts and were forced to exchange their meager surpluses to acquire goods they did not fashion. Wealth, therefore, flowed from some households into others, contributing to the differences in material well-being observed in the Naco data. Interestingly, this observation contrasts with the findings of Arnold (1991), who suggests that people turned to craftworking under conditions of relative impoverishment.

Power, as indicated earlier, does not clearly correlate with wealth outside La Sierra and must have been fought for using different resources. The ability to command labor in rural areas may well have hinged on senior positions within extended kin-groups and/or control of arable land by dint of first settlement (see also chapter 5). These contrasting processes yielded a dynamic, fluid politico-economic structure that can be glossed as heterarchical or hierarchical, depending upon which variables are highlighted (wealth or power) and how effective factions were at achieving their goals. As absolute supremacy and pure egalitarianism are rare achievements, heterarchy and hierarchy co-exist here, as they do everywhere, to varying degrees (see chapter 3).

Alliance formation and craft production are but two of the competitive processes that can generate heterogeneity in any society. Much more theory building must be accomplished before we can specify all the possible variables over which people contend, the consequences of such contests, and the ways in which these factors are combined under varying circumstances.

Adaptationist and political frameworks are best viewed as complementary vantage points from which to understand behavioral and material heterogeneity operating at variable scales. All societies are, to some extent, adjusted to their environments just as they provide arenas in which people, organized into blocs, contend for valued objectives, power, and the ability to control their own lives. The patterning we identify archaeologically, therefore, is a product of both integrative and competitive processes. Pursuit of one approach or another is justified as long as we remember that neither one will provide complete, unambiguous answers by itself. Each captures part of an ancient reality, not its totality.

Summary

It was not so long ago that we could speak confidently of lowland Maya rulers dominating a culturally homogenous peasantry through the agency of an equally uniform cadre of subordinates resident in minor ceremonial centers. Each tier of the settlement hierarchy served as venues for activities that mirrored, on smaller scales, those conducted at the next highest level. Wealth, power, and individual autonomy were closely related and declined down the hierarchy, with questions of identity rarely arising in our discussions.

There is no returning to this admirably simple model in Belize, or anywhere else. What we thought we knew about relations among site functions, wealth, power, social affiliations, and autonomy has been revealed as overly simplistic and, in some cases, just plain wrong. Ironically, it was the research conducted under the aegis of these misinformed assumptions that ultimately revealed their flaws. There is some comfort, albeit of a cold sort, in that recognition.

Having given up on the old model, we are forced to construct a new, more serviceable framework. As the volume contributors indicate through their work, the first step is definition of those variables whose complex intersections create the heterogeneity we now perceive in our data. Rather than characterizing these factors as deceptively neat polar oppositions (wealthy versus poor, elite versus commoner, and so forth), we are better off viewing them as continua whose values grade into one another. The first order of business, then, is to define the vectors relevant to describing ancient sociopolitical systems, determining their graduated expressions, and deriving ways of inferring these variable states from archaeological remains.

The social conditions pertaining at each site at specific points in time can then be reconstructed by specifying intersections among these varied continua. Characterizing particular settlements is, of course, not the ultimate goal of our investigations. Eventually, we must fit these individual pieces of the puzzle together to describe the sociopolitical systems of which even the largest center is but a part. These static pictures of sociopolitical organizations must ultimately be reimbued with the dynamism that characterized them in life. Time's importance can never be ignored, and the study of changing relations among social vectors is a crucial part of our descriptive efforts.

Accomplishment of these goals requires rethinking our field strategies (see chapter 2). In the Maya lowlands, assessing values for such factors as wealth, power, and site functions and their changes through time requires excavation. Survey defines the parameters of our research universe, specifies variations in the sizes and locations of ancient settlements, and suggests possible interpretations of observed differences. Survey alone, however, cannot provide the detailed information regarding the material patterns needed to test these notions and infer where particular social units fall out on the aforementioned vectors. Similarly, limited test pitting provides valuable data for constructing chronologies but does not yield the broad exposures of the activity areas required to describe ancient behaviors. Insights obtained from extensive lateral clearing of prehistoric deposits can, however, serve as reliable foundations for describing ancient societies, only if we have reason to believe that the areas sampled are representative of the full range of behaviors pursued within those units. But what are the entities that comprise our samples?

Some contributors, such as Conlon and Moore and Yaeger, argue that plazuela groups are the most appropriate units of analysis because they are the physical remains of that most basic of social entities, the household (for example, Santley and Hirth 1993; Sheets 1992; Wilk and Ashmore, eds. 1988). McAnany and her colleagues, along with Ashmore, remind us that there is more to the archaeological record than architecture; natural locales, such as caves, are also important elements of the social landscape. Most of us are still dealing with sites, though paying increasing attention to distinctions within these entities while simultaneously coming to view individual settlements as components of larger communities (see chapters 10, 4, and 9). We are, therefore, facing a continuum of potential investigative foci reaching from the isolated activity locus, situated within or outside architecturally defined settlements, all the way up to mega-communities, such as those centered on such political capitals as Calakmul, Caracol, Coba, and Tikal. What we select from this spectrum to study will depend on what we want to know. Research into intrasettlement variations in wealth, for example, will be conducted using a different set of analytical units than studies of integration within multisite communities. What is clear, however, is that no one person, possibly no one project, can investigate all of these levels simultaneously. The pictures we construct of ancient societies must be composites derived from the investigations of numerous researchers, each of whom conducts their studies in a manner that facilitates cooperation and mutual intelligibility.

In the course of dealing with the details of particular societies and their histories, we must never lose sight of possible regularities in associations among values ranged along different continua (see chapters 3, 7, 8, and 10, for examples of fruitful comparative analyses). The problem with earlier typologies was not that their creators posited predictable relations among such elements as wealth, power, and site function but that they assumed the invariability of these connections. The resultant formulations then obscured more than they revealed as we were tempted to force recalcitrant data into the neat categories our theories provided. The connections we seek are unknown to us now and are more likely to pertain under certain limited conditions rather than universally. Such restrictions do not lessen the significance of cross-culturally valid relations but only make them harder to discern. This volume is a testament to the potential of such comparative efforts.

Even as the work of description proceeds, we must be

aware that what we eventually see will be conditioned by the basic theoretical assumptions guiding our work (see chapter 1). Individual accounts and explanations of findings will continue to diverge considerably. Partly, this is owing to the generally unappreciated ingenuity the ancient lowland Maya exhibited in creating diverse social forms within a relatively small area. Such variability, however, is also a product of the different theories that we all use to filter observations and make sense of the material with which we are confronted. Contrary to popular belief, there is no reason to wring our hands in despair over these incongruities. They become problems only when we make them so by insisting that one, and only one, conceptual framework is an infallible guide to truth. As noted earlier, we are better served by acknowledging that each reasonable theoretical orientation provides insights into some truths not accessible from other vantage points. This does not make the truths we see any better than those perceived by our colleagues, just different.

At the center of this ongoing debate concerning description, comparison, and explanation of social diversity is the middle-level site. These centers, because they must be understood within both elite and rural contexts, serve as lightening rods for arguments over the structure of total societies. Grasping the nature, functioning, and history of intermediate settlements requires the modeling of both their relations to the notables who commissioned their monuments and the commoners in whose midst they were established. We can fool ourselves into thinking that political capitals are comprehensible when compared to their peers in other polities and that hamlets are best understood within their immediate ecological settings. Neither argument seems even remotely plausible for minor centers that can be described and explained only in relation to the total polities of which they were a part. This may be one of the reasons middle-level sites were so long ignored; we lacked, until recently, understandings of the contexts wherein they made sense. That minor centers are now getting their turn in the investigative spotlight reflects the maturity of a field whose practitioners are willing to take on the total polity analyses (Marcus 1993:170) needed to link rulers and ruled within a single frame of reference.

Each intermediate site, therefore, is a nexus where complexly related variables such as wealth, power, identity, and autonomy are interwoven into Gordian knots whose untying both frustrates and excites researchers. Judging by the chapters in this volume, the process of unraveling these skeins is well begun and promises great results.

Bibliography

Abrams, E.M.

1994 *How the Maya built their universe: Energetics and ancient architecture.* Austin: U of Texas Press.

Adams, B.

1998 Analysis of the Xunantunich Archaeological Project (XAP) human skeletal remains. Report on file, Cotsen Institute of Archaeology, University of California, Los Angeles.

Adams, R.E.W.

1981 Settlement patterns of the central Yucatan and southern Campeche regions. In *Lowland Maya settlement patterns*, edited by W.A. Ashmore, 211–258. Albuquerque: Academic Press.

1982 Rank size analysis of northern Belize Maya sites. In *The archaeology of Colha, Belize: 1981 interim report*, edited by T.R. Hester, H.J. Shafer, and J. Eaton, 60–64. San Antonio: Center for Archaeological Research, University of Texas.

Adams, R.E.W., and R.C. Jones

1981 Spatial patterns and regional growth among the Classic Maya cities. *American Antiquity* 46:301–322.

Adams, R.E.W., and F. Valdez, Jr., eds.

1995 *The Programme for Belize Archaeology Project, 1994 interim report.* San Antonio: Center for Archaeology and Tropical Studies and University of Texas.

Agrinier, P.

1983 Tenam Rosario: Una posible relocalización del clásico Maya Terminal desde el Usumacinta. In *Antropología e historia de los Mixe-Zoques y Mayas: Homenaje a Frans Blom*, edited by L. Ochoa and T.A. Lee, Jr., 241–254. Mexico: Universidad Nacional Autónoma de México and Brigham Young University.

Andrews, A.P.

1977 Reconocimiento arqueologico de la costa norte del Estado de Campeche. *Boletín de la Escuela de Ciencias Antropologicas de la Universidad de Yucatán* 4(24):64–77.

Andrews, A.P., and G. Vail

1990 Cronología de sitios prehispanicos costeros de la Peninsula de Yucatán y Belice. *Boletín de la Escuela de Ciencias Antropologicas de la Universidad de Yucatán* 18(104–105):37–66.

Angelini, M.L.

1998 The potter's craft: A study of Formative Maya ceramic technology at K'axob, Belize. Ph.D. dissertation, Department of Archaeology, Boston University, Boston.

Arnold, J.A., and A. Ford

1980 A statistical examination of settlement patterns at Tikal, Guatemala. *American Antiquity* 45:713–728.

Arnold, P.J., III

1991 *Domestic ceramic production and spatial organization: A Mexican case study in ethnoarchaeology.* Cambridge: Cambridge U Press.

Ashmore, W.A.

1981a *Lowland Maya settlement patterns.* Albuquerque: U of New Mexico Press.

1981b Some issues of method and theory in lowland Maya settlement archaeology. In *Lowland Maya settlement patterns*, edited by W.A. Ashmore, 37–69. Albuquerque: U of New Mexico Press.

1981c Pre-Columbian occupation at Quirigua, Guatemala: Settlement patterns in a Classic Maya center. Ph.D. dissertation, Department of Anthropology, University of Pennsylvania, Philadelphia.

1989 Construction and cosmology: Politics and ideology in lowland Maya settlement patterns. In *Word and image in Maya culture: Explorations in language, writing, and representation*, edited by W.F. Hanks and D.S. Rice, 272–286. Salt Lake City: U of Utah Press.

1991 Site-planning principles and concepts of directionality among the ancient Maya. *Latin American Antiquity* 2:199–226.

1992 Deciphering Maya architectural plans. In *New theories on the ancient Maya*, edited by E. Danien and R.J. Sharer, 173–184. Philadelphia: University Museum, University of Pennsylvania.

1993 Settlement archaeology at Xunantunich, Belize, Central America. Proposal submitted to National Science Foundation. August.

1998 Monumentos politicos: Sitio, asentamiento, y paisaje alrededor de Xunantunich, Belice. In *Anatomía de una civilización: Aproximaciones interdisciplinarias a la cultura Maya*, edited by A. Ciudad Ruiz, Y. Fernández Marquínez, J.M. García Campillo, Ma. J.I. Ponce de León, A.L. García-Gallo, and L.T. Sanz Castro, 161–183. Madrid: Sociedad Española de Estudios Mayas.

Ashmore, W.A., S.V. Connell, J.J. Ehret, C.H. Gifford, L.T. Neff, and J. VandenBosch

1994 The Xunantunich settlement survey. In Xunantunich Archaeological Project: 1994 field season, edited by R.M. Leventhal and W.A. Ashmore, 248–275. Report on file, Department of Archaeology, Belmopan, Belize, and Cotsen Institute of Archaeology at UCLA.

Ashmore, W., and A.B. Knapp, eds.

1999 *Archaeologies of landscape: Contemporary perspectives.* Oxford: Blackwell.

Ashmore, W.A., and J.A. Sabloff

1997 On spatial order in Maya civic plans. Paper presented at the Segunda Mesa Redonda de Palenque, Palenque, Mexico.

Ashmore, W.A., and R.R. Wilk

1988 Household and community in the Mesoamerican past. In *Household and community in the Mesoamerican past*, edited by R.R. Wilk and W.A. Ashmore, 1–27. Albuquerque: U of New Mexico Press.

Ashmore, W.A., J. Yaeger, and C. Robin

2001 Commoner sense: Late and Terminal Classic social strategies in the Xunantunich area. In *Collapse, transition, and transformation: New views of the end of the Classic period in the Maya lowlands*, edited by D.S. Rice, P.M. Rice, and A.A. Demarest. Denver: Westview Press.

Aveni, A.F.

1977 Concepts and positional astronomy employed in ancient Mesoamerican architecture. In *Native American astronomy,* edited by A.F. Aveni, 3–20. Austin: University of Texas.

Aveni, A.F., and H. Hartung

1986 Maya city planning and the calendar. *Transactions of the American Philosophical Society* 76(7).

Aveni, A.F., H. Hartung, and B. Buckingham

1978 The pecked cross symbol in ancient Mesoamerica. *Science* 202:267–279.

Awe, J.J.

1993 The Formative prehistory of the Belize Valley: A new perspective from Cahal Pech. Paper presented at the 58th Annual Meeting of the Society for American Archaeology, St. Louis, MO.

N.D.   Progress report of the 1998 season of the Western Belize Regional Caves Project.

Awe, J.J., and S. Brisbin

1993   Now you see it now you don't: The trials and tribulations of settlement survey at Cahal Pech, Belize. In *Belize Valley Archaeological Reconnaissance Project: Progress report of the 1992 field season*, edited by J.J. Awe, 1–9. Peterborough, Ontario: Department of Anthropology, Trent University.

Awe, J.J., M.D. Campbell, and J.M. Conlon

1991   Preliminary spatial analysis of the site core of Cahal Pech, Belize and its implications for lowland Maya social organization. *Mexicon* 13(2):25–30.

Ball, J.W., and J.T. Taschek

1990   *Settlement system and community organization in a Classic Maya realm: The 1988-90 SDSU Mopan–Macal Triangle Archaeological Project*. Preliminary Interim Report, No. 2. Belmopan, Belize: Department of Archaeology.

1991   Late Classic lowland Maya political organization and central-place analysis: New insights from the upper Belize Valley. *Ancient Mesoamerica* 2:149–165.

Barnhart, E.

1998   The map of Caye Coco. In *The Belize Postclassic Project 1997: Laguna de On, Progresso Lagoon, and Laguna Seca*, edited by M.A. Masson and R.M. Rosenswig, 93–106. Occasional Publication 2. Albany: Institute of Mesoamerican Studies, State University of New York.

Barrett, J.

1999   The mythical landscapes of the British Iron Age. In *Archaeologies of landscape: Contemporary perspectives*, edited by W.A. Ashmore and A.B. Knapp, 253–265. Oxford: Blackwell.

Barrett, J.W.

1999   Investigating structural architecture and phases of mound construction: Subop 5 and 15 excavations, Caye Coco. In *The Belize Postclassic Project 1998: Investigations at Progresso Lagoon*, edited by M.A. Masson and R.M. Rosenswig, 103–124. Occasional Publication 3. Albany: Institute of Mesoamerican Studies, State University of New York.

Bartlett, M.L., and P.A. McAnany

2000   "Crafting" communities: The materialization of Formative Maya identities. In *The archaeology of communities: A New World perspective*, edited by M.A. Canuto and J. Yaeger. London: Routledge.

Basso, K.

1996   *Wisdom sits in places*. Albuquerque: U of New Mexico Press.

Bawden, G.

1982   Community organization reflected by the household: A study of pre-Columbian social dynamics. *Journal of Field Archaeology* 9:165–181.

Beaudry, M., L. Cook, and S. Mrozowski

1991   Artifacts and active voices: Material culture as social discourse. In *The archaeology of inequality*, edited by R. McGuire and R. Paynter, 150–191. Oxford: Blackwell.

Becker, M.J.

1971   The identification of a second plaza plan at Tikal, Guatemala, and its implications for ancient Maya social complexity. Ph.D. dissertation, Department of Anthropology, University of Pennsylvania, Philadelphia.

1979   Priests, peasants, and ceremonial centers: The intellectual history of a model. In *Maya archaeology and ethnohistory*, edited by N. Hammond and G.R. Willey, 3–20. Austin: U of Texas Press.

1982   Ancient Maya houses and their identification: An evaluation of architectural groups at Tikal and inferences regarding their functions. *Revista Española de Antropología Americana* 12:111–129.

1983   Kings and classicism: Political change in the Maya lowlands during the Classic period. In *Highland-lowland interaction in Mesoamerica: Interdisciplinary approaches*, edited by A.G. Miller, 159–200. Washington, DC: Dumbarton Oaks.

1991   Plaza plans at Tikal, Guatemala, and at other lowland Maya sites: Evidence for patterns of cultural change. *Cuadernos de Arquitectura Mesoamericana* 14:11–26.

1992   Burials as caches; caches as burials: A new interpretation of the meaning of ritual deposits among the Classic period lowland Maya. In *New theories on the ancient Maya*, edited by E.C. Danien and R.J. Sharer, 185–196. Monograph 77. Symposium Series 3. Philadelphia: University Museum, University of Pennsylvania.

Beetz, C.P., and L. Satterthwaite

1981   *The monuments and inscriptions of Caracol, Belize*, Monograph 45. Philadelphia: University Museum, University of Pennsylvania.

Benavides Castillo, A.

1981   *Los aminos de Coba y sus implicaciones sociales (proyecto Coba)*. Mexico: Coleccion Cientifica, Arqueologia. Instituto Nacional de Antropologia e Historia.

Bender, B.

1998   *Stonehenge: Making spaces*. Oxford: Berg.

Bey III, G.J., T.M. Bond, W.M. Ringle, C.A. Hanson, C.W. Houck, and C. Peraza Lope

1998   The ceramic chronology of Ek Balam, Yucatan, Mexico. *Ancient Mesoamerica* 9:101–120.

Birchall, C.J., and R.N. Jenkin

1979   *The soils of the Belize Valley, Belize*. Supplementary Report, No. 15. Surbiton: Overseas Development Administration, Land Resources Development Centre.

Blanton, R.E.

1994   *Houses and households: A comparative study*. New York and London: Plenum.

Blanton, R.E., G.M. Feinman, S.A. Kowalewski, and P.N. Peregrine

1996   A dual-processual theory for the evolution of Mesoamerican civilization. *Current Anthropology* 37(1):1–14.

Borhegyi, S.F. de

1956   Settlement patterns in the Guatemala highlands: Past and present. In *Prehistoric settlement patterns in the New World*, edited by G.R. Willey, 101–106. Publications in Anthropology 23. New York: Viking Fund.

Boserup, E

1965   *Conditions of agricultural growth*. Chicago: Aldine.

1981   *Population and technological change: A study of long term trends*. Chicago: U of Chicago Press.

Bourdieu, P.

1973   The Berber house. In *Rules and meanings*, edited by M. Douglas, 98–110. Harmondsworth: Penguin.

1977   *Outline of a theory of practice*. Translated by R. Nice. Cambridge: Cambridge U Press.

Bradley, B.A.

1975   Lithic reduction sequences: A glossary and discussion. In *Lithic technology: Making and using stone tools*, edited by E. Swanson, 5–13. The Hague: Mouton Publishers.

Bradley, R.

1987   Time regained: The creation of continuity. *Journal of the British Archaeological Association* 140:1–17.

Brady, J.E.

1997   Settlement configuration and cosmology: The role of caves at Dos Pilas. *American Anthropologist* 99:602–618.

Brady, J.E., and W.A. Ashmore

1999   Mountains, caves, water: Conceptual landscapes of the ancient Maya. In *Archaeologies of landscape: Contemporary perspectives*, edited by W.A. Ashmore and A.B. Knapp, 124–145. Oxford: Blackwell.

Brady, J.E., J.W. Ball, R.K. Bishop, D.C. Pring, N. Hammond, and R.A. Housley

1998   The lowland Maya "Protoclassic": A reconsideration of its nature and significance. *Ancient Mesoamerica* 9:17–38.

Braswell, J.B.

1994   Investigations at Group D, Xunantunich, Belize, a nonroyal elite corporate group. In *Xunantunich Archaeological Project: 1994 field season*, edited by R.M. Leventhal and W.A. Ashmore, 214–247. Report on file, Department of Archaeology Belmopan, Belize, and Cotsen Institute of Archaeology at UCLA.

1998   Archaeological investigations at Group D, Xunantunich, Belize. Ph.D. dissertation, Department of Anthropology, Tulane University, New Orleans.

Brown, K.M., and J.F. Garber

2000   1800 years of construction–10 years of excavation: A summary view of the past decade of research at Blackman Eddy, Belize. In *The Belize Valley Archaeology Project: Results of the 1999 field season*, edited by K.M. Brown and J.F. Garber, 3–25. Report on file, Department of Archaeology, Belmopan, Belize, and Southwest Texas State University.

Brumfiel, E.M.
1987   Elite and utilitarian crafts in the Aztec state. In *Specialization, exchange, and complex societies*, edited by E.M. Brumfiel and T.K. Earle, 102–118. Cambridge: Cambridge U Press.
1991   Weaving and cooking: Women's production in Aztec Mexico. In *Engendering archaeology: Women and prehistory*, edited by J.M. Gero and M.W. Conkey, 224–251. Oxford: Blackwell.
1992   Breaking and entering the ecosystem–gender, class, and faction steal the show. *American Anthropologist* 94:551–567.

Brumfiel, E.M., and J.W. Fox, eds.
1994   *Factional competition and political development in the New World.* Cambridge: Cambridge U Press.

Bullard, W.R., Jr.
1960   Maya settlement pattern in northeastern Petén, Guatemala. *American Antiquity* 25:355–372.
1962   Settlement patterns and social structure in the southern Maya lowlands during the Classic Period. *Actas y memorias del XXXV Congreso Internacional de Americanistas* 1962:279–287. Mexico City.
1963   The British Honduras expedition, 1961: A progress report. In *1962 annual report, art and archaeology division, the Royal Ontario Museum,* 10–16. Toronto: Royal Ontario Museum.
1964   Settlement pattern and social structure in the southern Maya lowlands during the Classic period. *Actas of the 35th International Congress of Americanists* I: 279–287. Mexico City.

Bullard, W.R., Jr., and M. Ricketson-Bullard
1965   *Late Classic finds at Baking Pot, British Honduras.* Royal Ontario Museum Art and Archaeology Occasional Paper 8. Toronto: University of Toronto.

Cancian, F.
1972   *Change and uncertainty in a peasant economy: The Maya corn farmers of Zinacantan.* Stanford: Stanford U Press.

Carpenter, M., S.V. Connell, G. Cestaro, C. Campaigne, M. Eck, and B. Feld
1992   The Chaa Creek site report 1992. Report on file, Belmopan, Belize, and Cotsen Institute of Archaeology at UCLA.

Carr, R.F., and J.E. Hazard
1961   *Maps of the ruins of Tikal, El Petén, Guatemala.* Tikal Report 11. Monograph 21. Philadelphia: University Museum, University of Pennsylvania.

Chapman, J.
1994   Destruction of a common heritage: The archaeology war in Croatia, Bosnia and Hercegovina. *Antiquity* 68:120–126.

Chase, A.F.
1991   Cycles of time: Caracol in the Maya rsealm. In *Sixth Palenque Round Table, 1986*, edited by V.M. Fields, 32–42. Norman: U of Oklahoma Press.
1992   Elites and the changing organization of Classic Maya society. In *Mesoamerican elites: An archaeological assessment*, edited by A.F. Chase and D.Z. Chase, 30–49. Norman: U of Oklahoma Press.
1998   Planeación civica e integración de sitio en Caracol, Belice: definiendo una economia administrada del periodo clásico Maya. *Los investigadores de la cultura Maya* 6:26–44. Campeche: Universidad Autónoma de Campeche.

Chase, A.F., and D.Z. Chase
1985   Postclassic temporal and spatial frames for the lowland Maya: A background. In *The lowland Maya Postclassic*, edited by A.F. Chase and P.M. Rice, 9–22. Austin: U of Texas Press.
1987   *Investigations at the Classic Maya city of Caracol, Belize: 1985–1987.* Monograph 3. San Francisco: Pre-Columbian Art Research Institute.
1989   The investigation of Classic period Maya warfare at Caracol, Belize. *Mayab* 5:5–18.
1992   Mesoamerican elites: Assumptions, definitions, and models. In *Mesoamerican elites: An archaeological assessment*, edited by D.Z. Chase and A.F. Chase, 3–17. Norman: U of Oklahoma Press.
1994a   Maya veneration of the dead at Caracol, Belize. In *Seventh Palenque*

Round Table, 1989, edited by V.M. Fields, 53–60. San Francisco: Pre-Columbian Art Research Institute.
1994b   *Studies in the archaeology of Caracol, Belize.* Monograph 7. San Francisco: Pre-Columbian Art Research Institute.
1994c   Details in the archaeology of Caracol, Belize: An introduction. In *Studies in the archaeology of Caracol, Belize*, edited by A.F. Chase and D.Z. Chase, 1–11. Monograph 7. San Francisco: Pre-Columbian Art Research Institute.
1996a   More than kin and king: Centralized political organization among the Late Classic Maya. *Current Anthropology* 37:803–810.
1996b   The causeways of Caracol. *Belize Today* 10(3/4):31–32.
1996c   A mighty nation: How Caracol built an empire by cultivating its "middle class." *Archaeology* 49(5):66–72.
1998a   Late Classic Maya political structure, polity size, and warfare arenas. In *Anatomía de una civilización: aproximaciones interdisciplinarias a la cultura Maya*, edited by A. Ciudad Ruiz, Y. Fernández Marquínez, J.M. García Campillo, Ma. J.I. Ponce de León, A.L. García-Gallo, and L.T. Sanz Castro, 11–29. Madrid: Sociedad Española de Estudios Mayas.
1998b   Scale and intensity in Classic period Maya agriculture: Terracing and settlement at the "garden city" of Caracol, Belize. *Culture and Agriculture* 20(2):60–77.

Chase, A.F., N. Grube, and D.Z. Chase
1991   *Three Terminal Classic monuments from Caracol, Belize.* Research Reports on Ancient Maya Writing, No. 36. Washington, DC: Center for Maya Research.

Chase, D.Z.
1982   Spatial and temporal variability in Postclassic northern Belize. Ph.D. dissertation, Department of Anthropology, University of Pennsylvania, Philadelphia.
1986   Social and political organization in the land of cacao and honey: Correlating the archaeology and ethnohistory of the Postclassic lowland Maya. In *Late lowland Maya civilization: Classic to Postclassic*, edited by J.A. Sabloff and E.W. Andrews V, 347–377. Albuquerque: U of New Mexico Press.
1988   Caches and censerwares: Meaning from Maya pottery. In *A pot for all reasons: Ceramic ecology revisited*, edited by C.C. Kolb and L.M. Lackey, 81–104. Oxford: British Archaeological Reports.
1992   Postclassic Maya elites: Ethnohistory and archaeology. In *Mesoamerican elites: An archaeological assessment*, edited by D.Z. Chase and A.F. Chase, 118–135. Norman: U of Oklahoma Press.
1994   Human osteology, pathology, and demography as represented in the burials of Caracol, Belize. In *Studies in the archaeology of Caracol, Belize*, edited by D.Z. Chase and A.F. Chase, 123–138. Monograph 7. San Francisco: Pre-Columbian Art Research Institute.
1998   Albergando a los muertos en Caracol, Belice. *Los Investigadores de la Cultura Maya* 6:9–25.

Chase, D.Z., and A.F. Chase
1988   *A Postclassic perspective: Excavations at the Maya site of Santa Rita Corozal, Belize.* Monograph 4. San Francisco: Pre-Columbian Art Research Institute.
1992   An archaeological assessment of Mesoamerican elites. In *Mesoamerican elites: An archaeological assessment*, edited by D.Z. Chase and A.F. Chase, 303–317. Norman: U of Oklahoma Press.
1998   The architectural context of caches, burials, and other ritual activities for the Classic period Maya (as reflected at Caracol, Belize). In *Function and meaning in Classic Maya architecture*, edited by S.D. Houston, 299–332. Washington, DC: Dumbarton Oaks.
2000   Classic Maya warfare and settlement archaeology at Caracol, Belize. In *Estudios de Cultura Maya*. In press.

Chase, D.Z., A.F. Chase, and W.A. Haviland
1990   The Classic Maya city: Reconsidering the "Mesoamerican urban tradition." *American Anthropologist* 92:499–506.

Chase, S.M.
1992   South group plaza 1 and Nabitunich plaza group. In *Xunantunich Archaeological Project: 1992 field season*, edited by R.M. Leventhal, 35–55. Report on file, Department of Archaeology, Belmopan, Belize, and Cotsen Institute of Archaeology at UCLA.
1993   Excavations at the San Lorenzo group: The 1993 testing program and plaza group I. In *Xunantunich Archaeological Project: 1993 field season*, edited by R.M. Leventhal, 128–147. Report on file, Department of Archaeology, Belmopan, Belize and Cotsen Institute of Archaeology at UCLA.

Cheetham, D.T.
1994   Ancient roads, elite ritual and settlement patterns of the Maya: Recent evidence from Cahal Pech, Cayo, Belize. Paper presented at the 59th Annual Meeting of the Society for American Archaeology, Anaheim, CA.

Cheetham, D.T., J. Vinuales, J.T. Carlsson, T. Wallis, and P. Wilson
1993   Life in suburbia: Preliminary investigations of the Zopilote group, Cahal Pech, Belize. In *Belize Valley Archaeological Reconnaissance Project: Progress report of the 1992 field season*, edited by J.J. Awe, 152–172. Peterborough, Ontario: Trent University.

Ching, B., and G.W. Creed, eds.
1997   *Knowing your place: Rural identity and cultural hierarchy*. London: Routledge.

Clark, J.
1987   Politics, prismatic blades, and Mesoamerican civilization. In *The organization of core technology*, edited by J.K. Johnson and C.A. Morrow, 259–284. Boulder: Westview Press.

Clark, J.E., and M. Blake
1994   The power of prestige: Competitive generosity and the emergence of rank societies in lowland Mesoamerica. In *Factional competition and political development in the New World*, edited by E.M. Brumfiel and J.W. Fox, 17–30. New York: Cambridge U Press.

Clarke, D.L., ed.
1977   *Spatial archaeology*. London: Academic Press.

Claassen, C., and R.A. Joyce, eds.
1997   *Women in prehistory: North America and Mesoamerica*. Philadelphia: U of Pennsylvania Press.

Coe, M.D.
1965   A model of ancient Maya community structure in the Maya lowlands. *Southwestern Journal of Anthropology* 21: 97–114.

Coe, M.D., and R.A. Diehl
1980   The people of the river. In *the land of the Olmec*, Vol. 2, edited by M.D. Coe and R.A. Diehl. Austin: U of Texas Press.

Coe, W.R.
1965   Tikal, Guatemala and the emergent Maya civilization. *Science* 147:1401–1419.
1966   Review of prehistoric Maya settlements in the Belize Valley. *American Journal of Archaeology* 70:309–311.

Coe, W.R., and M.D. Coe
1956   Excavations at Nohoch Ek, British Honduras. *American Antiquity* 21:370–382.

Coe, W.R., and W.A. Haviland
1982   *Introduction to the archaeology of Tikal, Guatemala*. Tikal Report 12, Monograph 46. Philadelphia: University Museum, University of Pennsylvania.

Coggins, C.C.
1980   The shape of time: Some political implications of a four-part figure. *American Antiquity* 45:727–739.

Conlon, J.M.
1992   Beyond the castle walls: Preliminary report of the 1991 excavations at the Tzinic group, Cahal Pech, Belize. In *Progress report of the fourth season (1991) of investigations at Cahal Pech, Belize*, edited by J.J. Awe and M.D. Campbell, 69–90. Peterborough, Ontario: Department of Anthropology, Trent University.
1995   The final frontier: Settlement survey at the ancient Maya site of Baking Pot. In *Belize Valley Archaeological Reconnaissance Project: Progress report of the 1994 field season*, Vol. 2, edited by J.M. Conlon and J.J. Awe, 81–102. London: Institute of Archaeology.
1997   An analysis of ancient Maya consumption requirements and agricultural production potential at Baking Pot, Belize. In *Belize Valley Archaeological Reconnaissance Project: Progress report of the 1996 field season*, edited by J.J. Awe and J.M. Conlon, 7–20. Peterborough, Ontario: Trent University.
1997   Personal communication to Jason Yaeger.

Conlon, J.M., and J.J. Awe
1991   The Tzinic group at Cahal Pech, Belize: Preliminary comments on the 1990 season of investigations. In *Report of the third (1990) season of investigations at Cahal Pech, Belize*, edited by J.J. Awe and M.D. Campbell, 9–22. Peterborough, Ontario: Department of Anthropology, Trent University.

1995a   Estimates of population and agrarian potential for the ditched field irrigation system at Baking Pot, Belize. In *Belize Valley Archaeological Reconnaissance Project: Progress report of the 1994 field season*, Vol. 2, edited by J.M. Conlon and J.J. Awe, 63–80. London: Institute of Archaeology.
1995b   Ditched field agriculture at the ancient Maya site of Baking Pot and its implications for analyzing community organization. Paper presented at the 60th Annual Meeting of the Society for American Archaeology, Washington, DC.

Conlon, J.M., and A.F. Moore
1998   Plazuela groups of the Late Classic period: A comparison and contrast of community interaction and integration at Baking Pot, Belize. Paper presented at the 63rd Annual Meeting of the Society for American Archaeology, Seattle, WA.

Conlon, J.M., T.G. Powis, and B.M. Hohmann
1994   Ruler or ruled?: Status, land tenure, and nucleated settlement in the western periphery of Baking Pot, Belize. In *Belize Valley Archaeological Reconnaissance Project: Progress report of the sixth (1993) field season*, edited by J.J. Awe, 224–262. London: Institute of Archaeology.

Connell, S.V.
1993   Chaa Creek: Reconnaissance. In Xunantunich Archaeological Project: 1993 field season, edited by R.M. Leventhal. Report on file, Department of Archaeology, Belmopan, Belize; University of Pennsylvania; and Cotsen Institute of Archaeology at UCLA.
1994   Research at Chaa Creek, 1994. In Xunantunich Archaeological Project: 1994 field season, edited by R.M. Leventhal and W.A. Ashmore, 148–168. Report on file, Department of Archaeology, Belmopan, Belize; University of Pennsylvania; and Cotsen Institute of Archaeology at UCLA.
2000   Were they well connected? An exploration of ancient Maya regional integration from the middle-level perspective of Chaa Creek, Belize. Ph.D. dissertation, Department of Anthropology, University of California, Los Angeles.

Costin, C.L.
1991   Craft specialization: Issues in defining, documenting, and explaining the organization of production. In *Archaeological method and theory*, Vol. 3, edited by M.B. Schiffer, 1–56. Tucson: U of Arizona Press.

Creed, G.W., and B. Ching
1997   Recognizing rusticity: Identity and the power of place. In *Knowing your place: Rural identity and cultural hierarchy*, edited by B. Ching and G.W. Creed, 1–38. London: Routledge.

Crumley, C.L.
1987   A dialectical critique of hierarchy. In *Power relations and state formation*, edited by T.C. Patterson and C.W. Gailey, 155–169. Washington, DC: American Anthropological Association.
1995   Heterarchy and the analysis of complex societies. In *Heterarchy and the analysis of complex societies*, edited by R.M. Ehrenreich, C.L. Crumley, and J.E. Levy, 1–6. Archaeological Papers 6. Arlington, VA: American Anthropological Association.

Culbert, T.P.
1974   *The lost civilization: The story of the Classic Maya*. London: Harper and Row.
1991   Maya political history and elite interaction: A summary view. In *Classic Maya political history: Hieroglyphic and archaeological evidence*, edited by T.P. Culbert, 311–346. New York: Cambridge U Press.

Culbert, T.P., L.J. Kosakowsky, R.E. Fry, and W.A. Haviland
1990   The population of Tikal, Guatemala. In *Pre-Columbian population history in the Maya lowlands*, edited by T.P. Culbert and D.S. Rice, 103–121. Albuquerque: U of New Mexico Press.

Dahlin, B.H., and W.J. Litzinger
1986   Old bottle, new wine: The function of chultuns in the Maya lowlands. *American Antiquity* 51:721–736.

Deal, M.
1988   An ethnoarchaeological approach to the identification of Maya domestic pottery production. In *Ceramic ecology revisited, 1987: The technology and socioeconomics of pottery*, edited by C.C. Kolb, 111–142. BAR International Series 436. Oxford: British Archaeological Reports.

Demarest, A.
1992   Ideology in ancient Maya cultural evolution. In *Ideology and the evolu-*

tion of pre-Columbian civilization, edited by A. Demarest and G. Conrad, 135–157. Albuquerque: U of New Mexico Press.

1996   Closing comment. Current Anthropology 37:821–824.

1997   The Vanderbilt Petexbatun regional Archaeological Project 1989–1994: Overview, history, and major results of a multidisciplinary study of the Classic Maya collapse. Ancient Mesoamerica 8:209–227.

de Montmollin, O.

1987   Forced settlement and political centralization in a Classic Maya polity. Journal of Anthropological Archaeology 6:220–262.

1988a   Scales of settlement study for complex societies: Analytical issues from the Classic Maya area. Journal of Field Archaeology 15:151–168.

1988b   Settlement scale and theory in Maya archaeology. In Recent studies in pre-Columbian archaeology, edited by N.J. Saunders and O. de Montmollin, 63–104. BAR International Series 431. Oxford: British Archaeological Reports.

1989   The archaeology of political structure: Settlement analysis in a Classic Maya polity. New York: Cambridge U Press.

1995   Settlement and politics in three Classic Maya polities. Monographs in World Archaeology, No. 24. Madison, WI: Prehistory Press.

Donham, D.L.

1981   Beyond the domestic mode of production. Man 16:515–541.

Douglas, M.

1967   Primitive rationing: A study in controlled exchange. Themes in economic anthropology, edited by R. Firth, 119–147. A.S.A. Monograph 6. London: Tavistock.

1986   How institutions think. Syracuse, N.Y. : Syracuse University Press.

Dreiss, M.L., and D.O. Brown

1989   Obsidian exchange patterns in Belize. In Prehistoric Maya economies, edited by P.A. McAnany and B.L. Isaac, 57–90. Research in Economic Anthropology Supplement 4. Greenwich, CT: JAI Press.

Drennan, R.D.

1988   Household location and compact versus dispersed settlement in prehispanic Mesoamerica. In Household and community in the Mesoamerican past, edited by R.R. Wilk and W.A. Ashmore, 273–293. Albuquerque: U of New Mexico Press.

Dunham, P.S.

1990   Coming apart at the seams: The Classic development and the demise of a Maya civilization, a segmentary view from Xnaheb, Belize. Ph.D. dissertation, State University of New York, Albany.

Dunham, P.S., T.R. Jamison, and R.M. Leventhal

1989   Secondary development and settlement economics: The Classic Maya of southern Belize. In Prehistoric Maya economies, edited by P.A. McAnany and B.L. Isaac, 255–292. Research in Economic Anthropology Supplement 4. Greenwich, CT: JAI Press.

Dunnell, R.C., and W.S. Dancey

1983   The siteless survey: A regional scale data collection strategy. Advances in Archaeological Method and Theory 6:267–287.

Dunning, N.P.

1992   Lords of the hills: Ancient Maya settlement in the Puuc region, Yucatán, Mexico. Monographs in World Archaeology, No. 15. Madison, WI: Prehistory Press.

Dunning, N.P., and T. Beach

1994   Soil erosion, slope management, and ancient terracing in the Maya lowlands. Latin American Antiquity 5:51–69.

Dunning, N.P., and J.K. Kowalski

1994   Lords of the hills: Classic Maya settlement patterns and political iconography in the Puuc region, Mexico. Ancient Mesoamerica 5:63–95.

Dunning, N.P., V. Scarborough, F. Valdez, Jr., S. Luzzadder-Beach, T. Beach, and J.G. Jones

1999   Temple mountains, sacred lakes, and fertile fields: Ancient Maya landscapes in northwestern Belize. Antiquity 73:650–660.

Durkheim, E.

1933   Emile Durkheim on the division of labor in society. New York: Macmillan.

1938[1895]   The rules of sociological method. New York: Free Press.

Easton, D.

1959   Political anthropology. In Biennial review of anthropology, edited by B.J. Siegel, 210–262. Stanford: Stanford U Press.

Ehrenreich, R.M., C.L. Crumley, and J.E. Levy, eds.

1995   Heterarchy and the analysis of complex societies. Archaeological Papers 6. Arlington, VA: American Anthropological Association.

Ehret, J.J.

1995   The Xunantunich settlement survey test-pitting program. In Xunantunich Archaeological Project: 1995 field season, edited by R.M. Leventhal and W.A. Ashmore. Report on file, Department of Archaeology, Belmopan, Belize; University of Pennsylvania: and Cotsen Institute of Archaeology at UCLA.

1997   Settlement patterns and rural elite identity in an ancient Maya polity. Paper presented at the 62nd Annual Meeting of the Society for American Archaeology, Nashville, TN.

1998   Lineage, land, and loyalty: Implications of ancient Maya settlement complexity in the rural hinterlands of Xunantunich, Belize. Paper presented at the 63rd Annual Meeting of the Society for American Archaeology, Seattle, WA.

Eiseley, L.C.

1975   Charles Lyell. In Readings from Scientific American: Biological anthropology, compiled by S.H. Katz, 145–152. San Francisco: W.H. Freeman and Company.

Etheridge, B.

1995   Excavations at group B, structures A-2, A-3, A-4, and the stela house (A-16). In Xunantunich Archaeological Project: 1995 field season, edited by R.M. Leventhal and W.A. Ashmore. Report on file, Department of Archaeology, Belmopan, Belize, and Cotsen Institute of Archaeology at UCLA.

Escalona Ramos, A.

1946   Algunas Ruinas Prehispanicas en Quintana Roo. Boletín de la Sociedad Mexicana de Geografía y Estadística 61(3):513–628.

Falconer, S.E., and S.H. Savage

1995   Heartlands and hinterlands: Alternative trajectories of early urbanization in Mesopotamia. American Antiquity 60:37–58.

Fash, B., W.L. Fash, S. Lane, R. Larios, L. Schele, J. Stomper, and D. Stuart

1992   Investigations of a Classic Maya council house at Copan, Honduras. Journal of Field Archaeology 19:419–442.

Fash, W.L.

1983   Deducing social organization from Classic Maya settlement patterns: A case study from the Copán Valley. In Civilization in the ancient Americas: Essays in honor of Gordon R. Willey, edited by R.M. Leventhal and A.L. Kolata, 261–288. Albuquerque: U of New Mexico Press.

1988   A new look at Maya statecraft from Copan, Honduras. Antiquity 62:157–169.

1991   Lineage patrons and ancestor worship among the Classic Maya nobility: The case of Copan structure 9n-82. In Sixth Palenque Round Table, 1986, edited by V.M. Fields, 68–80. Norman: U of Oklahoma Press.

1994   Changing perspectives on Maya civilization. Annual Review of Anthropology 23:181–208.

Fash, W.L., and R.J. Sharer

1991   Sociopolitical developments and methodological issues at Copan, Honduras: A conjunctive approach. Latin American Antiquity 2:166–187.

Fedick, S.L.

1988   Prehistoric Maya settlement and land-use patterns in the upper Belize River area, Belize, Central America. Ph.D. dissertation, Department of Anthropology, Arizona State University, Tempe.

1989   The economics of agricultural land use and settlement in the upper Belize River Valley. In Prehistoric Maya economies of Belize, edited by P. McAnany and B. L. Isaac, 215–253. Research in Economic Anthropology Supplement 4. Greenwich, CT: JAI Press.

1995   Land evaluation and ancient Maya land use in the upper Belize River area, Belize, Central America. Latin American Antiquity 6(1):16–34.

Fedick, S.L., ed.

1996   The managed mosaic: Ancient Maya agriculture and resource use. Salt Lake City: U of Utah Press.

Feinman, G., and J. Marcus

1998   Introduction. In Archaic States, edited by G. Feinman and J. Marcus, 3–13. Santa Fe: School of American Research Press.

Feinman, G., and J. Neitzel

1984   Too many types: An overview of pre-state societies in the Americas.

In *Advances in archaeological method and theory*, edited by M.B. Schiffer, 39–102. New York: Academic Press.

Feld, S., and K.H. Basso, eds.

1996   *Senses of place.* Santa Fe: School of American Research Press.

Fields, V.

1995   Preliminary notes on the west façade of structure A-6. In *Xunantunich Archaeological Project: 1993 field season*, edited by R.M. Leventhal and W.A. Ashmore, 251–255. Report on file, Department of Archaeology, Belmopan, Belize; University of Pennsylvania: and Cotsen Institute of Archaeology at UCLA.

Flanagan, J.G.

1989   Hierarchy in "simple" egalitarian societies. *Annual Review of Anthropology* 18:245–266.

Flannery, K.V.

1967   Culture history versus culture process: A debate in American archaeology. *Scientific American* 217:119–122.

1976   Empirical determination of site catchments in Oaxaca and Tehuacan. In *The early Mesoamerican village*, edited by K.V. Flannery, 103–117. New York: Academic Press.

Folan, W.J.

1983   Urban organization and social structure of Coba. In *Coba: A Classic Maya metropolis*, edited by W.J. Folan, E.R. Kintz, and L.A. Fletcher, 49–63. New York: Academic Press.

1992   Calakmul, Campeche: A centralized urban administrative center in the northern Peten. *World Archaeology* 24:128–168.

Folan, W. J., E.R. Kintz, and L.A. Fletcher, eds.

1983   *Coba: A Classic Maya metropolis.* New York: Academic Press.

Folan, W.J., J. Marcus, and W.F. Miller

1995   Verification of a Maya settlement model through remote sensing. *Cambridge Archaeological Journal* 5:277–301.

Folan, W.J., J. Marcus, S. Pincemin, M. del Rosario Dominguez C., L. Fletcher, and A. Morales L.

1995   Calakmul: New data from an ancient Maya capital in Campeche, Mexico. *Latin American Antiquity* 6:310–334.

Foley, R.

1981   Off-site archaeology: An alternative approach for the short-sited. In *Patterns of the past*, edited by I. Hodder, G. Isaac, and N. Hammond, 157–183. Cambridge: Cambridge U Press.

Ford, A.

1981   Conditions for the evolution of complex societies: The development of the central lowland Maya. Ph.D. dissertation, Department of Anthropology, University of California, Santa Barbara.

1986   *Population growth and social complexity: An examination of settlement and environment in the central Maya lowlands.* Anthropological Research Papers, No. 35. Tempe, AZ: Arizona State University.

1990   Maya settlement in the Belize River area: Variations in residence patterns of the central Maya lowlands. In *Prehistoric population history in the Maya lowlands*, edited by T.P. Culbert and D.S. Rice, 167–181. Albuquerque: U of New Mexico Press.

1991   Economic variation of ancient Maya residential settlement in the upper Belize River area. *Ancient Mesoamerica* 2:35–45.

Ford, A., and S.L. Fedick

1992   Prehistoric Maya settlement patterns in the upper Belize River area: Initial results of the Belize River archaeological settlement survey. *Journal of Field Archaeology* 19:35–49.

Fortes, M.

1958   Introduction. In *The developmental cycle in domestic groups*, edited by J. Goody, 1–14. Cambridge: U of Cambridge Press.

Foster, G.M.

1965   Peasant society and the image of limited good. *American Anthropologist* 67:293–315.

Fowler, W.R., Jr.

1997   Introduction: The Vanderbilt Petexbatun Archaeological Project, 1989–1994. *Ancient Mesoamerica* 8(2):207–208.

Fox, J.W.

1987   *Maya Postclassic state formation: Segmentary lineage migration in advancing frontiers.* Cambridge: Cambridge U Press.

1994   Political cosmology among the Quiché Maya. In *Factional competition and political development in the New World*, edited by E.M. Brumfiel and J.W. Fox, 158–170. Cambridge: Cambridge U Press.

Fox, J.W., and G.W. Cook

1996   Constructing Maya communities: Ethnography for archaeology. *Current Anthropology* 37:811–821.

Fox, R.G.

1977   *Urban anthropology.* Englewood Cliffs: Prentice-Hall.

Freidel, D.A.

1981   The political economics of residential dispersion among the lowland Maya. In *Lowland Maya settlement patterns*, edited by W.A. Ashmore, 371–382. Albuquerque: U of New Mexico Press.

1986   Maya warfare: An example of peer polity interaction. In *Peer polity interaction and socio-political change*, edited by C. Renfrew and J.F. Cherry, 93–108. Cambridge: Cambridge U Press.

1999   Towards an archaeology of mayhem: Termination rituals in Maya centers. Paper presented at the 6th Maya Weekend, University of California, Los Angeles.

Freidel, D.A., and J.A. Sabloff

1984   *Cozumel: Late Maya settlement patterns.* Orlando: Academic Press.

Freidel, D.A., and V.L. Scarborough

1982   Subsistence, trade, and development of the coastal Maya. In *Maya subsistence: Studies in memory of Dennis E. Puleston*, edited by K.V. Flannery, 131–155. New York: Academic Press.

Freidel, D.A., and L. Schele

1989   Dead kings, living temples: Dedication and termination rituals among the ancient Maya. In *Word and image in Maya culture*, edited by W.F. Hanks and D.S. Rice, 233–243. Salt Lake City: U of Utah Press.

Freidel, D.A., L. Schele, and J. Parker

1993   *Maya cosmos: Three thousand years on the shaman's path.* New York: William Morrow.

Fry, R.E.

1980   Models of exchange for major shape classes of lowland Maya pottery. In *Models and methods in regional exchange*, edited by R.E. Fry, 3–18. Washington, DC: Society for American Archaeology.

Gamble, C.

1998   Palaeolithic society and the release from proximity: A network approach to intimate relations. *World Archaeology* 29:426–449.

Gann, T.W.F.

1918   *The Maya Indians of southern Yucatan and northern British Honduras.* Bureau of American Ethnology, Bulletin 64. Washington, DC: Smithsonian Institution.

Garber, J.F., and K.M. Brown

2000   A Baktun 8 carved stela from the lowland Maya site of Blackman Eddy, Belize. In *Belize Valley Archaeology Project: Results of the 1999 field season*, edited by K.M. Brown and J.F. Garber, 95–114. Report on file, Department of Archaeology, Belmopan, Belize, and Southwest Texas State University.

Garber, J.F., and D.M. Glassman

1996   The Belize Valley Archaeological Project: Results of the 1995 field season. Report on file, Department of Archaeology, Belmopan, Belize, and Southwest Texas State University.

Garber, J.F., W.D. Driver, and L.A. Sullivan

1993   Medium sized ceremonial centers in the Belize Valley: The Blackman Eddy example. Paper presented at the 58th Annual Meeting of the Society for American Archaeology, St. Louis, MO.

Garber, J.F., D.M. Glassman, W.D. Driver, and P. Weiss

1994   The Belize Valley Archaeological Project: Results of the 1993 field season. Report on file, Department of Anthropology, Belmopan, Belize, and Southwest Texas State University.

Garber, J.F., and R.M. Leventhal

N.D.   *Maya archaeology in the Belize Valley.* Unpublished manuscript.

Garduno Arguenta, J.

1979   Introduccíon al patron de asentamiento del sitio de Coba, Quintana Roo. Mexico, D.F.: Escuela Nacional de Antropologia e Historia.

Gerry, J.P.

1993   Diet and status among the Classic Maya: An isotopic perspective. Ph.D. dissertation, Department of Anthropology, Harvard University, Cambridge.

Gibson, E.C.

1986   Diachronic patterns of lithic production, use, and exchange in the southern Maya lowlands. Ph.D. dissertation, Department of Anthropology, Harvard University, Cambridge.

Giddens, A.
1985   *The constitution of society: Outline of the theory of structuration.* Berkeley: U of California Press.

Gifford, J.C.
1976   *Prehistoric pottery analysis and the ceramics of Barton Ramie in the Belize Valley.* Memoirs of the Peabody Museum of Archaeology and Ethnology 18. Cambridge: Harvard University.

Golden, C.W., and J.M. Conlon
1996   Archaeology in the plow zone: Results of salvage operations at the North Caracol Farm settlement cluster, Cayo, Belize. In *Belize Valley Archaeological Reconnaissance Project: Progress report of the 1995 field season*, edited by J.M. Conlon, 19–36. London: Institute of Archaeology.

Goldsmith, A.S.
1992   Report on the 1991 excavations at the K'ik' group, Cahal Pech, Belize. In *Belize Valley Archaeological Reconnaissance Project: Progress report of the fourth (1991) field season*, edited by J.J. Awe and M.D. Campbell, 9–34. Peterborough, Ontario: Trent University.

Gonlin, N.
1994   Rural household diversity in Late Classic Copan, Honduras. In *Archaeological views from the countryside: Village communities in early complex communities*, edited by G.M. Schwartz and S.E. Falconer, 177–197. Washington, DC: Smithsonian Institution.

Gossen, G.H., and R.M. Leventhal
1989   The topography of ancient Maya religious pluralism: A dialogue with the present. In *Lowland Maya civilization in the eighth century AD*, edited by J.A. Sabloff and J.S. Henderson, 185–217. Washington, DC: Dumbarton Oaks.

Graham, E.A.
1991   Women and gender in Maya prehistory. In *The archaeology of gender: Proceedings of the 22nd Annual Chacmool Conference*, edited by D. Walde and N.D. Willows, 470–478. Calgary: Archaeological Association of the University of Calgary.

Graham, E.A., G.D. Jones, and R. Kautz
1985   Archaeology and ethnohistory on a Spanish colonial frontier: An interim report on the Macal-Tipu Project in western Belize. In *The lowland Maya Postclassic*, edited by A.F. Chase and P.M. Rice, 206–214. Austin: U of Texas Press.

Graham, E.A., and D.M. Pendergast
1989   Excavations at the Marco Gonzalez site, Ambergris Cay, Belize, 1986. *Journal of Field Archaeology* 16:1–16.

Graham, I.
1967   *Archaeological explorations in El Peten, Guatemala.* Middle American Research Institute, Publication 33. New Orleans: Tulane University.

Gray, N.
2000   Into the darkness: Investigations of Maya chultunob from X-ualcanil (Cayo Y), Belize. M.A. thesis, Department of Anthropology, Trent University, Peterborough, Ontario.

Grube, N.
1994   Epigraphic research at Caracol, Belize. In *Studies in the archaeology of Caracol, Belize*, edited by D.Z. Chase and A.F. Chase, 83–122. Monograph 7. San Francisco: Pre-Columbian Art Research Institute.
N.D.   Recent epigraphic research at Caracol, Belize. In *Maya archaeology at Caracol, Belize*, edited by A.F. Chase and D.Z. Chase. Monograph 12. San Francisco: Pre-Columbian Art Research Institute.

Guderjan, T.H.
1997   Summary of the 1996 research and field season. In *The Blue Creek Project: Working papers from the 1996 field season*, edited by W.D. Driver, H.L. Clagett, and H.R. Haines, 1–11. San Antonio, TX: Maya Research Program, St. Mary's University.

Guderjan, T.H., ed.
1991   *Maya settlement in northwestern Belize: The 1988 and 1990 seasons of the Rio Bravo Archaeological Project.* San Antonio, TX: Maya Research Program and Labyrinthos.

Guderjan, T.H., and J.F. Garber
1995   *Maya maritime trade, settlement, and populations on Ambergris Caye, Belize.* San Antonio, TX: Maya Research Program and Labyrinthos.

Guderjan, T.H., M. Lindeman, E. Ruble, F. Salam, and J. Yaeger
1991   Archaeological sites in the Rio Bravo area. In *Maya settlement in northwestern Belize: The 1988 and 1990 seasons of the Rio Bravo Archaeological Project*, edited by T.H. Guderjan, 55–88. San Antonio, TX: Maya Research Program and Labyrinthos.

Gupta, A., and J. Ferguson
1992   Beyond "culture": Space, identity, and the politics of difference. *Cultural Anthropology* 7:6–23.

Haggett, P.
1965   *Locational analysis in human geography.* New York: St. Martin's Press.

Halperin, R.H.
1990   *The livelihood of kin: Making ends meet "the Kentucky way."* Austin: U of Texas Press.
1991   Karl Polanyi's concept of householding: Resistance and livelihood in an Appalachian region. *Research in Economic Anthropology* 13:93–116.

Hammond, N.
1975   Maya settlement hierarchy in northern Belize. In *Studies in ancient Mesoamerica II*, edited by J.A. Graham, 40–55. Contributions of the University of California Archaeological Research Facility, No. 27. Berkeley: Department of Anthropology, University of California.
1981   Settlement patterns in Belize. In *Lowland Maya settlement patterns*, edited by W.A. Ashmore, 157–186. Albuquerque: U of New Mexico Press.
1991   The discovery of La Milpa. *Mexicon* XIII:46–51.

Hammond, N., and M.R. Bobo
1994   Pilgrimage's last mile: Late Maya monument veneration at La Milpa, Belize. *World Archaeology* 26:19–34.

Hammond, N., and C. Miksicek
1981   Ecology and economy of a Formative Maya site at Cuello, Belize. *Journal of Field Archaeology* 8:259–269.

Hammond, N., K.A. Pyburn, J. Rose, J.C. Staneko, and D. Muyskens
1988   Excavation and survey at Nohmul, Belize, 1986. *Journal of Field Archaeology* 15:1–15.

Hammond, N., G. Tourtellot, S. Donaghey, and A. Clarke
1996   Survey and excavation at La Milpa, 1996. *Mexicon* 18:86–91.
1998   No slow dusk: Maya urban development and decline at La Milpa, Belize. *Antiquity* 72:831–837.

Hare, T.S., L. Campbell, and S. Durivage
1999   Mapping and 3-D modeling of Caye Coco. In *The Belize Postclassic Project 1998: Investigations at Progresso Lagoon*, edited by M.A. Masson and R.M. Rosenswig, 157–162. Occasional Publication 3. Albany: Institute of Mesoamerican Studies, State University of New York.

Harrison, P.D.
1990   The revolution in ancient Maya subsistence. In *Vision and revision in Maya studies*, edited by F.S. Clancy and P.D. Harrison, 99–113. Albuquerque: U of New Mexico Press.

Harrison, P.D., and R.E. Fry
2000   *Pulltrouser Swamp: The settlement maps.* Salt Lake City: U of Utah Press.

Harrison, P.D., and B.L. Turner II, eds.
1978   *Pre-Hispanic Maya agriculture.* Albuquerque: U of New Mexico Press.

Hart, G.
1992   Imagined unities: Constructions of "the household" in economic theory. In *Understanding economic process*, edited by S. Ortiz and S. Lees, 111–129. Monographs in Economic Anthropology 10. Lanham: University Press of America.

Haviland, W.A.
1963   Excavation of small structures in the northeast quadrant of Tikal, Guatemela. Ph.D. dissertation, Department of Anthropology, University of Pennsylvania, Philadelphia.
1966   Maya settlement patterns: A critical review. In *Archaeological Studies in Middle America*, 21–47. Middle American Research Institute, Publication 26. New Orleans: Tulane University.
1968   Ancient lowland Maya social organization. In *Archaeological studies in middle America*, 93–117. Middle American Research Institute, Publication 26. New Orleans: Tulane University.
1970   Tikal, Guatemala, and Mesoamerican urbanism. *World Archaeology* 2:186–198.
1981   Dower houses and minor centers at Tikal, Guatemala: An investigation into the identification of valid units in settlement hierarchies. In *Lowland Maya settlement patterns*, edited by W.A. Ashmore, 89–118. Albuquerque: U of New Mexico Press.
1982   Where the rich folks lived: Deranging factors in the statistical analysis of Tikal settlement. *American Antiquity* 47:427–429.

1988   Musical hammocks at Tikal: Problems with reconstructing household composition. In *Household and community in the Mesoamerican past*, edited by R.R. Wilk and W.A. Ashmore, 121–134. Albuquerque: U of New Mexico Press.

1997   On the Maya state. *Current Anthropology* 38:443–445.

Hayden, B., and A. Cannon

1982   The corporate group as an archaeological unit. *Journal of Anthropological Archaeology* 1:132–158.

Healy, P.F., K. Emery, and L.E. Wright

1990   Ancient and modern Maya exploitation of the jute snail (Pachychilus). *Latin American Antiquity* 1(2):170–183.

Healy, P.F., J.D.H. Lambert, J.T. Aranson, and R.J. Hebda

1983   Caracol, Belize: Evidence of ancient Maya agricultural terraces. *Journal of Field Archaeology* 10:397–410.

Hellmuth, N.

1971   *Possible streets at a Maya site in Guatemala.* Report Prepared for Foundation for Latin American Anthropological Research.

Hendon, J.A.

1987   The uses of Maya structures: A study of architecture and artifact distribution at Sepulturas, Copan, Honduras. Ph.D. dissertation, Department of Anthropology, Harvard University, Cambridge.

1991   Status and power in Classic Maya society: An archaeological study. *American Anthropologist* 93:894–918.

1992   The interpretation of survey data: Two case studies from the Maya area. *Latin American Antiquity* 3:22–42.

1996   Archaeological approaches to the organization of domestic labor: Household practice and domestic relations. *Annual Review of Anthropology* 25:45–61.

1997   Women's work, women's space, and women's status among the Classic-period Maya elite of the Copan Valley, Honduras. In *Women in prehistory: North America and Mesoamerica*, edited by C. Claassen and R.A. Joyce, 33–46. Philadelphia: U of Pennsylvania.

Hester, T.R., and H.J. Shafer

1984   Exploitation of chert resources by the ancient Maya of northern Belize, Central America. *World Archaeology* 16:157–173.

1991   Lithics of the Early Postclassic at Colha, Belize. In *Maya stone tools: Selected papers from the Second Maya Lithic Conference*, edited by T.R. Hester and H.J. Shafer, 155–162. Monographs in World Archaeology 1. Madison, WI: Prehistory Press.

Hill, P.

1986   *Development economics on trial.* Cambridge: Cambridge U Press.

Hirsch, E., and O'Hanlon, M., eds.

1995   *The anthropology of landscape: Perspectives on place and space.* Oxford: Clarendon Press.

Houk, B.

1996   The archaeology of site planning: An example from the Maya site of Dos Hombres, Belize. Ph.D. dissertation, Department of Anthropology, University of Texas, San Antonio.

Houston, S.D.

1987   Notes on Caracol epigraphy and its significance. In *Investigations at the Classic Maya city of Caracol, Belize: 1985–1987*, edited by A.F. Chase and D.Z. Chase, 85–100. Monograph 3. San Francisco: Pre-Columbian Art Research Institute.

1991   Appendix: Caracol Altar 21. In *Sixth Palenque Round Table, 1986*, edited by M.G. Robertson and W.M. Fields, 38–42. Norman: U of Oklahoma Press.

1993   *Hieroglyphs and history at Dos Pilas: Dynastic politics of the Classic Maya.* Austin: U of Texas Press.

1998   Classic Maya depictions of the built environment. In *Function and meaning in Classic Maya architecture*, edited by S.D. Houston, 333–372. Washington, DC: Dumbarton Oaks Research Library Collection.

Hyslop, J.

1990   *Inka settlement patterning.* Austin: U of Texas Press.

Iannone, G.

1992   Ancient Maya eccentric lithics: A contextual analysis. M.A. thesis, Department of Anthropology, Trent University, Peterborough.

1993a   Time among the thorns: Results of the 1992 field season at Zubin, Cayo District, Belize. In *Belize Valley Archaeological Reconnaissance Project: Progress report of the 1992 field season*, edited by J.J. Awe, 10–44. Peterborough, Ontario: Department of Anthropology, Trent University.

1993b   Eccentrics and the Maya middle class: Insights from the Bedran Group, Baking Pot. In *Belize Valley Archaeologica l Reconnaissance Project: Progress report of the 1992 field season*, edited by J.J. Awe, 225–236. Peterborough, Ontario: Department of Anthropology, Trent University.

1994   Ancient Maya social organization and the concept of the middle class: A critical review. In *Belize Valley Archaeological Reconnaissance Project: Progress report of the sixth (1993) field season*, edited by J.J. Awe, 3–31. London: Institute of Archaeology.

1996   Problems in the study of ancient Maya settlement and social organization: Insights from the "minor center" of Zubin, Cayo District, Belize. Ph.D. dissertation, Institute of Archaeology, University College, London.

1997   Exploring ancient Maya rural complexity: Continuing investigations in the upper Belize river region. In *The Social Archaeology Researc h Program: Progress report of the third (1997) season*, edited by G. Iannone, 3–20. Peterborough, Ontario: Department of Anthropology, Trent University.

Iannone, G., and J.M. Conlon

1993   Elites, eccentrics and empowerment in the Maya area: Implications for the interpretation of a peripheral settlement cluster near Cahal Pech, Cayo district, Belize. *Papers of the Institute of Archaeology* 4:77–89.

Ingold, T.

1993   The temporality of the landscape. *World Archaeology* 25:152–174.

Isaza, A., and P.A. McAnany

1999   Adornment and identity: Shell ornaments from Formative K'axob. *Ancient Mesoamerica* 10:117–127.

Jamison, T.R., and R.M. Leventhal

1997   Creating and holding a political center: Architecture and space at Xunantunich. Paper presented at the 92nd Annual Meeting of the Society for American Archaeology, Nashville, TN.

Jamison, T.R., and G.A. Wolff

1997   Excavations in and around plaza A-I and plaza A-II. In *Xunantunich Archaeological Project: 1994 field season*, edited by R.M. Leventhal and W.A. Ashmore, 25–47. Report on file, Department of Archaeology, Belmopan, Belize; University of Pennsylvania; and Cotsen Institute of Archaeology at UCLA.

Jones, C.

1977   Inauguration dates of three Late Classic rulers of Tikal, Guatemala. *American Antiquity* 42:28–60.

1991   Cycles of growth at Tikal. In *Classic Maya political history*, edited by T.P. Culbert, 102–127. Cambridge: Cambridge U Press.

Jones, G.D.

1989   *Maya resistance to Spanish rule: Time and history on a colonial frontier.* Albuquerque: U of New Mexico Press.

Joyce, R.A

1992   Images of gender and labor organization in Classic Maya society. In *Exploring gender through archaeology: Selected papers from the 1991 Boone Conference*, edited by C. Claassen, 63–70. Monographs in World Archaeology 11. Madison, WI: Prehistory Press.

1993   Women's work: Images of production and reproduction in pre-Hispanic southern Central America. *Current Anthropology* 34:255–274.

Keller, A.H.

1995a   Getting into Xunantunich: Investigations of the access points of Xunantunich. Paper presented at the First International Symposium on Maya Archaeology, Department of Archaeology, San Ignacio, Belize.

1995b   Getting into Xunantunich: The 1995 excavations of the access points and accessibility of Xunantunich. In Xunantunich Archaeological Project: 1995 field season, edited by R.M. Leventhal and W.A. Ashmore, 83–111. Report on file, Department of Archaeology, Belmopan, Belize; University of Pennsylvania; and Cotsen Institute of Archaeology at UCLA.

1997   Testing and excavation around *Sacbe* II and Group C. In *Xunantunich Archaeological Project 1997: The final field season*, edited by R.M. Leventhal, 96–115. Report on file, Department of Archaeology,

Belmopan, Belize; University of Pennsylvania; and Cotsen Institute of Archaeology at UCLA.

Kent, S.
1990   A cross-cultural study of segmentation, architecture, and the use of space. In *Domestic architecture and the use of space: An interdisciplinary cross-cultural study*, edited by S. Kent, 127–152. Cambridge: Cambridge U Press.

Killion, T.W.
1992   Residential ethnoarchaeology and ancient site structure: Contemporary farming and prehistoric settlement agriculture at Matacapan, Veracruz, Mexico. In *Gardens of prehistory: The archaeology of settlement agriculture in greater Mesoamerica*, edited by T.W. Killion, 119–149. Tuscaloosa: U of Alabama Press.

Killion, T.W., J.A. Sabloff, G. Tourtellot, and N.P. Dunning
1989   Intensive surface collection of residential clusters at Terminal Classic Sayil, Yucatán, Mexico. *Journal of Field Archaeology* 16:273–294.

King, E., and D. Potter
1994   Small sites in prehistoric Maya socioeconomic organization: A perspective from Colha, Belize. In *Archaeological views from the countryside: Village communities in early complex communities*, edited by G.M. Schwartz and S.E. Falconer, 64–90. Washington, DC: Smithsonian Institution.

Kirkby, A.
1973   *The use of land and water resources in the past and present Valley of Oaxaca, Mexico*. Museum of Anthropology. Memoir, No. 5. Ann Arbor, MI: U of Michigan.

Knapp, A.B., ed.
1992   *Archaeology, annales, and ethnohistory*. Cambridge: Cambridge U Press.

Knapp, A.B., and W.A. Ashmore
1999   Archaeological landscapes: Conceptualized, constructed, ideational. In *Archaeologies of landscape: Contemporary perspectives*, edited by W.A. Ashmore and A.B. Knapp, 1–30. Oxford: Blackwell.

Kohl, P.
1981   Materialist approaches in prehistory. *Annual Review of Anthropology* 10:89–118.

Kowalski, J.K.
1987   *The house of the governor*. Norman: U of Oklahoma Press.

Kosakowsky, L.J., K. Sagebiel, N. Hammond, and G. Tourtellot
1997   En la frontera: la cerámica de La Milpa, Belize. In *XI Simposio de Investigaciones Arqueológicas en Guatemala*, edited by J.P. LaPorte and H. Escobedo, 659–666. Guatemala City: Museo Nacional de Arqueología y Etnología.

Kuper, A.
1982   Lineage theory: A critical retrospect. *Annual Review of Anthropology* 11:71–95.
1988   *The invention of primitive society: Transformations of an illusion*. London: Routledge.

Kurjack, E.B.
1974   *Prehistoric lowland Maya community and social organization: A case study at Dzibilchaltun, Yucatan, Mexico*. Middle American Research Institute, Publication 38. New Orleans: Tulane University.
1976   The distribution of vaulted architecture at Dzibilchaltun, Yucatan, Mexico. *Estudios de Cultura Maya* 10:91–101.

Kurjack, E.B., and E.W. Andrews V.
1976   Early boundary maintenance in northwest Yucatan, Mexico. *American Antiquity* 41:318–325.

Larick, R.
1991   Warriors and blacksmiths: Mediating ethnicity in East African spears. *Journal of Anthropological Archaeology* 10:299–331.

Lathrap, D.W.
1985   Jaws: The control of power in the early nuclear American ceremonial center. In *Early ceremonial architecture in the Andes*, edited by C. Donnan, 241–267. Washington, DC: Dumbarton Oaks.

Laughlin, C.D.
1993   Fuzziness and phenomonology in ethnological research: Insights from fuzzy set theory. *Journal of Anthropological Research* 49:17–37.

LeCount, L.J.
1996   Pottery and power: Feasting, gifting, and displaying wealth among the Late and Terminal Classic lowland Maya. Ph.D. dissertation,

Departmant of Anthropology, University of California, Los Angeles.
1999   Polychrome pottery and political strategies in Late and Terminal Classic lowland Maya society. *Latin American Antiquity* 10(3):239–58.

LeCount, L.J., J. Yaeger, R.M. Leventhal, and W.A. Ashmore
2000   The Late and Terminal Classic chronology of Xunantunich, Belize. Unpublished Report.

Lefebvre, H.
1991 [1974] *The production of space*. Translated by D. Nicholson-Smith. Oxford: Blackwell.

Leventhal, R.M.
1979   *Settlement patterns at Copan, Honduras*. Ph.D. dissertation, Department of Anthropology, Harvard University, Cambridge, MA.
1996   The end at Xunantunich: The architecture and setting in the Terminal Classic. In Xunantunich Archaeological Project: 1996 field season, edited by R.M. Leventhal and W.A. Ashmore, 9–16. Report on file, Department of Archaeology, Belmopan, Belize; University of Pennsylvania; and Cotsen Institute of Archaeology at UCLA.
1993   Xunantunich Archaeological Project: 1993 field season. Report on file, Department of Archaeology, Belmopan, Belize; University of Pennsylvania; and Cotsen Institute of Archaeology at UCLA.
1996   Xunantunich Archaeological Project: 1996 field season. Report on file, Department of Archaeology, Belmopan, Belize; University of Pennsylvania; and Cotsen Institute of Archaeology at UCLA.
1997   Xunantunich Archaeological Project: 1997 field season. Report on file, Department of Archaeology, Belmopan, Belize; University of Pennsylvania; and Cotsen Institute of Archaeology at UCLA.

Leventhal, R.M., and W.A. Ashmore, eds.
1994   Xunantunich Archaeological Project: 1994 field season Report on file, Department of Archaeology, Belmopan, Belize; University of Pennsylvania; and Cotsen Institute of Archaeology at UCLA.
1995   Xunantunich Archaeological Project: 1995 field season Report on file, Department of Archaeology, Belmopan, Belize; University of Pennsylvania; and Cotsen Institute of Archaeology at UCLA.

Leventhal, R.M., and K.H. Baxter
1988   The use of ceramics to identify the function of Copan structures. In *Household and community in the Mesoamerican past*, edited by R. Wilk and W.A. Ashmore, 51–72. Albuquerque: U of New Mexico Press.

Leventhal, R.M., and L.J. LeCount
2001   Shifting political ritual at Xunantunich, Belize, during the Late and Terminal Classic. In *The Terminal Classic in the Maya lowlands: Collapse, transition, and transformation*, edited by D.S. Rice, P.M. Rice, and A.A. Demarest. Denver: Westview Press.

Leventhal, R.M., S. Zeleznik, T. Jamison, L. LeCount, J. McGovern, J. Sanchez, A. Keller, and J. Braswell
1992   Xunantunich: A Late Classic and Terminal Classic center in the Belize River Valley. Paper presented at *Palenque Mesa Redonda, Anniversario Katun, 1973–1993*, June 1993, Palenque, Mexico.

Levi, L.J.
1993   Prehispanic residence and community at San Estevan, Belize. Ph.D. dissertation, Department of Anthropology, University of Arizona, Tucson.
1996   Sustainable production and residential variation: A historical perspective on lowland Maya domestic economy. *The managed mosaic: Ancient Maya agriculture and resource use*, edited by S.L. Fedick, 92–106. Salt Lake City: U of Utah Press.
2000   Institutional frameworks for prehispanic Maya residential variation. Unpublished manuscript.

Levy, J.E.
1995   Heterarchy in Bronze Age Denmark: Settlement pattern, gender and ritual. In *Heterarchy and the analysis of complex societies*, edited by R.M. Ehrenreich, C.L. Crumley, and J.E. Levy, 41–53. Archaeological Papers 6. Arlington, VA: American Anthropological Association.

Lewis, B.
1995   The role of specialized production in the development of sociopolitical complexity: a test case from the Late Classic Maya. Ph.D. dissertation, Department of Anthropology, University of California, Los Angeles.

Lincoln, C.E.
1985   Ceramics and ceramic chronology. In *A consideration of the Early Clas-*

sic period in the Maya lowlands, edited by G.R. Willey and P. Mathews, 5–94. Albany: State University of New York.

López Varela, S.L.
1996   The K'axob Formative ceramics: The search for regional integration through a reappraisal of ceramic analysis and classification in northern Belize. Ph.D. dissertation, Institute of Archaeology, University of London.

Losch, A.
1954   *The economics of location*. New Haven: Yale U Press.

Loten, H.S.
1985   Lamanai Postclassic. In *The lowland Maya Postclassic*, edited by A.F. Chase and P.M. Rice, 85–90. Austin: U of Texas Press.

Low, S.M.
1995   Indigenous architecture and the Spanish-American plaza in Mesoamerica and the Caribbean. *American Anthropologist* 97:748–762.

Lucero, L.J.
1999   Water control and Maya politics in the southern Maya lowlands. In *Complex polities in the ancient tropical world*, edited by E.A. Bacus and L.J. Lucero, 34–49.Archaeological Papers 9. Arlington: American Anthropological Association.

MacKie, E.W.
1961   New light on the end of Classic Maya culture at Benque Viejo, British Honduras. *American Antiquity* 27:216–224.
1985   *Excavations at Xunantunich and Pomona, Belize. 1959-1960*. BAR International Series 251. Oxford: British Archaeological Reports.

MacNeish, R.S., S.J.K. Wilkerson, and A. Nelken-Terner
1980   *First annual report of the Belize Archaic Archaeological Reconnaissance*. Andover, MA: Robert F. Peabody Foundation for Archaeology, Phillips Academy.

Marcus, J.
1976   *Emblem and state in the Classic Maya lowlands*. Washington, DC: Dumbarton Oaks.
1982   The plant world of the sixteenth- and seventeenth-century lowland Maya. In *Maya Subsistence*, edited by K.V. Flannery, 239–273. New York: Academic Press.
1983a   On the nature of the Mesoamerican city. In *Prehistoric settlement patterns: Essays in honor of Gordon R. Willey*, edited by E.Z. Vogt and R.M. Leventhal, 195–242. Albuquerque, NM, and Cambridge, MA: U of New Mexico Press and Peabody Museum of Archaeology and Ethnology, Harvard University.
1983b   Lowland Maya archaeology at the crossroads. *American Antiquity* 48:454–488.
1992   Dynamic cycles of Mesoamerican states: Political fluctuations in Mesoamerica. *National Geographic Research and Exploration* 8:392–411.
1993   Ancient Maya political organization. In *Lowland Maya civilization in the eighth century AD*, edited by J.A Sabloff and J.S. Henderson, 111–183. Washington, DC: Dumbarton Oaks.
1995   Where is lowland Maya archaeology headed? *Journal of Archaeological Research* 3–53.
1998   The peaks and valleys of ancient states: An extension of the dynamic model. In *Archaic states*, edited by G.M. Feinman and J. Marcus, 59–94. Santa Fe: School of American Research.

Martin, S., and N. Grube
1995   Maya superstates. *Archaeology* 48(6):41–47.

Masson, M.A.
1993   Changes in Maya community organization from the Classic to Postclassic periods: A view from Laguna de On, Belize. Ph.D. dissertation, Department of Anthropology, University of Texas, Austin.
1997   Cultural transformation at the Maya Postclassic community of Laguna de On, Belize. *Latin American Antiquity* 8(4):293–316.
1999   Postclassic Maya ritual at Laguna de On Island. *Ancient Mesoamerica* 10:51–68.
N.D.   *In the realm of Nachan Kan: Postclassic Maya archaeology at Laguna de On, Belize*. Boulder: U of Colorado Press. In press.

Masson, M.A., and R.M. Rosenswig, eds.
1998   Postclassic monumental center discovered at Caye Coco, Belize. *Mexicon* 20(1):4–5.
1999   *The Belize Postclassic Project 1998: Investigations at Progresso Lagoon.*

Occasional Publication 3. Albany: Institute of Mesoamerican Studies, State University of New York.

Mathews, P.
1985   Maya Early Classic monuments and inscriptions. In *A consideration of the Early Classic period in the Maya lowlands*, edited by G.R. Willey and P. Mathews, 5–54. Publication 10. Albany: Institute of Mesoamerican Studies, State University of New York.
1991   Classic Maya emblem glyphs. In *Classic Maya political history: Hieroglyphic and archaeological evidence*, edited by T.P. Culbert, 19–29. New York: Cambridge U Press.

Mathews, P., and G.R. Willey
1991   Prehistoric polities of the Pasion region: Hieroglyphic texts and their archaeological settings. In *Classic Maya political history*, edited by T.P. Culbert, 30–71. New York: Cambridge U Press.

Mazzarelli, M.
1976   Ancient Maya food producing systems in the upper Belize Valley: Suggestions for strategies and implications for population. *Katunob* 9(3):63–81.

McAnany, P.A.
1993   The economics of social power and wealth among eighth-century Maya households. In *Lowland Maya civilization in the eighth century AD*, edited by J.A. Sabloff and J.S. Henderson, 65–89. Washington, DC: Dumbarton Oaks.
1995   *Living with the ancestors: Kinship and kingship in ancient Maya society*. Austin: U of Texas Press.

McAnany, P.A., and K. Berry, eds.
1999   Where the water meets the land: 1998 excavations in wetland fields and along transects at K'axob, Belize. Report on file, Department of Archaeology, Belmopan, Belize; University of Pennsylvania; and Cotsen Institute of Archaeology at UCLA.

McAnany, P.A., and S.L. López Varela
1999   Re-creating the Formative Maya village of K'axob: Chronology, ceramic complexes, and ancestors in architectural context. *Ancient Mesoamerica* 10:147–168.

McAnany, P.A., R. Storey, and A.K. Lockard
1999   Mortuary ritual and family politics at Formative and Early Classic K'axob, Belize. *Ancient Mesoamerica* 10:129–146.

McGovern, J.
1994   Excavations at Actuncan: 1994 Season. In Xunantunich Archaeological Project: 1994 field season, edited by R.M. Leventhal and W.A. Ashmore, 109–123 Report on file, Department of Archaeology, Belmopan, Belize; University of Pennsylvania; and Cotsen Institute of Archaeology at UCLA.

McGuire, R.
1983   Breaking down cultural complexity: Inequality and heterogeneity. In *Advances in archaeological method and theory*, edited by M.B. Schiffer, 91–142. New York: Academic Press.

McGuire, R., and D. Saitta
1996   Although they have petty captains, they obey them badly: The dialectics of prehispanic Western Pueblo social organization. *American Antiquity* 61(2):196–216.

McKillop, H.
1996   Ancient Maya trading ports and the integration of long-distance and regional economies: Wild Cane Cay in south-coastal Belize. *Ancient Mesoamerica* 7:49–62.

McKillop, H., and P.F. Healy
1989   *Coastal Maya trade*. Occasional Papers in Archaeology. Peterborough, Ontario: Trent University.

Michaels, G.H.
1987   A description of Early Postclassic lithic technology at Colha, Belize. M.A. thesis, Department of Anthropology, Texas A&M University, College Station.
1994   The Postclassic at Colha, Belize: A summary overview and directions for future research. In *Continuing archaeology at Colha, Belize*, edited by T.R. Hester, H.J. Shafer, and J.D. Eaton, 129–136. Texas Archaeological Research Laboratory Studies in Archaeology 16. Austin: University of Texas.

Michaels, G.H., and H.J. Shafer
1994   Excavations at operation 2037 and 2040. In *Continuing archaeology at Colha, Belize*, edited by T.R. Hester, H.J. Shafer, and J.D. Eaton,

117–129. Texas Archaeological Research Laboratory. Studies in Archaeology 16. Austin: University of Texas.

Mock, S.B.
1994   Yucatecan presence in northern Belize Postclassic ceramics at Colha. In *Continuing archaeology at Colha, Belize,* edited by T.R. Hester, H.J. Shafer, and J.D. Eaton, 9–16. Texas Archaeological Research Laboratory Studies in Archaeology 16. Austin: University of Texas.
1997   Preliminary ceramic analysis: Laguna de On 1996 season. In The Belize Postclassic Project: Laguna de On Island excavations 1996, edited by M.A. Masson and R.M. Rosenswig. Report on file, Department of Archaeology, Belmopan, Belize.
1998   Ceramics from Laguna de On, 1996 and 1997. In *The Belize Postclassic Project 1997: Laguna de On, Progresso Lagoon, and Laguna Seca,* edited by M.A. Masson and R.M. Rosenswig, 192–202. Occasional Publication 2. Albany: Institute of Mesoamerican Studies, State University of New York.

Moore, A.F.
1997   Intragroup comparative study of the ancient Maya in the periphery of Baking Pot: Report of the first season of investigations at the Atalaya Group. In *Belize Valley Archaeological Reconnaissance Project: Progress report of the 1996 field season,* edited by J.J. Awe and J.M. Conlon. Peterborough, Ontario: Trent University.
1998   The Atalaya group at Baking Pot: The second season of investigations. In *Belize Valley Archaeological Reconnaissance Project: Progress report of the 1997 field season,* edited by J.M. Conlon and J.J. Awe, 61–80. London: Institute of Archaeology, University of London.

Moore, J.H.
1993   Political economy in anthropology. *The political economy of North American Indians,* edited by J.H. Moore, 3–19. Norman: U of Oklahoma Press.

Morrill, R.L.
1974   *The spatial organization of society.* North Scituate: Duxbury Press.

Muhs, D.R., R.R. Kautz, and J.J. MacKinnon
1985   Soils and the location of cacao orchards at a Maya site in western Belize. *Journal of Archaeological Science* 12:121–137.

Mullen, A.M.
1999   Domestic feature excavations at subops 11, 14, 3b, Caye Coco. In *The Belize Postclassic Project 1998: Investigations at Progresso Lagoon,* edited by M.A. Masson and R.M. Rosenswig, 39–60. Occasional Publication 3. Albany: Institute of Mesoamerican Studies, State University of New York.

Murray, E.
1998   Spindle whorls from Laguna de On. In *The Belize Postclassic Project 1997: Laguna de On, Progresso Lagoon, and Laguna Seca,* edited by M.A. Masson and R.M. Rosenswig, 157–162. Occasional Publication 2. Albany: Institute of Mesoamerican Studies, State University of New York.

Neff, L.S.
1995   Excavations of structure A-20 on the Castillo, Xunantunich. In Xunantunich Archaeological Project: 1995 field season, edited by R.M. Leventhal. Report on file, Department of Archaeology, Belmopan, Belize; University of Pennsylvania; and Cotsen Institute of Archaeology at UCLA.

Neff, L.T., C. Robin, K. Schwarz, and M.K. Morrison
1995   The Xunantunich settlement survey. In Xunantunich Archaeological Project: 1995 field season, edited by R.M. Leventhal and W.A. Ashmore, 139–166. Report on file, Department of Archaeology, Belmopan, Belize; University of Pennsylvania; and Cotsen Institute of Archaeology at UCLA.

Nichols, D.L.
1996   An overview of regional settlement pattern surveys in Mesoamerica: 1960–1995. In *Arqueología Mesoamericana: Homenaje a William T. Sanders,* edited by A.G. Mastache, J.R. Parsons, R.S. Santley, and M.C. Serra Puche, 59–95. Mexico City: Instituto Nacional de Antropología e Historia, Arqueología Mexicana.

O'Brien, M., and T.D. Holland
1990   Variation, selection, and the archaeological record. In *Archaeological method and theory,* Vol. 2, edited by M.B. Schiffer, 31–79. Tucson: U of Arizona Press.

Oland, M.
1998   Lithic raw material sources at the southern end of the Freshwater Creek drainage. In *The Belize Postclassic Project 1997: Laguna de On, Progresso Lagoon, and Laguna Seca,* edited by M.A. Masson and R.M. Rosenswig, 163–176. Occasional Publication 2. Albany: Institute of Mesoamerican Studies, State University of New York.
1999a   Lithic raw material sources at the southern end of the Freshwater Creek drainage: A view from Laguna de On, Belize. *Lithic Technology* 24(2):91–110.
1999b   Preliminary analysis of lithics from Caye Coco, Caye Muerto and Progresso Lagoon 1998. In *The Belize Postclassic Project 1998: Investigations at Progresso Lagoon,* edited by M.A. Masson and R.M.Rosenswig, 144–156. Occasional Publication 3. Albany: Institute of Mesoamerican Studies, State University of New York.

Olwig, K.
1993   Sexual cosmology: Nation and landscape at the conceptual interstices of nature and culture; or what does landscape really mean? In *Landscape: Politics and perspectives,* edited by B. Bender, 307–343. Providence: Berg Press.

Ortner, S.
1984   Theory in anthropology since the sixties. *The Comparative Study of Society and History* 10:126–166.

Parsons, J.R.
1972   Archaeological settlement patterns. *Annual Review of Anthropology* 1:125–150.

Paynter, R.
1989   The archaeology of equality and inequality. *Annual Review of Anthropology* 18:369–399.

Pendergast, D.M.
1979   *Excavations at Altun Ha, Belize, 1964–1970,* Vol. 1. Royal Ontario Museum Publications in Archaeology. Toronto: Alger Press.
1981   Lamanai, Belize: Summary of excavation results, 1974–1980. *Journal of Field Archaeology* 8(1):29–53.
1985   Lamanai, Belize: An updated view. In *The lowland Maya Postclassic,* edited by A.Chase and P. Rice, 91–103. Austin: U of Texas Press.
1986   Stability through change: Lamanai, Belize from the ninth to the seventeenth century. In *Late lowland Maya civilization: Classic to Postclassic,* edited by J.A. Sabloff and E.W. Andrews V, 223–250. Albuquerque: U of New Mexico Press.

Pina Chan, R.
1978   Commerce in the Yucatec Peninsula: The conquest and colonial period. In *Mesoamerican communication routes and culture contacts,* edited by T.A. Lee and C. Navarrete, 37–48. Papers of the New World Archaeological Foundation 40. Provo, UT: Brigham Young University.

Pincemein, S., J. Marcus, L.F. Folan, W.J. Folan, M. del Rosario Dominguez C., and A. Morales L.
1998   Extending the Calakmul dynasty back in time: A new stela from a Maya capital in Campeche, Mexico. *Latin American Antiquity* 9(4):310–327.

Pohl, M.D., ed.
1985   *Prehistoric lowland Maya environment and subsistence economy.* Papers of the Peabody Museum of Archaeology and Ethnology 77. Cambridge: Harvard U Press.

Pohl, M.D., and J.M.D. Pohl
1994   Cycles of conflict: Political factionalism in the Maya Lowlands. In *Factional competition and political development in the New World,* edited by E.M. Brumfiel and J.W. Fox, 138–157. New York: Cambridge U Press.

Pohl, M.D., K.O. Pope, J.G. Jones, J.S. Jacob, D.R. Piperno, S.D. deFrance, D.L. Lentz, J.A. Gifford, M.E. Danforth, and J.K. Josserand.
1996   Early agriculture in the Maya lowlands. *Latin American Antiquity* 7(4):355–372.

Pollock, H.E.D.
1965   Architecture of the Maya lowlands. *Handbook of Middle American Indians* 2:378–440.

Pope, C.
1994   Preliminary analysis of small chert tools and related debitage at

Caracol, Belize. In *Studies in the archaeology of Caracol, Belize*, edited by D.Z. Chase and A.F. Chase, 148–156. Monograph 7. San Francisco: Pre-Columbian Art Research Institute.

Potter, D.R., and E.M. King
1995   A heterarchical approach to lowland Maya socioeconomics. In *Heterarchy and the analysis of complex societies*, edited by R.M. Ehrenreich, C.L. Crumley, and J.E. Levy, 17–32. Archaeological Papers 6. Arlington, VA: American Anthropological Association.

Powis, T.G.
1993   Special function structures within peripheral groups in the Belize Valley: An example from the Bedran Group at Baking Pot, Belize. In *Belize Valley Archaeological Reconnaissance Project: Progress report of the 1992 field season*, edited by J.J. Awe, 212–224. Peterborough, Ontario: Trent University.
1994   Sacred space and ancestor worship: Ongoing plaza investigations of two Middle Formative circular platforms at the Tolok group, Cahal Pech, Belize. In *Belize Valley Archaeological Reconnaissance Project: Progress report of the sixth (1993) field season*, edited by J.J. Awe, 122–146. London: Institute of Archaeology.

Proskouriakoff, T.
1960   Historical implications of a pattern of dates at Piedras Negras, Guatemala. *American Antiquity* 25:454–475.

Puleston, D.E.
1974   Intersite areas in the vicinity of Tikal and Uaxactun. In *Mesoamerican archaeology: New approaches*, edited by N. Hammond, 301–311. London: Duckworth.
1983   *The settlement survey of Tikal*. Tikal Report 13, Monograph 48. Philadelphia: University Museum,f University of Pennsylvania.

Puleston, D.E., and D.W. Callender, Jr.
1967   Defensive earthworks at Tikal. *Expedition* 9(3):40–48.

Pyburn, K.A.
1989   *Prehistoric Maya community and settlement at Nohmul, Belize*. BAR International Series 509. Oxford: British Archaeological Reports.
1998   Smallholders in the Maya lowlands: Homage to a garden variety ethnographer. *Human Ecology* 26:267–286.

Quezada, S.
1993   *Pueblos y caciques Yucatecos, 1550–1580*. Mexico: El Colegio de Mexico.

Rands, R.L., and R.L. Bishop
1980   Resource procurement zones and patterns of ceramic exchange in the Palenque region, Mexico. In *Models and methods in regional exchange*, edited by R. Fry, 19–46. SAA Papers 1. Washington, DC: Society for American Archaeology.

Rapoport, A.
1990   Systems of activities and systems of settings. In *Domestic architecture and the use of space: An interdisciplinary cross-cultural study*, edited by S. Kent, 9–20. Cambridge: Cambridge U Press.

Rathje, W.L.
1971   The origin and development of lowland Classic Maya civilization. *American Antiquity* 36(3):275–285.
1975   The last tango in Mayapan: A tentative trajectory of production-distribution systems. In *Ancient civilization and trade*, edited by J.A. Sabloff and C.C. Lamberg-Karlovsky, 409–448. Albuquerque: U of New Mexico Press.
1983   To the salt of the earth: Some comments on household archaeology among the Maya. In *Prehistoric settlement patterns: Essays in honor of Gordon R. Willey*, edited by E. Vogt and R.M. Leventhal, 23–34. Albuquerque and Cambridge: U of New Mexico Press and Peabody Museum of Archaeology and Ethnology, Harvard University.

Redfield, R.
1930   *Tepotzlan, a Mexican village: A study of folk life*. Chicago: U of Chicago Press.
1941   *The folk culture of the Yucatan*. Chicago: U of Chicago Press.
1953   *The primitive world and its transformations*. Ithaca, NY: Cornell U Press.
1955   *The little community: Viewpoints for the study of a human whole*. Chicago: U of Chicago Press.
1960   *The little community and peasant society and culture*. Chicago: U of Chicago Press.
1971 [1956] *Peasant society and culture: An anthropological approach to civilization*. Chicago: U of Chicago Press.

Reents-Budet, D.
1994   *Painting the Maya universe: Royal ceramics of the Classic period*. Durham, NC: Duke U Press.

Renfrew, C.
1975   Trade as action at a distance: Questions of integration and communication. In *Ancient civilization and trade*, edited by J.A. Sabloff and C.C. Lamberg-Karlovsky, 3–59. Albuquerque: U of New Mexico Press.

Rice, D.S.
1988   Classic to Postclassic Maya household transitions in the central Peten, Guatemala. In *Household and community in the Mesoamerican past*, edited by R.R. Wilk and W.A. Ashmore, 227–247. Albuquerque: U of New Mexico Press.

Rice, D.S., and T.P. Culbert
1990   Historical contexts for population reconstruction in the Maya lowlands. In *Precolumbian population history in the Maya lowlands*, edited by D.S. Rice and T.P. Culbert, 1–36. Albuquerque: U of New Mexico Press.

Rice, D.S., and P.M. Rice
1980   The northeast Peten revisited. *American Antiquity* 45:432–454.

Rice, P.M.
1980   Peten Postclassic pottery production and exchange: A view from Macanche. In *Models and methods in regional exchange*, edited by R. Fry, 67–82. SAA Papers, No. 1. Washington, DC: Society for American Archaeology.
1984   Obsidian procurement in the Central Peten Lakes region, Guatemala. *Journal of Field Archaeology* 11:181–194.
1987a *Pottery analysis: A sourcebook*. Chicago: U of Chicago Press.
1987b Economic change in the lowland Maya Late Classic period. In *Specialization, exchange, and complex societies*, edited by E.M. Brumfiel and T.K. Earle, 76–85. Cambridge: Cambridge U Press.

Ricketson, O.G.
1931   *Excavation at Baking Pot, British Honduras*. Contributions to American Anthropology and History, No. 1. Publication 403. Washington, DC: Carnegie Institute.

Ringle, W.M., and G. Bey
1992   The center and segmentary state dynamics: African models in the Maya lowlands. Paper presented at the Wenner-Gren Conference on the Segmentary State and the Classic Maya Lowlands, Cleveland State University, Cleveland, OH.

Robichaux, H.R.
1995a Ancient Maya community patterns in northwestern Belize: Peripheral zone survey at La Milpa and Dos Hombres. Ph.D. dissertation, Department of Anthropology, U of Texas, Austin.
1995b Survey in the peripheral zones of the La Milpa and Dos Hombres ancient Maya sites in northwestern Belize: The 1994 season. In *The Programme for Belize Archaeological Project: 1994 interim report*, edited by R.E.W. Adams and F. Valdez, Jr., 18–51. San Antonio: The Center for Archaeology and Tropical Studies and University of Texas.

Robin, C.
1997   Rural household and community flux at Classic Maya Xunantunich. Paper presented at the 62nd Annual Meeting of the Society for American Archaeology, Nashville, TN.
1998   Where people really live: Methods for identification of household spaces and activities. Paper presented at the 63rd Annual Meeting of the Society for American Archaeology, Seattle. WA.
1999   Towards an archaeology of everyday life: Maya farmers of Chan Noohol and Dos Chombitos Cik'in, Belize. Ph.D. dissertation, Department of Anthropology, University of Pennsylvania, Philadelphia.

Roscoe, P.
1993   Practice and political centralization. *Current Anthropology* 34:111–140.

Rosebury, W.
1989   *Anthropologies and histories: Essays in culture, history, and political economy*. New Brunswick, NJ: Rutgers U Press.

Rosenswig, R.M.
1999   Looter's trench documentation of architectural construction at Caye Coco. In *The Belize Postclassic Project 1998: Investigations at Progresso Lagoon*, edited by M.A. Masson and R.M.Rosenswig, 125–136. Occasional Publication 3. Albany: Institute of Mesoamerican Studies, State University of New York.

Rouse, I.
1972   Settlement patterns in archaeology. In *Man, settlement and urbanism*, edited by P. J. Ucko, R. Tringham, and G.W. Dimbleby, 95–107. London: Duckworth.

Rowlands, M.
1989   A question of complexity. In *Domination and resistance*, edited by D. Miller and C. Tilley, 29–40. London: Unwin Hyman.

Roys, R.L.
1957   *The political geography of the Yucatan Maya*. Publication 613. Washington, DC: Carnegie Institution.
1972   *The Indian background of colonial Yucatan*. New edition. Norman: U of Oklahoma Press.

Ruz Lhuillier, A.
1954   La pirámide-tumba de Palenque. *Cuadernos Americanos* 74:141–159.

Sabloff, J.A.
1975   *Excavations at Seibal, Department of the Peten, Guatemala: The ceramics*. Memoirs, Vol. 13, No. 2. Cambridge: Peabody Museum of Archaeology and Ethnology, Harvard University.
1983   Classic Maya settlement pattern studies: Past problems, future prospects. In *Prehistoric settlement patterns: Essays in Honor of Gordon R. Willey*, edited by E.Z. Vogt and R.M. Leventhal, 413–422. Albuquerque and Cambridge: U of New Mexico Press and Peabody Museum of Archaeology and Ethnology, Harvard University.
1996   Settlement patterns and community organization in the Maya lowlands. *Expedition* 38:3–13.

Sabloff, J.A., and W.A. Ashmore
2001   An aspect of archaeology's recent past and its relevance in the new millennium. In *Archaeology at the millennium: A sourcebook*, edited by G.M. Feinman and T.D. Price. New York: Plenum.

Sabloff, J.A., and W.L. Rathje
1975   The rise of a Maya merchant class. *Scientific American* 233:72–82.

Sabloff, J.A., and G. Tourtellot III
1991   *The ancient Maya city of Sayil: The mapping of a Puuc region center*. Publication 60. New Orleans: Middle American Research Institute, Tulane University.

Saitta, D.J.
1997   Power, labor, and the dynamics of change in Chacoan political economy. *American Antiquity* 62(1):7–26.

Sanchez, J.L.
1997   Royal strategies and audience: An analysis of Classic Maya monumental art. Ph.D. dissertation, Department of Anthropology, University of California, Los Angeles.

Sanders, W.T., ed.
1986/90 *Excavaciones en el area urbana de Copán*. Vols. 1–3. Tegucigalpa: Secretaria del Estado en el Despacho de Cultura y Turismo.

Sanders, W.T.
1992   Ranking and stratification in prehispanic Mesoamerica. In *Mesoamerican elites: An archaeological assessment*, edited by D.Z. Chase and A.F. Chase, 278–291. Norman: U of Oklahoma Press.

Sanders, W.T., and B.J. Price
1968   *Mesoamerica: The evolution of a civilization*. New York: Random House.

Sanders, W.T., and D. Webster
1988   The Mesoamerican urban tradition. *American Anthropologist* 90:521–546

Santley, R.S.
1994   The economy of ancient Matacapan. *Ancient Mesoamerica* 5(2):243–266.

Santley, R.S., and K.G. Hirth, eds.
1993   *Prehispanic domestic units in western Mesoamerica: Studies of the household, compound, and residence*. Boca Raton, FL: CRC Press.

Scarborough, V.L.
1993   Water management in the southern Maya lowlands: An accretive model for the engineered landscape. In *Economic aspects of water management in the prehispanic New World*, edited by V.L. Scarborough and B.L. Isaac, 17–69. Research in Economic Anthropology, Supplement 7. Greenwich, CT: JAI Press.
1994   Maya water management. *National Geographic Research and Exploration* 10:184–199.
1998   Ecology and ritual: Water management and the Maya. *Latin American Antiquity* 9:135–159.

Scarborough, V.L., M.E. Becher, J.L. Baker, G. Harris, and J.D. Hensz
1992   Water management studies at La Milpa, Belize. Report on file, Department of Anthropology, University of Cincinnati.

Scarborough, V.L., M.E. Becher, J.L. Baker, G. Harris, and F. Valdez, Jr.
1995   Water and land at the ancient Maya community of La Milpa. *Latin American Antiquity* 6:98–119.

Schama, S.
1995   *Landscape and memory*. New York: Knopf.

Schele, L.
1991   The demotion of Chac-Zutz': Lineage compounds and subsidiary lords at Palenque. In *Sixth Palenque Round Table, 1986*, edited by V.M. Fields, 6–11. Norman: U of Oklahoma Press.

Schele, L., and D.A. Freidel
1990   *A forest of kings: The untold story of the ancient Maya*. New York: William Morrow.

Schele, L., and P. Mathews
1998   *The code of kings*. New York: Scribner.

Schmidt, P.J.
1974   A new map and some notes on the Terminal Classic and Postclassic activities at Xunantunich, Belize. Paper presented at the International Congress of Americanists, Mexico.

Schortman, E.M.
1984   Archaeological investigations in the Lower Motagua Valley, Department of Izabal, Guatemala: A study in monumental site function and interaction. Ph.D. dissertation, University of Pennsylvania, Philadelphia.
1989   Interregional interaction in prehistory: The need for a new perspective. *American Antiquity* 54:52–65.

Schortman, E.M., and S. Nakamura
1991   A crisis of identity: Late Classic competition and interaction on the Southeast Maya Periphery. *Latin American Antiquity* 2:311–336.

Schultz, K.C., J.J. González, and N. Hammond
1994   Classic Maya ballcourts at La Milpa, Belize. *Ancient Mesoamerica* 5:45–53.

Schuster, A.M.H.
1997   The search for site Q. *Archaeology* 50(5):42–45.

Schwake, S.
1999   On the road: Excavations along the Maya sacbe at X-ual-canil, Cayo District, Belize. M.A. thesis, Department of Anthropology, Trent University, Peterborough, Ontario.

Schwartz, G.M., and S.E. Falconer
1994a   *Archaeological views from the countryside: Village communities in early complex communities*. Washington, DC: Smithsonian Institution.
1994b   Archaeological views from the countryside: Communities in early complex societies. In *Archaeological views from the countryside: Village communities in early complex communities*, edited by G.M. Schwartz and S.E. Falconer, 1–9. Washington, DC: Smithsonian Institution.

Scott, J.C.
1985   *Weapons of the weak: Everyday forms of peasant resistance*. New Haven: Yale U Press.

Seibert, J.
2000   Residential architecture as an indicator of social status among the ancient Maya of the Belize Valley. M.A. thesis, Department of Anthropology, Trent University, Peterborough, Ontario.

Shafer, H.J., and T.R. Hester
1983   Ancient Maya chert workshops in northern Belize, Central America. *American Antiquity* 48:519–543.
1988   Preliminary analysis of Postclassic lithics from Santa Rita Corozal, Belize. Appendix III. In *A Postclassic perspective: Excavations at the Maya site of Santa Rita Corozal, Belize*. Monograph 4. San Francisco: Pre-Columbian Art Research Institute.

Sharer, R.J.
1978   Archaeology and history at Quirigua, Guatemala. *Journal of Field Archaeology* 5:51–70.
1993   The social organization of the Late Classic Maya: Problems of definition and approaches. In *Lowland Maya civilization in the eighth century AD*, edited by J.A. Sabloff and J.S. Henderson, 91–109. Washington, DC: Dumbarton Oaks.

Sharer, R.J., W.L. Fash, D.W. Sedat, L.P. Traxler, and R. Williamson

1999   Continuities and contrasts in Early Classic architecture of central Copán. In *Mesoamerican architecture as a cultural symbol*, edited by J.K. Kowalski, 220–249. New York and Oxford: Oxford U Press.

Shaw, L.C., and E.M. King

1997   Research in high places: The hilltop center of Ma'ax Na, Belize. Paper presented at the 62nd Annual Meeting of the Society for American Archaeology, Nashville, TN.

Shaw, L.C., E.M. King, and B. Moses

1999   Constructed landscape as ideology: Archaeology and mapping at Ma'ax na in the three rivers region of Belize. Paper presented at the 64th Annual Meeting of the Society for American Archaeology, Chicago.

Sheets, P.

1992   *The Ceren site: A prehistoric village buried by volcanic ash in Central America*. Fort Worth, TX: Harcourt, Brace, Jovanovich.

1998   Place and time in activity area analysis: A study of elevated contexts used for artifact curation at the Ceren site, El Salvador. *Revista Española de Antropología Americana* 28:63–98.

Shipton, P.

1994   Land and culture in tropical Africa: Soils, symbols, and the metaphysics of the mundane. *Annual Review of Anthropology* 23:347–377.

Sidrys, R.V.

1983   *Archaeological excavations in Northern Belize, Central America*. Monograph 17. Los Angeles: UCLA Institute of Archaeology.

Smith, A.L.

1950   *Uaxactun, Guatemala: Excavations of 1931–1937*. Publication 588. Washington, DC: Carnegie Institute.

1977   Patolli, at the ruins of Seibal, Peten, Guatemala. In *Social process in Maya prehistory: Studies in honour of Sir Eric Thompson*, edited by N. Hammond, 349–363. New York: Academic Press.

1982   *Excavations at Seibal, Department of Peten, Guatemala: Major architecture and caches*. Memoirs of the Peabody Museum of Archaeology and Ethnology 15. Cambridge: Harvard University.

Smith, C.A.

1974   Economics of marketing systems: Models from economic geography. *Annual Review of Anthropology* 3:167–201.

1976   Exchange systems and the spatial distribution of elites: The organization of stratification in agrarian societies. In *Regional analysis*. Vol. II: *Social systems*, edited by C. Smith, 309–374. New York: Academic Press.

Smith, J.R.

1998   Geology and carbonate hydrogeochemistry of the Lower Mopan and Macal River Valleys, Belize. M.A. thesis, University of Pennsylvania, Philadelphia.

Smith, M.E.

1987   Household possessions and wealth in agrarian states: Implications for archaeology. *Journal of Anthropological Archaeology* 6:297–335.

1992   Rhythms of change in Postclassic Central Mexico: Archaeology, ethnohistory, and the Braudelian model. In *Archaeology, annales, and ethnohistory*, edited by A.B. Knapp, 51–77. Cambridge: Cambridge U Press.

1994   Social complexity and the Aztec countryside. In *Archaeological views of the countryside: Village communities in early complex societies*, edited by G.M. Schwartz and S.E. Falconer, 143–159. Washington, DC: Smithsonian Institution.

1998   Tlahuica ceramics: The Aztec-period ceramics of Morelos, Mexico. Report on file, Institute for Mesoamerican Studies, State University of New York at Albany.

1999   Comment on Hirth's "The Distributional Approach." Manuscript.

Smith, M.E., and C. Heath-Smith

1994   Rural economy in Late Postclassic Morelos. *Economies and polities in the Aztec realm*, edited by M.G. Hodge and M.E. Smith, 349–376. Studies on Culture and Society 6. Albany: Institute for Mesoamerican Studies, State University of New York.

Soja, E.

1985   The spatiality of social life: Towards a transformative retheorisation. *Social Relations and Spatial Structures*, edited by D. Gregory and J. Urry, 90–127. New York: St. Martin's Press.

Spencer, C.S., E.M. Redmond, and M. Rinaldi

1994   Drained fields at La Tigra, Venezuelan Llanos: A regional perspective. *Latin American Antiquity* 5(2):119–143.

Stahl, A.B

1993   Concepts of time and approaches to analogical reasoning in historical perspective. *American Antiquity* 58:235–260.

Stone, A., D. Reents, and R. Coffman

1985   Genealogical documentation of the Middle Classic dynasty of Caracol, El Cayo, Belize. In *Fourth Palenque Round Table, 1980*, edited by M.G. Robertson and E. Benson, 267–275. San Francisco: Pre-Columbian Art Research Institute.

Stone, G.D., R. McC. Netting, and M.P. Stone

1990   Seasonality, labor scheduling, and agricultural intensification in the Nigerian savanna. *American Anthropologist* 92:7–23.

Stuart, D.

1993   Historical inscriptions and the Maya collapse. In *Lowland Maya civilization in the eighth century AD*, edited by J.A. Sabloff and J.S. Henderson, 321–354. Washington, DC: Dumbarton Oaks.

Sullivan, L.A.

1997   Classic Maya social organization: A perspective from Las Abejas. Ph.D. dissertation, Department of Anthropology, University of Texas at Austin.

Sweely, T.

1998   Personal interactions: The implications of spatial arrangements for power relations at Ceren, El Salvador. *World Archaeology* 29:393–406.

Taschek, J.T., and J.W. Ball

1999   Las ruinas de Arenal: Preliminary report on a subregional major center in the western Belize Valley (1991–1992 excavations). *Ancient Mesoamerica* 10:215–235.

Thomas, J.

1991   *Rethinking the Neolithic*. Cambridge: Cambridge U Press.

Thomas, P.M., Jr.

1981   *Prehistoric Maya settlement patterns at Becan, Campeche, Mexico*. Middle American Research Institute Publication, No. 45. New Orleans: Tulane University.

Thompson, J.E.S.

1931   *Archaeological Investigations in the southern Cayo District, British Honduras*. Anthropology Series, Vol. 17, No. 3. Chicago: Field Museum of Natural History.

1966   *The rise and fall of Maya civilization*. Norman: U of Oklahoma Press.

1970   *Maya history and religion*. Norman: U of Oklahoma Press.

Thompson, J.E.S., H.E.D. Pollock, and J. Charlot

1932   *A preliminary study of the ruins of Coba, Quintana Roo, Mexico*. Publication 424. Washington, DC: Carnegie Institute.

Tourtellot, G.

1970   *The peripheries of Seibal, an interim report*. Papers of the Peabody Museum of Archaeology and Ethnology 16:405–421. Cambridge: Harvard University.

1982   Ancient Maya settlements at Seibal, Peten, Guatemala: Peripheral survey and excavation. Ph.D. dissertation, Department of Anthropology, Harvard University.

1988a   Developmental cycles of households and houses at Seibal. In *Household and community in the Mesoamerican past*, edited by R.R. Wilk and W.A. Ashmore, 97–121. Albuquerque: U of New Mexico Press.

1988b   *Excavations at Seibal, Department of Petén, Guatemala: Peripheral survey and excavation*. Memoirs of the Peabody Museum of Archaeology and Ethnology 16. Cambridge: Harvard University.

1993   A view of ancient Maya settlements in the eighth century. In *Lowland Maya civilization in the eighth century AD*, edited by J.A. Sabloff and J.S. Henderson, 219–241. Washington, DC: Dumbarton Oaks.

Tourtellot, G., A. Clarke, and N. Hammond

1993   Mapping La Milpa: A Maya city in northwestern Belize. *Antiquity* 67:96–108.

Tourtellot, G., N. Hammond, and S. Plank

1997   The city on the hill: Investigations at La Milpa, Northwestern Belize. Paper presented at the 62nd Annual Meeting of the Society for American Archaeology, Nashville, TN.

Tourtellot, G., N. Hammond, and J.J. Rose

N.D.   Reversal of fortune: Settlement processes at La Milpa, Belize. Paper presented at the 1st International Symposium of Maya Archaeology, San Ignacio, Belize, June, 1995. Department of Archaeology, Ministry of Tourism and the Environment, Belmopan, Belize.

Tourtellot, G., J.J. Rose, N. Grube, S. Donaghey, and N. Hammond
1994   More light on La Milpa: Maya settlement archaeology in northwestern Belize. *Mexicon* 16:119–124.

Tourtellot, G., J.J. Rose, and N. Hammond
1996   Maya settlement survey at La Milpa, Belize. *Mexicon* 18:8–11.

Tourtellot, G., J.A. Sabloff, and K. Carmean
1992   "Will the real elites please stand up?" an archaeological assessment of Maya elite behavior in the Terminal Classic period. In *Mesoamerican elites: An archaeological assessment*, edited by D.Z. Chase and A.F. Chase, 80–98. Norman: U of Oklahoma Press.

Tozzer, A.M., ed.
1941   *Landa's Relación de las Cosas de Yucatán*. Papers of the Peabody Museum of Archaeology and Ethnology 18. Cambridge: Harvard University.

Trigger, B.G.
1968   The determinants of settlement patterns. In *Settlement archaeology*, edited by K.C. Chang, 53–78. Palo Alto, CA: National Press.

Trombold, C.D., ed.
1991   *Ancient road networks and settlement hierarchies in the New World*. Cambridge: Cambridge U Press.

Tuan, Y.
1977   *Space and place: The perspective of experience*. Minneapolis: U of Minnesota Press.

Turner, B.L., and P. Harrison, eds.
1983   *Pulltrouser Swamp: Ancient Maya habitat, agriculture, and settlement in northern Belize*. Austin: U of Texas Press.

Turner, B.L., N.I. Turner, and R.E.W. Adams
1981   Volumetric assessment, rank ordering and Maya civic centers. In *Lowland Maya settlement patterns*, edited by W.A. Ashmore, 71–81. Albuquerque: U of New Mexico Press.

Vanden Bosch, J.C.
1992   Excavation of rubble mound features in the periphery. In Xunantunich Archaeological Project: 1992 field season, edited by R.M. Leventhal, 84–109. Report on file, Department of Archaeology, Belmopan, Belize; University of Pennsylvania; and Cotsen Institute of Archaeology at UCLA.
1993   Investigations of San Lorenzo's linear and cobble mounds. In Xunantunich Archaeological Project: 1993 field season, edited by R.M. Leventhal, 148–171 Report on file, Department of Archaeology, Belmopan, Belize; University of Pennsylvania; and Cotsen Institute of Archaeology at UCLA.

Villa Rojas, A.
1934   *The Yaxuna-Coba causeway*. Contributions to American Anthropology and History, No. 9. Publication 436 Washington, DC: Carnegie Institution.

Vogt, E.Z.
1970   *The Zinacantecos of Mexico: A modern Maya way of life*. London: Holt, Rinehart and Winston.
1976   *Tortillas for the Gods: A symbolic analysis of Zinacantan ritual*. Cambridge: Harvard U Press.
1981   Some aspects of the sacred geography of highland Chiapas. In *Mesoamerican sites and world-views*, edited by E.P. Benson, 119–142. Washington DC: Dumbarton Oaks Research Library and Collections.
1983a   Some new themes in settlement pattern research. In *Prehistoric settlement patterns: Essays in Honor of Gordon R. Willey*, edited by E.Z. Vogt and R.M. Leventhal, 3–20. Albuquerque and Cambridge: U of New Mexico Press and Peabody Museum of Archaeology and Ethnology, Harvard University.
1983b   Ancient and contemporary Maya settlement patterns: A new look from the Chiapas highlands. In *Prehistoric settlement patterns: Essays in honor of Gordon R. Willey*, edited by E.Z. Vogt and R.M. Leventhal, 89–114. Albuquerque and Cambridge: U of New Mexico Press and Peabody Museum of Archaeology and Ethnology, Harvard University.

Wailes, B.
1995   A case study of heterarchy in complex societies: Early Medieval Ireland and its archaeological implications. In *Heterarchy in complex societies*, edited by R.M. Ehrenreich, C.L. Crumley, and J.E. Levy, 55–69. Archaeological Papers 6. Arlington, VA: American Anthropological Association.

Walker, D.
1990   Cerros revisited: Ceramic indicators of Terminal Classic and Postclassic settlement and pilgrimage in northern Belize. Ph.D. dissertation, Department of Anthropology, Southern Methodist University, Dallas, TX.

Walling, S.
1993   Prehispanic Maya settlement at Tibaat, a residential complex associated with raised- and drained-fields at Pulltrouser Swamp, Belize. Ph.D. dissertation, Department of Anthropology, Tulane University, New Orleans.

Wauchop, R.
1934   *House mounds of Uaxactun, Guatemala*. Contributions to American Anthropology and History, No. 7. Publication 436. Washington, DC: Carnegie Institution.

Webster, D.
1997   City-states of the Maya. In *The archaeology of city-states: Cross-cultural approaches*, edited by D.L. Nichols and T.H. Charlton, 135–154. Washington, DC: Smithsonian Institution.
1998   Classic Maya architecture: Implications and comparisons. In *Function and meaning in Classic Maya architecture*, edited by S.D. Houston, 5–47. Washington, DC: Dumbarton Oaks Research Library and Collection.
1999   The archaeology of Copan, Honduras. *Journal of Archaeological Research* 7:1–53.

Webster, D., B. Fash, R. Widmer, and S. Zeleznik
1998   The skyband group: Investigation of a Classic Maya elite residential complex at Copan, Honduras. *Journal of Field Archaeology* 25:319–343.

Webster, D., and N. Gonlin
1988   Household remains of the humblest Maya. *Journal of Field Archaeology* 15:169–190.

Webster, D., N. Gonlin, and P. Sheets
1997   Copan and Ceren: Two perspectives on ancient Mesoamerican households. *Ancient Mesoamerica* 8:43–61.

Wells, E.C.
2000   Pottery production and microcosmic organization: The residential structure of La Quemada, Zacatecas. *Latin American Antiquity* 11(1):21–42.

Welsh, W.B.M.
1988   *An analysis of Classic lowland Maya burials*. International Series 409. Oxford: British Archaeological Reports.

West, G.
1999   Investigations at Structure I, Caye Coco. In *The Belize Postclassic Project 1998: Investigations at Progresso Lagoon*, edited by M.A. Masson and R.M. Rosenswig, 83–102. Occasional Publication 3. Albany: Institute of Mesoamerican Studies, State University of New York.

Wheatley, P.
1972   The concept of urbanism. In *Man, settlement, and urbanism*, edited by P.J. Ucko, R. Tringham, and G.W. Dimbleby, 601–637. London: Duckworth.

Wiessner, P.
1983   Style and social information in Kalahari San projectile points. *American Antiquity* 48:253–276.

Wilk, R.R.
1988   Maya household organization: Evidence and analogies. In *Household and community in the Mesoamerican past*, edited by W.A. Ashmore and R.R. Wilk, 135–152. Albuquerque: U of New Mexico Press.
1990   The built environment and consumer decisions. In *Domestic architecture and the use of space: An interdisciplinary cross-cultural study*, edited by S. Kent, 34–42. Cambridge: Cambridge U Press.
1991   *Household ecology: Economic change and domestic life among the Kekchi Maya in Belize*. Tucson: U of Arizona Press.

Wilk, R.R., and W.A. Ashmore, eds.
1988   *Household and community in the Mesoamerican past*. Albuquerque: U of New Mexico Press.

Wilk, R.R., and H.L. Wilhite
1991 The community of Cuello: Patterns of household and settlement change. In *Cuello, an early Maya community in Belize*, edited by N. Hammond, 118–133. Cambridge: Cambridge U Press.

Willey, G.R.
1956a The structure of ancient Maya society: Evidence from the southern lowlands. *American Anthropologist* 58:772–782.

1956b Problems concerning prehistoric settlement patterns in the Maya lowlands. In *Prehistoric settlement patterns in the New World*, edited by G.R. Willey, 107–114. New York: Wenner-Gren Foundation.

1965 Archaeological phases and ancient settlement. In *Prehistoric Maya settlements in the Belize Valley*, edited by G. Willey, W.R. Bullard, J.B. Glass, and J.C. Gifford, 561–581. Papers of the Peabody Museum of Archaeology and Ethnology 54. Cambridge: Harvard University.

1972 *The artifacts of Altar de Sacrificios*. Papers of the Peabody Museum of Archaeology and Ethnology 64: 1. Cambridge: Harvard University.

1980 Towards an holistic view of ancient Maya civilization. *Man* 15:249–266.

1981 Maya lowland settlement patterns: A summary view. In *Lowland Maya settlement patterns*, edited by W.A. Ashmore, 385–415. Albuquerque: U of New Mexico Press.

1997 Copan: Settlement, politics, and ideology. *Symbols* 37:5–8.

Willey, G.R., W.R. Bullard Jr., and J.B. Glass
1955 The Maya community of prehistoric times. *Archaeology* 8(1):18–25.

Willey, G.R., W.R. Bullard Jr., J.B. Glass, and J.C. Gifford
1965 *Prehistoric Maya settlements in the Belize Valley*. Papers of the Peabody Museum of Archaeology and Ethnology 54. Cambridge: Harvard University.

Willey, G.R., and R.M. Leventhal
1979 Prehistoric settlement at Copan. In *Maya archaeology and ethnohistory*, edited by N. Hammond and G.R. Willey, 75–102. Austin: Univerity of Texas Press.

Wobst, M.
1977 Stylistic behavior and information exchange. In *Papers for the director: Research essays in honor of James S. Griffin*, edited by C. Cleland, 317–442. Anthropological Papers 61. Ann Arbor: University of Michigan Museum of Anthropology

Wolf, E.R.
1957 Closed corporate communities in Mesoamerica and Java. *Southwestern Journal of Anthropology* 13(1):1–18.

1966 *Peasants*. Englewood Cliffs: Prentice-Hall.

1969 *Peasant wars of the twentieth century*. New York: Harper and Row.

Wright, A.C.S., D. Romney, R. Arbuckle, and V. Vial
1959 *Land in British Honduras: Report of the British Honduras land use survey team*. Colonial Research Publication 24. London: Her Majesty's Stationary Office.

Yaeger, J.
1992 Xunantunich settlement survey. In Xunantunich Archaeological Project: 1992 field season, edited by R.M. Leventhal, 110–126. Report on file, Department of Archaeology, Belmopan, Belize; University of Pennsylvania; and Cotsen Institute of Archaeology at UCLA.

1994 1994 fieldwork at San Lorenzo: Excavations at an outlier community. In Xunantunich Archaeological Project: 1994 field season, edited by R.M. Leventhal and W.A. Ashmore, 123–147 Report on file, Department of Archaeology, Belmopan, Belize; University of Pennsylvania; and Cotsen Institute of Archaeology at UCLA.

1995 San Lorenzo: Exploring the roles of communities in the upper Belize river valley. Paper presented at the First International Symposium on Maya Archaeology, Department of Archaeology, Belize.

1997 The 1997 excavations of plaza a-III and miscellanous excavation and architectural clearing in group a. In Xunantunich Archaeological Project 1997: The final field season, edited by R.M. Leventhal, 24–55. Report on file, Department of Archaeology, Belmopan, Belize; University of Pennsylvania; and Cotsen Institute of Archaeology at UCLA.

2000a Changing patterns of social organization: The Late and Terminal Classic communities at San Lorenzo, Cayo District, Belize. Ph.D. dissertation, Department of Anthropology, University of Pennsylvania, Philadelphia.

2000b The social construction of communities in the Classic Maya countryside: Strategies of affiliation in western Belize. In *The archaeology of communities: A New World perspective*, edited by M.A. Canuto and J. Yaeger, 23–142. London: Routledge.

2001 Untangling the ties that bind: The city, the countryside, and the nature of Maya urbanism. In *Beyond central places and ceremony: The archaeology of urban sites*, edited by M.L. Smith. Washington, DC: Smithsonian Institution. In press.

Yaeger, J., and M.A. Canuto
2000 Introducing an archaeology of communities. In *The archaeology of communities: A New World perspective*, edited by M.A. Canuto and J. Yaeger, 1–15. London: Routledge.

Yaeger, J. and S.V. Connell
1993 Xunantunich Settlement Survey. In *Xunantunich Archaeological Project: 1993 Field Season*, edited by R. M. Leventhal, 172–201. Report on file, Department of Archaeology, Belmopan, Belize; University of Pennsylvania; and Cotsen Institute of Archaeology at UCLA.

Yaeger, J., and L.J. LeCount
1995 Social heterogeneity and political integration in a Terminal Classic Maya community: On-going research at San Lorenzo, Belize. Paper presented at the 60th Annual Meeting of the Society for American Archaeology, Minneapolis, MN.

Yaeger, J., and C. Robin
N.D. Heterogeneous hinterlands: The social and political organization of commoner settlements near Xunantunich, Belize. In *Ancient Maya commoners*, edited by F. Valdez and J. Lohse. Austin: U of Texas Press. In press.

Yoffee, N.
1993 Too many chiefs? (or, safe texts for the '90s). In *Archaeological theory: Who sets the agenda*, edited by N. Yoffee and A. Sherratt, 60–78. Cambridge: Cambridge U Press.

Young, A.
1994 *The chocolate tree: A natural history of cacao*. Washington, DC: Smithsonian Institution.

Contributors

Wendy Ashmore
Department of Anthropology
University of California, Riverside

Gyles Iannone
Department of Anthropology
Trent University

Samuel V. Connell
Research Associate
Cotsen Institute of Archaeology at UCLA

Jason Yaeger
Department of Anthropology
University of Wisconsin-Madison

James M. Conlon
Institute of Archaeology
University of London

Allan F. Moore
Department of Archaeology
Belmopan, Belize

Patricia A. McAnany
Department of Archaeology
Boston University

Kimberly A. Berry
Department of Archaeology
Boston University

Ben S. Thomas
Department of Archaeology
Boston University

Laura J. Levi
College of Social and Behavioral Sciences
University of Texas, San Antonio

Gair Tourtellot
Department of Archaeology
Boston University

Gloria Everson
Department of Anthropology
Lyon College

Norman Hammond
Department of Archaeology
Boston University

Arlen F. Chase
Department of Sociology and Anthropology
University of Central Florida

Diane Z. Chase
Department of Sociology and Anthropology
University of Central Florida

Marilyn A. Masson
Department of Anthropology
SUNY-Albany

Edward M. Schortman
Department of Anthropology and Sociology
Kenyon College

Patricia A. Urban
Department of Anthropology and Sociology
Kenyon College